European environmental policy: the pioneers

Issues in Environmental Politics

series editors Tim O'Riordan, Arild Underdal *and* Albert Weale

As the millennium approaches, the environment has come to stay as a central concern of global politics. This series takes key problems for environmental policy and examines the politics behind their cause and possible resolution. Accessible and eloquent, the books make available for a non-specialist readership some of the best research and most provocative thinking on humanity's relationship with the planet.

already published in the series

Congress and air pollution: environmental politics in the US
   Christopher J. Bailey

Sustaining Amazonia: grassroots action for productive conservation
   Anthony Hall

The protest business? Mobilizing campaign groups
   Grant Jordan and William Maloney

Environment and the nation state: the Netherlands, the European
   Union and acid rain *Duncan Liefferink*

Valuing the environment *Raino Malnes*

Life on a modern planet: a manifesto for progress *Richard North*

Public purpose or private benefit? The politics of energy
   conservation *Gill Owen*

Environmental pressure groups in transition *Peter Rawcliffe*

Governance by green taxes *Mikael Skou Andersen*

European environmental policy: the pioneers
   Mikael Skou Andersen and Duncan Liefferink (eds)

The new politics of pollution *Albert Weale*

European environmental policy

The pioneers

edited by
Mikael Skou Andersen and Duncan Liefferink

Manchester University Press
Manchester and New York
Distributed exclusively in the USA by St. Martin's Press

Published by Manchester University Press
Oxford Road, Manchester M13 9NR, UK
and Room 400, 175 Fifth Avenue, New York, NY 10010, USA

Distributed exclusively in the USA by
St. Martin's Press, Inc., 175 Fifth Avenue, New York,
NY 10010, USA

Distributed exclusively in Canada by
UBC Press, University of British Columbia, 6344 Memorial Road,
Vancouver, BC, Canada V6T 1Z2

British Library Cataloguing-in-Publication Data
A catalogue record for this book is available from the British Library

Library of Congress Cataloging-in-Publication Data
European environmental policy: the pioneers/edited by Mikael Skou
Andersen and Duncan Liefferink
    p.   cm.—(Issues in environmental politics)
  Includes bibliographical references.
  ISBN 0–7190–5043–X
  1. Environmental policy—Europe.   I. Andersen. Mikael Skou.
II. Liefferink, Duncan.   III. Series.
GE190.E95E855   1997
363.7'0094—dc21   96–40303

ISBN 0 7190 5717 5 *paperback*

First published in 1997

01 00 99   10 9 8 7 6 5 4 3 2

GE
190
E95E87

Printed in Great Britain
by Biddles Ltd, Guildford and King's Lynn

Contents

List of contributors

Mikael Skou Andersen, Department of Political Science, Aarhus University, Arhus, Denmark.

Marko Joas, Department of Public Administration, Åbo Akademi, Åbo, Finland.

Annica Kronsell, Department of Political Science, Lund University, Lund, Sweden.

Volkmar Lauber, Department of Political Science, Salzburg University, Salzburg, Austria.

Duncan Liefferink, Department of Sociology, Wageningen Agricultural University, Wageningen, the Netherlands.

Heinrich Pehle, Department of Political Science, University of Erlangen-Nürnberg, Erlangen, Germany.

Marit Reitan, Department of Political Science, University of Oslo, Oslo, Norway.

Preface

EU environmental policy was formally founded with the European Council declaration made in Paris in October 1972, and especially in the last decade its environmental policies have developed at an unexpected speed. While the Cechini White Paper from 1985 scheduled about 300 new directives for the creation of the single market, no one policy document foresaw that about 150 legal acts relating to environmental policy would be passed in the period from 1987 to 1994, further extending environmental protection and thus affirming the position of environmental policy as one of the key areas within the EU. One of the reasons for the rapid development of EU environmental policy has been the marked differences among the various member states; between the forerunners with relatively developed domestic environmental policies and the latecomers with little or no national environmental legislation. The differences have had to be levelled out, and in this process the administrative and technical policy experiences of the forerunners seem to have had an upper hand in the harmonisation process.

The title of this book, *European environmental policy: the pioneers*, is not meant as a bold claim regarding the sophistication of environmental policy in a certain part of Europe, nor can the countries covered by this book be regarded as having developed particularly 'sustainable' economies and societies. What we are interested in is their political role in EU environmental policy-making, where they often have pushed for higher environmental standards, on the basis of their domestic policies.

It is our view that we cannot understand the promotion of

strategies and concepts at the EU level without understanding their origin in the domestic context. The basic idea of the book is to provide the reader with a deeper insight into domestic environmental policy-making, to trace the internal conflicts and dynamics that have made these countries develop their notions of environmental policy, and select the issues which are brought to Brussels for 'Europeanisation'. We think that such insights may provide a useful tool for better understanding and analysing the internal environmental politics of other EU member states, and hence for better understanding the policies they promote at the EU level.

The enlargement of the EU in 1995 with Austria, Finland and Sweden provided the occasion for the focus on the 'pioneers' since these three new member states had relatively developed domestic environmental policies and were expected to provide a significant impetus to EU environmental policy-making. Because alliances are rather crucial to policy-making in the EU, where decisions can be taken by qualified majority in the Council of Ministers, we found it logical to explore the domestic environmental policies of the previous environmental pioneers (Germany, the Netherlands and Denmark) as well, to investigate the coherency of a potential 'green bloc' in EU environmental decision-making. Norway is also included in the book, because Norway was expected to become a member, and because Norway is linked to the EU policy-making process, both through the European Economic Area arrangement and through its traditional partnership with the other Nordic countries.

The dynamics of the enlargement have been further explored in another book, *The innovation of EU environmental policy* from Scandinavian University Press, as well as in the final report from the project 'New member states and the impact on EU environmental policy'. The project, from which this book also stems, was funded by the European Commission's Socio-Economic Environmental Research Programme (contract CT 94-0385), and additional support was obtained from the Nordic Academy for Advanced Studies (NorFa). We would like to express our thanks to both organisations for their generosity.

The individual chapters have been written using a common analytical framework and were first presented at a workshop in April 1995 at Sandbjerg Manor, the conference facility of Aarhus University. As editors of this volume, we would very much like to thank the individual chapter authors for their efforts. We are also grateful for the linguistic assistance of Virginia A. Schildhauer, who translated the chapter on Germany into English, and of Judith Ugelow, who reviewed the remaining chapters, as well as for the skilful secretarial assistance of Anette Riber of the Political Science Department at Aarhus University. We would also like to express our thanks to Rebecca Crum from Manchester University Press for a pleasant and fruitful co-operation and to the series' editors, in particular Albert Weale, for their supportive attitude to this book.

Mikael Skou Andersen and Duncan Liefferink

Introduction: the impact of the pioneers on EU environmental policy

The new member states

When the European Union was enlarged with Austria, Finland and Sweden in 1995, it was widely expected that these new member states would give a significant impetus to EU environmental policy. Not least the environmental forerunners so far, i.e. Germany, the Netherlands and Denmark,[1] expected the three new member states to support a higher level of environmental protection in the EU, something which they had had difficulties achieving, particularly in the years since the 1992 Rio Summit. The Maastricht Treaty meant that from late 1993 qualified majority voting became the prevalent method of decision-making in environmental policy in the Council of Ministers, implying that the forerunners found themselves on the defensive on important issues, such as that of the packaging waste directive passed against their votes.[2] The other member states also felt that the enlargement would change the previous balance in environmental policy (Aguilar, 1997).

The immediate effect of the enlargement was that, in the case of mutual agreement, the (now) six forerunners in environmental policy were able to control a so-called blocking minority in the Council.[3] Although actual use of the qualified majority voting procedure has remained the exception rather than the rule, voting has become more common in the Council of Environmental Ministers since the Maastricht Treaty entered into force. More important than voting itself has been, as pointed out by Weiler (1991), the 'shadow of the vote' or perhaps rather, as would be the case here, the 'shadow of a blocking minority'. The six member states can, in case of mutual agreement, actually block the lowering of existing environmental standards. Thus the enlargement has changed *inter alia* the existing balance in the Council and has increased the propensity to give concessions to one or more of the 'greener' member states (Holzinger, 1997).

The new member states have been eager to influence EU environmental policy and to bring it up to a level of protection similar to that achieved domestically. As a potential lever to this purpose, the accession agreement allows the new member states a transitional period of four years during which they are permitted to maintain stricter environmental standards in specified areas.[4] During this period, EU environmental regulations are to undergo a review, in order possibly to bring the level of protection up to that of the new member states. These transitional measures strengthened expectations in the three new member states that their accession would promote a higher level of environmental protection (cf. Lindh, 1996, quoted from *Environment Watch* 4:2). Especially before the Swedish referendum on membership, the possible role which the new member states could come to play in EU environmental policy was used as an argument in favour of membership, and the Commission's recent and more reluctant attitude on this issue is likely to frustrate the domestic constituency (*Europe Environment*, 1996: 481, 6).

The three new member states each brought with them a comprehensive experience with domestic environmental policy, and the most fundamental impact expected from the enlargement was perhaps less connected to voting procedures or transitional agreements than to the general stimulus which the new member states could provide to environmental policy-making in the EU. The three member states have both well-developed domestic environmental policies and a long reputation for active international diplomacy in regional and global environmental issues.

This book examines and compares the priorities and strategies for domestic and foreign environmental policies of the three new forerunners (Sweden, Austria and Finland) with those of the former forerunners (Germany, the Netherlands and Denmark). The reason for the more general focus on this group of 'pioneers' in European environmental policy is connected to their historical role as catalysts in the EU policy-making process as well as in international environmental policy-making. It would be difficult to understand the role of the newcomers in the EU without a due understanding of the former forerunners in European environmental policy-making. Another important advantage of this broader approach is that it allows us to make a better analysis of the differences in the strategies of the various forerunners and of how they might complement each other.

Policy-making in the EU is a reciprocal two-level game in which an analysis of the link between domestic and supra-national policy-making is pertinent to a proper understanding of the process. On the one hand, there are 'Brussels politics', in which the member states, the different EU institutions and interest organisations are involved. On the other hand, there are 'domestic politics', which influence the official positions of the member states in the Council as well as the experiences and attitudes of individual nationals wherever they are based, be it in the Commission, the European Parliament, or in one of the numerous Euro-organisations. Despite the significance of domestic politics, it is often treated as a black box, not only in theories on international politics, but also by participants in the real political game. Negotiators are often misinformed about domestic politics, particularly about those of the other countries involved in negotiations, and generally do not do well in analysing each other's internal politics (Putnam, 1988: 452).

This book examines the domestic politics of environmental policy-making and analyses how the link is made to Brussels' politics by each of the pioneers in EU environmental policy. This introduction discusses the role of the pioneers and, more generally, the nature of the link between domestic politics and EU policy-making; and while it provides a key assessment of the domestic background and the strategic orientation of each of the pioneers, the remaining part of the book undertakes an in-depth examination of each of these six countries plus Norway. As a member of the European Economic Area (EEA), Norway is subject to most EU environmental directives, and although without formal votes, Norway has, in its own way, become a player in the game. We have, in another volume, chosen to focus more on the policy-making process in Brussels (Liefferink and Andersen, 1997).

The importance and role of pioneers in environmental policy-making

'Examples' and 'models' of solutions and strategies have traditionally played a significant role in environmental policy-making, both at the domestic and international levels. They seem to provide a stimulus to rethink established policies and to cause changes in beliefs concerning what is feasible. The examples set by the pioneers provide arguments for environmental advocacy coalitions to make policy-makers in other countries reconsider their priorities, but they also generate a practical and technical experience that can be useful elsewhere. The 'horizontal' development and dissemination of strategies and solutions at the national level is often mentioned as a precondition of a successful 'vertical' transfer to the international level (Jänicke, 1990: 230).

The 1972 Stockholm Conference, proposed by the Swedish government and organised under the auspices of the United Nations, is illustrative of the significance of both horizontal and vertical impacts. It succeeded in helping to pace the development of domestic environmental policies in the industrialised countries, since most of the governments which participated in the conference were eager to draw up their national policies in time for presentation at the conference. But there was also a vertical impact at the regional and international level.

At that time, it was mainly Japan, the USA and Sweden which stood as international pioneers in environmental policy, and their examples and experience became catalysts in the first phase of modern environmental policy. Japan's strict 1967 environmental protection law, created against a background of what was referred to as the ecological 'harakiri' of the 1960s, provided evidence of the need for industrial societies to remedy the impacts of pollution, while the establishment of the Swedish Agency for Nature Protection in the same year and the US Environmental Protection Agency in 1969 lent support to proponents in other countries who argued for independent institutional frameworks for pollution control, rather than interagency co-ordination of environmental policy (Kelley, Stunkel and Wescott, 1976; Tsuru and Weidner, 1985).

Gradually, international organisations responded to developments at the domestic level. The Organisation for Economic Co-operation and Development (OECD) established the polluter pays principle, aiming to eliminate the use of state subsidies for pollution control. At the Paris Summit in October 1972, the European Community issued an environmental policy declaration and mandated the Commission to draw up a proposal for the First Environmental Action Programme (OECD, 1975; Bungarten, 1978). From the late 1960s until October

1972, both the European Parliament and the Commission had passed resolutions in vain, to which the Council had been reluctant to react, and there is reason to assume that without the pressure invoked by the Stockholm Conference the process towards a common European Community environmental policy would only have become more protracted and difficult (Bungarten, 1978: 86). It was the spin-off from the simultaneous development of domestic environmental policies in the member states, catalysed by the Stockholm Conference, that paved the way for the decision made at the Paris Summit in October 1972. The establishment of EU environmental policy is thus illustrative of the fact that the impact of pioneers was indeed both 'horizontal' and 'vertical'; by their examples, the pioneers served as catalysts for the development of both domestic and international policies.

Since the birth of European environmental policy, persistent tension has, however, existed between environmental policy-making at the national level and at the European level. Domestic environmental policies reflected the issues and problems most urgent in the member states as well as their different regulatory styles and traditions (Johnson and Brown Gardner, 1976; Bungarten, 1978). The Community's environmental policy, without a clear basis in the treaty, developed more slowly and had, from the beginning, lost momentum compared with initiatives taken at the national level. Even if the time gap between the passing of, for example, national water pollution regulation in the member states and the basic framework directives on bathing and shellfish waters was only five or six years, Community policies had to cope with substantial national differences in environmental policy when defining a common approach (Andersen, 1994).

Besides the somewhat delayed development of Community environmental policy as compared with that of national environmental policies, domestic policies themselves developed at a different pace (see Bungarten (1978) for an overview of the early phase). The tempo difference in environmental policy-making was aggravated by the enlargement of the Community with Spain, Portugal and Greece in the 1980s. When Portugal and Spain entered the Community in 1986, neither of them had an environmental ministry or much experience in environmental administration, and EU regulations came to provide the foundation for pollution control in these countries (Font and Morata, 1992). The same applied to Greece, which had entered the Community in 1981 (Pridham *et al.*, 1995).

Between the 'latecomers' and the 'pioneers', one finds a number of member states with more issue-dependent and less predictable positions (Johnson and Corcelle, 1995: 8; Skjærseth *et al.*, 1992; Holzinger, 1994). The 'middle group' comprises Belgium, France, Italy, Ireland and Luxembourg. Belgium, Italy and Luxembourg have often joined forces with the forerunners, for instance, on the issue of climate policy (Huber, 1997), while Ireland has leaned more towards the latecomers, but has promoted a 'green' image (Coyle, 1994). France was from the beginning a rather reluctant participant in the development of EU environmental policy, but its domestic policies have become relatively developed, especially after an active period in the early 1990s (Bungarten, 1978; Larrue, 1992). The United Kingdom has a distinctive position, but has often joined forces with the latecomers due to the low priority assigned to environmental policy by the government – and in particular to a proper implementation of EU directives. The UK has nevertheless a higher institutional capacity for environmental policy-making than do the latecomers, a legacy from the early development of pollution control (Hill, 1983; Weale, 1996).

The differences among the member states relate not only to the general priority attached to environmental policy, but also to the strategies and concepts that have been developed in a national context. Each nation has a distinct regulatory style, which is a function of its more general policy style, and which causes the environment to be regulated very much in the same way as other areas of corporate conduct (Richardson, 1982; Vogel, 1986). The British use of quality standards in water policy is hence explained not only by the dilution opportunities offered by the vicinity to the sea, but is rooted more deeply in a distaste for rigid guidelines and in a general British propensity for co-operation and mutual adaptation. This approach differs considerably from the preference for command-and-control regulations in, for instance, Germany. It can sometimes be more difficult to define a common EU policy given such differences in regulatory traditions, than it is to reconcile different opinions about the level of environmental protection.

The tensions between domestic policy-making and EU policy-making, as well as the tensions between the different levels and strategies of environmental protection in the different member states (whether reflecting priorities or policy styles), contribute to the dynamics of European integration in this field, since environmental standards have an impact on the functioning of the single market as well. While it has often been pointed out in domestic debates that high environmental standards can affect the competitiveness of national industries negatively, it is also significant, from the EU point of view, that environmental standards can be used to create indirect barriers to free trade.

The pioneers have an interest in expanding their own level of protection to the whole of the EU while maintaining a right for themselves to be 'cleaner than the rest'. Once the domestic situation has led a country to adopt relatively high standards of environmental protection, there is a broad social interest in limiting the possible effects on competition by transferring similar environmental regulations to the EU level. National policy-makers can design domestic environmental policies to put pressure on the development of a European environmental policy, either by setting a good example or by affecting the functioning of the internal market.

The latecomers seem to be undecided as to whether they should prefer a more subsidiary approach, with generally less emphasis on the environmental dimension of the single market, or a more harmonised approach, with a higher level of protection combined with exemptions and side-payments. The latecomers do not generally oppose the pioneers maintaining their lead in environmental policy-making. High environmental standards are normally expected to influence the industrial competitiveness of the pioneers negatively, but if environmental standards may create barriers to trade, the other member states are more keen to put a brake on the pioneers. The ambiguity is embedded in the standing controversy over the legal basis in the EU treaty for environmental directives (Krämer, 1992). While directives passed according to the treaty's environmental articles (Article 130R-T) provide only a minimum level of protection that allows individual member states to take further measures, directives passed according to the internal market section (Article 100A) provide a harmonised level of protection, with the only opportunity for more far-reaching national measures being to invoke the so-called 'environmental guarantee' (Article 100A(4)).

The role of domestic politics in EU policy-making

There is by now a vast literature on comparative environmental politics. The first generation of fragmented case studies (Jänicke, 1978;

Downing and Hanf, 1983) was gradually succeeded by more systematic comparisons (Richardson and Watts, 1985; Vogel, 1986; Vogel and Kun, 1987; Weale *et al.*, 1991). Sectoral studies that compare national policies on water, air or other issues and concern the patterns of policy-making and implementation (Johnson and Brown, 1976; Lundqvist, 1980; Knoepfel and Weidner, 1985; Conrad, 1990; Boehmer-Christiansen and Skea, 1991) have been followed by studies that provide more encompassing analyses of national environmental policies (Baker *et al.*, 1994; Jänicke and Weidner, 1996) and systems of administration on a country by country basis (Jansen and Hanf 1996; Munk Christiansen, 1996). Other more recent types of study try to reach beyond the policy formulation and compare the outcome of environmental policies in different countries (Jänicke, 1990; Weale, 1992; Andersen, 1994). Few of these studies have discussed the impact of domestic policy-making on EU environmental policy-making. Studies of EU environmental policy-making have, on the other hand, tended to focus on 'Brussels politics' (Judge, 1992; Bennett, 1992; Liefferink *et al.*, 1993; Richardson, 1994), and the theoretical orientation has shifted from conventional international political theories towards policy analysis. The difficulty with this orientation is that it tends to treat member states as unitary actors and to overlook the significance of domestic politics, as has been revealed in some of the most comprehensive case studies available (Holzinger, 1994; Liefferink, 1996a).

The EU policy-making system is complex and difficult to conceptualise and, as Richardson has warned, almost any firm characterisations of the political processes are hence unreliable (Richardson, 1994: 139). It has perhaps been described most adequately as a set of nested games, almost as a set of Chinese boxes (Peters, 1992). The intergovernmental game among the member states is supplemented by an interinstitutional game involving the supra-national institutions (Council, Commission, Parliament and Court) as well as by a bureaucratic game involving Community and national civil servants, diplomats and experts. In this context, we are mainly preoccupied with the habitual intergovernmental game and the way that domestic policies link with policy-making at the EU level, but it does not imply that we disregard the importance of the other two games (cf. Rasmussen and Andersen, 1996).

In the literature on international politics as well as on EU integration, the intricate relationship between politics at the domestic level and the behaviour of states at the supra-national level is broadly acknowledged, but there are substantial differences in the way the relationship is conceptualised (Allison, 1971; Bulmer, 1983; Putnam, 1988; Moravcsik, 1993; Huelshoff, 1994; Hix, 1994). In particular neo-functionalism, once a predominant approach to studies of European integration, has been criticised for paying too much attention to the dynamics of 'spill-overs' and technocratic problem-solving and too little to those of domestic politics.

In an early article on the role of domestic politics in EU policy-making, Bulmer argued for the need to disaggregate the individual governments' positions in order to understand the outcome of the policy-making processes at the EU level: 'The domestic politics approach postulates that the pattern of negotiations in each national policy sub-structure sets the key, in which the relevant national minister (and interest groups) will behave in the upper decisional tier' (Bulmer, 1983: 358). National polities are the basic units of the Community, and Bulmer distinguishes between two different dimensions of domestic politics: structures and attitudes. 'Structures' refers to the more institutionalised patterns of decision- and policy-making, i.e. the institutional frameworks and standard operating procedures which have become established over time and which are characteristic of the national approach to policy-making. 'Attitudes' refers to the more immediate attitudes towards specific issues and policies and the opportunities linked with Europeanisation.

It is not surprising that Bulmer's viewpoint receives support from intergovernmentalists, who see member states as the basic policy-making units. Moravcsik thus argues that 'An understanding of domestic politics is a precondition for, not a supplement to, the analysis of strategic interaction among states' (Moravcsik, 1993: 481). Huelshoff goes further and argues, from a rational choice perspective, that national policy-makers who take part in decisions on regional integration are motivated most significantly by 'rewarding and protecting domestic groups upon which decision makers are dependent for political support and survival' (Huelshoff, 1994: 256).

A qualification to the significance attributed to domestic politics by intergovernmentalists is that, under some circumstances, the EU policy-making level may allow a government to 'escape' forces and interest groups at play on the domestic level. This may be the case when 'package deals' link different issues together in one decision, implying that some domestic interest groups may need to be sacrificed in order to reach concessions with other domestic interests. This may also be the case if qualified majority voting is used and a national government is down-voted, or perhaps even tacitly accepts to become down-voted because the protection of specific domestic interests is not feasible or suitable in the broader European context. Still, the basic implication in the above-mentioned literature is essentially a relatively simple, uni-directional relationship between domestic politics and policies at the EU level, the latter being a result of forces at play in the former (Evans *et al.*, 1993: 416). 'Domestic politics' gives zest to the analysis of international negotiations, but the complexity of the inter-play among the forces at the domestic level, some of which are transnational in character, tends to be simplified, although it may be rather crucial to a proper understanding (cf. Liefferink, 1996a).

The reciprocity of EU policy-making

Putnam (1988) offers a framework for analysing the relationship between domestic and international policies in which the two-level game is basically seen as a *reciprocal* relationship between concurrent negotiations in a domestic constituency and at the intergovernmental level. Although Putnam indicates that his theory might also be applic-able to the EU policy process, it has not been developed specifically for the purpose of EU studies. The reciprocal relationship in conven-tional international diplomacy among sovereign states is affected mainly by the need of negotiators to have an international agreement ratified by the domestic constituency and thus the need to negotiate simultaneously at two tables. Governments must, at their domestic negotiating table (level II), ensure support among a diverse spectrum of interests for the concessions and agreements that are reached at the international negotiating table (level I). The relationship between the two processes, which are going on interchangeably, is a mutual one:

> At the national level, domestic groups pursue their interests by pres-suring the government to adopt favourable policies, and politicians seek power by constructing coalitions among those groups. At the international level, national governments seek to maximize their own ability to satisfy domestic pressures, while minimizing the adverse consequences of foreign developments.
>
> (Putnam, 1988: 434)

The theory seeks to predict *ratification* of international agreements and, assuming only two negotiating governments, the outcome of international negotiations is likely to be ratified only if it falls within the overlap of the two 'win-sets' defined by the negotiators and the participants in each of the two domestic games. Putnam's theory explains how the range of solutions acceptable to the domestic constituency is defined. These 'win-sets' are determined by three variables: 1) the distribution of power, preferences and possible coalitions among level II constituents; 2) the level II political institutions; and 3) the strategies of the level I negotiators.

The first variable entails a relatively straightforward analysis of the political conditions at the domestic level: an identification of the political actors relevant to policy-making and the resources they control; as well as an investigation of the possible alliances between them. The institutions under focus in the second variable should be interpreted in the broadest sense and include not only formal institutions, but also informal institutions, i.e. developed meanings and concepts of specific policies as they have been cultivated domestically. The third variable, the strategies of the level I negotiators, concerns the ability to induce changes in the preferences of the domestic constituency in order to adapt to the direction of the international negotiations. Although the domestic constituency will usually serve to limit the range of opportunities open to the negotiators, negotiators can also utilise the tailwind from an international agreement to create changes in the perceptions and preferences of the domestic constituency. The possible reverberation underlines the reciprocity of the process.

Although the EU policy process is as much concerned with day-to-day policy-making as with high-level international policy negotiations, EU member state governments are, in a comparable way, involved in two games: the one at the EU level in Brussels; the other at the domestic level in the home capital. The reciprocity of the two-level game is, nevertheless, more pronounced in the EU policy-making process for at least four reasons.

First, the EU represents a carefully institutionalised forum for intergovernmental co-operation in which the same actors negotiate with each other repeatedly. The reiterative character of the process does not only explain the foretaste for issue-linkage and package deals, but also leads to better skilled and more experienced negotiators, who know better the positions of their partners as well as of their own domestic constituencies, and who are thus better informed about how to strategically maximise their impact on the bargaining process. There is reason to believe that member states and their governments will over time acquire considerable experience in how to manage and time domestic policy-making concurrently with the EU policy-making process.

Second, EU decisions differ from those resulting from more conventional international negotiations because they are legally binding for the member states and because they are based on qualified majority voting. The EU policy-making process is marked by fifteen member states, whose governments may enter into *ad hoc* coalitions with each other in order to build qualified majorities and to avoid becoming outvoted. In the latter case, governments may have to endure a decision that is not acceptable to the domestic constituency. While the reverberations from such decisions may be useful for inducing changes in the outcomes acceptable to the domestic constituency, they are generally not welcomed by member state governments. The use of qualified majority voting may, in other words, cause significant changes in the way the 'win-sets' are defined.

Third, the EU policy process involves participants other than the member states, e.g. the Commission, the European Parliament and a range of Euro-groups representing different interests. The triangular institutional relationship between the Council, the Parliament and the Commission especially increases the probability that member states will make concessions to interests of a more supra-national type. With the new procedures for co-operative decision-making, the Parliament has become more influential in the EU policy-making process, offering an additional venue for non-state actors to seek influence.

Fourth, although the EU political process is reciprocal, the two-level game is not necessarily simultaneous. Domestic policies may have been developed well before similar policies became a concern at the EU level, and if issues have already been negotiated and sorted out among the actors in the domestic constituency, it may complicate matters considerably if the issue is re-opened due to the need for an EU-wide agreement (Liefferink, 1996a). To member states which have become forerunners i.: environmental (or any other) policy, such time lags in the reciprocal game are difficult to avoid and also offer opportunities for influencing EU policy-making. Therefore, being a forerunner in the reciprocal two-level game of EU policy-making requires a reasonable timing between domestic policies and initiatives taken at the EU level.

Regulatory competition

In this reciprocal, reiterative and far from synchronous policy-making system, EU member states are committed to a detailed and minute harmonisation of standards and regulations to ensure the functioning of the internal market. In environmental policy, the harmonisation process depends on the ability to design positive integration measures rather than to dissolve national regulations. Because of the two-level character of the EU policy process, 'regulatory competition' among member states takes place long before negotiations are initiated in the Council (Héritier, 1992). As indicated above, the member states have developed rather different strategies for, and conceptions of, environmental policy, and regulatory competition concerns not only the agenda on the problems to be dealt with, but also the agendas on the basic regulatory philosophy and the policy instruments to be applied (Héritier, 1992: 438). Especially in the early preparatory phase of legislation, when national experts from the member states are called in to assist the Commission in drafting proposals, it is normal that the Commission looks to the member states for viable strategies and solutions to be transferred to the European level (Pellegrom, 1997). This mechanism seems to be crucial for bringing the policies and experiences from the domestic context into the integration process. Héritier thus points out that:

> In many of the Commission's working groups, experts from the most strictly regulated member states, who have better knowledge and *work together*, can (under the framework conditions of time pressure) better influence the decisions substantially than can the representatives of the less interested member states.
>
> (Héritier, 1992: 438, authors' translation)

This quotation points to two somewhat different mechanisms for bringing domestic experiences into the EU policy-making process.

First, the more strictly regulated member states, which have been innovators or forerunners on a specific issue, can support the development of EU policies on the basis of their domestic experiences. In an illustrative example of the relationship between domestic and EU policy, Bennett shows how the French system of risk assessment of industrial hazards was used as a model for the Seveso Directive because the French national policy was one of the most advanced in this field (Bennett, 1993).

Second, member states, governments and administrators learn

from their experience in EU policy-making and, having acknowledged that possible leads in domestic policies can be exported to the EU level, they have developed a set of strategies on how to cultivate and link domestic policies with EU policy-making. To these strategies, the more reciprocal relationship between domestic and EU policy-making is more relevant. In the above quotation, Héritier indicates that regulatory competition is a somewhat more intentional and deliberate process than one that offers the Commission only 'good ideas'. Héritier also points out how experts from the most strictly regulated member states can 'work together' to 'influence' the decisions, something which indicates the importance of closer alliances between member states as well as a more deliberate pushing of specific issues and solutions. Although there is no research available to support the claim, it is for instance notable within environmental policy how Denmark has been able to transfer its national Plan for the Aquatic Environment into the Urban Waste Water and Nitrate Directives, while the UK has in a similar way transferred its EMAS concept (Environmental Management and Auditing System) into the corresponding EU directive.

Forerunner and pusher strategies
In the following, distinction will be made between two different types of strategy for the articulation of 'green' positions in EU environmental policy-making. On the one hand, there are strategies primarily based on the domestic politics of the member states. These may be called 'forerunner' strategies and may range from simply defending existing national arrangements, by actively presenting them as 'examples' to others, to implementing unilateral measures as a way to provoke the EU. Strategies at the other end of the spectrum can be referred to as constructive 'pusher' strategies. This may involve, for example, putting issues on the agenda of the Council or lobbying the European Parliament.

The above given example of the French system of risk assessment seems to represent a domestic forerunner experience that has developed without an eye to the EU policy-making process. When, on the other hand, the Danish parliament decided unilaterally to introduce a CO_2 tax in 1991, it was more consciously argued that 'We think it benefits the EU process if we propose this now'. An element of regulatory competition was present too, since the proposers added that 'Being one of the first three or four countries preparing a proposal means we can indicate the lines of directions for how such taxes will be [designed] in the Community' (Bilgrav, 1991). In the discussion on car emission exhaust in the mid-1980s, Germany successfully pushed the EU policy-making process by threatening to introduce US standards unilaterally. The introduction of these standards would not only have set an example, but would also have closed off a substantial part of the European car market to other European car producers. By conflicting with the creation of the internal market, it represented an effective way of pushing the environmental policy-making process.

An important aspect of the 'pusher' role is the extent to which member states seek to build alliances with each other, something that the procedure of qualified majority voting seems to encourage. Normally alliances are created by working more or less along the same lines to promote similar concepts and principles, although 'inside Brussels tactics' also involve a more unpredictable element of horse-trading and log-rolling. It is of particular interest here that alliance-building in Brussels can be combined with unilateral action, i.e. forming a club that collectively sets an example, while at the same time pushing for joint action at the EU level. While the 'club strategy' has been used more often in international negotiations, e.g. for the protection of the ozone layer, to which end countries joined the Montreal Protocol, it has been less frequently used within the EU. However, the recent formation of a CO_2 tax club by the member states which had introduced such taxes domestically and simultaneously promoted an EU-wide tax, shows that the option can be utilised in cases that are sufficiently significant (*Europe Environment*, 1996: 471, 1).

More permanent alliances remain the exception as such alliances may antagonise other member states. The formation of alliances seems to depend a great deal on whether there is coherence in the domestic links to EU environmental policy. The coherence of these links depends not only on bold statements made by EU negotiators but also on the actual domestic political background, or, phrased in the words of Putnam, the 'win-sets' defined by the domestic constituencies. It does not make sense to draw these up in a formal sense, but in the following the domestic political background of the pioneers will be sketched, providing a profile of the foreign environmental policy strategies developed by each country. This is done on the basis of the empirical evidence presented in the chapters of the book.

Understanding the domestic polity

A broad range of domestic factors influence the EU policies of individual member states, and Schumann (1993) has summarised the insights of the comparative policy literature in a table (Table 1) that is useful for understanding in more depth the impact of the domestic polity on the shaping of the member states' specific EU policies. We do not intend to discuss this table as such, but it serves as a tool for structuring the first two of Putnam's variables, i.e. the political institutions as well as the powers and preferences at the domestic level. The third variable, i.e. the strategies at EU level, is treated in a following section. Here we use Schumann's classification to structure the presentation of the domestic basis for environmental policy-making, underlining in particular the differences. For a fuller account of the domestic background, we refer to the individual country chapters.

Table 1 *Domestic policies: important factors for member states' EU policy*

	Relatively stable	*Relatively unstable*
Country-specific	Socio-economic level Political culture; normative basis; attitudes to EU Structures and institutional framework Policy style (decision-making and implementation)	Current economic indicators Public opinion Government Current relations between main actors
Issue-specific	'Prevailing doctrines' Basic relations between state and interest groups Degree of policy integration	Experiences Recent conflict- and consensus-processes Topical problem pressure

Relatively stable, country-specific factors
The socio-economic level of development, as measured by indicators of gross national product etc., is quite similar among the pioneers, which belong to the more affluent group of EU member states. On

the other hand, the political culture and, in particular, the attitudes to European integration vary more. For example, the attitude towards European integration in Denmark and Sweden is more reluctant than among the other four pioneers, something which might explain the somewhat greater emphasis on the opt-out possibilities offered by the 'environmental guarantee' of the treaty (Article 100A(4)) in these two countries. Relatedly, Germany and the Netherlands belong to 'kern-Europa' and count themselves among the most 'loyal' supporters of European integration. Finland, partly out of general security concerns, and Austria also belong to the group of more 'loyal' members.

The political and institutional structures in Germany as well as in Austria are marked by the federal character of the political system. The German constitution assigns the responsibility for some environmental issues to the *Länder*, and the federal authorities are relatively weak in comparison with the stronger, more centralised environmental agencies and ministries in Sweden, Denmark and the Netherlands. Although Sweden, Denmark and the Netherlands established environmental ministries around 1970, Germany and Austria did not establish and consolidate their federal ministries until fifteen years later, at a time when it became evident that environmental problems were not just regional or local phenomena. This historical development might help explain why the environmental ministries in these two countries seem to have somewhat less autonomy and power *vis-à-vis* more traditional ministries of agriculture, industry, etc. and also need to confer more often with such ministries about their EU policies.

The policy styles vary considerably among all the countries in question, but especially in Germany, where the domestic heterogeneity and the importance of the regional authorities, i.e. the *Länder*, seem to have resulted in a somewhat different character. While both interest organisations and environmental non-governmental organisations are involved in formal consultations with the governments of the three Nordic countries and the Netherlands prior to new regulation and important EU initiatives, this is not the case in Germany. In a federal context, more regional interests must be accommodated, and consultation between the ministries in Bonn and the German *Länder* is an important axis in the environmental policy-making process. There is also less room to accommodate interest groups in the formal negotiations than in unitary states. Therefore, the German policy style is generally seen as less consultative than that of the other, more distinctly neo-corporatist, countries.

The German situation differs from that of Austria, whose federal system is weaker than Germany's (Lauber, this volume). The *Länder* in Austria are smaller and less autonomous, and the Austrian situation can, to a high degree, be explained by the role played by the two dominant political parties and their links to labour and industry, respectively (Lauber, this volume). There are also important differences among the smaller pioneers. In particular Denmark stands out as a country with unstable parliamentary coalitions and has less room for concertation of organised interests than Sweden and the Netherlands.

Relatively unstable, country-specific factors

Some observations of environmental policy-making based on more current developments can be added to these basic characteristics, and once again Germany stands out from the other pioneers. Following German reunification in 1990, the policy agenda became congested with issues related to developments in the new *Länder*, and although the German population remained among those most concerned with environmental issues within the EU (according to Eurobarometer), there was less room to accommodate these concerns. At the same time, the opening towards Eastern Europe made German industries more vulnerable to the relocation of industries, and relatively high factor costs triggered the 'standort Deutschland' debate. In the Nordic countries and the Netherlands, environmental issues remained considerably higher on the agenda, although these countries have also experienced a gradual decline in interest since the early 1990s. It is notable that environmental concerns have remained relatively high on the agenda in Sweden and Finland despite economic recession.

Changes of government have been less significant for the relative roles played by these pioneers than changes in environment ministers. It is noteworthy that the governments in both Germany and the Netherlands have recently appointed ministers who are less vociferous and forceful than were their former environmental ministers, Töpfer and Alders, who helped set the agenda in the early 1990s. In Finland, the Greens were elected into the government in 1995 and have since held the portfolio of the environment minister. But at the European level, Denmark, with the experienced Svend Auken, and Sweden took the lead.

Issue-specific, relatively stable factors

Environmental policy has probably become one of the most internationalised policy fields, with a universal tool-kit of policy concepts and strategies ranging from sustainable development to life cycle analyses. Nevertheless, comparative research has often pointed to substantial variations in the approaches to environmental policy across different countries. Although the international vocabulary and rhetoric normally finds its way into national environmental policy plans, it is usually not difficult to distinguish these basic, national differences (Downing and Hanf, 1983; Knoepfel and Weidner, 1985; Vogel, 1986; Vogel and Kun, 1987; Andersen, 1996; Jänicke and Weidner, 1996; Jansen and Hanf, 1996). Even if the group of pioneers in European environmental policy can be said to represent a group of 'most similar cases', there are some key differences worth drawing attention to. The concern with issue-specific, relatively stable factors at the national level is basically an interest in the special national traits of environmental policy.

In Germany and Austria, the emphasis on detailed, command-and-control-like regulations is an important characteristic (Pehle, Lauber, this volume). It is often explained by the desire to secure a 'Rechtsstaat' (constitutional state) after World War II and by the dominance of lawyers in public administration in these two countries (Weale, 1992), but the command-and-control approach also seems to be linked with the federal character of the regulatory system. For instance in water policy, uniform guidelines were already being demanded by industrial interests in the 1940s, as they preferred having a level playing field in all *Länder* (Andersen, 1994: 125). On the one hand, the richness of German standards in particular (as in the air pollution guidelines, TA Luft) has made these standards an important reference point for legislators across Europe. On the other hand, the tradition has been somewhat at a distance from, and difficult to integrate with, the more processual character of EU regulations in recent years (Pehle, this volume).

In Sweden and Denmark, a more flexible and integrated approach based on framework legislation and extensive consultations with interest groups has been practised for more than twenty years, a tradition which is very much linked with the distinct neo-corporatist tradition in these two countries. The Netherlands, in which consultations have always played an important role, moved towards a more integrated approach with the 1989 National Environmental Policy

Plan (NEPP), while regulations in Finland have remained somewhat fragmented across a number of sectoral laws. Nevertheless, these four countries have been more innovative in the use of new, more flexible policy instruments, in particular of an economic and voluntary type, in recent years, and have less difficulties with the more processual character of EU regulation. In the three Nordic countries, with their particularly strong welfare state tradition, the public sector seems to have come to play a more significant role in nursing pollution control than has been the case in Germany and the Netherlands, where more responsibility tends to be placed with target groups and private actors (Andersen, 1994).

Issue-specific, relatively unstable factors
Environmental concerns and priorities have changed over time and have been subject to the ups and downs of the issue-attention cycle. The media play an important role in bringing issues to the agenda, and due to the international orientation of these, in particular in the smaller member states, there is a tendency to focus on the same 'disasters' or environmental 'catastrophes' in all the countries. Forest die-back, the pollution of the Rhine, nuclear fall-out from Chernobyl, the death of seals, climate change and the Brent Spar platform are all examples of major environmental issues that have been subject to attention throughout Northern Europe and which have made policy-makers respond by tabling these for negotiations in Brussels, in one way or the other. Issues have been brought to the agenda with such rapid pace that there has been only limited time and attention with which to deal with them, but the pioneers have generally tried to act as 'pushers' at the EU level.

Despite the focus on global and regional environmental problems, each of the member states also has a more domestic agenda of issues. For a full account of these, we refer to the individual country chapters, but it might be indicative to point to the significance of acidification for Sweden, of transport issues for Austria, and of pollution from intensive livestocks for the Netherlands and Denmark, to understand the background for the initiatives taken by the individual member states in Brussels. Nevertheless, the environmental agenda is in constant flux, and it is noteworthy that during our interviews with officials in the national environment ministries, it was difficult for them to present formal lists of priorities.

The recent conflict and consensus processes regarding environmental policy-making at the domestic level nevertheless act as a general background for raising issues in Brussels. In this context, it might be useful to consider the significance of the response of national target groups to previous environmental policy measures. All the countries under scrutiny here have begun to move towards ecological modernisation of industries and have attempted to reconcile environmental protection with economic development. The industries which stand to lose from ecological modernisation have, however, gradually become more opposed to environmental policy measures. It seems that in Germany in particular these industries might be somewhat more influential and have succeeded in slowing down the pace of environmental policy-making.

Strategies at the European level

Many different terms are used to connote the approaches of the pioneers to environmental policy. Sweden speaks of *'förebild'* (example/model), while in Austria and Germany the approach is characterised by the expressions *'Vorreiter'* (forerunner) and *'Schrittmacher'* (pacemaker). The Netherlands uses the term *'gidsland'* (lead country); Denmark speaks of *'enegang'* (going alone), and while Norway is concerned about how to be a *'pådriver'* (pusher), Finland uses the term *'edelläkävijä'* (forerunner or pioneer). The differences are not only linguistic, but to some extent also reflect deeper strategic differences in the approaches conceptualised by the various pioneers (cf. the distinctions in the previous section on forerunner and pusher strategies). In the following section, the foreign environmental policy positions are explored. Since the concern here is with the more strategic foreign environmental policy orientations of the member states, these are treated one by one. First, we begin with the three new member states, and then review the other three, which have a longer experience with EU environmental policy, ending with an account of the position of Norway.

Sweden
Sweden's historical role as an international model in environmental policy was mentioned at the beginning of this chapter. Much could be said about this role, and it deserves more analysis than we can offer here (cf. Kronsell, this volume). Until Sweden became a member of the EU, this role was played by initiating international conferences

and other forms of co-operation on an *ad hoc* basis. Apart from the 1972 Stockholm Conference, Sweden has also initiated international environmental co-operation concerning air pollution and protection of the Baltic Sea (the Visby meetings). The Swedish government also supports the Stockholm Environment Institute, which is an international network of independent environmental think-tank institutes.

Sweden's role has been to act as a catalyst for international developments, and in this process Swedish experts and diplomats have come to play a significant role in providing scientifically based advice and international leadership. Sweden's role in the UN's International Panel on Climate Change, an advisory body with its secretariat in Stockholm headed by the Swede Bert Bolin, is a prominent example of this role, but so are the negotiations at the Rio convention at which the work of the Swedish diplomats stood out (Kjellen, 1994). Previous Swedish strategy has relied on a combination of international leadership (pushing) with domestic example-setting (being a forerunner), and this strategy has proved to be successful within air pollution control (see the account given by Kronsell, this volume). Climate policy does, however, provide a recent example of the difficulties with this approach. In 1991, Sweden decided to introduce a system of carbon-energy taxation comparable to that later proposed by the European Commission (a level of about US$100/ton CO_2). Although there were domestic taxation motives too, the intention was to set an example soon to be followed by other countries (SOU, 1989: 220). But the difficulties with securing joint action in practical climate policies and concerns about Sweden's competitiveness meant that Sweden had to lower its ambitions for the response to global climate change, and its level of carbon-energy taxation was substantially reduced in 1993 (Andersen, 1996).

Accession to the EU has provided Sweden with more formal possibilities of influencing and pushing wider regional and international arrangements, and the question is what role Sweden will come to play here. Before the referendum on membership, there was considerable concern that Sweden would have to lower its high domestic environmental standards. Both the four-year transitional period and the environmental guarantee were invoked to assure the Euro-sceptical and environmentally conscious population that 'Sweden will maintain its high environmental standards and at the same time, the EU will raise its ambitions in this field' (Dinkelspiel, quoted in

Europe Environment, 1994: 423). Immediately after having become a member, Sweden submitted a memorandum with a request to reduce air pollution and acidification, and a Swedish national expert was parachuted into the Commission for this purpose. Sweden has also formally worked out a policy for its intentions regarding EU environmental policy, but, like the other two new member states, Sweden has taken relatively careful steps during the first two years of membership (Liefferink, 1996b).

Austria

Austria became a *Schrittmacher* (pacemaker) (Österreichische Bundesregierung, 1995: 31) in environmental policy in the mid-1980s, when its domestic environmental policies were also consolidated. The role adopted in international environmental policy reflected Austria's more general foreign policy orientation of balancing neutrality with active international diplomacy to avoid isolation. Austria took the lead in establishing the international regime to protect the ozone layer by convening the diplomatic conference that led to the 1985 Vienna Convention for the Protection of the Ozone Layer, and Vienna has maintained its leading role on this issue (Lauber, this volume). Although Austria does perhaps lack Sweden's reputation, it has demonstrated in several ways a similar degree of active, international leadership in the last decade. By 1986 it had already introduced US standards for catalytic converters domestically, and had, for a long time, challenged the spread of nuclear power plants, particularly in Eastern Europe. The recent NEPP stressed Austria's involvement in global matters such as climate change and the United Nations Conference on Environment and Development (UNCED) process (Österreichische Bundesregierung, 1995: 20–3).

That the Austrian concerns extend beyond issues of immediate interest in the domestic context is well illustrated by the effort to develop a model for sustainable tropical timber imports by means of customs duties and a certification system (cf. Lauber, this volume). A law was passed prior to UNCED in 1992 for this purpose, and the law was intended to provide a model for other countries as well as to support the proposal for a forest convention to be negotiated in Rio. Due to lobbying by the International Timber Trade Organisation, the expected international forest convention was abandoned at UNCED and the Austrian initiative had little impact. When, after Rio, South East Asian countries began to threaten Austria with severe trade restrictions and protested to the General Agreement on Tariffs and Trade, the domestic custom duty was withdrawn. Similar to the Swedish difficulty with the carbon-energy tax prior to EU membership, the example of timber certification is hence illustrative of the difficulties involved with being a forerunner and pusher in a world where markets have become more open and interdependent and where formal influence in regional co-operation is lacking. Austria has subsequently tried to export the idea of a timber certification system to the EU, although with limited success until now (*Europe Environment*, 441: 102; 453: 125).

Euro-scepticism in Austria's population has not been experienced to the same degree as in Sweden and Denmark, and prior to the vote on membership, debate on the general implications for environmental protection was more limited than in Sweden (Lauber, this volume). Focus was mainly on the transit issue, because the western region of Tirol serves as a transport corridor for traffic between Germany and Italy, of which a large part is general north–south traffic from all of Europe. The accession agreement provided for an extension of the 1992 transit agreement between Austria and the EU of up to nine years. The EU has committed itself to reducing NO_x emissions from lorries by 60 per cent, while Austria has agreed to lift bilateral road transport quotas. Austria's interest in EU transport and infrastructure policies remains considerable, and Austria can be expected to keep pushing in this field, especially for a switch from road to rail. Austria can, therefore, be expected to provide an impetus not only to environmental policies (vehicle emissions) but also to transport policy, regional policy and the use of structural funds to integrate environmental concerns into these policies.

Finland

Of the three new member states, Finland has the most modest record as an environmental pioneer, but this does not preclude initiatives from Finland in the future. The lack of a sharp Finnish profile in international environmental policy can partly be explained by the relatively recent institutional consolidation of domestic environmental policies. Although Finland has nearly always joined the other Nordic countries in international environmental policies, it has not been possible to identify specific Finnish initiatives or proposals that have set the agenda for international environmental policy-making. Although Finland was the first country in the world to introduce a tax on CO_2 emissions, it has hardly perceived itself as a 'good example' that other countries could learn from. This somewhat humble attitude can probably best be understood given the historically difficult relationship Finland has had with Russia and the 'Finlandisation' of foreign policy-making in general.[5] The policy of 'active neutrality' and the leadership achieved through the Helsinki conferences in the 1970s on arms reductions were very much attuned to the Finnish role as a Soviet envoy (Arter, 1995: 364).

Foreign policy initiatives remain the prerogative of the Finnish President, and this initiative was cautiously managed from 1945 until 1995, when Russia's decline and Finland's membership in the EU broadened the space for foreign policy-making. Because foreign policy was an unusually sensitive issue that could create complications with Finland's difficult neighbour to the east, it seems obvious to link the absence of an active Finnish pusher role in environmental policy with the general paralysis in foreign policy. Combined with the late domestic institutionalisation of environmental policy (a Ministry of the Environment was not established until 1983), this may explain why, for many years, Finland was not a pusher but rather a follower of the other forerunners. It is not likely that international initiatives regarding the ozone layer or air pollution would have provoked reactions in Moscow, but the impression is rather that the general political climate in Finland was not favourable to such initiatives.

It remains to be seen whether the legacy from this period will continue to put its mark on Finland, also with respect to EU policy-making, or whether Finland will develop a more pro-active approach. Environmental policy was hardly an issue in the debate before the referendum on EU membership, a debate which focused on Finland's security concerns and the economic recession, both of which were linked with the collapse in the east (Arter, 1995; Joas, this volume). Situated at the rim of the EU, Finland has slightly different environmental concerns than the other forerunners. It shares with Sweden a concern for the Baltic Sea and the pollution from Russia and the Baltic republics. There is also concern about the presence of nuclear power plants on the Kola peninsula. The risk associated with nuclear power plants in the former Soviet republics is an issue that Finland is likely to find a shared interest in among the EU member states.

Germany

Germany became known as the 'engine' of EU environmental policy in the 1980s. This perception derived not only from the historical development of domestic environmental standards and from the economic significance of the German market in the Community as a whole, but also from the more intentional pusher role of the German government.

Germany combined the development of a domestic environmental policy with parallel efforts to push Community environmental policy, a strategy which to some extent explains the revitalisation of the latter in the early 1980s. Concern about the effects of acidification from air pollution, of which about 50 per cent originated outside Germany, caused the German government to follow a deliberate two-level strategy. Shortly after national regulations were proposed in 1982, Germany began an intensive lobbying campaign within the Community for a framework directive on air pollution (Bennett, 1992: 98). That was aided by the appointment of a German Environment Commissioner, Karl-Heinz Narjes. The Commission, which was already preparing an acidification policy, quickly developed a final proposal, and when Germany took over the Presidency of the Council in the first half of 1983, the issue was given high priority (Liefferink, 1996a). The activism which the German government displayed was very much linked with the domestic political setting, in which the new Green Party was making inroads on the voters from the traditional parties as a result of the forest die-back. These developments were coincidental with the approval of the 1983 Third Environmental Action Programme, which differed from previous such programmes by assigning environmental policy a more independent role, separate from concerns linked with ensuring free trade (Hildebrandt, 1992).

Occasionally, the German government has taken rather far-reaching measures domestically, without fully considering the implications for its EU partners. This was the case with the Waste Ordinance. The DUAL system was set up to deal with the waste that mounted up after German reunification had halted waste exports to the former GDR. Besides having implications for the internal market (requirements for foreign producers to comply with the green dot system), this ordinance also succeeded in turning the waste export stream towards Germany's EU partners.

However, Germany actually tends to prefer relatively harmonised solutions where possible and is less willing to take conscious unilateral action than most of the smaller member states. In the case of control of automobile exhaust, the most advanced measures, which had implications for the internal market as well, were put forward at the EU level (Holzinger, 1994). Although Germany threatened to adopt these standards unilaterally, such a step was never taken. Domestic measures consisted mainly of a system of smog alarms and traffic restrictions, which were more related to ozone problems (Prittwitz, 1990). A similar tendency can be seen in the case of the carbon-energy tax, which Germany supported actively at the EU level but did not introduce domestically.

The reason for the tendency to prefer common, harmonised solutions is probably less connected to Germany's self-perception as 'a devoted European'; the Bonn–Paris axis in environmental policy has until now had little significance (Pehle, this volume). A more straightforward explanation of Germany's lack of interest in 'green alliances' is probably that unilateral action with some of the smaller member states carries little weight in a German setting, both politically and economically (whereas joint action with Germany carries considerable weight, politically and economically, in the smaller member states). Germany has also shown little sympathy for the (predominantly Dutch) idea that groups of member states should jointly take unilateral measures.

The Netherlands

Although the Netherlands, as a smaller country, has formally carried less weight in Community institutions than Germany, the Netherlands has had its share of influence. Dutch influence has been based on the conceptual innovations in domestic environmental policies developed in the 1980s, e.g. in the ambitious NEPPs. New ideas and concepts were quickly conveyed into the Community institutions. In DG-XI, the environment directorate, the post of director-general has been held by Dutch nationals since 1986, and there is a conspicuous Dutch element in its staff as well. For instance, the Fifth Environmental Action Programme was deliberately modelled after the Dutch NEPP by a Dutch-led group (Kronsell, 1997).

Like Germany, the Netherlands has generally been inclined towards finding European solutions to environmental problems. For this purpose, the Netherlands has sometimes employed the distinctive Dutch technique of interest accommodation: complicated compromises, tailor-made to what is possible for each of the participants to accept and support. In response to opposition to the large combustion plants' directive, in particular from the UK, the Netherlands for instance proposed a differentiated scheme, with different reduction targets for different member states (Liefferink, 1996a). In another instance, the Dutch strategy suggested that a (willing) group of member states implement the targets of the Montreal Protocol, while the remaining member states be allowed to take weaker measures, to follow suit at a later stage (Bennett, 1992). While this approach has been successful for decades in accommodating the interests of the main political–clerical groupings in Dutch society, it has been much less so with respect to European environmental policy because of the reservations several actors have expressed against making policy at different speeds.

With a sense for tailor-made solutions, the Netherlands recently took the initiative to form a 'club' of the eight member states supporting the proposal for a European CO_2 tax.[6] The Dutch idea was that these member states should agree unilaterally to introduce some sort of carbon-energy tax, just as the Netherlands and the Nordic countries had already done. This club strategy was met with resentment, especially from Germany, which preferred to find a solution at the European level (Andersen, 1996).

Despite the Netherlands' active role as a pacemaker and pusher, the country has been prepared to make concessions to ensure that European solutions are reached:

> it may sometimes be necessary to moderate the Dutch position on the environment, aimed at achieving high community-wide standards, when this is necessary to reach agreement between member states, i.e. in the interest of the environment at the wider European level.
>
> (VROM, 1993)

Although the Dutch willingness to sacrifice the ideal for the workable should not be overestimated, the Netherlands has generally been less keen to insist on opt-outs, something which indicates the more compromise-oriented Dutch position.

Denmark
Denmark has been the most ambiguous of the original pioneers with regard to the development of a common environmental policy, and has been concerned that EU measures might prevent Denmark from

going further (Andersen, 1994; Johnson and Corcelle, 1995: 8). Denmark is a small country with only three votes in the Council of Ministers, and its preferences are perceived as carrying less weight than those of some of the larger member states. Policy-makers in Denmark have been anxious to secure leeway for a high domestic level of environmental protection, not only because environmental policy enjoys a considerable degree of support, but also because inroads to Denmark's autonomy on this point could provide ammunition for Denmark's strong and vociferous anti-EU movement. As the two referendums on the Maastricht Treaty showed, the Danish population is reluctantly European.

It was thus at Denmark's request that the environmental guarantee (Article 100A(4)) was inserted in the treaty at the intergovernmental conference in 1985. Article 100A(4) allows a member state that has been voted down to maintain its stricter domestic environmental regulations under specific circumstances, and Denmark wished to reserve the possibility for opting out in case internal market harmonisation measures interfered with desired environmental standards. The environmental guarantee played a significant role in the debate up to the 1986 referendum on the ratification of the Single European Act (Andersen, this volume). Nevertheless, Denmark has been cautious formally to invoke the treaty's environmental guarantee, something which was not done before 1995 (in the PCP case) (Pagh, 1994).

The example of vehicle emissions illustrates well the differences between the position of Denmark and that of Germany and the Netherlands in the 1980s. In 1985, Denmark blocked the Luxembourg Compromise on the Automobile Exhaust Directive, because it failed to introduce US standards for emissions control. Denmark joined instead the 'Stockholm group', which wanted to introduce US standards, and showed its disregard of Community environmental policy as the only Community member of this club to sign the declaration. (The other signatories were Sweden, Norway, Finland, Austria, Switzerland and Liechtenstein) (Liefferink, 1996a; Holzinger, 1994: 259.) Despite their principled support for stricter measures, Germany and the Netherlands did not sign, because of the incompatibility of the target with the Luxembourg compromise.

Since 1993, Denmark has taken a more active position in EU environmental policy. A change of government brought a more experienced and internationally oriented environmental minister, but there was also a regrouping among the Euro-sceptical Danes. In particular, the urban population started to react positively to the EU's more active position on international environmental policy in the early 1990s. The Danish government succeeded both in getting the new European Environment Agency located in Copenhagen and in getting the Commission's environment portfolio assigned to Ritt Bjerre-gaard. Denmark has actively tried to promote a Nordic group, consisting of Denmark, Sweden and Finland, within the Council of Ministers, and has actively played the role of pusher in EU environ-mental policy.

Norway
By the early 1970s, Norway had already adopted an active position in establishing international environmental conventions, notably the Oslo Convention of 1972 and the Paris Convention of 1974, both of which focused on the dumping of toxic waste in the North Sea. Along with Sweden, Norway also played a very active role in establishing an international regime for the control of air pollution and the reduction of acidification. As in Sweden, this effort was combined with domes-tic 'example-setting' in terms of strict standards for SO_2 emissions. By lending her name to the 1987 report from the World Commission for Sustainable Development, Prime Minister Gro Harlem Brundtland also helped position Norway in international environmental policy-making as one of the pioneers for creating a more sustainable devel-opment, and Norway has been an active 'mover' in the development of an international climate change policy. At the domestic level, this policy has been supported by the unilateral introduction of a CO_2 tax.

Norway's environmental image has been slightly disturbed by the whale issue; Norway has insisted on its right to hunt whales against the policy of the International Whaling Commission. Less noticed outside Norway has been the general reorientation of environmental policy in the early 1990s. In particular the Norwegian Finance Ministry has successfully argued for the use of cost–benefit analysis (Reitan, this volume). This approach led Norway to back out of its CO_2 stabilisation target, which proved to be costly to achieve for Norway's oil-intensive economy, and to support a joint implementa-tion approach, where CO_2 reductions can be effectuated in co-opera-tion with other countries, e.g. in Eastern Europe.

Environmental policy played a very significant role in the Norwegian referendum, where 37 per cent of the voters referred to environmental issues as the most important reason for voting as they did (Reitan, this volume). The opponents of membership argued that Norway could best maintain its forerunner role in international environmental policy by staying outside the EU, while the supporters argued for the need to influence EU environmental policy. Still, the increased integration of environmental and energy policies may face Norway with difficult dilemmas of reconciling economic and environmental policies and undermine its previous position as a forerunner.

As a member of the EEA, Norway has agreed to incorporate existing and future environmental directives in its national laws. Like the other European Free Trade Area countries, Norway is allowed a seat in the expert and implementation committees working under the auspices of the European Commission and may try to influence legislation there. Norwegian interest groups might also try to compensate for the lack of membership by seeking influence directly in Brussels. On the other hand, the other Nordic countries may see an interest in using Norway as a vehicle for traditional Nordic policies if these are blocked within the EU. The existence of a Nordic block, including Norway, in EU environmental policy-making became clear in the controversy over the Basle Convention in the spring of 1995 (Andersen, this volume).

Bringing the two levels together: the dynamics of the pioneers

The above analysis has focused on the domestic basis of EU environmental policy as well as the developed strategies of both the new member states and the former pioneers. It has been shown how the legacy of environmental policy-making in each of these countries has affected the concepts of environmental policy that are likely to be brought to the bargaining table in Brussels and how each of these countries has developed relatively individual strategies for conceptualising and influencing the relationship between their domestic environmental policy and the policy pursued at the EU level. In this final section, a short analysis will be made of the dynamics of EU enlargement for policy-making at the EU level. While the input of the pioneers to policy-making is relatively well known, it is relatively complex how this input will affect the decision-making process as well as the outcome. (We have dealt with the dynamics of enlargement in more detail elsewhere, in particular Liefferink and Andersen, 1997.)

The crucial question is to what extent the group of pioneers will be able to forge some kind of loose alliance with each other and, on the basis of their domestic policy experiences, provide a leadership in the Council that will be attractive to a broader group of member states. It depends very much on the degree of coherency in environmental policy-making among the pioneers. As already indicated, the degree of coherency is limited. To structure this final assessment of the coherency among the six countries, comparisons will be made using the following three elements (cf. Putnam, 1988):

- the domestic level: political institutions;
- the domestic level: distribution of power, preferences and possible coalitions; and
- the EU level: strategies of negotiators.

The domestic level: political institutions

Denmark, Sweden, the Netherlands and, to a lesser extent, Finland and Austria have relatively strong domestic environmental policy institutions, i.e. the environment ministries carry reasonable weight, and they have an autonomy which allows them to influence the positions of their respective countries at the EU level in Brussels. A process by which environmental policy is becoming integrated in other sectors of society has gradually begun, and, with the exception of Austria, each country has developed a coherent tradition for broad, processual environmental policy regulations, with successive and concurrent innovations that include life cycle policy and the use of economic instruments, for example.

In Germany, the Ministry of Environment carries less political weight and is restricted both by *Länder* competences and by the power of the more traditional ministries in Bonn (Foreign Policy, Finance, etc.). The existence of independent, advisory bodies at the federal level, such as the Council of Experts for Environmental Issues, cannot compensate for this. In particular the federal structure provides additional opportunities to block the decision-making process. Germany shares a regulatory style with Austria that, due to its emphasis on scientific-technical standards, differs considerably from that of the other pioneers, and although Germany has gone along with recent trends in environmental policy-making with the enactment of the Life Cycle Assessment Law, some of the new concepts and more procedural policy instruments have not been so quickly adapted into German legislation.

The domestic level: distribution of power, preferences and possible coalitions

Economic and industrial differences are pronounced between the six pioneers under consideration. In Germany, the Netherlands and Sweden, traditional smokestack industries within chemical, steel, and paper and pulp production are politically significant, while in Denmark and Austria, the commercial structure is more based on small- and middle-sized companies. Finland is the exception, with the significance of its forest industry. In Sweden and Denmark, in particular, and to a lesser extent in the Netherlands, the advocacy coalition of environmental and consumer organisations, business interests associated with environmentally friendly industries and political parties of 'green' orientation has become significant. One reason for the relative 'greening' of Swedish industry is the early institutionalisation of environmental policy. By the early 1970s, Swedish steel producers had already responded to taxes on energy use (and, as a result, found a niche in the stainless steel market) (Finansdepartementet, 1991).

In Sweden, both the rural Centre Party and a separate Green Party represent green interests; and while there are no green parties in Denmark and the Netherlands, other parties, some with influential positions in government, have responded to the greening of the electorate. (In the Netherlands notably D'66 and the Green Left, in Denmark the Social Liberals and the Socialist People's Party.) In Finland, Austria and Germany, separate green parties have been formed, but they are relatively small. And with the exception of Finland, where the Greens are in government, they have until now mainly gained influence at the regional or local level. It is safe to say that in all six countries the traditional parties have greened after the emergence of green or greenish parties on the political scene, and that it is an important part of the background for the relative advancement of their domestic environmental policies. The lack of enduring and stable parliamentary coalitions in Sweden, Denmark and the Netherlands may, however, explain the more easy penetration of green demands into official policy-making in these three countries.

The EU level: strategies of negotiators
It follows from the review of the policies of the six pioneers that their strategies as to how EU environmental policy can or should be influenced vary considerably. Denmark and Sweden are likely to remain the most outspoken pushers, which will at the same time choose, if necessary, to take advantage of the opportunities for opting out on harmonised measures to preserve a high national level of protection. The Netherlands and Austria will most likely give more priority to achieve solutions at a European level, and the Netherlands in particular may continue to exert its constructive pusher role, e.g. through tailor-made compromising. On some issues, in particular on the sensitive transit issue, Austria might be more vociferous and perform like Denmark and Sweden. Finland's role is the most difficult to predict. In the short run, Finland can be expected to continue as a follower of the group of pioneers, but in the longer run, Finland might develop a more result-oriented strategy to gain support for the issues that are important from a Finnish perspective.

With regard to Germany, it is doubtful whether it will still play the role as an 'engine' in EU environmental policy. The situation in Germany is complex since it differs considerably from that of the smaller member states. In particular, there is an asymmetry in the benefits (economically and in domestic politics) accruing to Germany and those accruing to the smaller member states from taking unilateral measures jointly. There are issues which Germany will keep pushing, but Germany has become more reluctant to take unilateral measures. For reasons that have to do with the integration process as a whole, Germany may also be concerned with how its partners, in particular France, would view the formation of a *de facto* environmental alliance among Germany and five, smaller, northern member states. In recent years, Germany has distanced itself from its former pusher role, and although there is still no Bonn–Paris axis in environmental policy, Germany now tends to work more closely together with France and the UK. By dismissing former Minister of Environment Klaus Töpfer, who was an experienced inspirator and critic of EU environmental policy, and appointing the less experienced Angela Merkel, Germany's Chancellor Helmut Kohl has indicated that Germany should take a more subordinate position in EU environmental policy in the future.

The contents of the book

The chapters in this book consist of two parts. In the first part, they each trace the historical development of environmental policy in the domestic political setting and analyse significant patterns and developments at the institutional and conceptual level in national environmental policy-making. In the second part, they each examine the foreign environmental policy-making process, paying attention to the role of various actors and institutions in the process of linking domestic environmental policies with international environmental policy-making, mainly, but not exclusively, in the context of the EU. The logic behind this structure is the conception of a reciprocal, intergovernmental two-level game as a significant aspect of EU policy-making. Although each chapter has been written according to a common set of guidelines, we have not tried to force upon the chapter authors the use of a rigid theoretical framework, but have allowed them to present the environmental policies of their own countries in a more explorative way, allowing emphasis to be placed on the developments which have proved to be significant in each of the countries under scrutiny here. As such, the book also presents itself as a reference work for further comparative analyses of environmental policy.

Notes

1 Most sources mention these three countries as the forerunners in EU environmental policy, e.g. Johnson and Corcelle, 1995: 8; Krämer, 1992.

2 The Single European Act from 1987 introduced decision-making by qualified majority voting for environmental measures related to the internal market, according to Article 100A of the treaty. The Maastricht Treaty expanded this method of decision-making in the Council to environmental policy in general (Article 130R-T), with the exception of energy, water resources and fiscal measures, where unanimity is still required.

3 The six forerunners hold the following number of votes in the Council of Ministers: Germany 10, the Netherlands 5, Denmark 3, Sweden 4, Austria 4, Finland 3. Twenty-six votes are sufficient to form a blocking minority (in some cases twenty-three, according to the Ioannina compromise). If the six join forces, they control twenty-nine votes.

4 For Austria, a transitional agreement on transit traffic may be extended for up to nine years.

5 Finland achieved independence from Russia in 1917. A large part of the Carelian region was lost to Russia as a result of World War II.
6 In addition to the six member states described here, Belgium and Luxembourg are also included.

References

Aguilar Fernandez, S. (1997), Abandoning a laggard role: new strategies in Spanish environmental policy, in D. Liefferink and M. S. Andersen (eds), *The Innovation of EU Environmental Policy*, Copenhagen, Scandinavian University Press.

Allison, Graham T. (1971), *Essence of Decision – Explaining the Cuban Missile Crisis*, Boston, Little, Brown and Company.

Andersen, Mikael Skou (1994), *Governance by Green Taxes: Making Pollution Prevention Pay*, Manchester and New York, Manchester University Press.

Andersen, Mikael Skou (1996), *The Domestic Politics of Carbon Energy Taxation*, unpublished manuscript, Aarhus, Department of Political Science.

Arter, D. (1995), The EU referendum in Finland on 16 October 1994: a vote for the West, not for Maastricht, *Journal of Common Market Studies*, 33:3, 361–410.

Baker, Susan, Kay Milton and Steven Yearly (eds) (1994), *Protecting the Periphery, Regional Politics and Policy*, special issue, London, Frank Cass.

Bennett, Graham (1992), Acid drops: the European Community's acid emissions control policy, in Bennett, *Dilemmas: Coping with Environmental Problems*, London, Earthscan, 92–132.

Bennett, Graham (1993), The implementation of EC environmental directives: the gap between law and practice, *The Science of the Total Environment*, 129, 19–28.

Bilgrav, Jens (1991), *Folketingstidende F*, sp. 3629; 3654; 6294.

Boehmer-Christiansen, Sonja and Jim Skea (1991), *Acid Politics: Environmental and Energy Policies in Britain and Germany*, London, Belhaven Press.

Bulmer, Simon (1983), Domestic politics and European Community policy-making, *Journal of Common Market Studies*, 21:4, 349–63.

Bungarten, H. H. (1978), *Umweltpolitik in Westeuropa*, Bonn, Europa Union Verlag.

Conrad, Jobst (1990), *Nitratdiskussion und Nitratpolitik in der Bundesrepublik Deutschland*, Berlin, Edition Sigma.

Coyle, Carmel (1994), Administrative capacity and the implementation of EU environmental policy in Ireland, in S. Baker *et al.* (eds), *Protecting the Periphery*, Essex, Frank Cass, 62–79.

Downing, Paul B. and K. Hanf (eds) (1983), *International Comparisons in Implementing Pollution Laws*, Boston, Kluwer-Nijhoff Publ.

Environment Watch Western Europe, bi-weekly newsletter, Arlington, MA, Cutter Information Corp.

Europe Environment, bi-weekly newsletter, Brussels, Europe Information Service.

Evans, P., H. Jacobson and R. Putnam (eds) (1993), *Double-edged Diplomacy*, Berkeley, University of California Press.

Finansdepartementet (1991), *Konkurrensneutral energibeskattning*, SOU 1991:90, Stockholm.

Font, Nuria and Francesc Morata (1992), Environmental policy in Spain, in A. I. Jansen and K. Hanf (1996), *Environmental Administration and Policymaking*, London, Harvester and Wheatsheaf.

Héritier, A. (1992), Policy-Netzwerkanalyse als Untersuchungsinstrument im europäischen Kontext, *Politische Vierteljahresschrift*, 34: 24, 432–47.

Hildebrandt, Philipp M. (1992), The European Community's environmental policy, 1957 to 1992: from incidental measures to an international regime?, *Journal of Environmental Politics*, 1:4, 13–44.

Hill, Michael (1983), The role of the British Alkali and Clean Air Inspectorate in air pollution control, in Paul B. Downing and Kenneth Hanf (eds), *International Comparisons in Implementing Pollution Laws*, Boston, Kluwer-Nijhoff Publ, 87–106.

Hix, Simon (1994), The study of the European Community: the challenge to comparative politics, *West European Politics*, 17:1, 1–30.

Holzinger, Katharina (1994), *Politik des kleinsten gemeinsamen Nenners? Umweltpolitische Entscheidungsprozesse in der EG am Beispiel der Einführung des Katalysatorautos*, Berlin, Sigma.

Holzinger, Katharina (1997), The influence of the new member states on EU environmental policy making: a game theory approach, in D. Liefferink and M. S. Andersen (eds), *The Innovation of EU Environmental Policy*, Copenhagen, Scandinavian University Press.

Huber, M. (1997), Leadership in the EU climate policy, in D. Liefferink and M. S. Andersen (eds), *The Innovation of EU Environmental Policy*, Copenhagen, Scandinavian University Press.

Huelshoff, M. (1994), Domestic politics and dynamic issue linkage: a reformulation of integration theory, *International Studies Quarterly*, 38, 255–79.

Jänicke, M. (ed.) (1978), *Umweltpolitik*, Opladen, Leske und Budrich.

Jänicke, M. (1990), Erfolgsbedingungen von Umweltpolitik im Internationalen Vergleich, *Zeitschrift für Umweltpolitik*, 3/90, 213–31.

Jänicke, M. and H. Weidner (1996), *Capacity Building in Environmental Policy: An International Comparison*, Berlin, Springer Verlag.

Jansen, A. I. and K. Hanf (1996) (in press), *Environmental Administration and Policymaking*, London, Harvester and Wheatsheaf.

Johnson, Ralph W. and M. Brown Gardner (1976), *Cleaning Up Europe's Waters*, New York, Praeger Publ.

Johnson, Stanley P. and Guy Corcelle (1995), *The Environmental Policy of the European Communities*, London, Graham and Trotman.

Judge, David (1992), *A Green Dimension for the European Community: Political Issues and Processes*, London, Frank Cass.

Kelley, D., K. Stunkel and R. Wescott (1976), *The Economic Superpowers and the Environment*, San Francisco, Freeman and Co.

Kjellen, Bo (1994), A personal assessment, in I. Mintzer and J. Leonard (eds), *Negotiating Climate Change*, Cambridge, Cambridge University Press, 149–74.

Knoepfel, Peter and Helmut Weidner (1985), *Luftreinhaltepolitik im internationalen Vergleich*, Band 1–6, Berlin, Edition Sigma.

Krämer, Ludwig (1992), *Focus on European Environmental Law*, London, Sweet and Maxwell.

Kronsell, Annica (1997), Policy innovation in the garbage can: the EU's Fifth Environmental Action Programme, in D. Liefferink and M. S. Andersen (eds), *The Innovation of EU Environmental Policy*, Copenhagen, Scandinavian University Press.

Larrue, Corinne (1992), *The Implementation of Environmental Policies by the French Administration*, paper delivered at a Workshop in Comparative Research on Environmental Administration and Policymaking, Drøbak, 11–14 June, Tours, Centre d'Etudes Supérieures d'Aménagement.

Liefferink, D. (1996a), *Environmental Policy and the Nation State: The Netherlands, the EU and Acid Rain*, Manchester and New York, Manchester University Press.

Liefferink, D. (1996b), *The New Member States and the Greening of EU Environmental Policy: Opportunities and Strategies in Brussels*, paper presented at the conference Scandinavia and the extended European Union, University of Surrey, Guildford, 7–8 June.

Liefferink, D. and M. S. Andersen (eds) (1997), *The Innovation of EU Environmental Policy*, Copenhagen, Scandinavian University Press.

Liefferink, D., P. Lowe and A. Mol (eds) (1993), *European Integration and Environmental Policy*, London, Belhaven Press.

Lundqvist, Lennart J. (1980), *The Hare and the Tortoise: Clean Air Policies in the United States and Sweden*, Ann Arbor, University of Michigan Press.

Moravcsik, A. (1993), Preferences and power in the European Community: a liberal intergovernmentalist approach, *Journal of Common Market Studies*, 31:4, 473–524.

Munk Christiansen, Peter (ed.) (1996), Governing the environment: politics, policy and organization in the Nordic countries, *Nord*, 1996:5, Copenhagen, Nordic Council of Ministers.

OECD (1975), *The Polluter Pays Principle*, Paris, OECD.

Österreichische Bundesregierung (1995), *Nationaler Umwelt Plan (NUP)*, Vienna, Österreichische Bunderregierung.

Pagh, P., 1994, Miljøgarantien efter PCP-dommen, *Ugeskrift for Retsvæsen*, 276–83.

Pellegrom, Sandra (1997), The constraint of daily work in Brussels: how relevant is the input from national capitals?, in D. Liefferink and M. S. Andersen (eds), *The Innovation of EU Environmental Policy*, Copenhagen, Scandinavian University Press.

Peters, Guy (1992), Bureaucratic politics and the institutions of the European Community, in Alberta M. Sbragia (ed.), *Europolitics*, Washington D.C., Brookings, 75–122.

Pridham, G., S. Verney and Konstadakopulos (1995), Environmental policy in Greece: evolution, structures and process, *Environmental Politics*, 4:2, 244–70.

Prittwitz, Volker von (1990), *Das Katastrophenparadox: Elemente einer Theorie der Umweltpolitik*, Opladen.

Putnam, R. (1988), Diplomacy and domestic politics: the logic of two-level games, *International Organization*, 42:3, 427–60.

Rasmussen, Lise Nordvig and Mikael Skou Andersen (1996), *An Institutional Analysis of the Policy-making Process in the Council: The Case of EU Environmental Policy*, working paper, Aarhus, Department of Political Science.

Richardson, J. (ed.) (1982), *Policy Styles in Western Europe*, London, Allen and Unwin.

Richardson, J. (1994), EU water policy: uncertain agendas, shifting networks and complex coalitions, *Environmental Politics*, 3:4, 139–67.

Richardson, J. and N. Watts (1985), *National Policy Styles and the Environment: Britain and West Germany Compared*, IIUG dp 85–16, Berlin, WZB.

Schumann, Wolfgang (1993), Die EG als neuer Anwendungsbereich für die Policy-Analyse: Möglichkeiten und Perspektiven der konzeptionellen Weiterentwicklung, *Politische Vierteljahresschrift*, 34, Sonderheft 24, 394–431.

Skjærseth, Jon Birger, Steinar Andresen and Jørgen Wettestad (1992), EF-landene og Norden i international miljøpolitikk, *Norsk miljøpolitikk og europæisk samarbeid, Forskernotater til Europautredningen*, Oslo, Fritiof Nansen Institutt, 31–84.

SOU (Statens offentliga utredningar) (1989), *Sätt värde på miljön*, SOU 21, Stockholm.

Tsuru, Shigeto and Helmut Weidner (1985), *Ein Modell für uns: Die Erfolge der japanischen Umweltpolitik*, Cologne, Kiepenheuer und Witsch.

Vogel, David (1986), *National Styles of Regulation: Environmental Policy in Great Britain and the United States*, Ithaca, Cornell University Press.

Vogel, David and Veronica Kun (1987), The comparative study of environmental policy: a review of the literature, in Meinolf Dierkes *et al.* (eds), *Comparative Policy Research*, Aldershot, Gower, 99–170.

VROM (Ministry of Housing, Physical Planning and Environment) (1993), *National Environmental Policy Plan 2*, The Hague, VROM.

Weale, Albert (1992), *The New Politics of Pollution*, Manchester, Manchester University Press.

Weale, Albert (1996), Capacity building in the United Kingdom, in M. Jänicke and H. Weidner, *National Environmental Policies – A Comparative Study of Capacity Building*, Berlin, Springer Verlag.

Weale, A., T. O'Riordan and L. Kramme (1991), *Controlling Pollution in the Round: Change and Choice in Environmental Regulation in Britain and West Germany*, London, Anglo-German Foundation.

Weiler, J. H. H. (1991), The transformation of Europe, *The Yale Law Journal*, 100:8, 2405–83.

1 *Annica Kronsell*

Sweden: setting a good example

Introduction

In the 1960s, policy-makers became increasingly aware of the problems associated with industrial processes and urbanisation. This resulted in a comparatively early institutionalisation of environmental concerns: the establishment of an environmental agency in 1967 and the promulgation of the Environmental Protection Act in 1969. The progressive stance that Swedish policy-makers took at that time has continued over the years. One argument presented here is that this progressiveness is partly due to the particular policy-making style in Sweden. Through co-operation and consensus-seeking processes, the interests and concerns of broad sectors of society have been effectively incorporated into policy-making. Furthermore, the particular status of independent agencies has left experts and bureaucrats more room to influence politics.

The development of a set of environmental institutions and pieces of legislation reflects the changing perception of environmental problems and solutions since the 1960s and can be ascribed to a number of different factors. First, simple trial and error and feedback mechanisms have revealed which strategies work in the best or the worst way. Learning has led to more informed, but also diversified perceptions of what environmental problems are. Second, economic factors have been very important. It is particularly noticeable that in any struggle over priorities, environmental concerns have lost out to economic ones. Third, geographical and atmospheric conditions have made Swedish territory particularly vulnerable to pollutants emitted from sources beyond its borders. This last factor has alerted Swedish policy-makers to keep a close watch on regional and international changes. Hence, the relationship with neighbouring states and the international community with regard to environmental issues has been particularly important. While Sweden has had a long-standing interest in encouraging international environmental co-operation (its initiative to hold the UN Conference on the Human Environment in Stockholm is evidence of this), it has also understood throughout that only by having its own domestic environmental policies in order could it expect others to do the same.

This chapter will start with a brief outline of the perception of environmental issues in Sweden. This account will be followed by a discussion of the different strategies used and the institutional responses to these. The political traditions and policy styles that contributed to the way environmental issues became organised will also be presented. Since international issues have been especially prominent on the Swedish environmental agenda, the remainder of the chapter will look more specifically at the foreign policy dimension of environmental policy. Emphasis will be placed on relationships with Western European states and the EU. The analysis of the foreign policy dimension will also look at perceptions of international environmental problems, the strategies proposed by Swedish policy-makers for solving these problems, and the type of institutions responsible for dealing with this dimension.

Perceptions of environmental issues

It is important how problems are perceived because this informs and influences the strategies employed to solve these problems. Environmental issues have been on the political agenda in Sweden since the 1960s. Since then, perceptions of environmental problems have changed considerably. Although it is possible to describe these different perceptions chronologically, this would be somewhat deceptive. One way of perceiving a problem is not immediately replaced when a new one appears. Rather, different perceptions tend to co-exist with one another, i.e. a certain way of viewing environmental problems and the strategies to solve them – all of which became popular and highly salient during a certain time – can still have value at another time. For example, the nature conservation aspect of environmental concerns described below may not be the usual way of approaching this problem today, but it is still feasible and widely accepted, as evidenced by the continued setting aside of nature reserves and national parks. In the following, the different perceptions and responses of Swedish policy-makers will be accounted for. Since this is based only on the view of the policy-makers, a number of perceptions will be excluded. This means that the views expressed by, for example, radical ecologists or *laissez-faire* economists will not be accounted for.

Conservation and preservation of nature

The development of environmental policy in Sweden can be historically traced back to two separate fields: nature conservation and the development of technical and chemical control policies (Lundgren, 1989). By the turn of the twentieth century, state property had been set aside for national parks. Towards the middle of the century, concern for the environment was focused on the need for natural reserves for recreational and aesthetic purposes in times of rapid industrialisation and urbanisation. During this period with nature conservation, some institutionalisation took place. General guidelines adopted by the government in 1963 included setting aside areas for recreation and outdoor life, especially in the most urbanised areas; preserving certain areas representative of the traditional landscape; and guaranteeing free access to the beach front. The Governmental Nature Conservation Board was set up in 1963 and charged with the administration and monitoring of conservation efforts around the country. In 1964, the government passed a nature conservation act. Simultaneously, they began to develop an increasing and expanding set of policies to control the use of chemicals.

Pollution as a health problem

At the turn of the century, the side effects of industrial development, particularly water pollution, were becoming visible. The water pollution problem was mainly due to the discharge of untreated sewage into lakes and rivers from industry and households. Water pollution was discussed in parliament a number of times between 1902 and 1908, but it was decided that water pollution was not sufficiently important and urgent to demand legislative measures. A rather weak piece of legislation on water pollution came in 1941 (Ds 1989: 32). Conditions were dramatically improved when municipalities, instead of relying on dilution, set up sewage treatment plants.

The Swedish translation of Rachel Carson's book, *Silent Spring*, in

1963 contributed to the debate on mercury in the environment, along with other Swedish books on the theme of poisons and pollutants in the ecosystem. Nevertheless, mercury pollution was still perceived mainly as a health problem by the majority of the public. High mercury levels had been found in birds' eggs and in fish, both main staples in the Swedish kitchen. Scientists subsequently showed that these concentrations originated from totally different sources. Mercury in wild birds was due to their place at the end of the food chain, in poultry it was due to the treatment of grains with mercury compounds, and in fish it was due to the use of mercury in the paper and pulp industry, which was then disposed of into the fishing waters. This made some people realise that toxins could indeed transcend and travel far away from the original source and affect human health; it started to become more apparent that the problem of environmental pollution was not a local, isolated phenomenon. The mercury debate put environmental issues on the political agenda as issues in their own right. In 1965, the government issued a prohibition against the use of alkyl mercury in seed grain treatment, and in 1966 it prohibited the use of phenyl mercury in the paper mill industry (Lundqvist, 1974).

The transnational character of pollution
Thus, the mid-1960s marked a turning point in the perception of pollution problems. In the 1960s and during the following decade, the debate was intense and the activities connected to environmental issues were many. For example, the problem of acid rain was already recognised by many in the 1950s, especially by the scientific community, but it was still perceived as a local problem that could be solved either by building higher smokestacks or by reducing the sulphur content of heating oil. It was not until the 1960s that the scientist, Svante Odén, managed to convey the message that acidification was a problem far more extensive than that. Relying on diverse scientific observations, he linked local urban air pollution to data showing the effects of sulphur emissions on water and land. Odén, together with a few other scientists and policy-makers who had already become aware of some of the dimensions of this problem, was successful in lobbying and convincing government officials and the general public of the possible implications as well as the origin of the acidification problem. Legislation passed in 1968 forbidding the burning of heating oil containing more than 2.5 per cent sulphur and the early

engagement with the acidification problem can be attributed to key persons who managed to bridge the gap between the scientific community and the bureaucrats and politicians (Lundgren, 1991).

After having passed this piece of legislation in 1968, Sweden turned towards the international arena to try to persuade other countries to take action. By 1968 it had become obvious to individuals and groups in Sweden that a major part of the acidification problem was created beyond Swedish borders, particularly in the Ruhr region and in Great Britain. It was difficult, however, to win support for the claim that sulphur in fossil fuels caused damage to forests in distant places, far from the emission source. Environmental problems were still generally thought of as rather local phenomena. Yet Swedish policy-makers believed that if Sweden could not set an example, it would have no grounds on which to argue that other countries should work towards reducing the sulphur content of fossil fuels. Nonetheless, it took some time before the acidification problem was recognised internationally and almost twenty years before an international agreement was signed showing a commitment to begin to solve this problem (Lundgren, 1991).

The understanding of the transnational character of environmental problems occurred relatively early among key policy-makers in Sweden. It was induced by the stark realities that Sweden was particularly vulnerable to pollution from outside sources and gave policymakers a strong impetus to engage in international activities to encourage environmental accords at the international level. An early example is the UN Conference on the Human Environment, held in Stockholm in 1972, initiated by the Swedish delegation to the UN, and headed by Ambassador Sverker Åström (UD, 1969: 126). Engagement in international activities has been a tradition ever since.

Overtaken by the energy crisis
Because of the oil embargo in 1973–1974, much of the commitment to general environmental problems dwindled and was taken over by the energy debate. Energy had been considered the motor of industrialisation and modernisation in Sweden. To keep this motor running, the availability of cheap energy had been guaranteed by different types of subsidies and tax reduction schemes made available to Sweden's energy-intensive industries, for example, the wood, pulp and steel industries (SOU, 1956; SOU, 1970). The oil embargo created an oil crisis in Sweden, and the most important concerns

became the dependence on fossil fuel and Sweden's subsequent vulnerability to external politics. This concern was magnified by the increased understanding of limited resources in general, as articulated in the debates in relation to the influential and apocalyptic visions of the 1972 Club of Rome report, *Limits to Growth* (Meadows *et al.*, 1974).

Energy conservation was a very important response to this concern about limited energy resources. Very broad and far-reaching measures, albeit some temporary ones, were carried out in an effort to conserve energy. Various types of research projects and initiatives aimed at developing alternative energy sources were initiated. Energy conservation methods and insulation techniques were encouraged by governmental funds and subsidies. In addition, petrol was rationed, television transmission was stopped at 10 p.m., people were encouraged by campaigns to save water by showering together rather than alone, and every other street light was turned off. This was the first time that environmental issues had become extremely personal. The personal became the political, as strategies appealing to individual responsibilities showed how individual actions could have political consequences. The energy crisis was not perceived in environmental terms, but it did, nevertheless, have effects contributing to a sounder use of natural resources. Perhaps most importantly, it led to a new understanding of resources as finite and to the realisation that international actions have concrete effects on individuals, and it showed that personal actions make a difference.

Apart from energy conservation and the development of alternative energy sources, an increasing reliance on nuclear energy became another strategy aimed at reducing Sweden's dependency on foreign fuel sources. Nuclear energy had been introduced in Sweden without much controversy. On the contrary, the possibilities were perceived as endless and the problems few (SOU, 1956; SOU, 1970). The development of nuclear energy on a large scale started in 1975. In response to the growth of the nuclear energy sector, the general energy debate evolved into a nuclear energy debate, most intensely in the late 1970s. While there were dispersed protests throughout the 1970s, the issue became most controversial after the Three Mile Island nuclear accident in 1979 (Jahn, 1992: 391). The main conflict was between those who emphasised the benefits of clean and cheap nuclear energy and those who envisioned serious problems with highly toxic nuclear waste and the risk of accidents at nuclear energy sites. It was a very salient debate, and in 1980 it culminated with the fourth referendum in Swedish history. As we shall see later, this referendum and the campaign preceding it became vital to the development of the Green Party. Nuclear energy has more than doubled its share of total energy production since the referendum (Jahn, 1992: 392), and the relationship between the energy and environmental sectors has remained conflictual. The decision to phase out nuclear energy is still contested and is being re-evaluated today as Sweden is faced with economic problems.

Moving from a sectorial approach towards integrative policies
Although other types of environmental issues remained somewhat in the background during the energy debates, environmental regulation constantly developed. The policy development was related to various environmental topics, but within different and separate sectors which were inadequately co-ordinated. As a result, it became increasingly difficult for some parts of industry, businesses and farmers to know which laws applied to their activities. In short, the variance in, and incoherence of, the different pieces of what could be labelled environmental legislation made it very difficult for the actors affected by the laws to keep within them. What was needed was a broad and embracing piece of legislation that could connect nature conservation, physical planning, chemicals and toxins, energy, traffic and species preservation. The Environmental Protection Act of 1969 had, of course, been an attempt at this, but a very incomplete one. It contained no provisions that took the rapid deterioration of the natural environment into account. Different sector goals were often in conflict and would sometimes directly contradict environmental goals. The environmental policy system lacked co-ordination capabilities, the division of responsibilities was vague, and environmental competence was lacking in different sectors (SOU, 1987).

In response to this lack of cohesion on environmental issues, the government presented a bill entitled 'Environmental policy in the 1990s' (Prop. 1987/88). This bill was the first attempt to view environmental policy in a collective sense. This subsequently led to an investigation of how best to co-ordinate the various pieces of environmental policy. The bill also related current Swedish environmental policy to the ideas of the Brundtland Report and adopted the report's recommendation of sector responsibility. The idea was to involve different policy sectors, such as agriculture and traffic departments, in the work with environmental problems by setting up target levels of emissions. As a result, sector responsibility has become a principle in the environmental activities of the 1990s, but this has only accentuated the need for a legislative environmental framework that can accommodate sectoral interests without creating a conflict between different sector goals and environmental goals.

Recognising these problems, the government commissioned an inquiry to find an environmental code that could co-ordinate these separate laws and regulations and contribute to a more coherent environmental policy and effective implementation. A number of commissions and subsequent consultations have led to the proposition of an environmental code (Prop. 1994/95).[1] When the Social Democrats were elected into government in September 1994, the bill was sent back to a committee for revision. This first proposal for an environmental code was considered insufficient because, first, it contained only a superficial investigation of the integration of water, agricultural and forest policies. Second, the problem of the responsibility for pollution and sanctions against pollutors was not considered well developed. Finally, the role of particularly environmental non-governmental organisations (NGOs) in litigation and in the policy process needed to be strengthened (Dir. 1994). A new proposal for an environmental code is expected in 1997. Even though the aim is to strengthen environmental legislation further, the much needed efforts to reinforce the environmental dimension of Swedish politics have also been postponed.

Environmentalism goes to the market
During the 1980s, administrative regulation was, to an increasing degree, supplemented by different types of charges and taxes (Sterner, 1994). These market-based solutions indicated that environmental problems were perceived in economic terms and to an increasing degree included in the economic discourse. The politicians began to recognise that the economic value of natural resources could be calculated, and hence incorporated into economic language and calculations. Pollution problems and resource depletion started to become associated with market failure, corrected for by setting the 'right' price. In making environmental issues a market matter, the ethical dimension so important to environmentalism was removed. However, it emerged again towards the end of the 1980s: environmental concerns moved up on the public and political agenda.

By this time, early environmental policies had succeeded quite effectively in reducing certain types of pollution, such as the pollution of bathing water in lakes and the sea and emissions into the air from factories. Focus now changed towards a more production process-oriented environmentalism. The impact of aerosols on the ozone layer and the problems of bleaching processes in paper production precipitated. With amazing speed, this led to the phasing out of certain bleached paper products. This happened without legislative or economic instruments, but rather through consumer initiatives, NGO campaigns and alerts, which managed to influence industry to change both the production processes and the products on the market. Once again, individual responsibility moved into the debate. This time, environmentally conscious consumers were made aware that they could reduce pollution by buying or boycotting certain products, possibly guided by different types of eco-labels. This approach to the problem has been very successful and very visible and it also fits very nicely with business ideology: that it is demand which creates supply. With this development in environmental concerns, the responsibility for action moved beyond the state to the individual.

Another example showing that environmental 'policy' is increasingly moving outside the legislative context is the focus and reliance on individuals at the local level as the primary agents of change. This is particularly apparent in the work on Agenda 21 (Bäckstrand *et al.*, 1996). The Agenda 21 strategy in Sweden means that environmental regulation and action takes place in a local context, i.e. in the municipal administration, in schools, and at the level of consumers and grassroots organisations. The activities are based on education, information, agreements and voluntary action rather than on legislation. Environmental politics has become very personal and part of the daily life of the Swedish population.

Since the early 1990s, with the increasing budget deficit, the debate has centred more and more on economic recession and unemployment as the most urgent issues confronting society. It has not overshadowed environmental concerns completely because environmental issues are highly prioritised by certain groups, particularly young people and women. For example, in the debates preceding the referendum on EU membership in November 1994, environmental concerns were of the utmost importance and widely discussed. The main fears expressed were that Sweden would no longer be able to impose strict domestic legislation in the field of environmental issues and would instead be forced towards more lax environmental restrictions.

It is apparent that the perception of environmental problems has changed considerably over the years. The way that environmental issues have been perceived has influenced the responses and strategies suggested. The most important responses which have been generated are nature conservation, chemical control, international co-operation, an efficient use of energy, integration of environmental concerns in other sectors, and responsible individual action. These responses have subsequently been turned into a set of policies and regulations. Due to changing perceptions, a whole range of strategies have become practice. Measures such as laws, administrative regulations, environmental taxes and user charges, environmental principles and guidelines, eco-labelling and information, co-exist today in what could be defined broadly as the Swedish environmental institutional context.

The basic characteristics of the institutional context

The move away from a strict focus on isolated areas of pollution, such as those of water and air, brought with it a broader approach to pollution problems. The separate governmental boards, the nature conservation board, the water inspection board and the air protection board, which had operated independently of one another when dealing with pollution problems, were all merged into one agency in 1967 under the name: Naturvårdsverket (the Swedish Environmental Protection Agency, SEPA). Two years later came the first piece of environmental legislation, the Environmental Protection Act, regulating air, noise and water pollution. Air and noise had not been regulated before. The Environmental Protection Act was the first of its kind to include a set of pollution sources, but it was rather typical of the early stages of environmental legislation in that it was mainly set up to combat point source emissions. This means that it regarded mainly isolated production techniques, while there was no concern for the product itself or the waste generated. The law was expected to be enforced within the administrative structure. Koncessionsnämnden (the National Franchise Board for Environmental Protection) was set up in 1969 under the jurisdiction of SEPA with the task of issuing permits and directives on emission levels and other related

industrial activities. A separate Environment and Energy Ministry
was set up as late as 1987, when Sweden's first Environmental Minister, Birgitta Dahl, was appointed. The first environmental statistics
came in the *Yearbook of Environmental Statistics* of 1975 (SOU,
1980).

Environmental concerns at the political level
Ever since the turn of the century, organised protests and social
movements have been incorporated effectively in Swedish policy-
making (Micheletti, 1991: 144–6). At the political level, the stable
five-party structure is illustrative of this. These five parties were
strongly affiliated with different organised interests. The Social
Democratic Party, for example, had – and still has – very strong ties
with the Labour Union (Landsorganisationen); the Agrarian Party
(Centerpartiet) had ties with the Farmers' Association (Lantbrukar-
nas Riksförbund); and the Conservative Party (Moderaterna) had ties
with the Employers' Association (Svenska Arbetsgivarföreningen).
But environmentalist concerns were not adequately accommodated
within this five-party structure. In 1988, the lack of accommodation
led to a sensational feat: the Green Party managed to break the five-
party dominance that had lasted for seventy years, because the wide
public interest in, and concern for, environmental issues was not
adequately reflected in the political programmes of the traditional
parties: they were aligned 'on one single scale: the left–right axis'
(Vedung, 1988: 81).

The Agrarian Party was the only party in parliament with an
ideology that deviated from the left–right ideological line because it
had its base in a rural electorate. The party's concerns to preserve the
countryside and decentralise decision-making could accommodate a
green profile; this became the strategy employed by the Agrarian
Party's leaders in the 1960s. Because of this and its stand against
nuclear energy, the Agrarian Party gained extreme popularity in the
1976 election and attracted voters with environmentalist and anti-
nuclear values. The Agrarian Party gained 24 per cent of the seats in
parliament, and this shifted the orientation from the socialist coalition, which had lasted for forty-four years, to the bourgeois coalition. As part of a coalition, the Agrarian Party did not succeed in
stopping nuclear energy, and it was forced to compromise on its
general environmental profile. As a result, its popularity declined
rapidly (Gaiter, 1991: 6–23; Vedung, 1988).

During the campaign against nuclear energy, which preceded the 1980 referendum, the different movements opposing nuclear energy collaborated in the 'People's Campaign Against Nuclear Power' (Moberg, 1980). Although the alternative supported by the campaign lost in the referendum, the People's Campaign brought together, mobilised and organised different grassroots movements. This paved the way for the formation of an environmentalist party, the Green Party (Miljöpartiet–De Gröna), which was founded in 1981. During the 1982 and 1985 elections, the Green Party had already gained seats in many municipal councils (Bennulf and Johnsson, 1993: 30), but it was in the 1988 elections that the Green Party was finally elected for parliament with more than the 4 per cent needed for parliamentary representation.

On 1 January 1987, the government established a joint Environment and Energy Ministry as a step in the direction towards fulfilling the ambitions of the Brundtland Report. This ministry was given the responsibility of co-ordinating environmental issues. Apparently, the co-ordination of energy and environmental issues by one ministry was too difficult, and by 1990 energy issues had been repatriated to the Industrial Ministry (Loftsson *et al.*, 1993: 71). The Environmental and Natural Resource Ministry, which is rather small and employs 150 staff members, has the responsibility for environmental issues, while the other ministries also have environmental responsibilities, but ones more specific to their sectors.

Environmental issues and the administrative institutions
SEPA is the central administrative agency responsible for environmental protection issues and nature conservation. Since it is an agency, SEPA is directly responsible to the government and not to the Environmental Ministry. Together with a set of other administrative bodies, SEPA's role is to implement governmental and parliamentary decisions in the environmental area. SEPA plays a very decisive role in environmental politics, and it is sizably larger than the ministry: its staff is close to 500 employees. These staff members are civil servants, the majority of which are scientific experts, and their employment is not substantially affected by changes at the political level.

The tasks and responsibilities of SEPA have developed in phase with the understanding of, and concern for, environmental issues. SEPA has changed from being an issue-specific organisation, dealing

mainly with conservation issues, to an organisation which co-ordinates, monitors and offers information. In the 1960s and 1970s,
SEPA had to do most of the work on environmental issues on its
own. It not only had to develop and lobby concrete proposals for
legislation, but had also to monitor the implementation of existing
environmental policies. At the same time, SEPA had to build up an
expertise in a number of fields to deal with environmental problems
created in the domain of other policy sectors.

The work of SEPA in the 1990s is centred around rather broad
and long-term environmental issues. In this respect, SEPA plays an
important role in advising the government and the Ministry of the
Environment. The role of the international secretariat of SEPA has
become increasingly important because the integration of international and domestic environmental activities and policies has become
highly prioritised. Increasing demands for sector responsibility have
given SEPA more of a co-ordinating and supervisory role with respect
to what is being done in different sectors; hence, SEPA is moving
away from specialised and direct involvement in specific environmental concerns. Instead, its responsibility is moving towards motivating environmental concerns in different sectors, following up on
existing policies, and co-ordinating different types of sector activities
both in its relationship with the government and with different societal actors (SOU, 1991, 32: Chapter 2). Furthermore, extensive
decentralisation has increased the responsibility of the municipalities
for implementing environmental policies. In light of this development, the responsibilities of the central administration have begun to
change.

The National Franchise Board for Environmental Protection has a
more restricted mandate than SEPA: SEPA always has the right to
appeal a Franchise Board decision. The role of the Franchise Board is,
nevertheless, a very important one. It is the central government
agency granting permits for large-scale environmentally hazardous
activities. It was set up in conjunction with the Environmental
Protection Act of 1969 as a board with court-like procedures. The
Franchise Board proceedings consist of 'hearings' during which a
decision is taken on what type of conditions should apply to the
industrial activities in question. Although it is not an open hearing,
its members represent society's interests: the board consists of several
lawyers, one technical expert, one representative from environmental
and conservation interests, and another representative either from

industry or from the municipalities, depending on the issue. Typically, economic issues, such as economic productivity, employment prospects and technical feasibility, are weighed against environmental issues. After all, the Franchise Board was never meant to be a strictly environmental board, but rather a forum where compromise could be reached between different interests.

The result is hypothetically a compromise, representing a typical example of the Swedish tradition of co-operation and consensus in decision-making, where the use of boards with representatives from a set of predetermined interests in society is common. However, although the Franchise Board is mandated to restrict and control industrial practices according to the Environmental Protection Act, it has not always pushed industrial enterprises to use the cleanest technology. In addition, it might be argued that while SEPA is busy issuing strict environmental regulations, the Franchise Board does, at times, work against this, exempting industry from this legislation.

The National Chemicals Inspectorate (Kemikalieinspektionen) is an agency that issues regulations under the Act on Chemical Products. The inspectorate monitors the use of chemical products both by advising companies on the use of chemicals and by requiring approval before new chemicals can be used. It investigates the health and environmental risks associated with the use of different chemical products, such as insecticides, fertilisers and pesticides, as well as regulating their use. The introduction of the precautionary principle in 1990 has worked to the inspectorate's advantage. Precaution has been a standard principle in the evaluation and control of chemical products and has, together with the substitution principle, guided the legislation on chemical products since 1985 (SOU, 1994, 133: 51–6). Substitution means that chemical products that *can* be substituted with products less dangerous to the health and the environment *must* be substituted. These principles have empowered the Chemicals Inspectorate actually to deny permission to use particular substances if they cannot be proven harmless. The effects would have been completely different if the burden of proof had been reversed, making the inspectorate responsible for proving that the substance was actually harmful. The EU recommends the use of the same principles, the difference being that in the EU it is not legislatively binding.

The implementation of the precautionary and substitution principles has, in the early 1990s, been particularly effective with respect to the agricultural sector. This can be attributed, at least partly, to the independent status of the agency. Had the insecticide/pesticide division been a subsection of, for example, the Agricultural Ministry, conflicts over different interests and priorities would have been more likely (interview, September 1994). In the area of insecticides, pesticides and fertilisers, both regulatory and educational mechanisms have been used simultaneously. The inspectorate has given farmers information about products in order that they may substitute the chemicals they use by less hazardous ones. By not only implementing laws, but also providing information, the inspectorate has developed a collaborative relationship both with different agricultural bodies and directly with farmers. Since chemicals are approved on a yearly basis, products approved for use one year might not be approved the next year when norms are stricter and new substitutions have been found. The independent status of the agency strengthens its means for enforcing rather strict environmental controls on chemicals. This, together with a tradition of negotiation with affected parties, has enabled Sweden to achieve one of the strictest controls of chemicals in the world.

In this section, the institutions responsible for environmental issues have been described. The next section will attempt to explain why these institutions have assumed the roles and ways of working that they have. The explanation can be found in an important, and perhaps distinct, Swedish political tradition of policy and institutional style.

Swedish political traditions and environmental policy

Since the 1930s, the idea of *folkhemmet* has been the fundamental idea underlying the creation of the welfare state. This was the utopian vision of the social democratic project, a way of operationalising a classless society and trying to realise it through social engineering. It was a vision of society as a community based on solidarity, equality and care for the weak, the poor and the disadvantaged. However, the idea of *folkhemmet* also became a metaphor that legitimised rather paternalist and interventionist decision-making towards the general public during the more than forty-four years of uninterrupted social democratic government (Eduards, 1991: 161–81). The decision-making process did accommodate organised interests but, nevertheless, excluded many groups and interests, which never became a part of the established elite. As long as the belief in the creation of the welfare state remained the vision of the general public as well, consensus prevailed (FRN, 1993: 40). Environmental concerns can, perhaps, provide the new vision legitimising governmental intervention (FRN, 1993: 73).

The apparent success of the project of *folkhemmet,* particularly in the 1950s and until the 1970s, came out of a conviction among the public and the elites that it was possible to plan and engineer an equal and just society based on solidarity (Hirdman, 1989). This conviction also affected the way that international politics was carried out: establishing solidarity with the Third World through, for example, foreign aid; being an international critic, particularly during the Vietnam War; and setting 'a good example' in the international context. Environmental concerns fit quite neatly into this picture because the Swedish have a long tradition of living close to nature, as reflected in the principle of public access to private land. I would argue that the Swedish project aimed at creating a 'perfect society' and exporting the model as a 'good example' to the rest of the world was made possible mainly because of the economic prosperity in post-war Sweden. The policy style that emerged during this period was one of co-operation and consensus. Through negotiations between the most important actors, compromises could be reached that were more constructive and beneficial to all than if the relationship had been adversarial. One could argue that this was only 'fair weather politics' and that as long as the economy was growing and all interests could be paid off through, for example, employment, wage increases, political or administrative appointments and different social support systems, the model worked. Another argument might be that such modernist politics does not function in a post-modern era. Post-modern politics lacks the universal unity, the homogeneous identity and the belief in hierarchical, standard solutions which the 'Swedish model' presupposes (Micheletti, 1991: 145).

Independent agencies

A very strong tradition has been the belief in planning and social engineering. Many actors have adhered to a conviction that societal change can be made through rational and scientific methods. This has meant a strong reliance on expertise in providing solutions to problems, and the agencies have provided much of this expertise. Regarding environmental issues, scientific expertise has been particularly prominent. Framework laws were set up because of the belief that experts in the administrative structure were best at solving social problems and have been commonly used in Sweden with increasing frequency since the 1960s. A framework law in the Swedish context contains goals, general guidelines and principles which are to be filled with more specialised regulations by the government, by the administration and often by individual municipal councils. This reliance on framework laws means that a political problem is transformed into an administrative problem, which is then settled by an expert in the administrative structure, i.e. the interpretation of the law is entrusted to the one applying the law (Ericsson, 1985: 22 and 76). Due to the use of framework laws coupled with the independence of the administrative level, experts and bureaucrats within SEPA have been able to work out environmental legislation without much political intervention and without creating conflicts with other sectors. This has also meant that the general public has been rather less engaged in these issues, the solutions have become rather technocratic and disparate, and the involvement with other sectors has become more difficult.

The role of organised interests

The co-operation and consensus model relies on the inclusion of a broad range of organised interests in planning and decision-making. Generally, interest organisations have been recognised as legitimate participants in the decision-making process. They are involved in the formal policy process through a system of referrals (*remissförfarandet*), but there are also less formal aspects of their involvement. A drawback to this involvement is often that it can make the consensus-seeking processes in which legislation is formed more time-consuming (Ruin, 1982).

Due to paternalist politics and the belief in expertise, interest representation has not been of a grassroots kind, but has mainly included well-established organisations, such as the labour unions, the employers' union and the farmers' union. The number of organisations has increased over the years, not only because of the addition of 'new' social movements: environmentalist, feminist and peace movements; but also because of the growth within existing organisations. As a consequence, it has been difficult to decide whom to include in the decision-making process without making it more cumbersome and tedious. In any case, the broad population has never had the privilege of deciding which organisations to involve. Such choices have been limited to the governmental and administrative levels. While the corporatist tradition has enabled more traditional and established organisational interests to participate in environmental policy planning, environmental NGOs have been far more marginalised (Ericsson, 1985: 65; Lundqvist, 1981). The hearings of the Franchise Board, which are limited to the affected parties, exemplify this: only those who own private property that can be damaged through a polluting activity can participate. There has been no provision for environmental litigation, and thus individuals or NGOs cannot call for the enforcement of environmental legislation in order to protect the public interest (Westerlund, 1992: 93–7; Ericsson, 1985: 62).

The role of organised interests in the policy process has tended to reduce conflicts by including rather than excluding the critics and opponents of policy proposals and by tying them closely to the administrative and governmental apparatus. On the other hand, since not all groups, but only representatives from certain groups, have been included, only the interests and criticism of the strongest, best organised groups have been heard.

Co-operation and consensus

In Swedish policy-making, there is a long tradition of seeking consensus between opposing groups and interests through negotiations. In this process, mutual trust is built. This is why it is possible to let industry control its own emission levels. Licences and emission levels granted to polluting industries by either the Franchise Board or the county administrations are followed up mainly through self-control. This does not mean, however, that the relationship between the economic sector of society and those representing environmental interests has been harmonious or even free of conflict, or that industry can be trusted not to cheat on emission targets. It only illustrates the tradition of meeting, discussing and seeking agreement among organised interests.

To increase the legitimacy of the previous decision models, which have been elitist and top-down, the government has passed legislation related to planning for the municipal level in the form of negotiations with the spontaneous involvement of concerned or interested actors rather than only predetermined well-established interests. Legitimising negotiations as a decision process has to be understood as part of the general tendency towards decentralisation, which has given the municipalities more power to decide, for example, over physical planning. However, large projects still remain under state jurisdiction. The major concern expressed about negotiation as a method of deciding physical planning is related to the problems of democratic accountability and transparency (FRN, 1993: 25). In many municipalities, the interdependence between the private sector and the administration is asymmetric, and leverage is often on the side of industry and business, leading to unwanted compromises on environmental concerns. In other words, the municipal administration often does not have sufficient power and resources to secure the implementation of environmental regulations and often has too much to lose since industry and business provide revenue and employment. This aspect is becoming increasingly important in the light of the more recent tendency to delegate more responsibility to the local level.

This can be said generally about the co-operation and consensus process of decision-making, where compromises can be reached and mutual trust developed between actors with, more or less, conflicting interests, so that hostile conflicts leading to stalemates can be avoided. On the other hand, if environmental issues are essential to individual and societal survival, as environmentalists will argue, then such compromises might be detrimental.

Distribution of competence between the national and local level
The twenty-four county administrations, which are regional branches of the central government, are responsible for environmental protection within their territories. They are responsible for overseeing the activities which the National Franchise Board has sanctioned within their territories and, furthermore, can give permits to environmentally hazardous activities on a smaller scale which are not under the jurisdiction of the Franchise Board. However, since the 1980s, more and more of these types of activities have been delegated to the municipalities. The general tendency was that municipalities should play a larger role in environmental protection. Each municipal government was to make sure that its different policy sectors, such as industry, waste management, traffic and energy, take environmental aspects into account. The main responsibility was to lie with the municipal environmental and public health committees as well as with their planning and building committees.

Overall framework legislation has gradually replaced detailed guidelines from government and parliament, allocating a greater degree of freedom to county councils and municipalities to formulate and implement public programmes on the basis of local conditions. By the early 1970s, decisions on land use had already been somewhat decentralised and this was becoming more and more common. Decentralisation was subsequently incorporated in the law on building and planning of 1987. By 1981, the same trend towards decentralisation could be seen with the implementation of the health aspects of the Environmental Protection Act: the right to monitor was delegated to the municipalities. A number of other changes have also given municipalities more autonomy and have subsequently made it more difficult for government agencies to interfere in municipal jurisdiction, even if activities violated current national legislation (Westerlund, 1991: 45). The increasing emphasis on the role of municipalities and county administrations culminated in the new Local Government Act of 1991. This new law has strengthened the autonomy of municipalities even more.

While municipalities had previously been required by the central administration to have a health and environmental board, the new Local Government Act allowed municipalities to determine their own municipal organisation, i.e. which agencies and boards they wanted to establish. In government circles, there was apprehension that, with increased municipal independence, environmental issues would be organised out or subordinated under local government boards with the responsibility for land use and planning. However, the majority of the 286 municipalities kept their health and environmental boards (SOU, 1993: 19).

In general, it has been difficult to translate the national environmental goals decided by parliament into local goals. It has also been argued that there is no efficient communication system between the national and local level with regard to national goals and action programmes for the environment (SOU, 1993: 19). SEPA has often been commissioned by the government to prepare action plans to implement the nationally established environmental goals. However, these recurrent action plans have seldom included guidelines to implement goals at levels other than the national one. Local organisations have not participated in the formulation of the national action plans and, as a consequence, national environmental goals are often unknown at the local level (SOU, 1993: 19; interviews, October 1994).

One explanation of the problems of co-ordination and communication is the legacy of a centralist expert bureaucracy. Central agencies, staffed by experts, have defined and organised environmental issues around a number of narrowly defined sectors. These technocratic national agencies had developed a rather detailed system of rules designed for the local municipal administrators, who often worked in isolation. The new Local Government Act represents a paradigmatic shift away from the hierarchical mentality of central control towards locally based solutions (Hjern, 1993).

A more pessimistic view of the decentralisation wave has been heard in the public debate. The new code words for municipal organisation – local adaptation, flexibility, efficiency, competition, leadership and goal steering – represent a shift from a public interest perspective to a management perspective. The new promised autonomy and the dream of abolishing the large central hierarchy could lead to smaller hierarchies and fragmentation. The networks that result are often seen as an ideal of organisational development, but they also present dangers. They have informal working strategies and are not accountable to the public (Amnå, 1993).

The relationship between the economy and the environment

Swedish politics in the mid-1990s are focused mainly on economic concerns. The large Swedish budget deficit, the high unemployment rate and the unstable krona has put economic concerns at the top of the political agenda. The recurrent problem is the lack of resources, which is accentuated in times of recession when environmental and employment goals compete for resources. Between 1989 and 1994, state grants for environmental protection decreased (Prop. 1993/94, 111, Annex 2: 220). In the last election, in 1994, the electorate favoured two parties: the Moderates and the Social Democrats. As Jahn (1995) argued, materialist values had become predominant. This was also indicated by a survey (Bjurulf, 1996) in which well over 85 per cent of the electorate, irrespective of age, class and gender, rated employment as the most important political issue. On the other hand, the Green Party was simultaneously voted into parliament and a large section of the population seemed to have taken environmental issues quite seriously once again. The switch has made it increasingly apparent, at least in the rhetoric of some industrialists and labour union members, that a clean environment and access to raw materials and natural resources are necessary for economic development. Moreover, the environmental strategies used and proposed today have become closer to economic strategies and have, in this sense, made the relationship between the two more harmonious.

Sustainable development
The way that sustainable development was perceived after the Brundtland Report and the way it was conceived in the post-Rio debate differs in many respects. The Brundtland version of sustainable development was made equivalent to sustainable growth and was as such seen as the solution to both the developmental crisis and the ecological crisis of poor and rich countries. Growth *per se* was not questioned, but was perceived as necessary in order to allocate resources for environmental management.

The discussion after the United Nations Conference on Environment and Development (UNCED) conference proposed a change in thinking about growth. In 1993, the Swedish government presented a proposal with guidelines for the operationalisation of sustainable management using an ecocycle approach to environmental planning (Prop. 1992/93). It was an attempt to introduce a cyclic rather than a linear approach to societal development, and traditional growth scenarios, predictions and figures were not approximated. The long-term aim is to use the ecocycle approach to resource management in all planning processes (SOU, 1994, 7: Chapter 2). Since the ecocycle principle is based on ecological and biological science, this marks a new era in Swedish environmental protection and resource conservation (SOU, 1994, 133: 29). In practice, this means that recycling and the re-use of raw materials become very important for the realisation of a sustainable society. Emphasis on the use of renewable resources is central. This principle was developed in the Ecocycle Bill of 1993.

A major accomplishment with the emphasis on ecocycle has been the introduction of producer responsibility, whereby the producer, and not the consumer or the municipality, is responsible for the life cycle of a product. So far, producer responsibility has been applied to only a limited number of products, but the general idea is to expand this responsibility (Prop. 1994/95, 10: 160). The intention is to involve the producers in the responsibility for products and, particularly, the waste that the product generates as it is consumed.

Other ministries and sectors have been affected by these new ideas, but not substantially, as only a few minor changes have been initiated.

One initiative aimed at integrating environmental concerns in the budgetary process affects the Ministry of Finance, which became obliged to add a state of the environment report to the yearly budget proposal, starting in 1991. But the report was more of a separate addendum and did not influence economic scenarios and proposals in general (cf. LU, 1995). Another initiative has been work on the green gross domestic product (GDP), which started in 1990 (SOU, 1991: 37). The green GDP is, however, still at an experimental stage in Sweden.

Environmental charges and taxes

In the late 1960s, environmental protection was dominated by governmental and administrative legislation which regulated the emission levels from a few large pollution sources. The first type of economic motivation came in the 1970s in the form of subsidies for environmental investments in the industrial sector and for municipal sewage plants.

Environmental charges in general have been used in Swedish legislation for a long time. Sewage and garbage charges are an example of this. Lundgren claims that Sweden has been very active in using charges to finance administrative environmental control. Such user charges have mainly had a financing purpose, however, and have not been intended as steering mechanisms, even though they have had positive effects on the environment (Lundgren, 1989: 91–3).

Taxes on energy were already in use in 1957, but taxes on coal, oil and peat were used to finance the nuclear energy sector and had nothing to do with environmental concerns (Lundgren, 1978: 42–9; SOU, 1970: 114). From the energy proposition of 1975, it is apparent that the government had come to realise that a high level of energy consumption led not only to high production, but also to environmental problems and dependency on imported oil. Hence, systems for subsidising alternative energy and energy conservation were developed. The energy taxes referred to above as well as the petrol tax have subsequently been changed into a set of differentiated taxes, depending on the lead and sulphur contents of fuels and petrol.

In 1978, an inquiry on environmental costs (SOU, 1978) recommended the use of economic instruments and administrative regulations to combat national or regional pollution in two cases: when the total emission level had to be reduced and when it was of less importance where the reduction took place. Since 1978, the major point emissions have been located and lowered substantially. Because most of today's pollution problems are related to diffuse emissions from diffuse sources, there is a renewed interest in economic instruments as an additional method of reducing pollution levels (SOU, 1989: 21; SOU, 1989: 83; SOU, 1990: 59). In addition, they have also been very effective. Taxes on leaded fuels and the taxes on sulphur have been successful in environmental terms. The consumption of leaded fuels has practically disappeared and emissions of sulphur have been eliminated (Sterner, 1994: 24).

The system of environmental charges and taxes is rather extensive. The major part was developed and instigated during the 1980s (Organisation for Economic Co-operation and Development (OECD), 1989; OECD, 1994). The purpose of user charges has mainly been to contribute to the financing of the environmental bureaucratic apparatus in connection with its control and other administrative functions. This is in line with the general tendency to try to finance administrative activities through user charges rather than through the general budget. The conclusion of the government report on economic instruments (SOU, 1990, 59: 134) is that user charges have, in general, been so low that they have not substantially influenced the use of, for example, oil, non-returnable packaging or fertilisers. Only a minor part of the charges have been ear-marked for special environmental projects.

On the other hand, the taxes developed during the 1980s have been used to reduce specific environmental problems. In connection with the latest tax reform, additional environmental taxes were introduced. It was, however, the explicit intention of the government to reduce the total tax burden, hence environmental taxes and user charges were a part of the general budget and provided the funds to make up for a reduction in income, capital and other taxes. With this reform, 18 million SKr. would be obtained through energy and environmental taxes rather than through income taxes (Christiansen and Lundqvist, 1995: 13–15; Prop. 1990/91: 55). Although this tax shift was intended to stimulate conservation, reduce energy consumption and encourage the use of alternative energy resources in the long run, it did not benefit the environment directly. There is an ongoing debate among the parties and in parliament about a green tax shift. This would shift the tax burden from income to natural resource use. Hence labour would become cheaper and natural resources more expensive, and this would, as with other environmental taxes, be expected to lead to a more efficient use and re-use of natural resources as well as to higher employment rates.

The strategies proposed for environmental legislation have become more similar to economic reasoning. The linking of economic development and environmental concerns in the sustainable development discourse and strategy, as well as the use of economic incentives and disincentives to curb the use of natural resources, are obvious examples of the use of economic ideas to solve environmental problems.

Foreign environmental policy

Once domestic environmental policies and instruments had managed to reduce pollution levels in Sweden, it became increasingly evident that Sweden was, to a great extent, also affected by pollutants coming from sources external to the country as such. Domestically, SO_2 emissions, heavy metal deposition and organo-chlorine substances had been reduced substantially. The greater part of the substances causing what was perceived as the most urgent problems, i.e. acidification and eutrophication, was found to originate in foreign countries. This motivated Sweden to pursue environmental strategies with an increasing emphasis on encouraging co-operation on regional and international accords.

In order for Sweden's environmental goals to be fulfilled, the emission levels of NO_x and SO_x had to be reduced at the international level. It was particularly important to have the Northern European countries sign international agreements on these environmental problems. The report following the Brundtland Commission's report (Ds, 1989), the report to the UNCED (SOU, 1991: 55) and the governmental report developed as a response to the Rio conference (SOU, 1992) all emphasised the role that the industrialised world had to play in reducing both the environmental impact and the depletion of natural resources. This role is to set examples by reducing pollutants and toxins at home, signing international agreements and developing technology for environmental protection. The reports stressed the responsibility of the industrialised countries to work for sustainable development.

Important themes on the foreign policy agenda
Acidification represents one of the biggest pollution problems, and both lakes and soil are affected. In some areas, the input of acid substances is four to five times above the critical level (SOU, 1990,

88: 38; SOU, 1991, 55: 24). This makes the problem acute since the Swedish soil and bedrock do not have a high buffering capacity. However, acidification is not a unique Swedish problem, but affects most of Europe, Canada and China. The problem is not new either; by 1967, the Swedish Minister of Industry had already introduced the issue at the OECD (Lundgren, 1991: 83). But, as pointed out earlier, it was much more difficult to convince politicians and scientists internationally than it was to convince them at home, where the sulphur content of oil was already regulated in 1967, making 'a world record of its kind' (Lundgren, 1991: 195).

Since the late 1960s, it has been in the interest of Swedish politicians and bureaucrats to try to involve as many countries as possible in the work aimed at decreasing sulphur emission levels co-operatively. Strict national legislation had been insufficient since 80–90 per cent of the sulphur deposition came from sources located outside the country. In the Swedish report to the UN conference in Stockholm in 1972, the major issue was acidification and so it remained. Even though an investigation made by the OECD showed how SO_2 could move over great distances, the general opinion was that it did not affect the environment noticeably. The OECD countries did not seem to want to take the issue seriously, and it was brought up again in 1979 by Norway at the UN Economic Commission for Europe. In 1982, Sweden arranged a conference on acidification, at which consensus was finally reached that sulphur emissions contributed to large-scale environmental damages. Subsequently, when Germany realised that its forests were dying because of acidification, it allied itself with Sweden and Norway (Lundgren, 1991: 195–7). Under the Convention on Long-Range Transboundary Air Pollution, a protocol on the control of sulphur emissions was signed in 1985, and another on NO_x emissions was signed in 1988. Acidification remains the most highly prioritised area for international co-operation (SOU, 1992: 47), which is not surprising since SEPA estimates that the level of SO_x and NO_x emissions in Europe must diminish by 70 per cent for Swedish acidification levels to remain at current levels (SNV, 1993b: 8). Work to encourage further reductions will go on within the EU with the expected help of the coalition partners, i.e. the Netherlands, Germany, Finland and Austria, and internationally, with Norway and Switzerland hopefully joining as concerned parties (SOU, 1994, 7: 117, 210–17).

Eutrophication is another important problem. It is caused by excessive amounts of nitrogen deposits emanating mainly from two sources: from agriculture in the form of ammonia, which is distributed over shorter distances, and NO_x which is emitted by motor vehicles, the burning of fossil fuels in combustion plants and through industrial processes. Eutrophication has not affected all of Sweden equally, but has been most severe in the southern part. However, the effects have not been as serious as in the agriculturally intensive areas of Europe: the Netherlands and Denmark. Nevertheless, 80 per cent of the NO_x has come from sources beyond the Swedish borders (SOU, 1994, 7: 24).

The problems of eutrophication, especially of the Baltic Sea, are severe. The Baltic Sea is an inland sea with a small outlet and brackish water. As such it does not have the same water exchange frequency as the open sea. Its brackish nature makes it a superb habitat for a diversity of marine species. Due to both nitrogen and phosphorous emissions, it has been affected by eutrophication and has a dead, deoxygenated sea floor. The eutrophication of the Baltic Sea is, to a large degree, a result of sewage discharges into the rivers flowing into the Baltic Sea. Most of this pollution comes from Poland and Russia. Only a small part is due to atmospheric deposition (SOU, 1990, 88: 51).

Climate change has been one of the most important global environmental problems (another one being the preservation of biodiversity) with which Sweden is concerned. In comparison with acidification and eutrophication, it does not appear to be perceived as an immediate problem for the country itself. A little more sunshine, warmer temperatures and longer growing seasons could be perceived as attractive to people who live with temperatures below the freezing point for six months a year. This illustrates only partly how deceptive problem formulation can be. A closer look at climate changes reveals that CO_2 emissions are the largest contributor to global warming, and these emissions are largely a result of the fossil fuel combustion that takes place when producing electricity, when powering industrial processes and when transporting vehicles. But combustion also leads to SO_x and NO_x emissions, the first of which contributes to acidification, and the second of which contributes to eutrophication. So neither the problems nor the solutions are straightforward.

Though 80 per cent of the anthropogenic sources of CO_2 emissions in 1990 came from the burning of fossil fuels, Sweden has maintained a low profile with regard to CO_2 emissions. It is true that by 1990 CO_2 emissions from industry and the energy sectors had already been cut by 33 per cent compared with the 1970 levels. It is also true, however, that CO_2 emissions from the transportation sector increased, both in relation to the total and in absolute terms (SOU, 1994, 7: 32). But what is more important, Sweden's energy consumption per capita is high (Jahn, 1995). Moreover, its current reliance on nuclear energy is to be phased out by 2010 according to a parliamentary decision made in 1980. These two facts make Sweden fairly dependent on either increased fossil fuel consumption or a re-evaluation of the nuclear energy decision, since no serious investments have been made in alternative energy sources.

Current measures to combat acidification, eutrophication and global warming are insufficient both at the national, regional and international levels (SOU, 1994, 7: 39). But these areas are politically very controversial; strong and influential interests are at stake both within Sweden and internationally. CO_2 taxes are a sensitive area in Swedish politics because industry is very energy-intensive. Since 1993, CO_2 taxes have been lowered and differentiated for industry so that the CO_2 taxes paid by the consumers are more than two-thirds higher than those paid by industry (Sterner, 1994: 22). Some measures will probably be introduced in the near future, however. The development of catalysing technology and a variety of policies to control and reduce emission levels from cars and the burning of fossil fuels are highly prioritised areas. The traffic sector has been targeted in an EU strategy emphasising the need for technical improvements for cleaner emissions, such as better catalytic converters on cars. Interestingly, it does not mention the need to reduce private transportation and airline traffic or to invest in collective transportation systems (Ds, 1994: 134).

Regulation of goods and products
Another area highly prioritised for international co-operation is the regulation of products. As has been shown in the previous sections, policies regulating the use of chemical products and chemicals in production processes are important and rather well developed domestically. With the new ecocycle approach and the precautionary and substitution principles, this means increasing emphasis on products, their content, their toxicity and their packaging.

Sweden is a net export country. Different types of regulations on products have implications for international trade in different ways. Strict domestic environmental regulations can be beneficial in the sense that they can force Swedish industry and production into a leading role in environmental technology and environmentally sound products on the market. This depends on whether consumers in other countries demand or are interested in products which are 'environmentally sound'. But the industrial sector fears that high environmental standards will lead to higher production costs. This can be detrimental to competition with products on the world market not subject to the same environmental regulations. Anticipation of higher product costs as a result of stricter regulation is often an argument used by industrial interests to protest against such regulations.

There are many unresolved issues when it comes to the General Agreement on Tariffs and Trade (GATT) as to the extent tariffs can be levied on products for reasons of environmental protection. This can be perceived as trade restrictions. This is a problem for Sweden within the EU market, but also because Sweden has historically supported and encouraged free trade in general. The concern is whether Sweden will be able to restrict the import of products that do not fulfil the domestic environmental restrictions. Explicit ambitions in the EU strategy are not to lower Swedish levels of environmental protection. A difficult problem is environmentally hazardous production: it might be rather difficult for Sweden to impose restrictions on imports that do not live up to the Swedish environmental regulations, but even more difficult to limit imports for which the production process is known to be environmentally hazardous, but located outside Swedish borders.

Sweden has played a very active role in the international work on chemical control both in the UN, OECD and EU. GATT is furthermore expected to play an increasing role in the regulation of chemicals in regard to trade barriers (SOU, 1994, 7: 228). But EU membership limits the role that Sweden can play because the EU often speaks with one voice in these organisations. Sweden's possibilities of maintaining an environmental profile are, therefore, limited.

Preferred international policy levels
Ever since the early 1970s, Sweden has taken pride in setting an example as an environmentally progressive country. The general

belief expressed by policy-makers has been that for Sweden to be able to pressure other countries to adopt stricter environmental standards, it has been necessary to show 'a good example'. The high international profile that Sweden has achieved in this context is naturally related to the more general role of pursuing an active foreign policy, which began during the time of the social democratic project. These activities have not been based on altruism alone, and probably not on a concern for the situation of less advantaged countries either. Other factors that played an important role were: Sweden's trade dependency as a small country, its neutrality policy based on trust in Sweden's good intentions, and the vulnerability to pollution from sources beyond its geographical borders.

International environmental co-operation remains important and Swedish policy-makers will continue working for international environmental accords when possible outside and within the EU. The Swedish approach to international environmental co-operation in the 1990s is directed more towards a regional emphasis than a global one. This can be said for Swedish foreign policy in general and for environmental policy in particular. The tendency is to move towards regional types of co-operation when possible, under the umbrella of more embracing international accords or conventions. The problem with a regional emphasis is, obviously, that it might exclude certain key actors.

Since the EU Commission increasingly tends to represent its member states in international negotiations, Sweden's possibilities of pursuing a more environmentally progressive role could be restricted given that an EU stance would entail finding a compromise among the member states. The strategy developed entails work both inside the EU to pressure the member states for the most progressive environmental policy possible, and at the international level. When not directly possible, it could be done via co-operation with Nordic and other states that are non-members, encouraging them to pursue the Swedish position. Hence, some type of multilevel, simultaneous strategy is prescribed. SEPA is expected to handle international co-operation and EU environmental co-operation in addition to its ongoing responsibilities with the existing personnel and within its financial budget (SNV, 1994). The conclusion is that, in practice, the strategy will have to be compromised, and most of the environmental work will be geared towards the EU and the Northern European region. Work with global environmental issues will most likely take place under the EU umbrella in intergovernmental organisations and through the foreign aid budget.

The institutional context and policy style in foreign environmental policy-making

When international environmental co-operation began in the 1970s, few organisations dealt with environmental issues internationally. There were only a few conventions, and the policy-makers responsible for these issues consisted of a small group. Environmental issues were considered to be low on the political agenda and were thus left to experts in the agencies rather than to the politicians. This has, at times, facilitated co-operation between actors who would otherwise have had great difficulty in co-operating on other more politicised issues. Increasingly it has been shown that what at first appeared to be of a scientific nature has had important political consequences not apparent until conventions had been implemented at the national level. Experts from the Ministry of the Environment and SEPA, having had the mandate to negotiate international environmental agreements, have trodden on territory reaching far beyond the environmental sphere. This was the case, for example, with the agreement on the discharge levels of chlorinated organic substances into water. The Swedish representatives agreed to, and signed, a convention with a far more radical position than the Ministry of Industry, the Ministry of Finance and the important pulp industry would have accepted (Noreland, 1993).

Environmental issues are becoming more and more politicised and involve an ever larger set of actors. At the same time, environmental problems are perceived as more complex and thus demand the input of more expertise. The politicisation of environmental issues has increased, and the number of conventions, organisations and conferences has risen. The national organisations responsible for environmental foreign policy have expanded as a result of this. It has been difficult to establish a clear division of responsibilities. The foreign policy dimension of environmental issues involves, to a great extent, the same organisations as in national environmental policy. This is true particularly if the international work is of a technical or highly specific nature. Now that environmental policy-making involves other sectorised interests as well, a larger number of actors have to be consulted prior to the development of a Swedish position. The organisations responsible for the development and implementation of national and regional environmental legislation and regulation are also involved when it comes to international environmental issues, i.e. the Ministry of the Environment, SEPA and the National Chemicals Inspectorate. In addition, the Ministry of Foreign Affairs and various departments within this ministry are involved.

Ever since 1972, the Ministry of Foreign Affairs has had a strong position in international environmental co-operation because it has been responsible for relations with international organisations and the UN system. It has also attached considerable importance to this work. Until 1991, very little use had been made of the diplomatic missions in regard to environmental co-operation. Only at rather large embassies had a staff member been assigned environmental issues as part of his or her tasks. The competence and the qualifications at the embassies had been low regarding environmental issues. To solve this problem, the position as an environmental attaché was instated in 1991 for the EU delegation in Brussels and for the Embassy in Bonn. In February 1996, the Swedish Permanent Representation in Brussels had two environmental attachés.

Within the Ministry of the Environment and Natural Resources, there is a specialised, small, international secretariat. This unit is smaller than the one devoted to international environmental issues at the political department of the Ministry of Foreign Affairs. Because of its size, the international secretariat has not been able to act as a co-ordination centre of international activities. Instead, the different divisions within the Ministry of the Environment have taken the responsibility for the co-ordination of the international dimension or aspects of their activities. The large number of departments and actors involved has led to some problems with the co-ordination of positions and issues. However, the Swedish government is rather small relative to the size of other countries' governments, so that within the field of international environmental co-operation, the individuals may have come from different ministries, but they have worked with this issue for a long time, have built the structure and are therefore very familiar with it. Even though complaints can be made about the possibilities of planning activities with the current system, the people involved know each other and the system very well and can communicate informally across departments and divisions (SOU, 1990, 88: 160–3).

In response to EU membership, the Ministry of the Environment has set up fourteen *EU* 'preparatory committees' dealing with different environmental issues and including representatives from the different ministries and SEPA. A reference group with representatives from interest organisations, business and administrative authorities is attached to each committee. These preparatory committees are responsible for the working out of Swedish opinions and suggestions related to EU Commission proposals. They also have to deliver a Swedish opinion to the environmental attachés attending the Committee of Permanent Representatives' (COREPER's) working groups as well as assisting the Minister of the Environment in the Council. The most important strategies here are to work towards a consensus for a Swedish position, to be well prepared and to have the position well grounded within the agency and the ministry (SNV, 1994: 5). It is still undecided whether the positions coming out of these preparatory committees should be subject to review (*remissförfarandet*) by a number of agencies and organised interests, as has been the tradition. In their effort to reach consensus and be well prepared, the committees have relied less and less on this principle (interview, January 1995). However, in a governmental publication, it was stated that all Commission proposals aimed at COREPER and Council deliberations would, upon receipt, be sent out for review by all concerned parties in Sweden (R & D, 1995: 14).

As with national environmental activities, the greater part of international environmental activities take place at the agency level, i.e. in SEPA. Due to its involvement with product regulation, the National Chemicals Inspectorate also has an international orientation (SOU, 1990, 88: 163). The control of chemicals of various sorts, such as pesticides and toxic chemicals, is a matter of high priority for Sweden and has been discussed earlier in this text. The Chemicals Inspectorate is the agency responsible for most questions concerning chemicals, while in the EU these types of questions are handled by a number of different directorates. Since chemicals are often regulated through Article 100a, it becomes a concern for Sweden. It means that it might be difficult, if not impossible, to pursue a stricter and different policy on chemicals than the EU. Furthermore, the precautionary and substitution principles do not apply to chemicals in the EU. The result of the negotiation on EU membership was unclear as to whether the substitution principle could still apply nationally. It was quite clear, however, that Sweden's stricter regulations on pesticides and insecticides could not continue in the EU. Swedish taxes on chemical fertilisers were not in harmony with EU policies, and the taxes were lowered in anticipation of EU membership. In concrete terms, this meant that chemical fertilisers became 25 per cent cheaper, and the result was an increase in the use of fertilisers in the fields (Nielsen, 1994: 57). Recalling that eutrophication of the marine environment is partly due to agricultural effluents high in nitrogen and phosphate, this increase has been detrimental to previous efforts aimed at grappling with eutrophication.

The strategy employed so far to encourage chemical standardisation at the international level will continue both at the international level and within the EU itself. Voluntary standardisation by the European standardisation organisation (CEN) has become increasingly common because international trade becomes much easier with similar norms for products in every country. The consequence of a particular EU directive could be the adaptation of standards and standardisation, which is then no longer voluntary. The Chemicals Inspectorate is involved in the standardisation proceedings along with concerned companies and branch organisations, which are very active participants (SOU, 1994, 7: 187). Environmental concerns and precautions are not high on the standardisation committees' agendas. On the contrary, environmental interests are marginal and the work in the committees is dominated by industrial and business interests (SNV, 1993a).

The principle of substitution expressed in Swedish environmental law does not seem to be applicable to products under harmonisation directives since no similar principle exists at the EU level. In areas where Sweden has a more strict control of chemical products, it has received a period of grace[2] during which the EU will review Swedish legislation to see if the stricter Swedish standards could be applied to the EU. The Ministry of the Environment hopes, and seems quite optimistic, that Swedish standards will be accepted. This will be an advantage to Swedish producers, and it will satisfy the public concern to keep high environmental standards even with EU membership. This issue is still very much up in the air. It will depend on how skilfully Sweden can lobby for stricter standards and to what extent other EU member states and organisations will join Sweden in that effort. In the pre-referendum debate, a lot of faith was put in the possibility of keeping higher standards than the rest of the EU because of the environmental guarantee. According to a critic, this will not be possible; the environmental guarantee seems to have been only an illusion imagined by the Swedish government (Nielsen, 1994: 47). However, in the strategy developed by the ministry, it is uncompromisingly stated that Sweden will not lower any norms domestically and will work to raise the level of environmental regulation in the EU further towards Swedish standards (Ds, 1994: 126). Table 2 shows quite clearly the difference in environmental ambitions between Sweden and the EU. With these figures in mind, it becomes comprehensible why some critics claim it unrealistic to think that the EU would adopt Swedish standards or let Sweden maintain high standards domestically. On the other hand, it also shows that if Sweden can play a forerunner role and push the other member states in the same direction, then it would, indeed, mean quite a leap towards stricter environmental standards.

Table 2 *Environmental goals in Sweden and the EU*

Substance	Sweden reduction by year	EC/EU reduction by year
Sulphur	80% 1980–2000	35% 1985–2000
Nitrogen Oxides	30% 1980–1995	30% 1990–2000
Hydrocarbons	50% 1988–2000	30% 1990–1999
Ammonia	25% 1990–1995	–
Carbon dioxide	stabilise at 1990 level by year 2000	–

Source: SOU, 1994, 7:65.

The debate about EU membership

Environmental issues were highly prioritised by the Swedish population in the debate preceding the referendum in November 1994. Survey statistics showed that environmental issues were most important, followed by the concern for how EU membership would influence the principle of public right to access private land (*allemansrätten*), which could be classified as a nature conservation issue (SOU, 1994, 7: 13). Concern for this public access right had to do with a fear that it would not be respected within the framework of EU legislation. That aspect was cleared up rather quickly because there is no EU legislation regulating this type of access to land. Furthermore, land use and land property issues are closely related to issues of sovereignty, one of the issue areas which have so far been left largely untouched by EU jurisdiction. Nevertheless, during membership negotiations, the concern was so strong that Dinkelspiel, the Minister of European Affairs, felt compelled to spell out clearly the strong traditions regarding public access to land. He also stated that Sweden did not intend to compromise that right or have anyone interfere with it. The more important concern expressed among the public and often aired in the debate was the question of whether Sweden would be allowed to keep its environmental legislation with EU membership or whether it would have to adopt lower environmental standards. As stated earlier, the government relied heavily on the possibility of keeping such standards on the basis of the environmental guarantee even though others said that this would be impossible. It is now quite clear that the environmental guarantee could not be adhered to regarding chemicals, because they are subject to standardisation directives. The prospects of pursuing or at least maintaining higher environmental standards are better regarding minimum directives.

At the parliamentary and governmental level, the environment also became one of the major issues of concern and debate. Prior to the referendum, there were two campaigns: the 'yes' and the 'no' campaign. The campaign was very intense. The 'no' side was strongly affiliated with environmental interests and groups, and the 'yes' side was backed by business interests and had more resources at its disposal. The yes campaign started out weakly; opinion polls showed that more than 60 per cent of the population was against EU membership. This was the situation until a few months prior to the referendum. In the end, the only parties against EU membership were the Green Party and the Left Party. The conclusion is that even though environmental issues were highly salient in the discussion, in the end it was economic concerns, unemployment, a budget deficit and trade dependence on EU countries that finally decided the outcome.

Sweden has emphasised its leading role as an environmentally progressive country both in the debate prior to the referendum and in the texts produced on the topic. Sweden appears to be willing to play this role also in European co-operation by insisting on keeping existing high environmental standards and setting new ones. In this respect, there is a high level of reliance on the possibilities of the environmental guarantee in EU law (Article 100a: 4), which allows countries to set higher standards for environmental reasons. It is unclear how and to what extent this is really a guarantee since trade and free competition still appear to be prioritised over environmental concerns (SOU, 1994, 7: 49, 182–5; Jörgensen, 1992: 14).

The Swedish governmental strategy is to continue to work for high environmental standards also after joining the EU. Sweden will strive to secure and maintain environmental regulation nationally, while pursuing environmental goals perhaps together with coalition partners such as Germany, Denmark and the Netherlands within the EU. On the condition that Sweden will actually pursue the strategies and ambitions expressed in the pre-referendum debate as well as in various documentation on the subject, it would be possible for Sweden to maintain high standards nationally and persuade other countries, and perhaps the whole EU, to adopt similar policies. It appears to be contingent on the extent to which the government is willing to do so, the type of resources allocated for environmental activism and lobbying at the EU level, and the extent to which the government is willing also to advocate high environmental standards in different international arenas. The problem is that there is no general consensus supporting a progressive environmental policy. Instead, many actors see an opportunity for using the laxer environmental legislation in most areas of EU policy and in the member states to argue for similar regulation in Sweden. An example is when Volvo demanded that the Franchise Board license a higher solvent emission level using precisely the argument that the EU had lower standards (Nielsen, 1994: 54).

Conclusions

Sweden has reduced pollution and environmental degradation within the country substantially by using progressive and innovative strategies. This chapter has analysed how this has been possible by looking at the perceptions of environmental problems as well as the institutional responses to these perceptions. The conclusion is that certain characteristic features of Swedish policy and institutional style have facilitated this development. The most important of these features are: the autonomous agencies, the inclusion of organised interests and the co-operation and consensus style of policy-making. Environmental concerns have, through these mechanisms, been effectively absorbed into (particularly) the administrative apparatus and turned into solutions that have been neither too conflictual nor too challenging for the dominant actors in Sweden. So far, these solutions and strategies have been comparatively successful in reducing pollution from various sources within the country and in applying comparatively high levels for future policies.

One argument raised in the chapter is that these developments were made possible because of the economic progress in Sweden from the 1950s to the 1980s. Today, when different actors airing different concerns compete for scarce resources, environmental priorities tend to lose out. However, the relationship between the economy and the environment has been relatively harmonious and of late the political tendencies to decentralise decision-making to the local level, the use of economic instruments and the focus on environmentally conscious individual action as a strategy seem to bring economic and environmental ideas more closely together.

Being a forerunner in the environmental field means that pollution problems generated within the country itself were effectively reduced rather early. Two aspects were important in explaining the active role that Sweden played in international and regional environmental co-operation. One reason is Sweden's vulnerability to pollution sources outside its borders caused by unfortunate wind and water currents. This naturally led to an interest in having other countries taking environmental problems seriously by adopting similar legislation. The other reason was the general pattern of engagement in international issues and co-operation that had become a kind of Swedish foreign policy style. That Swedish policy-makers still perceive Sweden as a forerunner country and as a good environmental example is clear both in the strategies developed for EU policy and for international co-operation.

Notes

1 Proposed by the four-party coalition government composed of Moderaterna (the Conservative Party), Folkpartiet (the Liberal Party), Centern (the Agricultural Party) and Kristdemokraterna (the Christian Democratic Party).

2 The period of grace is four years for a number of chemicals that are more strictly regulated in Sweden, for example, classification and notification of pesticides and insecticides, limits on the use of arsenic, cadmium, PCP and restrictions on batteries (Nielsen, 1994: 65).

References

Amnå, E. (1993), Vad innebär organisation och roller i kommunerna för miljöpolitiken?, *Planera för en bärkraftig utveckling*, Stockholm, Byggforskningsrådet.

Bäckstrand, K., A. Kronsell and P. Söderholm (1996), Organisational challenges to sustainable development, *Environmental Politics*, 5:2, 209–30.

Bennulf, M. and S. Holmberg (1990), The Green breakthrough in Sweden, *Scandinavian Political Studies*, 13:2, 165–84.

Bennulf, M. and L. Johnsson (1993), *Miljöpolitik*, Lund, Studentlitteratur.

Bjurulf, B. (1996), *Serviceuppfattning och Serviceuppskattning*, unpublished manuscript, Lund, Department of Political Science.

Carson, Rachel (1963), *Silent Spring*, Harmondsworth, Penguin Books.

Christiansen, P. M. and L. J. Lundqvist (1995), *Environmental Policy Organisation, Instruments and Styles in the Nordic Countries*, paper presented for the Conference: New Nordic Member States and the Impact on EU Environmental Policy, Sandbjerg, Denmark, 6–9 April.

Dir. (1994, 134), *Miljöbalkens nya direktiv*, Stockholm, the Swedish Government.

Ds (1989: 25), *Svensk Politik för en Miljövänlig och Hållbar Utveckling – En redovisning med inriktning mot Världskommissionens rekommendationer*, Stockholm, Ministry of Environment and Energy.

Ds (1994: 126), *Det svenska miljöarbetet i EU*, Stockholm, Ministry of Environment and Energy.

Ds (1994: 134), *Svenskt samarbete med Central och Österuropa*, Stockholm, the Foreign Ministry.

Eduards, M. L. (1991), The Swedish gender model: productivity, pragmatism and paternalism, *West European Politics*, 14:3.

Ericsson, L. (1985), *Ett surt regn kommer att falla – Naturen, myndigheterna och allmänheten*, Lund, Bokbox Förlag.

FRN (Forskningsrådsnämden) (1993: 5), *Beslutsprocesser för stora project – Långsiktiga konsekvenser för miljö och regional utveckling*, Stockholm, the Swedish Research Council.

Gaiter, P. J. (1991), *The Swedish Green Party, Responses to the Parliamentary Challenge 1988–1990*, Stockholm University, International Graduate School, Master's thesis.

Hirdman, Y. (1989), *Att lägga livet till rätta – studier i svensk folkhemspolitik*, Stockholm, Carlsson.

Hjern, B. (1993), Är lokal demokratisk miljöpolitik egentligen önskvärd? *Planera för en bärkraftig utveckling*, Stockholm, Byggforskningsrådet.

Holmgren, K. (1988), Sweden, in D. Rowat (ed.), *Public Administration in Developed Democracies: a Comparative Study*, New York and Basel, Marcel Dekker.

Interview, September 1994, with Vibeke Bernson, head of insecticide and pesticide division of the National Chemicals Inspectorate.

Interviews, October 1994, with three members of the Environmental Delegation from the Municipality of Lund, Sweden.

Interview, January 1995, with Kirsten Mortensen, Director of the International Secretariat of SEPA, on telephone.

Jahn, D. (1992), Nuclear power, energy policy and new politics in Sweden and Germany, *Environmental Politics*, 1:3, 383–417.

Jahn, D. (1995), *The Social Paradigms of Environmental Performance: the Scandinavian Countries in an International Perspective*, paper for the Sandbjerg workshop on New Nordic Member States and the Impact on EC Environmental Policy, Denmark, 6–8 April.

Jamison, A., R. Eyerman and J. Cramer (1990), *The Making of the New Environmental Consciousness. a Comparative Study of the Environmental Movements in Sweden, Denmark and the Netherlands*, Edinburgh, Edinburgh University Press.

Jörgensen, C. E. (1992), *EG:s miljöpolitik inom kemikalieområdet*, Stockholm, Naturskyddsföreningen.

Loftsson, E., J. Hedrén, R. Hjorth and M. Löwgren (1993), *Svensk Miljöpolitik*, Lund, Studentlitteratur.

LU (1995), *Långtidsutredningen*, Stockholm, government report.

Lundgren, L. J. (1978) Energipolitik i Sverige 1890–1975, *Energi och Samhälle*, Stockholm, Sekretariatet för framtidsstudier.

Lundgren, L. J. (1989), *Miljöpolitik på längden och tvären – Några synpunkter på svensk miljövård under 1900–talet*, Solna, SEPA.

Lundgren, L. J. (1991), *Försurningen på Dagordningen*, Solna, SEPA and the Swedish Research Council.

Lundqvist, L. J. (1974), *The Case of Mercury Pollution in Sweden*, The Committee on Research Economics, Report 4.

Lundqvist, L. J. (1981), *The Hare and the Tortoise: Clean Air Policies in the United States and Sweden*, Ann Arbor, University of Michigan Press.

Meadows, Donella, Dennis Meadows, Jorgen Randers and William W. Behrens III (1974), *The Limits to Growth*, London, Pan Books, 2nd edition.

Micheletti, M. (1991), Swedish corporatism at a crossroads: the impact of new politics and new social movements, *West European Politics*, 14:3.

Moberg, Å. (1980), *Så började 80–talet-Dagbok från folkkampanjen*, Stockholm, Prisma.

Nielsen, K. (1994), *Gröna stjärnor eller blå dunster? Om EU och miljön*, Uddevalla, Miljöförbundet.

Noreland, L. (1993), *International Negotiations: a Short-cut to Domestic Power?*, Master's thesis, Lund University, Department of Political Science.

OECD (1989), *Economic Instruments for Environmental Protection*, Paris, OECD.

OECD (1994), *Environment and Taxation: the Cases of the Netherlands, Sweden and the United States*, Paris, OECD.

Petersson, O. (1994), *Swedish Government and Politics*, Stockholm, Fritzes.

Prop. (1987/88:85), *Miljöpolitiken inför 90–talet*, government bill.

Prop. (1990/91:90), *En god livsmiljö*, government bill.

Prop. (1992/93:180), *Om riktlinjerna för en kretsloppsanpassad samhällsutveckling*, government bill.

Prop. (1993/94:111), *Med sikte på hållbar utveckling:genomförandet av*

besluten vid FNs konferens om miljö- och utveckling UNCED, government bill.
Prop. (1994/95:10), Miljöbalk, government bill.
R & D (1995, 14), Regering & Departement, journal published by the State Chancellery.
R & D (1995, 22/23)
Ruin, O. (1982), Sweden in the 1970s: policy making becomes more difficult, in J. Richardson (ed.), Policy Styles in Western Europe, London, Allen & Unwin.
SNV (Statens Naturvårdsverk) (1993a), Konsekvenserna för svenskt miljöarbete av den ökade, förändrade och internationaliserade standardiseringen, Solna, SEPA.
SNV (1993b), Försurning – ett evigt problem, eller finns det hopp?, Rapport 4232, Solna, SEPA.
SNV (1994), EU-Strategi, Solna, SEPA.
SOU (Statens Offentliga Utredningar), Swedish Official Report, Report from Parliamentary Commissions of Inquiry.
SOU (1956:58), Bränsleförsörjningen i Atomåldern.
SOU (1970:13), Sveriges Energiförsörjning.
SOU (1978:43), Miljökostnader.
SOU (1980:24), Bättre miljöinformation.
SOU (1987:32), För en bättre miljö.
SOU (1989:83), Ekonomiska styrmedel i miljöpolitiken, Energi och trafik.
SOU (1990:59), Sätt värde på miljön – Miljöavgifter och andra ekonomiska styrmedel.
SOU (1990:88), Sweden's Role in International Environmental Cooperations: New Goals and Opportunities.
SOU (1991:32), Naturvårdsverkets uppgifter och organisation.
SOU (1991:37), Räkna med miljön! Förslag till natur -och miljöräkenskaper.
SOU (1991:55), Sveriges Nationalrapport till UNCED 1992.
SOU (1992:104), Vår uppgift efter Rio – Svensk handlingsplan inför 2000-talet.
SOU (1993:19), Kommunerna och miljöarbetet.
SOU (1993:27), Miljöbalk.
SOU (1994:7), EU, EES och miljön.
SOU (1994:133), Miljöpolitikens principer.
Sterner, T. (1994), Environmental tax reform: the Swedish experience, European Environment, 4:6, 20–5.
UD (1969), Förenta Nationernas generalförsamlings möte, Stockholm, Kungliga Utrikesdepartementet.
Vedung, E. (1988), The Swedish Five-Party Syndrome and the environmentalists, in K. Lawson and P. H. Merkl (eds), When Parties Fail: Emerging Alternative Organisations, Princeton, Princeton University Press.
Westerlund, S. (1991), EG:s miljöregler ur svenskt perspektiv, Stockholm, Naturskyddsföreningen.
Westerlund, S. (1992), EG och makten över miljön, Stockholm, Naturskyddsföreningen.

2   *Volkmar Lauber*[1]

Austria: a latecomer which became a pioneer

Historical overview

As in most industrial countries, environmental regulation in Austria has a long history, if only with regard to specific problems. Measures for the protection of forests (against excessive felling of trees, against damaging smoke) can be found centuries back. A clause of the Civil Code – enacted in 1811 – contains a legal remedy against pollution from nearby installations. The second half of the nineteenth century saw the rise of associations that devoted themselves fully or in part to the protection of nature.

Between the two world wars, Austria underwent two decades of de-industrialisation, economic decline and high levels of unemployment. Rapid industrialisation came with the *Anschluss* to the Third Reich in 1938; World War II and its aftermath brought new hardships. This long period of stagnation, which followed the collapse of the Austro-Hungarian Empire in 1918, left its mark on the population and its leaders: henceforth, economic growth, the expansion of material welfare and a policy of consensus were accorded a central place. In fact, during the first decades after World War II, industrial and economic growth reached record levels and was among the highest in the Organisation for Economic Co-operation and Development (OECD) countries. As a result, in terms of per capita income, Austria is by now one of the dozen or so wealthiest countries in the world. This consensus on growth, however, brought with it a certain amount of political immobility, which lasted roughly until the 1980s, particularly with regard to the two large parties, the social partners and the state bureaucracy.

During the decades of the 'economic miracle,' i.e. the 1950s and

1960s, there was little concern about environmental problems, which seemed to be inseparably connected with the new affluence. At the time of the Stockholm Conference in 1972, an empathy with nature in the Austrian context was viewed by many as anti-modern, reactionary or worse (a result of the Nazi propaganda which had 'appropriated' nature as part of its blood-and-soil myth). By contrast, the Ministry of Public Health and Environmental Protection was set up in 1972 by Chancellor Kreisky, who had begun a long period of social democratic rule two years earlier, to show a supposedly modern, technocratic approach. In fact, the establishment of this ministry was mostly an act of symbolic politics: the ministry remained practically without powers for about a decade and a half, almost without personnel for the task of environmental protection, and was rebuffed when it requested to be involved in the preparation of environmentally relevant legislation being undertaken by other ministries. The comprehensive environmental protection act that it prepared over several years never saw the light of day.

The first important environmental issue in Austria was that of radiation from nuclear power plants. After the first oil crisis in 1973–1974, the Austrian government decided to build a whole series of such plants. This led to the greatest wave of political mobilisation since the war and finally to a vote in a referendum in 1978 in which nuclear power was narrowly defeated;[2] nuclear power generation was subsequently banned by law. One such plant, in Zwentendorf on the Danube, had already been completed by then, and the governing Social Democrats and organised business and labour made considerable efforts to put it into operation. These efforts were not abandoned until after the Chernobyl disaster in 1986.

The conflict over this plant defined the two camps for years to come: it was the 'environment' versus the 'economy'; the environmentalists (who were not yet organised as a political party) versus organised business and labour (the most important social partners). Public sector electric utilities were strongly involved in this conflict (they promoted nuclear power); this helped to politicise all forms of electricity generation. In subsequent years, opposition also arose against the construction of thermal and hydro-electric plants.

The next important environmental issue was *Waldsterben*, i.e. forest die-back, primarily caused by acid rain. This led to strong public pressure for clean air legislation, which was passed in several stages in the 1980s. The decade opened with the Act on Steam Boiler

Emissions, which was successively tightened by several decrees and replaced in 1988 by the Clean Air Act for Steam Boilers, which contained standards more stringent than EU regulations (OECD, 1995: 36). Catalytic converters for automobiles were required by a 1985 law, well in advance of related EU regulations; when the legislation had been passed, the Austrian government expected the EU to adopt similar regulations in the near future (Martischnig, 1990: 76–80). However, legislation was not the only instrument used in clean air politics. Because of very strong public pressure, many electric utilities – which were exclusively in the public sector at that time – were forced by their federal or provincial owners to install powerful pollution control equipment even beyond the legal requirements. All this laid the ground for the development of a domestic clean air technology industry, which became quite successful.

Electricity generation became a cause for nation-wide environmental mobilisation once more in the mid-1980s. This time, the controversy centred on a hydraulic dam at Hainburg, the economic usefulness of which was doubtful and which would have destroyed some of the Danube's last wetlands. When the management of the utility (supported by the Construction Workers' Union) tried to force the issue after a highly controversial permit procedure, another large wave of mobilisation led to a severe political crisis. The government stepped in, the dam project was postponed indefinitely, and the ecology movement celebrated another victory over the utilities and the industrial social partners. For the ecology issue, this was a major breakthrough, and now the government clearly felt the need to respond to a concern that enjoyed such strong support. As a side effect of this event, the Austrian Society for Environment and Technology (Österreichische Gesellschaft für Umwelt und Technik, ÖGUT) (Eltbogen, 1986: 167–70) was set up to facilitate a dialogue between leading industrial firms, ministries, scientists and environmental activists. In a parallel development, the Greens experienced a surge of voter sympathies, and by 1986 they were represented in the federal parliament.

The years that followed were characterised by important changes in the institutional structure of environmental politics. Organised business and labour suffered two major defeats at both Zwentendorf and Hainburg. The two large political parties, the Social Democratic Party (Sozialdemokratische Partei Österreichs, the largest party since 1970) and Conservative People's Party (Österreichische Volkspartei) accepted the consequences, took care to loosen the ties to 'their' respective interest associations (see below), and developed green currents of their own in an effort to avoid losing an electorate clearly sympathetic to environmental concerns. Several important pieces of legislation were consequently passed in a short time span. Towards the end of the decade, the Ministry of the Environment, Youth and Family was set up and granted greater powers than its predecessor; environmental ombudsmen institutions were created in most provinces and ambitious bills were drafted (but not passed) to institutionalise citizen participation in administrative proceedings (Lauber, 1991; Höll, 1994).

Since the late 1980s, several issues have stood out in the environmental discussion: truck freight transit across the Alps, nuclear power in Eastern Europe and the question of climate change. These issues have been perceived as international in character. In addition, the domestic issues during this time period have been the problems of waste (waste dumps, incineration plants), pesticides and chemicals, and air quality (because of the ozone problem).

The 1990s also brought a new generation of laws that affected the structure of environmental policy-making. Here, the impact of the EU and its recent approach of relying on the instrument of information was clearly observable. In 1993, both the Environmental Information Act and the Environmental Impact Assessment and Citizen Participation Act were passed. And in 1995, an EU regulation on voluntary environmental auditing of business firms was adopted (EMAS). Unlike most Austrian environmental legislation passed so far, these laws – enacted in the perspective of imminent EU membership or soon after accession (in 1995) – do not prescribe technical standards, but count on the effect of public information (and sometimes participation) to 'civilise' industrial and technological development. If the perspective of EU membership led to the above pieces of legislation, it also led to – at least momentarily – a standstill in other areas. Now, the main emphasis was on the adaptation to EU accession and to intensified competition from Eastern Europe in basic industries, and on the curtailing of expenditures to stabilise the growing budget deficit. This clearly limited new environmental initiatives. On the other hand, efforts at deregulation (as in the case of industrial permits) also remained largely unsuccessful.

Austrian environmental policy relies primarily on command-and-control measures and on subsidies. The government share of environmental expenses has been unusually high (about 57 per cent in 1991), in fact so high as to question seriously the applicability of the polluter pays principle (OECD, 1995: 86–8 and 99). Some taxes considered to be eco-taxes today originally served other purposes, most importantly the taxes on mineral oil and on motor vehicles. These made up more than three-quarters of the eco-taxes in 1993, which altogether amounted to about 8 per cent of the gross federal revenue (OECD, 1995: 91). In 1995, all political parties discussed the ecological tax reform intensively; however, the subsequent political crisis over the budget buried this discussion.

Over time, a trend towards greater policy integration can be identified. Austrian environmental law has consisted mostly of punctual regulatory measures; special laws have been prepared and administered by a variety of ministries on items such as used lubricants, detergents, etc. Only in recent years have more comprehensive measures cut across different fields (laws on environmental information, on environmental impact assessment and citizen participation, on environmental auditing and, to some extent, on waste management). More recently, an effort was made to integrate environmental goals into sectors: a national environmental plan, inspired by the Dutch example, was prepared and launched in June 1992 to co-ordinate the long-term planning of environmental policy. The working groups preparing this plan included members from federal and provincial administrations, the social partners, the scientific community and environmental organisations, all of whom sought to achieve consensus. However, the plan is not binding and is vague on some points (OECD, 1995: 25–6 and 95). A draft bill on environmental liability supporting the polluter pays principle and allowing for at least a partial shift of the burden of proof (inspired by the Japanese model) was prepared in the early 1990s, but became a victim of the recession that began in 1992 and intensified the business community's resistance to the bill.

The 1995 OECD report on environmental performance in Austria recommended a reduction of the cost and administrative complexity: by simplifying environmental legislation (in particular permit procedures for industrial projects); by integrating economic and environmental policies in a better way; by introducing new economic instruments and expanding the use of voluntary agreements (they are currently used mainly to promote recycling efforts by industry); by strengthening the co-ordination among various ministries and levels of government; and by adopting legislation on environmental liability based on the polluter pays principle. These steps would improve cost-effectiveness and thus prepare the ground for further progress (OECD, 1995: 95–9 and 162–3). In 1995, the new Minister of the Environment, Bartenstein, announced reform efforts in this direction.

In retrospect, the development of environmental policy in Austria is marked by a long period of stagnation followed by a breakthrough in the mid-1980s. The stagnation was probably a result of the fact that the political leaders and social partners were almost single-mindedly set on pursuing economic growth and distributional stability. These were the central goals of public policy, and this course was not challenged by the social movements or other forces until fairly late. This in turn may have resulted from the fact that Austrian politics in the post-war decades was marked by the strong hold that the two large parties and the social partners exerted over state and society, not only in the immediate administrative sphere, but also in the media (radio, TV, party newspapers), in public education, in the provision of subsidised housing and in a substantial part of the economy.

Reforms in the 1960s and 1970s began to make Austria more liberal (Lauber, 1996: 253–6). The social movements of the 1970s, and in particular the ecology movement, helped loosen the duopoly of the parties and social partners at a time when this duopoly was beginning to weaken due to the effects of generational change. They thus prepared the way for new priorities. The late 1980s brought a period of major change: the decline of the power of the traditional parties now became manifest. In the environmental area, a series of structural changes occurred during this period, of which the strengthening of the environment ministry and the rise of environmental organisations were the most important. Since then, Austrians have enjoyed being told they are pioneers in this area.

The institutional and political context

Consociationalist politics
Since World War II, Austrian politics have typically been characterised as consociationalist (Luther and Müller, 1992) to convey the search for consensus that for long characterised relations between the two major parties (the Social Democrats and the Conservative

People's Party, which governed in grand coalitions from 1945 to 1966 and again from 1987 onwards) and the four large corporatist groups, the 'social partners'. These social partners comprise the three large organisations with obligatory membership (the Chambers of Commerce, of Agriculture and of Labour) and the Trade Union Federation. These social partners have traditionally acted jointly in matters of economic and social policy, defusing the distributional conflicts which tore Austria apart during the inter-war years. Pragmatic consociationalism has become a widespread practice that has gone beyond the above actors; it also played a role when the ecology movement first arose. For example, there was never an escalation of violence as in Germany or France over nuclear power or similarly controversial projects.

The influence of the social partners is largely informal; if they arrive at an agreement, they can usually count on the support of their respective parties (the Chambers of Commerce and Agriculture are close to the People's Party, the Chamber of Labour and the Trade Union Federation are close to the Social Democrats). However, in the case of the power plant projects at Zwentendorf and Hainburg, these organisations suffered their most important defeats in the environmental area because, as mentioned above, the two parties strove for greater independence as a result of popular resistance to the power plants. Consequently, the social partners also explored and developed environmental programmes of their own.

The two large parties historically gathered 89–90 per cent of the vote in parliamentary elections; by the mid-1990s, they attracted only about two-thirds of the vote. The remaining vote went to three other parties, the largest of which is the Freedom Party of Jörg Haider (on the right wing, with regular excursions into Nazi traditions). The two other rather small parties are the Liberal Forum (which split away from the Freedom Party in 1993) and the Greens, now the smallest party in parliament.

Federalism
Austria is a federal state and consists of nine provinces or *Länder*. Except for matters concerning the environment, the distribution of power is heavily tilted towards the federal government, much more so than in Germany, Switzerland or the United States. Most laws and decrees (decrees are enacted by a ministry or a provincial government on the basis of a law) are applied at the lowest level by district

authorities; their decisions can be appealed to higher administrative levels (provincial and/or federal) and eventually to a court of public law (Administrative Court or Constitutional Court). Finally, there is the level of the municipalities, which have powers of their own. Authority in matters concerning the environment is distributed over the three levels.

The constitution of 1920/29 did not mention environmental protection, and it was not mentioned in the constitution until 1984. Until 1984, this field was 'annexed' to other matters explicitly characterised as federal or provincial. In several constitutional amendments (1983, 1988 and 1993), the powers of the federal government in the environmental area were increased, but dispersion still prevails. Thus, the federal government is in charge, for example, of emmission protection, air quality (except for emissions from heating systems), hazardous waste, permits for industrial installations, steam boilers and engines, water law, forests, mining, traffic and legislation on environmental impact assessment. The provinces are in charge most notably of nature protection, non-hazardous waste (in part), airborne emissions from heating systems, zoning, construction norms (insulation, promotion of solar heating) and the administration of environmental impact assessments (Welan, 1995). The municipalities handle such matters as waste collection and disposal, sewage and sometimes municipal enterprises for public transportation, water, gas, electricity and district heating.

At the federal and provincial levels, environmental powers are further subdivided by administrative units. Thus, there is a federal environment ministry, but environmental questions related to energy policy, mining, tourism or road construction (and a few other issues) are handled by the Ministry of Economic Affairs. The Ministry of Agriculture and Forestry is in charge of water legislation, water management and groundwater; and the Ministry of Health handles drinking and bathing water quality and protection against radiation and toxic substances. This list could be continued. Ministries are usually closely linked to 'their' polluters, with whom they share a common understanding of priorities and a network of mutual support.

Federal level   When the Federal Ministry of Public Health and Environmental Protection was established in 1972,[3] nearly all the powers in the field had already been appropriated by other, more powerful ministries. This state of affairs remained unchanged for fifteen years, during which the minister and a small staff of a few dozen persons working with environmental affairs undertook only symbolic politics and preparatory activities. Expert advice in the environmental area was provided by the Austrian Federal Institute of Health, (Österreichisches Bundesinstitut für Gesundheitswesen, ÖBIG) set up in 1973 with a rather modest staff. This situation changed only when a Federal Environmental Agency (Umweltbundesamt, UBA) was established in 1985, and when, in 1987–1988, the environment ministry acquired its first real powers and resources after the reshuffling of governmental tasks resulting from the 1986 elections, when the new grand coalition came to power. The Ministry of Environment, Youth and Family is now in charge of general environmental policy, air quality (emmissions), waste, chemicals, the allocation of environmental funds to the provinces and of part of environmental inspection (OECD, 1995: 25). It has a staff of about 300. In many situations, the environment ministry has to share its power with other federal agencies, usually the Ministry of Economic Affairs, which has the upper hand because it is politically more weighty, partly due to its constituency. The environment ministry, on the other hand, still lacks a strong constituency of its own. However, its role was strengthened through EU membership, for it now co-ordinates more policy areas at the European level than it is in charge of at home (Steiner and Trattnigg, 1996).

As stated above, the environment was not mentioned in the constitution until 1984. At that time, anti-Hainburg activists collected signatures for a popular initiative[4] to secure a constitutional right to environmental quality, which could serve as a basis for lawsuits. The government responded with a constitutional law which declared comprehensive environmental protection to be one of the basic goals of the state. While this law is largely symbolic, it is not entirely devoid of significance; it is occasionally invoked by the courts to support decisions favourable to the environmental cause.

Some environmental statistics date back to the 1970s. In 1985, the UBA was created to monitor and collect environmentally relevant statistics (the UBA now operates most of the federal environmental databases) and to provide advice to the environment minister on measures to reduce and prevent pollution, a task previously fulfilled by the ÖBIG. In 1995, the UBA had a staff of about 200 (OECD, 1995: 25). Statistics are published regularly, and an environmental data catalogue has existed since 1995, in accordance with the Environmental Information Act of 1993.

Provincial and local levels   Provinces have their own environmentally relevant legislation on physical planning, soil, construction codes, emissions from heating systems, non-hazardous waste (in part) and protection of nature. In addition, they administer much federal legislation. By far the largest number of civil servants dealing with environmental issues work at the provincial or municipal level – many more than at the federal level (OECD, 1995: 86).

Between 1984 and 1993, most provinces established an office of the environmental ombudsman or Umweltanwaltschaft, which may take up environmental concerns in administrative proceedings governed by provincial law. These ombudsmen have access to all relevant documents, may formulate objections, and in some provinces they may appeal to the highest courts of public law. In 1993, the environmental ombudsmen were granted similar rights in federal proceedings governed by the Law on Environmental Impact Assessment and Citizen Participation. The intention behind the creation of these offices was to avoid institutionalising a citizen participation which seemed highly unpredictable (Kok, 1989: 143–65; Stolz, 1990). But because of their weak political position, most ombudsmen have been rather tame so far. Even so, efforts have been made lately to weaken them further (*Salzburger Nachrichten*, 14 November 1995).

The main actors: parties, interest groups, citizens

Political parties
Today, all political parties in Austria profess a commitment to sustainable development, although their understanding of this concept varies greatly according to their priorities. The Social Democrats have been strongly protective of industry as the basis of full employment and of wage-earner interests; they 'greened' considerably in the 1980s, though at times reluctantly. The Conservative People's Party has been divided into three leagues: business, wage-earners and farmers. During the second half of the 1980s, the People's Party developed the slogan of the 'eco-social market economy', a slogan definitely lacking specificity, but associated with green initiatives – the introduction of market instruments in environ-

mental policy, support for an energy tax on fossil fuels (to promote biomass), and the creation of a national park on the Danube to preclude the Hainburg plant. Even Jörg Haider's Freedom Party discovered the green vote and came forward with green ideas, although the party has been best known in recent years for its xenophobic and right-wing politics.

These three parties developed their environmental platforms in the late 1980s. Shortly thereafter, conditions changed radically. The fall of the Iron Curtain and the war in former Yugoslavia led to immigration from Eastern and South-eastern Europe. Together with the onset of the economic recession in 1992, this led to intense fears of unemployment. Those feelings were, on the other hand, skilfully exploited by the Freedom Party. The two big parties, afraid of losing voters to the Freedom Party, followed suit. In this climate, new environmental initiatives by the government coalition fell by the wayside. Much energy was spent on taking over EU environmental regulations or on resisting EU policies that would have worsened conditions in Austria. In 1995, the grand coalition fell apart over budget consolidation. In the ensuing election campaign, which was dominated by the issue of austerity and by the question of whether Austria would henceforth be governed by a conservative bloc (the People's Party and the Freedom Party), environmental issues were almost completely neglected. In the December 1995 elections, the Social Democrats received about 38 per cent of the vote, the People's Party slightly more than 28 per cent, and the Freedom Party close to 22 per cent.

Green parties emerged in Austria around 1980. They obtained their first representation in a provincial parliament in 1984 and entered the federal parliament in 1986 as a very small party. But the Greens were divided into two different political organisations: one leftist, the other quite conservative. This division and the resulting in-fighting considerably weakened their impact. Only in the elections of 1994 did the 'leftist' Green Party (Green Alternative) prevail, while the conservative Greens became insignificant. It was not until that campaign that the Green Alternative achieved a modern image; for a long time, the party had been equated (not always for good reasons) with the rejection of industrial society and a preoccupation with direct democracy.[5] In 1994, they attracted 7.3 per cent of the vote, after having received 4.8 per cent in 1986 and 1990 (Lauber, 1995). However, their success was short-lived. During the campaign for the

1995 parliamentary elections, they dropped from 10 per cent support back to the 4.8 per cent they had held in 1986 and 1990; internal divisions had arisen. Because the strength of the Greens has resided in appealing to public or parliamentary opinion, their role is likely to be curtailed by EU membership; EU institutions seem less sensitive to such appeals (Steiner and Trattnigg, 1996).

The most recent Austrian party in parliament, the Liberal Forum, was founded in 1993 by Freedomite members of parliament opposed to Haider's xenophobic and anti-EU course (Müller, 1996). Although not a green party, it is rather pro-environment in its orientation, without the leftist touch of the Greens. In 1995, it received 5.5 per cent of the vote after receiving 6 per cent in 1994.

Interest groups
It is in this area that the role of the four social partners stands out as an almost unique institution, viewed internationally. They play a special role in the legislative process (bills are normally negotiated with them before being sent to parliament) and also in administration. This search for agreement is at the very core of consociational politics. However, Austrian politics have become less consensus-oriented during the last decade, and environmental policy-making is a case in point (Talos, 1993: 173–8). The Chambers of Commerce and Labour and the Austrian Trade Union Federation (Österreichischer Gewerkschaftsbund) have long had a reputation of being anti-environmental. This has changed during the last decade, and the environmental subdivision of the Chamber of Labour has become a prominent promotor of environmental concerns, even if its proposals have not always been in agreement with the official line of the organisation. In late 1994, the Chamber of Labour even supported an ecological tax reform, provided that compensation could be found for the poor and for energy-intensive industries. The Chamber of Commerce, though often bent on slowing down environmental reform, now assists its members with information and training and negotiates voluntary agreements with the government to promote recycling at the industrial level (OECD, 1995: 95). Of the four social partners, it has the strongest influence on environmental policy-making. The Chamber of Agriculture defends the interests of the farmers and has played a significant role in promoting biomass (mostly woodchips) for space heating (Austria – along with Denmark – is one of the leading European countries using this fuel). It has long

pushed for a tax on fossil fuels to make renewable biomass more competitive.

In addition to the social partners, there are other large interest groups, especially the Association of Austrian Industrialists and associations of industrialists within particular sectors (Talos, 1996). Like the Chamber of Commerce, they usually resist further environmental reform, which they view as a threat to Austrian industry. Further progress, they argue, should be achieved only in step with the EU and in taking account of competition from Eastern Europe. But at the practical (sometimes local or regional) level, many firms develop new technologies less damaging to the environment, often with the help of public funding. If successful, they usually work to have their new standards applied to the whole branch.

High domestic standards and the development of special technical solutions have made the branch of environmental technology increasingly important, and it has also contributed significantly to exports. In relative terms, this branch is more important in Austria than it is in Germany or Switzerland. This industry supports strict regulation (Köppl and Pichl, 1995).

Tourism (more important in Austria than in any other industrial country) has of course its own interest in preserving the environment. However, tourism also tends to overuse the environment for its own purposes, especially in sensitive alpine areas.

Environmental organisations

In Austria, the first environmental organisations arose in the second half of the nineteenth century (the Alpine Club in 1862, the Friends of Nature in 1895, the Nature Protection Society in 1913). An Austrian Office of the World Wildlife Fund was set up in 1963, and the Austrian Society for the Protection of Nature and the Environment (Österreichische Gesellschaft für Natur- und Umweltschutz, ÖGNU), an umbrella organisation for the (by now more numerous) nature protection associations, was created in 1973. A broad founding wave of modern environmental organisations took place between the late 1970s and the late 1980s (Friends of the Earth, Greenpeace, Global 2000). After Hainburg in 1985, the Forum of Austrian Scientists for Environmental Protection, the Austrian Ökologie-Institut for Applied Environmental Research, and the ÖGUT described above were founded (Fischer-Kowalski and Payer, 1995: 565). More specialised organisations followed, such as the Austrian Traffic Club

(Verkehrsclub Österreich), which developed counter-expertise to challenge the traditional lobbying monopoly of the automobile associations. Several groups have organised the opponents of nuclear power, and there have been a great variety of other organisations and initiatives.

The need for co-ordination and efficient action and the need to be represented in Brussels have led to co-operative efforts. Also, the environment ministry has looked for a constituency of its own to acquire more political weight. Environmental organisations have usually been very critical of the ministry and have tended to criticise it even for misdeeds that it could not have prevented because of its own powerlessness. Partly for these reasons, the idea of an environment chamber was born, both to protect environmental interests and to create links between the ministry and the environmental organisations (Krott and Traxler, 1993). The new institution would have been given the right to participate at an early stage in the drafting of bills and government decrees, to demand environmental information from public authorities, to participate in administrative proceedings and to provide legal services to members or citizen initiatives involved in lawsuits (*Standard*, 3 September 1993). But after a brief discussion, the idea was abandoned. The governing coalition parties were afraid of the potential power of such an institution; in turn, the more activist environmental organisations were concerned about the compromises that such a semi-official status might require. The more activist groups are now organised on their own and set up the Ökobüro in 1993. Both the ÖGNU and the Ökobüro are members of the European Environmental Bureau in Brussels.

Though the plans for an environmental chamber have been shelved, contacts between government agencies and environmental organisations seem to have become more normal as these organisations have become stronger and less hostile towards government over the last ten years. Increasingly, the environmental movement has shifted its energy from protest towards formulating plausible alternatives. On the other hand, policy-making in Brussels is less open to environmental organisations than it is in Vienna; this creates a new challenge.

Activist citizens

Since the state is often not genuinely interested in securing environmental protection, it is crucial that actors outside the state structure

have the right to insist on the application of environmental law. In
Austria, such provisions are contained in various administrative laws
regulating business installations. After Hainburg, a general right of
citizen participation in administrative proceedings was discussed; the
idea was to achieve an early consensus on particular projects rather
than to fight out the issue on every construction site. After many
different projects (Meyer, 1994: 469–93), the Act on Environmental
Impact Assessment and Citizen Participation was passed in 1993. For
certain very large projects, it combined an environmental impact
procedure with citizen participation and a concentrated (and stream-
lined) permit procedure. Provincial ombudsmen, the local municipality, neighbouring municipalities, and initiatives consisting of at least
200 citizens from the relevant municipalities were given the right to
participate in the proceedings and to appeal the decisions to the
highest courts. While this was an important step in the expansion of
standing rights for citizens, it was limited by the fact that only a few
dozen very large projects were likely to fall under the scope of this
law every year. For all other projects, the Ministry of Economic
Affairs has tried drastically to curtail standing rights, so far with
limited success (Meyer, 1994: 472–3 and 492–3).

National style and beliefs

National style in environmental policy
Although the search for consensus has been the dominant trait of
Austrian policy-making, a somewhat different pattern has characterised environmental legislation. Environmental laws and decrees
have usually been prepared by experts from the ministries in charge
(Environment, Economic Affairs, Agriculture and Forestry) in close
co-operation with business representatives. Since 1986, all three
ministries have been held by the People's Party, which has also dominated the Chamber of Commerce. Particularly in the case of decrees,
the other social partners played a much lesser role than the one they
play, say, in economic and social welfare matters. Disagreements that
could not be solved were settled towards the end of the process at the
political level by the chief negotiators of the coalition parties. Environmental organisations rarely took part in this process. When they
did impose themselves as actors, their involvement came only in the
administrative phase after the rule-making had been completed or an
administrative decision had been taken, because they could muster a

significant protest potential or could credibly threaten legal action, raising the spectre of a crisis of legitimacy, as in the case of Hainburg.

Many public laws have provided only a framework and have needed to be specified by decree from the relevant ministry or ministries before they could be made applicable. In theory, administrative decisions should be fully determined by those laws and decrees. In practice, the exercise of discretion is unavoidable. In the past, this discretion was frequently exercised to the detriment of the environment; the civil servants in charge were under pressure from economic interests and also from hierarchical superiors usually affiliated with one of the two big parties (who in turn were linked to specific producer interests). Political interventions in administrative proceedings motivated by economic interests were not unusual and were viewed as normal (Guggenberger, 1991). During the last decade or so, however, civil servants seem to have emancipated themselves to some extent, becoming more independent. They have also been able to rely on more independent and more critical environmental experts than they could in the past (Svoboda, 1988: 6).

Austria has among Europe's highest ratios of law graduates among its civil servants; this goes hand-in-hand with a practice that relies strongly on command-and-control measures and is averse to economic instruments. The civil service apparatus is quite thorough (if sometimes slow), and its decisions are usually respected. In the past, some form of accommodation for polluters was common; this seems to have declined in recent years as support for environmental regulation has spread throughout Austrian society.

Despite the strongly legalistic administrative culture, there is not much reliance on the courts. The courts of public law (the Administrative and the Constitutional Courts) are the authority of last resort for appeals in administrative proceedings, but the criteria for who may bring an appeal are still quite restrictive. Criminal courts play a negligible role. Polluters usually go free or pay insignificant fines. The group most commonly fined are farmers who spread excessive amounts of liquid manure; they are convicted of water pollution.

In the search for solutions that are less cumbersome than formal law, business has pressed for other instruments. One of these is the instrument of voluntary agreement. By 1995, over seventeen such agreements had been negotiated and signed between government and business or industry, particularly for achieving specific recycling goals. Because of their flexibility, voluntary agreements were judged as very promising by the OECD report. However, some organisations, such as the Chamber of Labour, have had important reservations because these agreements have not been published (as they are in the Netherlands), making it difficult to judge their success (Glatz, 1995). In fact, the OECD links its recommendation for the wider use of such agreements to transparency and to the introduction of monitoring mechanisms (OECD, 1995: 95, 98 and 163).

Environmental protection and economic growth
Until the mid-1980s, economic growth and environmental protection were commonly presented as antagonistic in public discussion. Those who supported growth connected it with the belief in the blessings of industrial society, in particular increased material production, a higher standard of living, full employment and competitiveness on international markets. In this view, pollution was either portrayed as insignificant or its control was presented as a luxury that could be financed only out of high rates of economic growth. In contrast, support for the environment was frequently identified with a fundamental rejection of industrial society, full employment and a high standard of living in favour of some sort of return to nature. Remarkably, economic logic was widely ignored by both sides in the discussion. Environmentalists tended to ignore it because they viewed it as inherently prejudiced in favour of business, and businessmen often did so because they were not prepared at first to question their methods of production or because they did not see the economic potential residing in a more efficient use of resources.

Towards the end of the 1980s, another logic began to transcend this antagonism. In this logic, the environment and economics were no longer viewed as contradictory. Business firms began to strive for a 'green' image, and some producers began to take pride in the high environmental standards which they had often accepted reluctantly. Increasing efficiency using new technology was more and more identified as a singularly appropriate way to satisfy both economic and environmental criteria. Measures to this effect were promoted early on in the area of energy policy, but their potential began to be realised more widely only in the second half of the 1980s. This was assisted by the fact that larger firms at least were now required to designate a person within the firm as responsible for environmental questions; later on a similar responsibility for waste was also created.

The late 1980s and early 1990s also saw a founding wave of environmental consultancy firms (Martinuzzi, 1994: 17). By the 1990s, special programmes had been set up to fine-tune the technology of particular firms in such a way as to reduce both resource consumption and financial expenditure; investment costs were recovered in a short time, often within months (BMWF/BMU, no date). It is expected that eco-audits will reinforce this trend. In some areas, resource consumption declined substantially. Energy consumption by industry in 1992 was the same as in 1973, while industrial production had increased by 70 per cent. If overall energy consumption went up during this period, this was mostly due to growth in transport and heating (OECD, 1995: 101).

The two big parties reworked their thinking (more than their actual behaviour) on this subject in the late 1980s; this was reflected in many, specific proposals in their programmes for the 1990 parliamentary elections. There was a real outpouring of ideas. Both government parties promised efforts against nuclear power plants in neighbouring countries, public information on environmental data and measures to avoid waste, as well as the construction of incineration plants, the promotion of public transport and restrictions on car traffic in city centres. The Social Democrats also stressed the need for a law on environmental liability and for a reduction of specific emissions (VOCs: 50 per cent reduction by the year 2000; CO_2: 25 per cent reduction by 2005), and were prepared to impose restrictions on business firms. The People's Party stressed economic incentives, particularly as a new approach to the waste problem; it also proposed discontinuing partially halogenated CFCs and PVC for packaging. It created a new slogan – the 'eco-social market economy'. Both parties addressed many other questions. The opposition parties took a similar approach; not surprisingly, the Greens had the most far-reaching programme with the most radical proposals. These programmes were almost an environmentalist's paradise (Goetz and Faulhaber, 1991). In 1994 and 1995–1996, the environment did not enjoy a comparable priority.

Against the background of the previous antagonism, the idea that economic growth and environmental protection might converge amounted to a real discovery for many leaders and most of the general public. In the discussion about an ecological tax reform in 1994–1995, what seems to have surprised most was the argument – formulated in studies both by Greenpeace and by the Austrian Institute for Economic Research – that such a reform would positively affect economic growth and employment and also diminish resource consumption (Bach *et al.*, 1994; Köppl *et al.*, 1995). The idea began to spread that high technical standards as well as eco-taxes might promote leadership in the development of an environmental technology industry, which already represented an asset for exports. In 1995, this industry had a business volume of about ECU 1.5 billion, almost half of which was exported. It comprised 250 firms with a total employment of 11,000. Waste management and environmental consulting added another ECU 1 billion (Köppl and Pichl, 1995; *Salzburger Nachrichten*, 13 October 1995).

However, this realisation of an at least partially parallel logic of economic and environmental criteria has not yet been anchored very solidly. The economic difficulties that started in 1992 led to several business proposals to scale down environmental protection or to postpone legislation in this area. It seems that, in difficult times, the pattern which defines economy and environment as antagonistic tends to re-emerge.

Foreign environmental policy

Austria is a small country that has been committed to a policy of active neutrality since 1955. To compensate for its lack of power and to avoid isolation, it has consciously sought an active role in international affairs, particularly in the framework of the UN and other international organisations, and has looked for co-operation with like-minded countries (Kramer, 1996: 151–2). This attitude can also be found in the environmental area. Thus, Austria convened the diplomatic conference that led to the 1985 Vienna Convention for the Protection of the Ozone Layer; it chaired this conference and the one that led to the adoption of the 1987 Montreal Protocol; and it hosted a follow-up conference in Vienna in December 1995. It also took initiatives to accelerate the phasing out of partially halogenated CFCs (OECD, 1995: 143–4) and has taken the lead in reducing airborne pollution. On several occasions, it has sought to promote the Earth Charter. It is one of the largest donors (in relative terms) to the Global Environmental Facility, along with Norway and Switzerland (*ibid.*: 147 and 154). Since about 1990, it has challenged the development of nuclear power. In Europe, Austria was among the first countries to require catalytic converters for automobiles (in 1985) and is currently pleading for restrictions on long-distance freight transport by trucks, going against the grain of EU policy. For Eastern Europe, it has offered programmes to help reduce air pollution, promote energy efficiency and develop renewable sources of energy. In recent years, the Austrians – i.e. the political leaders, the media and much of the public – have liked to view their country as a driving force in the international environmental area. The OECD report has concluded that this view is not unrealistic (*ibid.*: 151).

Major issues

In the 1970s and 1980s, few environmental issues were regarded as having a strong international dimension. This was true for transboundary air pollution and for car exhaust emissions (given the difficulty of a small country in tackling such an issue on its own). The first organised opposition in Austria to nuclear power took place in the early 1970s and involved a Swiss reactor near the Austrian border. In the 1990s, the number of international issues multiplied rapidly. Four of them are discussed here: transboundary air pollution, nuclear power, truck transit and climate change.

Transboundary air pollution The first important international issue was probably transboundary air pollution from sulphur and nitrogen oxides. The Convention on Long-Range Transboundary Air Pollution, which Austria ratified, was developed quite early (in Geneva in 1979). As a domestic issue, acid rain first developed in the context of *Waldsterben*. Austria is a net importer of these pollutants; almost all of its acid deposition (about 95 per cent) can be traced to emissions from abroad.

For this reason, Austria has actively pressed for international agreements providing significant emission reductions (Oslo Protocol, Sofia Declaration); its own national reduction targets go still further. Within the framework of the Geneva Convention, Austria has taken various initiatives. In the Working Group on Technology, it has advocated (along with Switzerland and Germany) particularly high standards for best available technology with regard to the emission of VOCs, SO_x, NO_x and dioxin (Umweltbundesamt, 1993: 586–90). It has also supported pollution control in neighbouring Eastern European countries by means of technical and financial assistance, as in Slovakia (Novaky) and in Slovenia, where one single power plant (Sostanj) emits more sulphur than all of Austria (OECD, 1995: 31–5, 140–1 and 151; *UBA-Info*, March 1995: 13–15).

Nuclear power   There was a considerable radioactive fall-out in some parts of Austria after Chernobyl (though not as much as in Scandinavia); this sealed the fate of Austria's only nuclear power plant in Zwentendorf. There was also considerable mobilisation against nuclear facilities in neighbouring countries, first against a nuclear reprocessing plant under construction in Bavaria, where Austrian citizens participated in on-site demonstrations and legal proceedings. After strong pressure, the federal government raised a formal legal objection along with about 420,000 Austrian citizens (Fischer-Kowalski and Payer, 1995: 565). After the plans for the Bavarian reprocessing plant had been scrapped in 1989, the anti-nuclear movement focused on other nearby plants that were considered unsafe.

When, after the fall of the Iron Curtain, Eastern and Central European governments continued with the construction of Russian-designed nuclear reactors, there was another strong wave of mobilisation in Austria, directed especially against plants close to the Austrian border in the Czech Republic and in Slovakia. In 1990, the Austrian government declared that it would seek to promote a nuclear power-free zone in Central Europe and started a policy that opposed the modernisation of stalled Russian-designed reactor projects in that region with Western safety equipment. Such modernisation was promoted by international lending institutions, such as the European Bank for Reconstruction and Development, which provided the finances for such projects. The Austrian government argued in detailed studies that non-nuclear technology and efficiency would be more economic; at the same time, it made efforts in those countries to help promote energy conservation and renewables (Leutgöb, 1995a, b). So far, the Austrian position seems to have managed to delay certain projects (Wedmore, 1995).

Truck freight traffic   Freight traffic across the Alps, between Germany and Italy, has a long tradition and has long been an important source of income in Tyrol, the Austrian province that lies between those two countries. For decades after World War II, the construction of new roads and motorways was viewed very positively, as a part of general progress. In Tyrol, most of the local population actually welcomed the motorway across its territory when it was opened in the early 1970s; it was expected to produce income from freight and tourism. In fact, three additional major transit routes were originally planned across Tyrol; but in the 1970s, local resistance stopped the other projects in opposition to the preference of the provincial leadership (Bertsch, 1991). Similar protests took place later against north–south transit routes across other provinces. In Tyrol, local resistance also stopped plans to expand transit by rail. The resistance was a reaction to the steady growth of pollution and noise that had resulted from traffic in narrow and densely populated Alpine valleys. But even in 1984, transit freight traffic was not yet a theme that could decide the outcome of a provincial election.

In subsequent years, however, citizen initiatives against traffic increases were highly successful in their efforts at mass mobilisation. *Waldsterben* was an important concern; so was human health. People demanded a reduction in truck traffic and a partial shift to rail. Soon thereafter (in 1987), the discussion on Austrian EU membership started. By this time, the EU had begun to liberalise traffic; this led to bans on quantitative limitations and established the principle of free choice of transport means. As a result, it was clear that a durable regulation of the transit traffic question would have to be made before Austria's accession was decided. Political leaders, especially from Germany, strongly urged Austria not to interfere with the freedom of traffic, declaring that such a policy would hurt Austria's prospects of EU membership.

The Conservative People's Party of Tyrol, with its solidly established majority, had long favoured road traffic and at first ignored the protest movement. Because of this lack of sensitivity, it lost almost a quarter of its voters in the 1989 provincial election. After the election, it joined the other parties in advocating traffic reductions in negotiations with the EU to arrive at a solution that would endure after Austria's accession. These negotiations lasted from December 1987 until October 1991; citizen initiatives kept up their pressure during this time and afterwards. An agreement was made in 1991 but, as discussed below, the EU insisted on renegotiating this agreement in 1994, and Austria had to accept a watered-down version.

The agreement of 1991, the Transit Treaty, aimed at reducing transit truck emissions by 60 per cent by the year 2003, starting from a politically agreed base level of pollution in 1991, which served in the calculation of 'eco-points' (pollution rights) for trucks. In addition, a ceiling was placed on the number of trucks in transit, at 108 per cent of the 1991 level. There is some indication that the base levels of pollution and traffic were systematically overestimated to allow for additional increases in actual traffic, as much as 50 per cent according to a 1995 study (*Standard*, 30 November 1995). The agreement specified earlier commitments made by Austria, Germany and Italy to build an appropriate rail infrastructure for absorbing traffic increases and expressly provided for the subsidisation of rail traffic, which would otherwise have contradicted EU law. In addition, Austria and the EU signed a declaration of intent to charge full cost for truck traffic, including, in a second phase, external (and in particular environmental) costs, but only after more detailed consultations (Sickinger and Hussl, 1993).

The EU insisted on renegotiating this agreement after Austria's accession in 1994. In the meantime, the problem had intensified because Switzerland had banned all heavy truck transit through Swiss territory after 2004 in a referendum, raising concerns for France and Austria about 'bypass' transit. In the negotiations of 1994, Austria, which had wanted to preserve the 1991–1992 Transit Treaty in its entirety, consented to a reduction in the duration of that agreement by at least one year and to the reduction of road taxes to the EU level. The clause of the Transit Treaty according to which Austrian road pricing could, after 1997, include all external (and in particular environmental) costs was replaced by a simple declaration of the EU Council that it would ask the Commission to propose a framework that could durably solve the environmental problems of freight traffic and to introduce specific measures that included external costs. This was celebrated as a major success by the Austrian delegation, which argued that it had persuaded the EU to adopt an ecological transport policy. Declarations on the need for rail infrastructure were also restated in 1994 and were included in the new Trans-European Networks.

During the first year after Austria's accession to the EU, truck freight transit increased by about 14 per cent (*Standard*, 27 December 1995); however, it still did not reach the 'inflated' estimate of 1991 and could thus not be checked by legal restrictions. On the other hand, train freight traffic decreased. In December 1995, the EU Commission submitted a Green Paper on internalising external costs of traffic (Commission, 1995), but at a press conference, Traffic Commissioner Kinnock made it clear that this would take another ten to fifteen years (*Standard*, 22 December 1995). In the meantime, Austria had increased the truck toll on the Brenner route twice (in

1995 and 1996); after the second increase, Kinnock announced that the Commission would probably take Austria to the European Court of Justice for charging fees in excess of Council Directive 93/89/EEC on vehicle taxes, infrastructure tolls and charges of 1993 (*Standard*, 21 February 1996). Intense political pressure came from Germany as well as from freighters. However, the Austrian government was prepared to stick to its policy (Bundesregierung, 1995: 26 and 114). Within Austria, the leaders of the anti-transit movement made it clear that they were alive and well and ready for new activism. Within the framework of the Alpine Convention, Austria made another effort to prevent further traffic increases, trying to make its neighbours renounce motorway projects that would lead right up to the Austrian border. Italy and Germany were, however, not prepared to renounce their projects, so the stage was set for further conflict.

Climate change   This issue emerged in Austria in around 1990. Discussions centred on two measures: legislation to protect rain forests and ecological tax reform. CO_2 emissions in Austria have varied only slightly since 1973. Both per capita and per unit of GDP, they are below the OECD average, mostly because of Austria's large share of renewable energy; about one-quarter of primary energy comes from hydropower or biomass (OECD, 1995: 33–4). However, these emissions are scheduled to increase by 10 to 15 per cent over the next ten to fifteen years unless action is taken to stabilise them (Musil, 1993; BMUJF, 1994: 96–102); their reduction will require an even greater effort. To achieve the Toronto target of a 20 per cent reduction from the 1988 level by the year 2005, Austria would have to reduce its current CO_2 emissions by about 28 per cent (*UBA-Info*, December 1995: 5).

Austria is one of the countries that support strong measures to reduce CO_2 emissions on the international scene. The federal government supports the Toronto target and included it in the 1993 Energy Report and the 1994 National Climate Report. In Europe, similarly ambitious goals were set only by Germany (which benefits from reductions in its newly incorporated eastern provinces), Denmark and Luxembourg (*Acid News*, February 1995: 11). When it became clear before the United Nations Conference on Environment and Development (UNCED) in Rio that due to US opposition there would be no climate convention with more ambitious targets, a group of like-minded countries led by Austria, Switzerland and Norway were able at least to introduce the goal of reducing emissions to the 1990 level by the year 2000. Austria ratified the Framework Convention on Climate Change in 1994. However, in line with the EU, it did not support the AOSIS (Alliance of Small Island States) proposal at the Berlin conference in 1995 to reduce emissions by 20 per cent from the 1990 level by the year 2005.

In domestic politics, however, little decisive action has been taken so far, and it is increasingly obvious that the government is not seriously committed to the envisioned goal, although it has not abandoned it either. At the local and regional level, many municipalities and eight out of nine provincial governments have become members of the Climate Alliance and have thus committed themselves to a 50 per cent reduction of CO_2 emissions by the year 2010 (*Klimabündnis Rundbrief*, 3, 1995: 6). In some municipalities, this has led to remarkable activities.

Part of the CO_2 problem stems from the destruction of tropical rain forests, an issue that attracted some attention in Austria in the late 1980s. Actually, only a small part of this destruction is due to timber exports (most often, forests are actually burned). Though Austria's per capita imports of tropical wood were far below the OECD average, restrictions were decided in 1991 on all wood harvested through non-sustainable management practices. This law was accompanied by a programme to set up sustainable forest management projects intended to benefit indigenous rain forest populations. This law was voted unanimously and supported by the major environmental organisations. It was meant to serve as a model for other countries and to show Austria's commitment to the UNCED goals just a few days before the conference opened (*Salzburger Nachrichten*, 29 May and 24 June 1992). During a parliamentary discussion, it was pointed out that Austria's position would inevitably meet with resistance from economic interests and that Austria should therefore be prepared for such pressures.

In the meantime, preparation for the UNCED conference had taken a very different turn. The planned forest convention with its obligatory measures was scrapped at the last moment upon the insistence of Third World countries and the International Timber Trade Organisation, which claimed that the real issue at stake was whether anyone had the right to tell a country how to manage its own natural resources. Instead of a convention, a legally non-binding 'statement of principles' – Friends of the Earth called it a 'chainsaw charter' –

was adopted, supposedly because of practical problems in defining sustainable practices. This statement banned boycotts on unsustainable forest products and other unilateral measures restricting trade with such products on the grounds that this would violate the General Agreement on Tariffs and Trade (GATT) (*Financial Times*, 11 and 15 June 1992). In late 1992, several South East Asian countries protested against the mandatory label for tropical wood contained in Austrian law. They threatened to leave the organisation or move to expel Austria, and later on they took their protest to GATT (Ludwig, 1993: 128; Umweltbundesamt, 1993: 606). Out of concern for its exports to that region, Austria rescinded its law and passed a new one, which provided only for a voluntary label for wood harvested from sustainably managed forests – tropical, temperate or boreal. Relations with Indonesia and Malaysia soon normalised again, but there was considerable irritation in parliament.

Given the insignificance of Austrian imports of tropical timber, the emotional intensity of that controversy may seem surprising; but the issue was not only symbolic. If the UNCED had adopted the Forest Convention as planned, the Austrian law could indeed have represented a model; presumably, it was for this very reason that several export countries reacted so violently. It seems that somewhat similar legislation was considered in several other European countries. Austria would have done well to seek allies for its cause (perhaps forsaking prestige). The issue illustrates the difficulty of helping indigenous populations or of promoting sustainability against the will of the governments in charge.

The climate change issue also stimulated the debate on ecological tax reform. In Austria, proposals regarding such a reform date back to the early 1980s. A 1995 study by the Austrian Institute of Economic Research listed some three dozen fairly detailed proposals for such a tax reform over the previous decade (Köppl *et al.*, 1995: 16–36). After the 1990 parliamentary election, the government, while recognising the importance of economic instruments, declared that it wanted to proceed only in step with other Western European countries on the issue of energy taxation. However, action by the EU or by neighbouring countries was not forthcoming, and in 1995 a large discussion took place in which all political parties took part. The three opposition parties (the Greens, the Liberal Forum and the Freedom Party) presented plans for an ecological tax reform (tax increases on energy compensated essentially by a reduction in the taxation on labour). However, the parties in government, which in the meantime had shown some willingness to accept this approach, became more and more cautious. After the coalition government had fallen apart over the issue of austerity, the reform was postponed once more; what remained was a modest tax on oil products in 1995 and on gas and electricity in 1996, both without compensation. Austria officially continues to support EU efforts to increase energy efficiency by CO_2 taxation because in this way distortions in the competitiveness of national economies can be minimised. But the government has ignored the advice given by the prestigious Institute of Economic Research that an ecological tax reform conducted in a revenue-neutral way (by reducing taxes on labour) need not hurt, and may actually improve, the prospects of the country's economy.

The preparation of foreign environmental policy

The most important institutional actors in international environmental policy are the Ministry of Foreign Affairs and the environment ministry. Within the EU, policy formulation is made directly by the line ministries, which are in immediate contact with the EU organs concerned; however, the environmental ministry benefits from the EU structure of environmental policy.

The Ministry of Foreign Affairs formally represents the Austrian position abroad. In some instances, its diplomatic missions play an important role in day-to-day contacts with organisations such as the United Nations Environmental Programme in Nairobi, the United Nations Economic Commission for Europe in Geneva and the OECD in Paris; in those cases, they also represent the environment ministry. The Ministry of Foreign Affairs formally authorises the Austrian delegations at international conferences, gives valuable material support and co-ordinates activities if several Austrian ministries are affected by a particular issue and take part in its negotiation; in such cases, the Ministry of Foreign Affairs makes sure that they arrive at a uniform Austrian position. It also supports other ministries by placing at their disposal its experts on international law. It does not, however, interfere with the composition of delegation teams or with substantive work, except when this work involves questions of international law.

The international division of the environment ministry carries out most of the substantive work in the field of foreign environmental policy. For many years, this was the task of a single person who had been in the ministry from its inception; by 1995, however, the international division counted some two dozen persons. It co-ordinates the substantive work in cases where several ministries are in charge of a particular subject matter and prepares the Austrian position. Because of the 'messy' situation regarding the distribution of environmental powers, the environment ministry can – and often does – seek the initiative in many areas that arguably 'belong' to other ministries. In practice, it also entertains many direct, informal contacts with the ministries of other countries and international organisations without using the channels of the Ministry of Foreign Affairs. In international negotiations, it receives its mandate from the Ministry of Foreign Affairs to which it notifies the positions arrived at.

At the UNCED – an intergovernmental, not just an interministerial conference – Austria was represented by the Chancellor (the head of the government) plus the Ministers of Foreign Affairs and the Environment. The conference, in turn, was prepared domestically by a commission to which representatives of all ministries were invited, along with representatives of the provinces, the social partners and environmental organisations. At the Berlin climate conference in 1995, the Austrian delegation included not only representatives from several ministries, but also representatives from the Chamber of Commerce and two environmental organisations. Similar practices exist in other areas (as in the negotiation on the Transit Treaty).

In the framework of the EU, things are different. Here, relations with EU authorities are handled directly by the line ministries. Austria's permanent representation in Brussels consists of two representatives from most ministries, exceptions being made for foreign affairs (thirteen), economic affairs (seven) and finance (four), with some ministries having only one representative. The delegation also includes the four social partners (five representatives of the Chamber of Commerce, two of the Chamber of Labour, one each for the other two), the Association of Austrian Industrialists, one delegate from the provinces, one from the cities and one from the National Bank (Lamport and Lughofer, 1995: 242–4). However, they do not take part in negotiations. The presence of the social partners is, in fact, meagre compensation for the decline in their influence resulting from the transfer of policy agendas from Vienna to Brussels (Falkner, 1993; Korinek, 1994: 139–40).

At the EU level, the environment ministry has often succeeded in seizing the initiative to establish contacts with EU authorities, even when the subject matter has arguably 'belonged' to another ministry (but again, the demarcation is not always clear in the environmental field). It has also insisted on being consulted when other ministries formulate positions affecting environmental policy (e.g. when the Ministry of Finance formulated the Austrian position on environmental taxation). In this, it is helped by the EU institutional structure. The directorate general in charge of environmental matters (DG-XI) deals, for example, with water, which means that the Council of Ministers of the Environment also handles this issue. In that case, the Austrian environment ministry occupies the leading position in an area in which it has no powers domestically. Its position is limited, though, by the fact that most of the experts are in the Ministry of Agriculture and Forestry, which is in charge of most water issues at the domestic level (Steiner and Trattnigg, 1996).

A major issue in EU policy-making is that of control, by the Austrian parliament, of ministers taking part in the European Council and, particularly, in its legislative process. In 1994, a constitutional amendment was adopted that mandated ministers to inform the lower house of parliament about all projects and to give it an opportunity to formulate a position on the subject (Article 23e of the federal constitution). The minister is then constitutionally bound by instructions from parliament if the project concerns matters that are the object of federal legislative powers (even in the case of an EU regulation, which is applicable without any legislative activity by the Austrian parliament). He may deviate from such instructions only 'for compelling reasons of foreign or integration policy', a rather vague criterion. In matters not relating to legislative projects, the obligation to comply with the instructions carries primarily political weight.

This constitutional amendment was inspired by the Danish example. There is a difference, however. In Denmark, parliamentary control with ministers engaged in EU policy-making has been a long-standing practice based on universal consensus. The Austrian opposition parties did not trust the government enough (especially in EU matters) for such a solution; they insisted on a constitutional amendment as the price for their consent to the constitutional law on EU accession, for which the government needed a two-thirds parliamentary majority, which it could not muster by its own strength at that time (Trattnigg and Waibel, 1995). In one case, at least, Article 23e proved a somewhat clumsy instrument. The EU Council debated the transport of livestock. The Austrian parliament wanted a particularly strict regulation and instructed the minister accordingly. The paradoxical result was that the advocates of strict regulation in the European Council lost out because the Austrian minister could not join them, being bound to still higher standards. Detailed instructions had produced a result opposite to that which had been intended.

The debate on EU membership and environmental policy

Austria formally applied for EU membership in 1989; the main reason for this step was the fear of being excluded from the single market scheduled for the early 1990s. About two-thirds of Austria's foreign trade was already with the EU, and in the second half of the 1980s there was concern, first in industry and later also among the government parties, that the Austrian economy might not come out of the structural crisis which had beset it since 1983–1984 after decades of superior performance. Soon a second reason was added: the fall of the Iron Curtain and the new insecurity resulting from tensions and war in the former Yugoslavia (Kramer, 1996: 163 and 173–5).

Among the population, this application was met with substantial reservations right from the outset. These reservations were primarily of an economic nature: some people feared stepped-up competition in the event of EU membership, or a less favourable treatment by public policy as in the case of agriculture; there was concern about lower standards of social welfare and fear of deflationary policies after Maastricht. Another major theme was the future of Austrian neutrality: would it survive EU accession? Citizen initiative groups, environmental organisations and the Greens contributed to the environmental theme; they argued that the EU was an organisation set on maximising economic growth without much regard for democratic decision-making, social welfare or environmental protection; later on, the Greens also stressed that Austria's neutrality was needlessly put at risk. For these reasons, they argued that Austria should remain outside the EU and should work to transform the EU into a more democratic organisation that would be more sensitive to environmental and social welfare considerations. Their slogan was 'Yes to Europe, no to the EC' (Grüne Bildungswerkstatt, 1993). However, one Green member of parliament favoured accession, arguing that

Austria (together with the new Scandinavian member states) could strengthen the forces of ecological reform within the EU. The government and its constituent parties (the Social Democrats and the People's Party) responded by claiming that Austria would not only be able to maintain its high environmental standards within the EU, but would also serve as a model for other member states. In their propaganda, they brushed aside most environmental criticisms of the EU as simply exaggerated and focused on the more basic – i.e. economic – issues. But they did treat environmental issues seriously in the negotiations.

Despite the near unanimity of the government and the social partners in favour of EU membership, public opinion surveys showed some ambivalence, though the supporters were somewhat more numerous for most of the five years preceding the vote on EU membership in June 1994. A substantial part of the electorate was simply undecided until a very late point in time (Plasser *et al.*, 1995; Kramer, 1996: 174). Under these conditions, the negotiations on the Transit Treaty with the EU – which started in 1989 and ended in 1991 (with ratification in 1992) – took on particular significance. They were the most visible indication of how serious the EU was about the environment, and the results were not always encouraging.

Other environmental themes concerned the question of what would happen to higher Austrian standards after accession. The Greens – who are usually quite critical of Austria's environmental legislation – now argued that the standards would have to be diluted as a result of membership; by contrast, they could be upgraded if Austria stayed outside. Anti-nuclear groups conjured up the spectre of nuclear power plants being built on Austrian territory on the basis of EU laws, and the Greens pointed out that Austria, by joining the EU, would also join Euratom and thus contribute large amounts of money to nuclear power programmes.

As to the other opposition parties, the Freedom Party had supported an application for membership for decades, but (under its autocratic leader, Jörg Haider) became more and more critical of accession in the 1990s, even against the preference of its own supporters. This was one reason why some parliamentary deputies left this party and set up the Liberal Forum in 1993 – a group with environmental sympathies, but even more strongly pro-EU, supporting the government on this issue (Schaller, 1994: 49–74; Kunnert,

1993: 76 and 100). The Liberals were prepared to place their trust in future European environmental policy.

At the start of negotiations in February 1993, the Austrian Foreign Minister stressed the interests that Austria needed to protect the most: the survival of its comparatively small-structured agriculture, its high standards in social welfare and its environment, the sensitive alpine ecology and, in particular, the Transit Treaty intended for the latter's protection (*Salzburger Nachrichten*, 3 February 1993). Environmental issues were dealt with under the headings of energy, environment, agriculture and transportation.

In the field of energy, Austria's major concern regarded nuclear power. The federal government declared its intention to lead the struggle for a nuclear-free zone in Central Europe, primarily by helping Eastern European reform states to renounce nuclear power. In particular, Austria wanted to maintain its legal ban on nuclear power plants. This led to a common declaration in September 1993 that recognised the freedom of the member states of Euratom to decide on their own whether to use nuclear power or not. It was also clarified that Austria need not admit imports of radioactive waste (Bericht der Bundesregierung, 1994: 20–1).

With regard to environmental standards (mostly for products), a package was agreed upon with the following content: Austria (and the other new members) would have the right to maintain stricter standards in certain areas for a four-year transition period. During this time, the EU would review its own standards with a view to achieving the highest possible level. After this date, Austria would take over the *acquis* and could maintain higher standards only to protect specifically listed goals and only if free trade between member states was not inhibited or discriminated against. Austria added a unilateral declaration according to which it could request an extension of the four-year transition period if the EU had not, by that date, completed its review process. This environmental package was agreed upon in December 1993 (Bericht der Bundesregierung, 1994: 6–10).

Two large issues remained to be solved until the very end; because of their highly controversial nature, they were decided at the highest level during the ministers' meeting in March 1994. They concerned agriculture and transit traffic. In agriculture, farmers and food industries were expected to lose income as a result of accession. However, EU subsidies to sustainable farming practices were to provide a major impulse to organic-biological farming, an area where Austria is leading Europe, with about 10 per cent of its farmers following this practice (Vogl and Heß, 1996; Bericht der Bundesregierung, 1994: 22). The issue that was discussed most intensely in domestic politics was that of transit traffic. According to some surveys, 65 per cent of the population (and a considerably higher percentage in Tyrol) were prepared to reject accession if the Transit Treaty was modified to Austria's disadvantage. The results achieved in the end, although presented as a success by the Austrian negotiating team, were viewed with considerable scepticism in Tyrol, where the governor at first withheld his support for accession until the government had given sufficient guarantees for the expansion of rail infrastructure (*Standard*, 3 March 1994). This scepticism may yet prove legitimate. However, in the rest of the country, surveys showed a clear increase in support for accession, once the negotiation results had been presented by the government in Vienna as a kind of triumph. This even led to momentary EU euphoria.

Yet, the leaders of the Greens – and for different reasons, the Freedom Party – recommended a negative vote in the referendum of June 1994, though some dissenters among the leadership of both parties favoured membership. Since the outcome of the vote seemed far from certain (*Financial Times*, 8 June 1994), the eventual two-thirds majority in favour of accession, motivated primarily by the expectation of economic advantages, came as a surprise (Kramer, 1996; *Standard*, 14 June 1994). After this unambiguous vote, the Green deputies in parliament announced that they would now vote for the ratification of the accession treaty and would concentrate on efforts, in co-operation with the Austrian government, to transform the EU from the inside, to make it more democratic and its public policy more sensitive to the environment and social welfare (*Standard*, 14 June 1994).

The Austrian government seemed at first to be serious about making good on its promise – formulated in response to Green criticism – of trying to reform EU structures. An internal government paper on the intergovernmental conference of 1996 argued that the success of the EU in the years to come would strongly depend on whether it could deal successfully with the most important contemporary issues, i.e. unemployment and environmental protection. The EU treaty should be modified to help achieve better results in those areas. Most other policy items of the first pillar (energy, tourism, the economic and currency union, and agricultural and regional policy) were viewed as less important or less appropriate for discussion at this point, whereas several highly specific proposals were formulated in the environmental field: to anchor the concept of sustainable development in Article 2 of the treaty (among the goals of the EU) and to list sustainability or environmental protection in other articles of the treaty (Articles 36 and 39). Austria also favours an extension of the powers of the European Parliament in all areas of environmental policy (as a body more sympathetic to the environmental cause) and greater leeway for national measures in this area (Bundeskanzleramt, 1995: 5–18).

These proposals reflect the situation prevailing after the October 1994 election, when the Greens and the Liberal Forum were still celebrating their electoral successes and growing support; they could take the government on its word. But although the 1995 elections have weakened those forces (in particular the Greens), the government has stuck to its proposals. Perhaps they also illustrate the enthusiasm of a neophyte member; other EU countries favour similar reforms but do not want to bring up the subject for fear of possible setbacks. Finally, the proposals could be seen as an adaptation of Austrian politics to the EU structure: the energies of the domestic forces for environmental reform can thus be deflected towards actors in Brussels (who can be blamed if success is not forthcoming), while at the same time this kind of 'environmental nationalism' can serve to attract Green voters to the government parties. (Such mechanisms may help to explain – and not just in Austria – the success of the formula of sustainable development in international politics simultaneously with its relative lack of substance when it comes to domestic reforms.) Still, Austria does seem to want to give this formula a stronger environmentalist content than the EU, despite its own Fifth Environmental Action Programme, has done so far.

Notes

1   I would like to thank Martina Schuster from the Ministry of Environment, Youth and Family for an interview that helped me understand foreign environmental policy-making, and Wolfgang Lauber and Karin Hofer for their comments on earlier versions of this chapter.
2   Party politics played a role here, as the Conservative People's Party

hoped that Chancellor Kreisky would resign in the case of a negative outcome of the referendum.

3   The name of the ministry has been changed several times since then. Its current name is the Ministry of Environment, Youth and Family. At some point, it was also called the Ministry of the Environment. In the text, the term 'environment ministry' will often be used in order to signify the ministry responsible for the environment.

4   This is a way for the electorate to initiate a law, and it is very rarely attempted. See note 5.

5   Direct democracy is contrasted with representative democracy. Two major instruments of direct democracy in Austria are: popular referendums on particular issues, such as EU membership and nuclear power plants, and popular initiatives as a way to start the legislative process.

References

Bach, S., B. Praetorius and J. F. Mayer (1994), *Zur Übertragbarkeit der Ergebnisse der DIW-Studie 'Wirtschaftliche Auswirkungen einer ökologischen Steuerreform auf Österreich'*, Berlin, Deutsches Institut für Wirtschaftsforschung (DIW)/Vienna, Energieverwertungsagentur (EVA).

Bericht der Bundesregierung über das Ergebnis der Verhandlungen über den Beitritt Österreichs zur Europäischen Union (1994), Vienna, Bundeskanzleramt.

Bertsch, J. (1991), Transitwiderstand in Tirol, in H. Koch and H. Lindenbaum, *Überrolltes Österreich*, 167–78.

BMUJF (Bundesministerium für Umwelt, Jugend und Familie) (1994), *Nationaler Klimabericht der österreichischen Bundesregierung*, Vienna.

BMwA (Bundesministerium für wirtschaftliche Angelegenheiten) (1993), *Energiebericht 1993 der österreichischen Bundesregierung*, Vienna, BMwA.

BMWF/BMU (Bundesministerium für Wissenschaft und Forschung/ Bundesministerium für Umwelt) (no date, probably 1995), *Prepare Österreich. Initiative für innovatives und umweltbewußtes Wirtschaften*, Vienna, BMWF/BMU.

Bundeskanzleramt (1995), *Leitlinien zu den voraussichtlichen Themen der Regierungskonferenz 1996*, Vienna.

Bundesregierung (1995), *Weißbuch der österreichischen Bundesregierung. Österreich in der Europäischen Union*, Vienna.

Commission of the European Union (1995), *Toward Fair and Efficient Pricing in Transport*, COM (95) 691 fin., 20 December.

Eltbogen, U. (1986), *Umweltschutzinstitutionen in Wien und Umgebung*, Vienna, Wirtschaftsuniversität.

Falkner, G. (1993), Sozialpartnerschaftliche Politikmuster und europäische Integration, in E. Talos (ed.), *Sozialpartnerschaft*, Vienna, Verlag für Gesellschaftskritik, 79–102.

Fischer-Kowalski, M. (1988), *Öko-Bilanz Österreich*, Vienna, Falter Verlag.

Fischer-Kowalski, M. and H. Payer (1995), Fünfzig Jahre Umgang mit der

Natur, in R. Sieber, H. Steinert and E. Talos (eds), *Österreich 1945–1995*, Vienna, Verlag für Gesellschaftskritik, 552–66.

Glatz, H. (1995), *Österreichische Umweltpolitik. Eine kritische Einschätzung der Instrumente.* Informationen zur Umweltpolitik No. 111, Vienna, Chamber of Labour.

Goetz, M. and T. Faulhaber (1991), Papierflut, unter ihrem Wert gehandelt. Die Wahlprogramme der politischen Parteien zu den National-ratswahlen 1990 im Vergleich, *Österreichisches Jahrbuch für Politik 1990*, Vienna, Verlag für Geschichte und Politik, 285–309.

Grüne Bildungswerkstatt (1993), *Ja zu Europa, Nein zur EG*, Vienna.

Grüner Club (1994), *Kritische Bilanz zur Umsetzung des Regierungsübereinkommens 1990 und Grüne Erfolge*, Vienna.

Guggenberger, G. (1991), *Probleme der österreichischen Luftreinhaltepolitik*. Unpublished Master's thesis, University of Salzburg.

Höll, O. (1994), The Austrian case, in O. Höll (ed.), *Environmental Cooperation in Europe*, Boulder, Westview, 281–96.

Kofler, T. and O. Stocker (1985), *Öko-Insel Österreich? Umweltpolitik auf dem Prüfstand*, Vienna, Böhlau.

Kok, F. (1989), Die Umweltanwaltschaft als Instrument der Umweltpolitik, in H. Dachs and R. Floimair (eds), *Salzburger Jahrbuch für Politik 1989*, Salzburg.

Köppl, A. and C. Pichl (1995), *Wachstumsmarkt Umwelttechnologien*, Vienna, WIFO/BMwA.

Köppl, A. *et al.* (1995), *Makroökonomische und sektorale Auswirkungen einer umweltorientierten Energiebesteuerung in Österreich*, Vienna, Österreichisches Wirtschaftforschungsinstitut (WIFO).

Korinek, K. (1994), Interessenvertretungen im Wandel, in P. Gerlich and H. Neisser (eds), *Europa als Herausforderung*, Vienna, Signum, 133–58.

Kramer, H. (1996), Foreign policy, in V. Lauber (ed.), *Contemporary Austrian Politics*, Boulder, Westview, 151–200.

Krott, M. and F. Traxler (1993), *Verbandsorganisation im Umweltschutz*, Vienna, BMJUF.

Kunnert, G. (1993), *Österreichs Weg in die Europäische Union*, Vienna, Staatsdruckerei.

Lamport, C. and S. Lughofer (1995), *Keine Angst vor Brüssel*, Vienna, Ökobüro.

Lauber, V. (1991), Umweltpolitik, in H. Dachs *et al.* (eds), *Handbuch des politischen Systems Österreichs*, Vienna, Manz, 558–67.

Lauber, V. (1995), The Austrian Greens, *Environmental Politics*, 4:2, 313–19.

Lauber, V. (1996), Conclusion and outlook, in V. Lauber (ed.), *Contemporary Austrian Politics*, Boulder, Westview, 253–61.

Leutgöb, K. (1995a), Kontrahenten entdecken gemeinsame Interessen, *EVA Quartalsbericht*, 1995/4, 20–1.

Leutgöb, K. (1995b), Sachliche Argumente in einer hitzigen Auseinandersetzung, *Soziale Technik*, 1995/4, 14–16.

Ludwig, K. (1993), Hört auf, den Wald zu zerstören!, in Gesellschaft für bedrohte Völker (ed.), *Land ist Leben*, Vienna, Dachs.

Luther, K. and W. C. Müller (eds) (1992), *Politics in Austria. Still a Case of Consociationalism?*, London, Frank Cass.

Martinuzzi, A. *et al.* (1994), *Öko-Consulting in Österreich*, Vienna, BMU.

Martischnig, K. (1990), *Österreichs umweltaußenpolitische Aktivitäten im bilateralen und multilateralen Bereich*, unpublished doctoral dissertation, University of Salzburg.

Meyer, M. (1994), Umweltverträglichkeitsprüfung und Bürgerbeteiligung, *Österreichisches Jahrbuch für Politik 1993*, Vienna, Verlag für Geschichte und Politik, 469–93.

Müller, W.C. (1996), Political parties and movements, in V. Lauber (ed.), *Contemporary Austrian Politics*, Boulder, Westview, 23–58.

Musil, K. (1993), *Energieprognose des WIFO und CO_2-Reduktionsszenario*, Vienna, BMwA.

OECD (1995), *Environmental Performance Reviews: Austria*, Paris, OECD.

Onz, C. (1988), *Sozialistische Umweltpolitik*. Zeitdokumente 49, Vienna, Zukunft Verlag.

Plasser, F., F. Sommer and P. A. Ulram (1995), Entscheidung für Europa. Analyse der Volksabstimmung über den EU-Beitritt Österreichs 1994, *Österreichisches Jahrbuch für Politik 1994*, Vienna, Verlag für Geschichte und Politik, 325–54.

Pleschberger, W. (1988), *Umweltanwaltschaft – Bürgerbeteiligung – Verwaltungsreferendum*, Vienna, ÖGNU.

Schäfer, E. (1993), *Umweltanwaltschaft und Umweltkontrolle*, Vienna, BMUJF.

Schaller, C. (1994), 'Ja' oder 'Nein' zu 'Europa'?, in A. Pelinka (ed.), *EU-Referendum*, Vienna, Signum.

Sickinger, H. and R. Hussl (1993), *Transit-Saga. Bürgerwiderstand am 'Auspuff Europas'*, Innsbruck, Kulturverlag.

Steiner, G. and R. Trattnigg (1996), *Die österreichischen umweltpolitischen Akteure im Mehrebenensystem Österreich – Europäische Union: Veränderungen im Politiknetzwerk*, Vienna, unpublished manuscript.

Stolz, A. (1990), Umwelt-, Natur- und Landschaftsschutzanwälte im österreichischen Recht – Möglichkeiten und Grenzen einer 'mediatisierten Bürgerbeteiligung', in M. Zenkl (ed.), *Bürger Initiativ*, Vienna, Böhlau, 148–86.

Svoboda, W. R. (1988), *Vollzugsdefizite im Umweltschutz II*. Informationen zur Umweltpolitik 48, Vienna, Chamber of Labour.

Talos, E. (1996), Corporatism – the Austrian model, in V. Lauber (ed.), *Contemporary Austrian Politics*, Boulder, Westview, 103–24.

Talos, E., K. Leichsenring and E. Zeiner (1993), Verbände und politischer Entscheidungsprozeß – am Beispiel der Sozial- und Umweltpolitik, in E. Talos (ed.), *Sozialpartnerschaft*, Vienna, Verlag für Gesellschaftskritik, 147–85.

Trattnigg, R. and S. Waibel (1995), *Die Mitwirkungsrechte des österreichischen Nationalrats in der EU*, Vienna, unpublished manuscript.

UBA-Info. Monthly publication by the Federal Office of the Environment.

Umweltbundesamt (1993), *Umweltkontrolle und Bestandsaufnahme. Umweltkontrollbericht*, Vienna, BMUJF.

Vogl, C. and J. Heß (1996), Ein Land stellt um!? Entwicklungen und Perspek-
    tiven des Biolandbaus in Österreich, *Ökologie und Landbau*, 24:1,
    27–32.
Wedmore, L. D. (1995), The political costs of Mochovce, *Transition*, 1:10
    (23 June), 46–50.
Welan, M. and M. Kind (1995), *Umwelt und Recht in Österreich*. Diskus-
    sionspapier 42-R-95, Vienna, Universität für Bodenkultur.

Finland: from local to global politics

Introduction

It is obvious that environmental policies in different countries are themselves different as a result of factors characterising the respective political systems. But one aspect often forgotten in cross-national comparisons of environmental policies and politics is the difference in the state of the environment and thus the need for environmental protection. In the following, the main features of the state of the environment in Finland today will be described as a means towards understanding why Finnish environmental policy has the shape that it has.

The area of Finland is 338,145 km². It is the fifth largest country in the EU and has a population of 5.1 million inhabitants. Population density is quite low; there are only 16 inhabitants per km² on average, and the largest population centres are in the south of the country and along the Baltic Sea coastline. For example, almost 25 per cent of the total population is located in the County Uusimaa surrounding the metropolitan area of Helsinki; here, the population density is 131 inhabitants per km². However, many parts of the country are very sparsely inhabited. Because local industrial activities are at a minimum in these areas, environmental damage is only minor. Damage from agriculture and forest cultivation is an exception, however. Of the total mainland area, about 8 per cent is cultivated, 10 per cent is covered by water, 69 per cent is covered by forests (5 per cent of which are made up of old natural forests) and 13 per cent is classified otherwise, mostly as non-use areas. In fact, most of the land is inhabitable (Wahlström *et al.*, 1992: 183; *Finland i siffror '94*, 1994).

The state of the environment in Finland is generally good and has always been good in comparison with many other countries. As an example, the air quality is generally better in Finland than in most other industrialised countries. This is partly due to a favourable geo-ecological position, the small population, the low level of agricultural production and an industrialisation process that did not begin until the mid-nineteenth century. However, the energy-intensive industry structure, combined with a rather cold climate, raises some specific problems. For example, energy supply is problematic. Indigenous energy sources, i.e. water power, peat and wood, account for about 30 per cent of annual energy production, whereas the rest, about 70 per cent, is imported (72 per cent oil, 9 per cent coal, 9 per cent natural gas and 8 per cent electricity). Four nuclear power plants supply as much as all water power together, i.e. about 20 per cent of electricity production. The largest energy consumers are industry, heating and traffic, consuming 44 per cent, 22 per cent and 14 per cent of the total, respectively (Ympäristötilasto – Environment Statistics, 1994: 74; Luonnonvarat ja Ympäristö, 1995: 15).

Water pollution levels (BOD7) are rather high per capita and per BNP due to the relatively large share of paper and pulp industries. In addition, the discharges of nutrients and oxygen-demanding substances are a problem, mostly in the coastal regions of Finland. More than 50 per cent of nutrient discharges are derived from agricultural production in the coastal regions, although 25 per cent are derived from municipal sewage treatment plants, and 15 per cent are derived from industry and peat-cutting (Ympäristötilasto – Environment Statistics, 1994: 129; Kämäri, 1991: 53).

Despite the relatively low level of pollution from a global point of view, it is different from an EU point of view. Levels of air emissions of No_x and SO_2 per capita and per BNP are slightly higher than the EU average. This is also the case with CO_2 emissions. However, Finland still remains a net receiver of most common air pollutants from the EU and the European Free Trade Area (EFTA) countries. Considerable environmental risks also arise from Finland's geographic proximity to the Kola Peninsula, Carelia and St Petersburg regions to the east and the Baltic states to the south (Luonnonvarat ja Ympäristö, 1995: 17; Wahlström *et al.*, 1992: 183–4).

A short history of Finnish environmental policies and politics

The Finns first became aware of nature in the late nineteenth century during the romantic period in Finland's cultural history. Finnish nature was seen as something special and worthy of protection. But, as always, the politicians delayed acting on these new ideas. In the beginning, environmental problems were regarded only as an emerging need for nature conservation, although the signs of early industrialisation were already visible in the largest communities. Actually, until the 1960s, environmental policy was seen almost entirely in terms of problems of nature conservation and public health. Thus, the general development of environmental policies in Finland can be divided into phases depending on the main objectives of the time period (Hermanson and Joas, 1996: 104–11).

The early years: to the 1960s
Although only minor in impact, the first written rules regulating the relationship between man and the environment can be found in the Swedish constitution of 1734. This act was also valid in Finland during the Russian period and in the early twentieth century. The first actual (public health) measures to control pollution problems due to increasing urbanisation and industrialisation were taken by the senate in 1879. Still, the environmental policies of the nineteenth century were first and foremost a question of nature conservation and were considered of minor importance. The first nature reserves were established in Finland during the early nineteenth century. This involved the scenic ridge of Punkaharju. In 1803, the Russian Czar prohibited logging here, and in 1840 the area became state-owned. The first person to respond to the demand for nature conservation on a large scale was the Finnish arctic explorer Adolf Erik Nordenskiöld, who did so in a speech in 1880. His speech brought a dualistic view of nature to the Nordic countries – some relatively small pristine areas should be protected from economic exploitation. In the late nineteenth century, the idea of making reserves was discussed, for example, in nature organisations such as the Societas pro Fauna et Flora (Järvikoski, 1993: 6–10 and 1991: 164). But the relatively slow process of establishing nature reserves and the late start of the nature conservation movement are both often seen as the result of Russian rule in Finland in the nineteenth and early twentieth century, despite partial autonomy.

In 1910, a forest protection commission proposed a larger nature park programme, and gradually a nature conservation area was established in the Malla mountain region in Lapland. But it was the declaration of independence in 1917 that made large-scale nature protection possible. The first years of independence accelerated the interest in nature in Finland, and in 1923 the progressive Nature Conservation Act was introduced, an act still in force today. However, for political reasons new areas of protection were not established until 1938 (Järvikoski, 1993: 14–22).

The forestry sector – i.e. logging, transporting and processing – has been the most important part of the Finnish economic system since the beginning of industrialisation. According to some observers, this fact has made it the environmental blind spot in Finnish society. For a long time, the forestry industry has been energy-intensive, polluting air and water, employing only relatively few people and centrally governed – all factors that contribute to environmental problems. The environmental impact of the forestry industry was regulated modestly in the early twentieth century. For a long time, forestry and nature protection were seen as closely interrelated and not at all in conflict with each other. But from the time of early independence, the forest industry has been regulated, mainly to prevent damage to its economic value (Donner-Amnell, 1991: 265–80; Raumolin, 1990: 20).

In addition to conservation goals, this first period of environmental policies may best be characterised by a 'good neighbour' policy. You could pollute as much as you wanted to as long as it did not harm nearby neighbours. This policy was manifest in the Public Health Act of 1927 and the Neighbourhood Act of 1923. During the following fifty years, only minor policy changes were made (Environmental Protection in Finland, 1988: 111–13).

Pollution awareness: 1960–1970
Although the environmental debate remained at an elitist level during the 1950s and 1960s, public opinion was awakened by both a handful of severe environmental accidents during the period and by the gradual worsening of the environment. Water pollution from large chemical and mechanical wood-processing industries and untreated municipal sewage had become a significant health hazard to people living in and around larger cities or industrial communities. In 1961, public and environmental pressures made the Cabinet adopt

an extensive Water Act for the first time, meant to control water-polluting activities using a permit procedure. The building of munic-ipal sewage treatment plants also began during this era (Wahlström *et al.*, 1992: 330). The Public Health Act was revised in 1965, incor-porating a decree controlling drinking water standards, air pollution control and noise abatement provisions. New physical instruments for controlling point source pollution were introduced in a renewed Planning and Building Act.

The publication of two books also served to make the public aware of the seriousness of ensuing environmental problems. Rachel Carson's book *Silent Spring* was issued in Finnish in 1963 and the Club of Rome report (Meadows *et al.*) was issued in 1972, both of which had an alarming effect (Järvikoski, 1991: 168; Oittinen, 1993: 173).

Movement took place on the domestic scene as well. Alarm bells were rung by Pentti Linkola, a pioneer in the field of ecology, in the early 1960s. He is still active today, although his arguments and goals have changed during the last thirty-five years. He has shifted from being a pacifist, environmentalist and critic of modern society to an advocate of pure ecofascism. Yet, he still manages to become headline news. Today Linkola is often seen as one of the most impor-tant, but highly controversial, environmental discussants in Finland (Oittinen, 1993: 171–7).

Efforts to achieve a better environment did not occur in Finland until the 1960s, and were facilitated by new public interest in envi-ronmental questions and the worsening of the pollution situation in general, at least in industrialised communities. However, it is impor-tant to remember that the economic situation in Finland during the 1960s made the industrialists more interested in pollution control – the war debts had been paid in the 1950s, and the economy was growing faster than ever.

The institutionalisation of environmental policy: 1970–1983
The National Board of Waters was created in 1970 as the first administration unit with some environmental duties. The thirteen years that followed can be characterised as the main institutionalisa-tion phase of the environmental sector. During this phase, there were severe splits within the parties about the administrative structure of environmental responsibilities (see below). Many important policy reforms were set aside until the debate about the shape of the admin-istration had been finished. Major reforms in this period were

concentrated in the last five years and included the new Waste Management Act (1978) and the Air Pollution Control Act (1982). This period ended with the creation of the Ministry of the Environment in 1983.

Environmental activism and the 'green' movement began in Finland during this period. Poorly organised *ad hoc* groups gathered during the summers of 1979 and 1980 to prevent the drainage of a relatively significant waterfowl habitat, Lake Koijärvi, in southern Finland. The Koijärvi protest was followed by several others around the country during the early 1980s and even later, although the level of activism shifted during these first years. The most active period was 1979–1981. A second wave of activism emerged in the late 1980s (Rannikko, 1993: 24–8). A new period of environmental activism, a third wave, began in the mid-1990s. For example, during the winter of 1994–1995, nature activists gathered at Kuusamo using civil disobedience to stop the logging of specific areas of virgin state woods owned by private landowners.

The building of an environmental sector: 1983–1995
The Ministry of the Environment has turned out to be an active participant in environmental politics in Finland. It has co-operated with, and even partly co-opted, environmental activist groups, while at the same time working with the rest of the administration. In many conflict situations, the ministry's standpoint has followed the nature activist line of action. At times, legislative bills proposed by the ministry have turned out to be too progressive for the established parties.

National environmental policy during the 1980s was sector-based. For example, new regulations were introduced and adopted in the Soil Materials Act to regulate the use of natural resources, and partial reforms were made in many other areas. Nature reserves were also enlarged, and administrative reforms continued. For example, local environmental administration was enlarged in 1986. The institutionalisation phase continued during this time within the central administration.

The transboundary and global character of current environmental problems somewhat changed Finnish policies during the late 1980s and early 1990s, so that today international and global objectives are seen as even more important than purely national ones. But environmental protection standards are, as a rule, already very high in

Finland, as they are in the other Nordic countries, and this is why the most effective help for the environment can be found in pollution prevention in Eastern Europe.

Environmental policy in Finland seems to have remained a high priority area despite the economic crisis in the early 1990s. Cut-backs in public spending affected environmental administration, but not any differently from how they affected other policy areas. Relatively speaking, the most affected areas were the large welfare sectors, such as health and social policy. With respect to the environment, however, evidence of this high priority is found in the Declaration of the new Cabinet formed by the Lipponen 'Rainbow' coalition; this declaration represents a step towards a sustainable society, promoting the concept of sustainable development within most social areas.

Institutions in the environmental policy field

The institutionalisation process

Although the institutionalisation of environmental policy is a late phenomenon in Finland, its start can be timed to the same period as that of most other Western democracies: the late 1960s and the early 1970s. Prior to 1970, Finland had no single administrative body with comprehensive environmental responsibility; environmental matters were handled by many different ministries, although many cases were handled by the Ministry of Agriculture and Forestry.

During 1970, the European Year of Environmental Protection, the Cabinet set up an *ad hoc* environmental protection commission whose task it was to plan the forthcoming environmental administration. Co-ordination, however, was still a long way off. The National Board of Waters was established in 1970 with specific duties in water pollution control. The commission proposed an enlargement of environmental administration, which resulted in the establishment of the Environmental Protection Department and the Environmental Protection Council within the Ministry of the Interior in 1973. The Ministry of Agriculture and Forestry still had a division for the management of natural resources. At the regional level, environmental matters were subordinated to several units, i.e. to the water districts (in 1970) and to the supervisor of environmental protection at the county offices (since 1973) (Storsved, 1993b).

The institutionalisation process was considerably delayed due to a prolonged political fight about the competence of the forthcoming

Ministry of the Environment. The political divide was between rural-based political forces, the centre party (Suomen Keskusta, KESK), rather small rural-dominated parties and the Central Union of Agricultural Producers and Forest Owners (Maa-ja Metsätaloustuottajain Keskusliitto, MTK), on the one side, against urban-based forces, the Social Democratic Party (Suomen Sosialidemokraattinen Puolue, SDP) and the conservative National Coalition Party (Kansallinen Kokoomus, KOK), on the other side. Industry and trade unions remained neutral or leaned slightly towards the urban view. This divide can be called the environmental ideological dimension in the Finnish environmental debate, a split that is still visible in environmental debates concerning, for example, landowners' rights.

The rural side supported a narrow solution and thus limited competence for the new ministry, while the urban view supported broad competence for the ministry. The question of competence was also a political one given that new responsibilities would be ones previously handled by the Ministry of the Interior, traditionally dominated by the SDP, and the Ministry of Agriculture and Forestry, dominated by the KESK. The SDP/KESK Cabinet could not reach a compromise, and in the end the decision was turned over to parliament, a very uncommon procedure in Finland. After a protracted debate, lasting for more than ten years and including several commission reports and investigations, the Ministry of the Environment was finally founded on 1 October 1983. For the first time, a major part of environmental care could be handled within one administrative sector.

In the end, the conflict resulted in a relatively large ministry, whose influence touched many, less traditional environmental matters, such as building, planning and housing, not only nature protection and conservation. The National Board of Waters was subordinated to the new ministry and remained the central agency handling most environmental matters. However, the other ministries involved, especially the Ministry of Agriculture and Forestry, were left with a few limited environmental duties (Persson, 1983; Storsved, 1993a).

The legal framework
The legal and constitutional practice of changing the existing constitution has been very limited in Finland. The Finnish constitution includes four basic acts of law, all enacted during the first eleven years of independence. The two most important ones are the Form of

Government Act of 1919 and the Parliament Act of 1928. Reforms have involved mostly minor, often symbolic, time-limited changes. However, in the early 1990s, the need to reform the constitution changed. And in 1995, for the first time since 1919, new basic citizen rights were introduced in the constitution. One of the new rights is the right to a sound environment – a rule stressing not only the right to, but also the responsibility for, the environment (1995 revision of the Form of Government Act 1919 14a §). The constitution, on the other hand, strongly protects the right to private property, including the right to use natural resources freely, and this has often been considered a major disadvantage, especially in nature conservation.

Finland lacks a specific and comprehensive environmental law, such as Sweden has, in which all environmental legislation is concentrated into one major act. Instead, the core of Finnish environmental legislation is composed of about thirty individual sector-based acts and more than 300 ordinances and cabinet decisions. This has been a problem for the co-ordination of protection activities and the coherence of environmental policy. There have been minor efforts to co-ordinate at least some of the policy procedures (e.g. the permit procedure), but no major attempts to create a comprehensive environmental act have been made. However, many new or renewed environmental acts have been effected during the last two years, along with a major administrative reform (Rouhinen, 1991: 225; Koskinen, 1994: 8; Hermanson and Joas, 1996: 131).

To a certain degree, criminal law in Finland lacks the teeth for punishing environmental offences, even if these offences are obvious in many cases. A rough estimation indicates that only 1–2 per cent of all environmental crimes are subject to public prosecution and taken to court. There are several reasons for this. There is a lack of resources, a lack of judicial competence, and Nordic political and administrative traditions do not include an extensive use of courts, contrary to the Anglo-Saxon tradition. Negotiations and consensus-seeking are the main strategies used in implementing environmental laws. In the mid-1980s, of the few cases actually handled, about 75 per cent resulted in some kind of, often very mild, punishment; about 25 per cent of cases were dismissed. Of the cases handled by the criminal or water courts, more than 50 per cent were only minor waste management offences, 20 per cent were more serious waste management crimes and about 25 per cent were water crimes (Träskman, 1992: 162–3 and 181).

Central government: the political level
In parliament, i.e. the highest, collective, political decision-making
level in Finland, environmental matters are handled in the same way
as other matters. Standing committees are supposed to possess the
specialised knowledge required in the legislation process. However, a
specific, permanent standing committee for environmental questions
was first introduced to parliament in late 1990 (Parliamentary
Working Directive 1058/90). Prior to that, environmental matters
were most often handled by the Standing Committee for Agriculture
and Forestry or some other sector-related committee.

Central administration: a system under change
On 17 June 1993, the Cabinet decided to reform the central administrative system in Finland. The goal of the reforms was to streamline
substantially the central administration, by moving central agency-
level duties where possible to the regional or local level or to the
ministry level depending on the matter, and thus make the administration more efficient. The remaining agencies were changed into
research and development centres. As part of the Cabinet decentralisation and deconcentration plan, the environmental administration
was also reformed during 1993–1995 in order to simplify it and
make it more effective. Former dual structures, covering supervision
and control independently, were made substantially simpler and
more easy to govern by moving both duties into a single decision-
making body (Statsrådets beslut om åtgärder..., 1993: 5–10).

The Ministry of the Environment The competence of the Ministry
of the Environment is rather large, and its administrative duties cover
most environmental sectors (Nuuja *et al.*, 1993: 2/IV), such as:

- nature and landscape conservation;
- water administration (protection, usage, care, planning,
  research);
- environmental protection (air protection, noise abatement, waste
  management, oil and chemical damage, environmental research);
- open-air life and other recreation usage of the environment; and
- planning, building and housing administration.

The Ministry of the Environment is divided into five main departments: Environmental Policy, Environmental Protection, General

Management, Land Disposal, and Housing and Building. The aim of the Environmental Policy Department has been to integrate environmental policies. The department's main duties have thus been policy-oriented programme planning. The main programmes have included sustainable development, environmental economics, the planning of environmental policy instruments and environmental awareness and information. The department has also co-ordinated research and technology policies in the environmental sector. The Environmental Protection Department has mainly been responsible for the core activities in environmental protection. Its main target areas have been industrial and energy production, communities and agriculture. Special attention has been paid to environmental risks and damage. Several advisory bodies specialising in different sectors of environmental protection have been attached to the department. International contacts in related areas have been co-ordinated through this department. However, the control of international affairs in general and foreign relations has been in the hands of the General Management Department, if not the Ministry for Foreign Affairs. The Land Disposal Department has mainly been concerned with land disposal planning at the national level, regional community structure and land disposal, and research in communities as living environments. The department also has responsibility for the care and protection of nature, common pool resources, culture landscapes and the environment, as well as related recreational activities (Vuosikirja, 1995: 60; Hermanson and Joas, 1996: 158–60).

In late 1994, the staff of the Ministry of the Environment numbered about 295, not including short-time vacancies or trainees. Over ten years, the staff has grown by only 85 persons. The administrative reform will increase the number of ministry personnel because some staff from the central agency will be moved to the ministry. The staff consists of persons with backgrounds in the natural sciences (21 per cent), the social sciences (30 per cent) and technical studies (18 per cent) (Hermanson and Joas, 1996: 121).

The central agency level: Finnish Environment Institute   Prior to the latest administrative reform, the central agency handling environmental matters was the National Board of Waters and Environment. Known as the National Board of Waters before 1986, it was mainly responsible for water administration. After the 1986 reform, it took its new name and became responsible for environmental administration on a broader scale as well. However, according to the Cabinet decision of 1993, the agency ceased to exist as a central agency as of 1 March 1995. The agency was transformed into the Finnish Environment Institute. Most of its former administrative duties were moved to the new regional environment centres. Only a few administrative duties were left within the institute, such as the regulation of chemical and international waste transportation and the combat of oil spills. Some duties were moved to the Ministry of the Environment or to the Ministry of Agriculture and Forestry, and some research-related tasks were moved from the ministry to the institute. The main tasks of the new unit are, thus, environmental research and development, environmental monitoring, education, information and planning. The central agency level in housing and building was also reformed into the Housing Fund of Finland (Statsrådets beslut om åtgärder..., 1993; Ympäristöhallinnon uudistaminen, 1994: 50; Rusanen, 1993: 13).

Other sector interests   Several other state administration units are still charged with a few limited environmental administration duties despite the effort to concentrate them within a single environmental administration. While the ultimate responsibility lies, however, most often in the Ministry of the Environment, the expert knowledge units may often be administratively subordinated to another ministry. Naturally, there is and has been close co-operation between the different administrative units *vis-à-vis* the environment within the state administration but, as in any bureaucracy, conflicts can occur. Questions concerning forestry, agriculture and nature reserves/protection and questions concerning energy and industry often pit the Ministry of Agriculture and Forestry and the Ministry of Trade and Industry, respectively, against the Ministry of the Environment.

The regional environmental administration
Before the 1995 administrative reforms, regional environmental administration was split up between two relatively independent authorities: the county offices (twelve government administration units) and the water and environmental districts (thirteen regions). Regional environmental administration began with the introduction of water districts in 1970. Environmental supervisors were set up in the county offices in 1973, and this function was gradually enlarged.

In 1982, environmental protection sections were founded, and in 1992 these became departments. These units had responsibility at the regional level for administrating and supervising the protection of the environment and nature, planning and building, housing and waste management. The water and environmental districts had responsibility for monitoring and administering water courses and their use (Nuuja *et al.*, 1993).

The 1995 administrative reforms at the regional level joined the two units into regional environment centres, as described above; these were environmental administration units with combined and enlarged duties and competence. The enlarged competence followed from the reform at the agency level, during which several centralised duties were reassigned to regional level. Some limited ministerial duties were also moved to the new districts. The thirteen regional environment centres (divided almost according to the former water districts) are administratively subordinate to the Ministry of the Environment, but in some limited matters also to the Ministry of Agriculture and Forestry. The new centres are regional, public, full-service units with duties that include controlling the environment and providing information, advice and other services to local municipalities, public organisations, manufacturing and other firms, private citizens and municipalities (Statsrådets beslut om åtgärder..., 1993: 48; Ympäristöhallinnon uudistaminen, 1994: 98).

The role of local government
The municipalities are autonomous, democratic units within the public administration system in Finland. They have, for example, the right to collect municipal taxes without any legal limit. The municipalities are thus important environmental actors with duties in, for example, the environmental permit-issuing process, waste management organisation, air quality, land- and soil-use, noise abatement control and environmental health supervision. However, in most cases, the municipalities have only executive tasks when implementing national environmental legislation, such as issuing environmental permits according to national emissions guidelines. But to a certain extent, they possess the power to conduct their own independent environmental policy, especially in land-use planning and information activity (Nuuja *et al.*, 1993: 29–30/IV).

Environmental administration and decision-making in the municipalities are handled by many different bodies depending on the matter. The highest political decision-making unit working with environmental questions is the Municipal Council, an elected unit. But the most important bodies for preparing and deciding environmental matters are the four sector boards: the Environmental Protection Board, the Health Board, the Board for Technical Affairs and the Building Board. The Executive Board plays an important role as the highest executive body within local government. About 75 per cent of all 455 municipalities have chosen to organise their environmental administration within the primary municipality, and of those 67 per cent within the technical sector. In smaller municipalities, 15 per cent have chosen municipal federations and 10 per cent have chosen municipal co-operation. Most municipalities employ specific environmental officials, adding up to 500 full-time or part-time posts today. In addition, the municipalities also employ three times as many environmental health officers who work with environmental supervision to a certain extent (Joas, 1995: 7–10).

Public environmental opinion
Traditionally, public interest in nature has been high in Finland. Most Finns have their roots in the countryside and maintain an active relationship with nature, although almost two-thirds of the population live in towns or cities today. The concern for the environment is high as well. According to a public survey made in the autumn of 1993, environmental problems are the second most severe problems in Finnish society, just after unemployment. The survey respondents were most concerned about problems related to nuclear energy (25 per cent), water pollution (13 per cent), former USSR air pollution (12 per cent) and air pollution in general (11 per cent). Three out of four respondents urged for more international co-operation with neighbouring areas. The solutions called for were systematic and deep changes in society, technical innovation and research. The most often quoted reason for environmental problems was the too dominant economic sector (80 per cent). At the same time, almost 35 per cent said that the environment could be protected only if economic growth was sufficient. The respondents believed that they could change their habits in a more sustainable direction if they could get more information (75 per cent), but also if stricter rules or legislation were enacted (80 per cent). The questionnaire also measured environmental attitudes and activity, e.g. 80 per cent of the respondents were willing to pay more for environmentally sound consumer goods,

and 84 per cent said that they collect problem waste quite regularly (Kaila-Kangas *et al.*, 1994).

Environmental and business interest organisations

The historical roots of the most important environmental interest organisations can be traced to the organisations for nature conservation established in the late nineteenth century. The two nation-wide civic organisations mainly concerned with nature protection are the Finnish Association for Nature Conservation (Suomen Luonnonsuojeluliitto, SLL, founded in 1938) and Nature and Environment (Natur och Miljö). Jointly, they had about 40,000 members in the late 1980s. Another organisation of international origin is the Finnish chapter of the Worldwide Fund for Nature, founded in 1972. Activist groups such as Greenpeace grew in importance during the 1980s, but lost economic support and members in the 1990s due to the economic depression. They have received media attention a handful of times with their direct action operations, but they still remain a marginal phenomenon in Finnish society. Other active environmental groups are fragmented single-issue groups that have managed to get considerable attention over the last twenty years in relation to a few environmental conflicts (cf. the Koijärvi case). There are also more sector-oriented organisations, such as the nuclear energy-opposed alternative movement (Hermanson and Joas, 1996: 129–30).

In the traditional Nordic democratic and corporatist policy-making model, interest organisations as well as traditional political parties have always played an important role in shaping public policies. This influence is also clear in Finland. Interest organisations have officially taken part in the policy formulation process on several occasions: 1) interest groups have been represented on specific commissions preparing new legislation affecting varied interests; 2) interest groups have received commission reports sent for comments; and 3) interest groups have participated in permanent advisory commissions or delegations. The commissions consisted mostly of representatives from the state administration, but traditionally strong interest groups, i.e. trade unions, business organisations and municipalities, have also had considerable representation. Expert views are often represented by faculty members at universities. Traditional environmental organisations, i.e. the SLL, have also been represented on most commissions, especially during the 1980s and 1990s. The variety of interest representation seems to have expanded during the early 1990s; for example, Greenpeace was chosen to participate in the Finnish National Commission on Sustainable Development.

The largest business organisations and trade unions are almost always invited to participate in commissions and delegations handling environmental questions – questions that could harm their interests. The three most influential organisations are the Central Organisation of Finnish Trade Unions (Suomen Ammattiliittojen Keskusjärjestö, SAK – the largest federation of industrial trade unions), MTK (representing farmer, forest and landowner interests) and the Confederation of Finnish Industry and Employers (Teollisuuden ja Työnantajain Keskusliitto, TT – representing business and industrial interests). Naturally, their environmental views and programmes reflect their interests and goals. At the programme level, the SAK professes sustainable development, but in practice the organisation seems less eager to promote, for example, environmental taxes. The MTK promotes rural sustainable development – nature should remain a clean and renewable asset and should not be polluted by factories. The TT and its predecessor, the Federation of Industries, stand mostly for a productionist world view, although they emphasise sustainable development in a technical sense. All of these organisations were in favour of a fifth nuclear reactor when the matter was discussed and rejected in parliament in 1993 (Koskinen, 1994: 68–73).

Both the old, but especially the new, interest organisations play an important role in the shaping of public opinion. As pressure groups, the environmental organisations are often the most active in getting media attention for environmental conflicts (Hermanson and Joas, 1996: 136).

The parties and the environment
The established political parties reacted against the serious environmental problems rather late in Finland, and this gave the green movement a start that was stronger than that of many other green movements in Western Europe. However, since then, all established parties have managed to create environmental programmes. However, their late introduction and the belief that the established parties did not have the will to seek radical solutions to environmental problems clearly benefited the introduction of the green movement in Finland.

For the most part, the 'greening' of the whole party field since the 1970s followed the patterns found in the other Nordic countries. The agrarian or centre parties took on an agrarian ecological role; the conservatives took on a 'green' market orientation; and the social democrats took on a 'green' welfare state orientation. In addition to the programme of the Green League Party (known as the Greens), the most ecological orientation in Finland could actually be found in the programmes of the Left Wing Alliance (Vasemmistoliitto, VAS), the former mainstream communists (Jaatinen, 1991: 52–3; Koskinen, 1994: 83–5).

The origin of the green movement in Finland seems to be domestic rather than international. This is contrary to the experience of many other green movements in Europe, which mostly followed the German example. The early green movement got its members and ideas from many, heterogeneous social groups: the 1960s new left movement, new radical protection of nature, anti-nuclear, local ecological and environmental groups (as at Koijärvi), the radically weakened liberals and political youth organisations. The participation of the disabled in the green movement was also strong from its very start. Today the supporters of the mainstream Greens, the party favouring a mainstream orientation, are mostly young, well educated and urban (Borg, 1991: 184–6).

Ideological disagreements split the green movement into two major factions in 1988. The split could be seen as an ideological divide (cf. the divides inside the German Greens) between a fundamental ecological orientation that spoke for very radical solutions and a mainstream movement that was more willing to seek compromises in order to gain popular support and the means to influence other parties. The supporters of the fundamental ecological orientation, a rather strong part of the early movement, formed a separate party called the Ecological Party (Ekologinen Puolue Vihreät, EPV) (Borg, 1991: 188). The split has remarkably favoured the mainstream Greens, who have received stronger electoral support than the EPV. However, the EPV gained one seat at the parliamentary elections in the spring of 1995 due to a rather populist candidate.

The electoral history of the green movement in Finland has been short, but quite successful. A 'green' list was put up for the first time in municipal elections in Helsinki in 1976, but it was in the 1980 municipal election in Helsinki that the first seat was won. The national breakthrough came in the 1983 parliamentary election when the 'green' list gained two seats (out of 200). The next parliamentary election in 1987 gave the Green movement four seats in parliament. The increase in the support for the Greens at the elections in the late 1980s and early 1990s was visible both at national and especially at local elections. The 1992 municipal election was a great success for the Greens. Nationally, they got 6.9 per cent of the electoral support, but the support was especially high, up to 15–18 per cent of all votes cast, in the large cities of southern Finland and their surroundings. In these main support areas the Greens seem to have gained a position in the 'normal' party system (Borg, 1991: 191–3).

The March 1995 parliamentary election can be seen as an election which stabilised the electoral situation of the Greens. Although the party actually lost some support and a seat (it won nine seats in comparison with ten in 1991), it managed to gain new support areas in the countryside. It was invited to join Prime Minister Paavo Lipponen's (SDP) five-party 'rainbow' coalition Cabinet along with the SDP, the KOK, the Swedish People's Party (Svenska Folkpartiet i Finland, SFP) and the VAS. Pekka Haavisto, former Green League Party leader, became Minister of the Environment. President Ahtisaari, who is a strong actor in the Cabinet-building process, was willing to have the Greens in the Cabinet – exerting their influence though the election winner, the SDP.

The environmental agenda today

Central themes in the environmental debate in Finland are topics common to all Western states, including, for example, the concept of sustainable development, biodiversity and other concepts defined at the United Nations Conference on Environment and Development (UNCED) in Rio in 1992. Ever since the 1960s, global environmental problems have been regarded as being of central importance to Finland. The post-Brundtland Report discussions were active, and the post-UNCED discussions have started lately as the agreements made in Rio are being implemented nationally. Other common Western discussions are the ongoing debate about new policy instruments and the connection between the economy and the environment. There are, of course, also some nationally important topics, such as the concept of sustainable forestry including biodiversity and the basic energy solution (Wahlström *et al.*, 1992: 337–51; Vuosikirja, 1993: 45–57).

New environmental policy instruments

So far, traditional legal instruments, in addition to traditional information and physical instruments, have dominated environmental control in Finland. The most common regulatory mechanisms in Finland have been individual environmental permit and acknowledgement procedures (co-ordinated, simplified and renewed in 1992) and self-control of polluting industries, in combination with general emission level guidelines, mandatory rules and authority supervision. In the late 1980s, a discussion about new environmental policy instruments also began in Finland. A limited number of new economic instruments were introduced during the early 1990s, but a majority still wants a broader scale of these to be implemented in the future. According to the Cabinet programme, environmental taxes will be the main regulatory instrument in the future (Wahlström *et al.*, 1992: 330–5).

In 1990, Finland introduced a CO_2 tax on coal and other combustion fuels, probably the first country in the world to do so. The tax level is still very modest, only about FM25 per ton of coal. Indigenous energy sources, i.e. wood and peat, are exempt from this tax. Although taxes and charges on traffic, i.e. fuel taxes, automobile purchase taxes and charges and car user charges, have traditionally been very high in Finland, they have been raised mostly for fiscal purposes. The fuel tax has, however, been graded depending on the fuel lead content, but since 1994 there have been no leaded fuels on the market. Cars with low emission levels got tax rebates, but since the early 1990s, all petrol-driven cars on the market have been equipped with catalytic converters. Other taxes and charges with positive environmental effects have been the disposable bottle tax, the pesticide charge, the waste oil charge and the water protection charge. Before Finland became a member of the EU, taxes on fertilisers, electricity and charter flights were relatively high. In 1995, these taxes yielded almost FM15.6 billion, an increase of FM4.2 billion from 1993.

In waste management, a few economic instruments have also been introduced. One of them has resulted in the recycling of both domestic and imported beverage industry bottles, a programme that has been effective for years. For other bottles and glassware, a successful recycling campaign started in the mid-1980s, and in 1995 a similar recycling campaign began for household metal wares. Participation in the programme for the recycling of bottles, glassware and household metal wares has been voluntary for the individual, but residences with more than two households are guided by economic benefits. The recycling of paper is also rather effective; a large part of all paper products is circulated for recycling purposes. Finland also imports recycled paper because domestic resources are not sufficient for the large paper industries (Hermanson and Joas, 1996: 152; Luonnonvarat ja ympäristö, 1995: 4–6).

The further use of economic instruments was discussed by several expert commissions and working groups in the early 1990s. In 1991, for example, a working group proposed an environmental taxation of air emissions (SO_x and NO_x) and water emissions (P, N, BOD7 and Cl) to start in 1995. The proposed taxes and charges would have raised the price of electricity by 20 per cent to 50 per cent, depending on the user. But the economic recession postponed these rather radical plans. Despite the recession, levels of energy taxation were raised in the 1994 budget on all fuels except domestic energy sources (wood and peat). In 1993, a governmental expert committee proposed, in addition to energy taxation, an environmental damage fund, higher charges for non-recycled waste and economic instruments to guide environmental protection in rural areas. Environmental accounting has been an ongoing discussion in Finland within the environmental administration and among activist groups. It must be emphasised, however, that the introduction of economic instruments is, in fact, only in its infancy in Finland, as it is in most other Western countries (Wahlström *et al.*, 1992: 333–5, 344–5; Implementation of Agenda 21 in Finland, 1994: 27–8).

In addition to traditional information campaigns, the use of communicative instruments is just beginning in Finland. The first steps were taken in 1995, when the Ministry of the Environment made an agreement with the beverage industry about the recycling of cans. The ten-year programme of the Ministry of the Environment emphasises the enlarged use of communicative instruments, such as voluntary agreements and environmental leadership, in harmonious combination with other instruments. The environmental labelling system has been further developed since 1989, when the Nordic swan symbol was introduced (Vuosikirja, 1995: 41; Implementation of Agenda 21 in Finland, 1994: 28).

The concept of sustainable development and Agenda 21
The Brundtland Report initiated a broad debate about the future of society in Finland. Economic growth was at an all-time high in

Finland when the report came out, and environmental values were more important than economic ones. The Cabinet responded to the report by appointing the Finnish Commission on Environment and Development in 1987, which issued a report in the spring of 1989. This report led to a politically important report submitted by the Cabinet to parliament in 1991. The Cabinet report contained a set of guidelines on how to achieve the sustainable development goals set up by both the Finnish and the World Commissions on Environment and Development (Hållbar utveckling och Finland, 1990: 5).

The Cabinet report acknowledged the multi-reason character of the environmental problems that should, thus, be handled in a broad time perspective and not only through *ad hoc* measures. The report took up measures at the local, national, regional and global levels, but these were framed mostly as political goals and not as actual programmes. During the five years that have passed since the Cabinet report was published, some goals that were at least partly inspired by the Brundtland Report have been achieved. Since 1993, legislation has been much improved, as prescribed in the guidelines. For example, the Environmental Impact Assessment Act and the Programme for Environmental Protection in Agriculture have been introduced (Hållbar utveckling och Finland, 1990: 19–23).

The implementation of agreements reached during the UNCED conference started in Finland about two years after the conference. The climate change convention was ratified nationally in August 1994, and the biodiversity convention was ratified in October 1994 (Luonnonvarat ja ympäristö, 1995: 28–9). To control and guide the implementation of UNCED decisions and especially Agenda 21, the Cabinet established the Finnish National Commission on Sustainable Development in June 1993. This high-level commission was chaired by the Prime Minister, and its executive committee consisted of five central ministers. The commission also included representatives from the central, regional and local government authorities, from the scientific and educational community, private organisational interests and the media. The Commission published a report in 1994 about how to implement UNCED decisions in Finland in the short and in the longer term. The political goals were presented by the Cabinet to parliament in an official Cabinet report, *Charting Finland's Future Options*, in October 1993 (Vuosikirja, 1993: 15–16; Implementation of Agenda 21 in Finland, 1994: 34–6).

One of the main ideas in the concept of sustainable development is to achieve a fundamental change at the local level. This was made even more clear during the UNCED process. Local government is very strong in Finland, and it is very important to make local authorities emphasise local sustainable development. Therefore, the Ministry of the Interior together with other central government units and the Association of Finnish Local Authorities initiated a municipal sustainable development pilot project in 1991. Despite the pilot character and the limited number of participating municipalities (eleven municipalities and three municipal associations), this project made the Finnish municipalities discuss the possibility of achieving a 'sustainable development municipality'. Some municipalities have been active in starting environmental projects of their own in addition to those related to the pilot project described above. So far, the local 'Agenda 21' idea has initiated only about thirty actual projects – a figure that is, however, increasing (Kunnat Kestävää Kehitystä Etsimässä, 1994: 19; Valanta, 1992: 85–95).

In the spring of 1995, the Lipponen Cabinet stressed environmental themes in its Cabinet declaration. Special emphasis was put on sustainable development, although this might only have been a catchphrase. In any case, it was meant to be not only a goal for the environmental sector, but also an inter-sector goal. In its declaration, the Cabinet promised to work actively for a higher level of environmental protection inside the EU, and it promoted best available technology, the precautionary and polluter pays principles, and the extended use of economic instruments in Finland and internationally.

Local topics

In addition to the global issues and administration reforms discussed earlier, two major local topics dominated the environmental agenda during the early 1990s, one of which was sustainable forestry in Finland. Green activist groups, such as chapters of Greenpeace in Central Europe, where Finnish forest industry products (pulp and paper) find their largest market, have put forestry methods in the limelight of the environmental debate. These groups have been supported by several local activist groups in Finland, and several conflicts have occurred between forest-owners and nature activists during the last five years. Although forestry is based on sustainable principles, so that the amount of trees planted by the forest-owner must equal the amount felled, the new mechanical forestry methods are a threat to the biodiversity of Finnish forests; only a small proportion of them are protected in a virgin state. The forestry authorities recommend softer methods, such as selective cutting, but economics often have first priority. The problem is hard to handle when private ownership is protected by the constitution and a major part of the forests is owned by farmers and other private interests (Wahlström *et al.*, 1992: 341).

The second topic is the ongoing energy debate. Since the early 1980s, industry has wanted a new nuclear power plant, but the politicians have not been willing to make a choice. The Cabinet washed its hands by passing the decision on to parliament in the early 1990s. Parliament voted narrowly not to build a fifth nuclear reactor, but the debate did not end with that vote. The problem is that basic energy sources are still needed; no basic solutions other than domestic sources of minor importance have been promoted by the Cabinet, and consumption will increase in the near future.

Finland's foreign environmental policy agenda

The awareness of transboundary environmental problems, the need for global sustainable solutions and the knowledge of the limited impact of domestic policies in environmental protection has highlighted the need for international co-operation in solving environmental problems. Since the early 1980s, the Finnish Cabinet has acknowledged this need. For example, the 1987 Cabinet programme stated that: 'The Government will promote the efforts to strengthen international cooperation within environmental protection' (Environmental Protection in Finland ... 1988: 339).

Finland has participated rather actively in the development of international environmental law and today takes part in most multilateral conventions and multilateral and bilateral treaties concerning environmental problems. Since the International Treaty on Whaling (Washington, 1946), Finland has signed almost thirty major, multilateral, environmental treaties (Luonnonvarat ja ympäristö, 1995: 28–9; Wahlström *et al.*, 1992: 356).

Since the early 1990s, international efforts have been emphasised even more than before. Global issues, such as problems of climate change, the ozone layer and biodiversity, are still gaining in importance, but more traditional international issues, such as transboundary emissions, are also seen as important in Finland. The almost catastrophic environmental situation in Eastern Europe has raised a special need in Finland for international environmental co-operation on a regional basis, e.g. intensified co-operation with areas contiguous to Finland. The activity plan of the Ministry of the Environment (1994–1997) put special emphasis on regional co-operation (Kola, Carelia and St Petersburg in Russia and Estonia), on Baltic Sea co-operation and on EU co-operation. Some of the most important international topics of environmental protection for Finland will be discussed in the next sections. The discussion will also be about the main international organisations through which the Finnish government can act in addressing relevant problems.

Global issues
The focus on the international environment in Finland has shifted from regional/international transboundary emissions to more fundamental issues, such as climate change and biodiversity, the main UNCED themes.

Transboundary pollution in general   Traditional questions of transboundary pollution played a central role in Finland during the initial phase of international environmental co-operation. Finland had suffered from pollution imports both from the east and the west, but it had also been a pollution exporter itself. It was in Finland's interests to take an active part in the international community's effort to control pollution.

Stable and valuable environmental co-operation takes place between the Nordic countries. This makes sense given that Finland and Sweden, for example, are in a similar geo-environmental situation and have a similar industrial structure. In 1974, environmental co-operation was introduced into the Helsinki Act, and in 1976 the Nordic Environmental Protection Treaty was signed. The Nordic Council of Ministers adopted a joint environmental programme in January 1989 with politically binding goals for environmental protection including not only pollution control. The Nordic countries have also co-operated about environmental problems in Eastern Europe (Rumpunen, 1994: 43; Wahlström *et al.*, 1992: 175–6).

Pollution control at the European level became more important when Finland became a member of the EU. Originally, the UN Economic Commission for Europe (ECE) was the main arena in which Western European states could discuss environmental problems and European environmental co-operation with Eastern European states. In addition to the reduction of transboundary pollution, special areas of attention for Finland were clean technologies, water pollution control, environmental impact assessment and nature conservation. The importance of the ECE has declined, however, with the reforms in the East.

Although the Conference/Organisation on Security and Co-operation in Europe was also active in the debate on environmental problems in Europe, the new area of interest for the Finnish environmental policy is EU environmental co-operation. Before joining the EU, the Ministry of the Environment had already emphasised close co-operation with the EU in environmental matters and openly declared its intentions to influence future EU policies in a more sustainable and precautionary direction (Environmental Protection in Finland ..., 1988: 346; Vuosikirja, 1993: 28).

Biodiversity and forests   In preparation for the UNCED meeting, the Finnish government listed its most important goals: 1) to change global production and consumption patterns; 2) to reduce global poverty and population growth; 3) to achieve sustainable forestry; 4) to develop international development and environmental funding systems; and 5) to emphasise the UN in environmental and developmental questions. It was recognised that sustainable forestry could be achieved only if biodiversity was taken into account (Numminen, 1992: 11).

The Finns have always considered themselves to be at the forefront in developing effective and sustainable forestry, and for the UNCED meeting four goals were proposed. The first was to acknowledge the multi-usage possibilities of forests in the context of total protection of forest areas. The second was that special attention be paid to tropical and borealic forests. The third was that the total global forest area not diminish in size after 2005. And the fourth was that sustainable forestry take into account the multitude of species, thus following the biodiversity agreement. The biodiversity agreement was nationally ratified in Finland in October 1994 (Numminen, 1992: 14–15; Ympäristö, 1995: 27).

Climate change policies   Climate change problems due to CO_2 emissions have turned out to be problematic for Finland. While the government has acknowledged the severity of the problem, not least in Finland and the borealic forest region, it has also struggled with an economic crisis and an energy situation based mostly on imported combustion fuels. At the UNCED meeting, Finland backed the EU goal of freezing emissions by the year 2000 at the 1990 level. But in Berlin in 1995, Finland was not prepared to go any further. The Berlin achievements were considered good according to a delegate from the Ministry of the Environment. Another delegate representing the Ministry of Trade and Industry stated that the results were very problematic for Finland. Besides Portugal, Spain and Greece, Finland is one of the EU members that will have major problems in achieving the level agreed on in Rio because emissions are expected to increase by about 30 per cent by the year 2000 if no new nuclear plants are built or if no electricity is imported (Numminen, 1992: 21; *Turun Sanomat*, 4 August 1995; Ympäristö, 1995: 35; Tirkkonen and Wilenius, 1995: 30–1).

Global activities are concentrated mainly with the UN and its specialised bodies. A central forum for global environmental co-operation is the United Nations Environmental Programme (UNEP), in which Finland has been a very active, but also selective, participant. The Nordic countries have often co-operated within the UN specialised bodies. Finland has supported a broad-scale agenda for UNEP, with special emphasis on global environmental problems and environmental problems in developing countries (Environmental Protection in Finland ..., 1988: 344–6; Vuosikirja, 1993: 29).

Regional issues
Despite the global character of the most severe environmental problems, Finland has also found regional co-operation extremely important, mainly because the encompassing environmental problems in the former USSR endanger not only the population there, but, to a large extent, also the populations of Finland and other neighbouring countries. The first steps taken to combat these problems were connected with the Helsinki Commission (HELCOM), the pride and joy of the Finnish government in environmental co-operation.

Marine pollution in the Baltic Sea   Since the signing of the Helsinki Convention in 1974 and the foundation of HELCOM, which monitors compliance with the convention, Baltic Sea co-operation has been of major importance for the Finnish political leadership. It has been a cornerstone in the new Eastern Europe environmental aid project discussed below. The Baltic Sea co-operation agreement is a broad-scaled, international treaty that deals with most of the pollution sources affecting this vulnerable marine environment. In specific cases, the treaty has already given results, e.g. in reduced levels of heavy metals in the Baltic Sea. The convention was renewed in 1992 (Wahlström *et al.*, 1992: 173).

The special case: Eastern European environmental problems The pressure emerging from the environmental problems of the former USSR – primarily Russia and Estonia – has grown constantly in Finland during the last ten years. At an expert level, the problems were acknowledged even earlier, but the political situation made it almost impossible to discuss these problems with the USSR at that time. Special problem areas for Finland are the nearby areas of the Kola Peninsula (nuclear power plants and metal industries), Carelia (paper and pulp industry) and the St Petersburg region (over 5 million inhabitants 200 km from the Finnish border and nuclear power plants). Finland has more than 1000 km of common border with Russia and has been a net receiver of transboundary pollution in general, for example heavy metals and ammonia nitrogen. However, due to wind conditions Finland is a net exporter of NO_x to Russia. The environmental threats caused by unstable nuclear power plants and ageing nuclear weapon systems are also important. For example, the Chernobyl accident caused considerable damage in Finland. Estonia has considerable point source pollution problems along the Baltic Sea coastline (Hiltunen, 1994: 7–31; Luonnonvarat ja ympäristö, 1995: 17).

Environmental co-operation between Finland and the USSR, and later between Finland and Russia and Estonia, can be divided into three main phases: 1) a phase of scientific co-operation during the Cold War period from the 1960s; 2) a phase after the mid-1980s in which Finland used strategies of persuasion and pressure; and 3) a phase since the early 1990s in which Finland has supported and financed pollution control. The last phase emerged when it was finally understood just how deep and severe the environmental problems were in the former Soviet areas. Even minor environmental protection investments made in these areas are more effective in protecting the Finnish environment than are any investments made in Finland (Hiltunen, 1994: 33–4; Vuosikirja, 1993: 17–18).

As part of this third phase, the Ministry of the Environment set up a special Eastern Europe project unit inside the ministry to co-ordinate the efforts made in Russia and Estonia. Considerable economic investments in environmental aid have already been made and are planned in the near future by the Finnish government. In the first step, 1991–1992, most of the aid was given to Estonia, but later increasing amounts were also given to Russia. The co-operation with the neighbouring areas is conducted both at the central level and at the local level, where projects have been developed on the basis of local needs and wishes. Finland has co-operated closely with the other Nordic countries in co-ordinating aid to the area. The results of this co-operation cannot yet be properly estimated according to Hiltunen (1994: 50), but pollution-level monitoring has, at least, been updated. In the late autumn of 1993, all in all seventy-seven different environmental co-operation projects had been initiated between Finland and Estonia (twenty of them in the form of direct investments) and ninety between Finland and Russia (twelve of them in the form of investment projects). The political priority of this co-operation seems to remain high. Problematic in the co-operation with Russia is, of course, the totally different levels of problem perception. What Finland interprets as major problems are regarded as only minor ones by Russia (e.g. nuclear power plants) (Hiltunen, 1994; see also Susiluoto, 1991 about the USSR's problem perception).

A regional, multilateral co-operation project has been started with the aim of solving arctic environmental problems (inside Russia). The project is known as Arctic Area Environmental Co-operation. A joint declaration and protection programme were adopted in Rovaniemi in 1991 by eight arctic countries or areas (Rumpunen, 1994: 43).

Foreign (environmental) policy institutions

The presidency
In Finland, the presidency is the highest decision-making body in matters concerning general foreign relations, according to the constitution (the Form of Government Act 33§). In practice, the president has been able to control and co-ordinate not only central foreign and security policy guidelines, but also some details, at least concerning the most important relations. When the constitution was drawn up, foreign relations were left – probably by tradition – entirely in the hands of the president (Jyränki, 1981: 208–15; Nousiainen, 1991: 389).

In practice, presidential foreign policy-making has shifted a lot. Before World War II, the Finnish presidents used to leave the conduct of foreign policy to their Cabinet or foreign minister. But since then, the president has taken on a more comprehensive leadership in foreign affairs. It is, of course, impossible for the president to control all relations, but all major decisions must be approved by him. There are two limitations to the president's foreign policy power: 1) treaties needing national jurisdiction must be approved by parliament, and 2) decisions of war and peace must be approved by parliament. According to the constitution, the Cabinet as a collective body has no foreign policy decision-making power and neither do the ministers as sector representatives. The Cabinet is forced to trust in the president's goodwill in conducting foreign policy (Jyränki, 1981: 217; Nousiainen, 1991: 389–94).

The president gives negotiation directives when international treaties, such as environmental conventions and treaties, are being discussed. He can also give the authority of signature to a Cabinet minister or another government official. The president is also free to meet foreign political leaders and negotiate with them without Cabinet approval, and he often has direct channels to officials at the Ministry for Foreign Affairs that do not require consulting the Minister for Foreign Affairs first (Nousiainen, 1991: 391–4).

At the moment, the foreign policy-making position of the president is being discussed for the first time since 1917 because of Finland's EU membership. The scope of foreign relations in the EU is so broad that the political establishment is ready to decrease the presidential powers and increase those of the prime minister. The borderline between foreign and domestic matters also becomes blurred due to EU membership. However, the question of EU representation remains unresolved. But since the SDP came into power, the dispute between Prime Minister Lipponen (SDP) and President Ahtisaari (SDP) has been put aside, and both will attend top EU meetings.

The role of the Ministry for Foreign Affairs

The role of the Ministry for Foreign Affairs is also very central to foreign policy-making in Finland. The constitution gives the Minister for Foreign Affairs a co-ordinating role in foreign policy, while it stipulates that 'all messages to foreign powers or to the Finnish ambassadors abroad' should pass via him. In practice, the Ministry for Foreign Affairs controls the initial phases of international agreements almost totally since it co-ordinates the delegations that take part in the negotiations and delivers the agreements to further internal proceedings (Nousiainen, 1991: 389).

While the amount and scope of foreign contacts continued to increase in Finland during the 1980s, the role of the Ministry for Foreign Affairs became even more problematic. From the 1960s to the present, the Ministry for Foreign Affairs has grown more rapidly than the rest of the state administration. At the same time, internationalisation within domestic ministries has increased as well. Nonetheless, the Ministry for Foreign Affairs has managed to maintain its position as the leading unit in foreign relations. The co-ordination mechanisms have been stronger than the forces of decentralisation in Finland (Karvonen and Sundelius, 1987; Joas, 1994a).

This means that the Ministry for Foreign Affairs also has a strong role in co-ordinating foreign environmental relations between Finland and other countries. Since 1990, the ministry has had a specific Office for International Environmental Affairs with a staff of five persons attached to the central Political Department (Numminen, 1992: 5). According to the Head of the Environmental Office in the ministry, Asko Numminen (telephone interview, 20 February 1995), the division of labour between the Ministry of the Environment and the Ministry for Foreign Affairs is flexible but structured. The main field of interest for the Ministry for Foreign Affairs is global environmental co-operation, e.g. related to UN and especially UNCED activities. Large-scale international agreements are, at an early initial phase, handled through the Ministry for Foreign Affairs because of its neutral role in speaking for national interests. At the later implementation and supervision stages, the matters are moved to the Ministry of the Environment for further proceedings and negotiations. This is a normal way of handling the line between the politics and administration of international affairs. Politically sensitive environmental matters, e.g. civil and military nuclear safety near Finnish border areas and the global discussion of Norway's whaling, are handled by the Ministry for Foreign Affairs as far as political co-ordination is concerned. The EU Secretariat within the Ministry for Foreign Affairs has its own environmental unit in close co-operation with the Ministry of the Environment, and this mostly handles environmental co-operation inside the EU.

The role of other specialised ministries

The importance of specialised ministries in shaping foreign policy has grown in Finland since the narrow boundaries set at the end of World War II were weakened during the 1950s. According to Karvonen and Sundelius (1987), however, the real expansion in the foreign contacts of domestic ministries took place in the late 1960s in Finland. In another, earlier study, Karvonen (1984: 146) noted the following: 'The scope of Finnish foreign policy has expanded greatly, and Finnish government and society have experienced a general process of internationalization. This has meant that a great number of new issues and actors have appeared on the foreign relations agenda; it is often hard to tell whether a specific question constitutes a foreign policy issue or not.'

In the later study, Karvonen and Sundelius (1987: 161) continued: 'This study has shown that a transformation of the Swedish and Finnish policy-making structures in the direction of increased inter-nationalization has occurred during the post-war period.'

Their study shows that the whole range of sectors increased their international contacts. Quite naturally, the Ministry of Education seemed to be the most active, but other domestic ministries had significant international contacts as well (especially the Ministries of Finance and Agriculture). The Ministry of the Environment, although just founded at the time of the Karvonen and Sundelius study, also showed a large variety of international contacts. In the beginning, the international activity of the ministry was directed towards Nordic co-operation and Baltic Sea co-operation. But UN bodies, such as UNEP and HABITAT (the United Nations Centre for Human Settlements), also played a certain role for the ministry. European contacts were conducted through the ECE, the Organisa-tion for Economic Co-operation and Development (OECD) and the Council of Europe. The vast activities of the new-born ministry were considered a foreign policy co-ordination problem in a Commission report published in 1984 (Karvonen and Sundelius, 1987: 73–4).

A later study focusing on the amount of international contacts in the domestic ministries in the early 1990s found that the Ministry of Education and the Ministry of the Environment were by far the most 'international' units within the domestic state administration. The latter had more contacts on a multilateral basis, while the former was more active in bilateral contacts. The Ministry of the Environment's contacts to organisations were conducted mostly through the same organisations as in the beginning, i.e. through the ECE, the OECD, the International Union for the Conservation of Nature, the United Nations Development Programme and, of course, HELCOM and UNEP. Nordic and EFTA contacts were also important. The contact pattern of the Ministry of the Environment towards other countries was characterised as problem-oriented and modern. Most contacts were with Estonia and Russia, on the one hand, and with developing countries, on the other hand. The numerous contacts with Russia and Estonia had resulted from the Cabinet's environmental aid plan (Helander, 1993: 83–98).

An important indicator of Finnish foreign policy activity is political visits. The number of visits tells us about the general political activity of the Cabinet and about the variety of this activity. Active ministers with many foreign contacts travel a lot. The international activity of the Minister of the Environment seems to be equal to that of other 'domestic' ministers. The minister goes abroad on official political visits three to four times a year on average. In comparison, the activity rate within, for example, the educational sector is almost the same. The most active ministers in international exchange are, of course, the Minister for Foreign Affairs and the Minister for Foreign Trade. The activity of the Minister of the Environment was mostly directed to Eastern European countries (58 per cent of all visits during the period examined), and only a few of the visits were to Nordic and Western European countries. This is due to the early start of Eastern European environmental aid projects and the political realities of the Cold War period (Joas, 1994b: 12).

According to the Ministry for Foreign Affairs, the division of labour between the two central ministries today gives the Ministry of the Environment the role of regional and non-controversial case actor since this ministry mostly handles co-operation within the EU, the ECE and the OECD. Except for politically sensitive cases, all regional matters are handled by the Ministry of the Environment. More often, the Ministry of the Environment gets the role of implementing and providing technical knowledge, whereas the Ministry for Foreign Affairs co-ordinates the initial phase, contributing with its political competence. The co-operation between these two units seems to work rather well – better than between the Ministry for Foreign Affairs and other domestic ministries.

In conclusion, the international activities of the Ministry of the

Environment seem to be relatively many, and seem to have grown in number during most of the twelve years that the ministry has existed.

EU membership and environmental policy

Environmental themes played only a minor role in the EU membership debate prior to the membership referendum on 16 October 1994, at least at the public level. The environmental effects of membership were discussed, however, at the level of experts. Critical views were presented by, for example, Antti Vahtera, the environmental columnist in the *Helsingin Sanomat*, the largest daily newspaper in Finland (Vahtera, 1993), but those opposing EU membership were unable to attract broader public attention to the environmental debate. The result of the referendum was that 56.9 per cent voted for membership and 43.1 per cent voted against it. The turnout percentage was 74 per cent (Pesonen, 1994a; see also Jahn and Storsved, 1995).

The domestic membership debate and the lack of environmental issues

In the Finnish membership debate, environmental issues appeared to be set aside, and the agenda differed somewhat from that of the other Nordic countries. The scene was set, of course, by the media. Political facts colouring the debate were the very deep economic crisis in Finland (with an unemployment rate of about 20 per cent) and the geo-political position of Finland, which shares a border and a long history of conflicts with Russia. The media covered several issues equally, if one uses the coverage in the *Helsingin Sanomat* and the Finnish News Information Services as an indicator. According to a panel survey conducted four times before the referendum, the public responded differently to these issues, however. Those against EU membership stressed issues of democracy and sovereignty, equality and agriculture, and those in support of membership emphasised issues such as Western European cultural identity, employment, economy and security policy. Environmental issues were mentioned by less than 2 per cent of the panel (Aula and Rosenblad, 1995: 6–12).

A similar pattern could be found in a study that focused on the referendum turnout. An inquiry of 1600 voters showed that those voting for membership stressed mainly the economic gains of membership (52 per cent) and the possibility of influencing EU decisions (40 per cent). Other relevant issues in the debate seemed to be the cultural aspects of membership (22 per cent) and the security gains that membership would bring (30 per cent). Those voting against membership stressed primarily issues related to the possible loss of decision-making independence (54 per cent) and possible economic drawbacks to the agricultural sector (29 per cent) and industry (19 per cent). Other motivations were, for example, beliefs that immigration to Finland would increase and that social welfare would lose (both 11 per cent). Environmental problems were mentioned as a reason to vote no, but only by 7 per cent of the voters. A small majority seemed to believe that the environment would actually be better off if Finland joined the EU. However, the debate prior to the referendum seemed to have only a minor effect on the voters since less than 5 per cent changed their opinion during the last month of the campaign (Pesonen, 1994b: 87; Sänkiaho and Säynässalo, 1994: 102).

The party scene was divided in Finland prior to the referendum, and many parties were also divided internally. In some cases, the party leadership was in strong support of a different view to that of its voters. The most strongly pro-membership parties were the conservative KOK and the SFP, of which 89 per cent and 85 per cent, respectively, voted for membership. However, a faction of the SFP, the peasants, strongly opposed membership. Only the leadership of the SDP seemed to support membership: until the referendum, a large part of its voters had not chosen sides yet. In the end, however, the voters followed the leadership, and 75 per cent voted for EU membership.

Most voters opposing membership were members of protest parties, such as the Christian Union (Suomen Kristillinen Liitto, SKL) and the former communist VAS. The SKL leadership was strongly opposed to membership, and 96 per cent of the party's voters followed its opinion. The VAS was divided on this question, although 66 per cent of its voters voted no. However, the party most divided in the referendum was the KESK. From a leading governmental position, its party leadership declared that Finland could only benefit from EU membership. Nonetheless, almost 60 per cent of both the party members and voters were very strongly opposed to membership because of the possible economic losses to agriculture. The Greens were divided into two almost equally large groups on the membership issue, both at the leadership level and at the voter level, and its party leadership gave its members no suggestions (Sänkiaho, 1994: 167–9).

EU environmental policy and Finland

General beliefs in Finland seem to be: that the EU does not affect the possibilities of pursuing national environmental policies; that EU environmental policy is effective only if the members implement it properly; and that national policies can retain their importance because of the subsidiarity principle in environmental matters. The problem related to free trade is, of course, acknowledged in Finland, but the belief is still strong that national policies do matter, based on the Danish example (Alho and Widgrén, 1994: 109–10; Rumpunen, 1994: 65).

In general, the EU environmental rules seem to fit rather well to the Finnish environmental policy system. Some of the rules are stricter and some are more lenient, and this is acknowledged also by critics of the EU (Vahtera, 1993: 168–9).

The European Economic Area (EEA)   The EEA arrangement has forced Finland to follow EU directives as minimum guidelines in environmental questions, but left room as such to follow stricter national rules. However, the main problem with the arrangement is that Finland, or any other EEA state, has had no actual possibility of affecting the EU policy-making process. The EEA has left its members outside EU environmental co-operation. The agreement has also left out policy sectors important to the environment, such as foreign affairs, energy policy and agriculture. The main effects of the EEA on Finnish environmental policy have been that EU directives have forced Finland to enforce stricter rules than before with respect to:

- *drinking water*, for which stricter rules were based on general EU norms;
- *waste management*, for which stricter definitions of waste, re-use, the recycling of waste, packaging norms, etc. were imposed (Waste Management Act 1994);
- *environmental impact assessment*, which was required for the first time in accordance with the EU directive (Environmental Impact Assessment Act 1994);
- *noise abatement* and *chemical handling*, which required stricter and new technical rules; and

- *biotechnical rules*, for which legislation had not previously existed in Finland.

The list indicates that Finland has been forced to make some central environmental rules stricter than before. Waste management was one of the key areas within which Finnish rules had to be strengthened a lot. The municipalities shut down many older dumping grounds in 1993 before the stricter rules were implemented (Rumpunen, 1994: 47–9; *Turun Sanomat*, 19 April 1994).

The EU membership treaty   The negotiation round between the EU and the countries recently applying for membership was unique; environmental questions had not been discussed in earlier negotiations with the UK, Denmark, Spain, Portugal and Greece. The environmental questions not handled previously in the EEA treaty concerned: 1) swimming and drinking water quality, 2) radiation safety, 3) energy, 4) regional policy and – maybe most importantly – 5) nature conservation. The EU considered the Finnish nuclear waste disposal prohibition, the stricter maximum sulphur levels in fuels and the fuel taxation grading as possible trade barriers, but the Finnish point of view was, however, considered the rule. In its EU membership agreement, Finland was allowed to prohibit radioactive waste import even from the EU countries, and Finnish fuel taxation levels were allowed as long as the minimum EU tax level was not passed. The sulphur levels could be maintained during a transition period of two years, giving the EU time to change its rules in the direction of the Finnish ones. The subsidiarity principle was followed in the swimming water question. While the EU took a principle standpoint on environmental questions, it declared its intention to try to place most environmental rules at the same level as the Finnish (and other Scandinavian) ones over a transition period of three years. EU common regional and agricultural policy will also have an effect on Finnish environmental policy; for example, a substantial amount of agricultural subsidies are given for environmental investments (Rumpunen, 1994: 73–5).

The most problematic area for Finland turned out to be nature conservation, for which the EU's rules are relatively strict. The Finnish programmes as such seem to be in order; but due to older legislation (from 1923), many of the follow-up functions are very poorly organised. The position of the (private) landowner is very well protected in the Finnish constitution and, therefore, also in the old Nature Conservation Act; EU norms highlight the benefits for society. The EU's Habitats Directive will force Finnish standards to be set at a more nature-friendly level. A new, much stricter act is under preparation in Finland, but it seems to be delayed because of the 'normal environmental split' between rural landowners (the KESK) and urban officials and workers (the KOK and the SDP) in the parliamentary proceedings (*Turun Sanomat*, 1 June 1994; Rumpunen, 1994: 74).

In the international arena, Finnish membership seems to give Finland a broader scale of opportunities to act for higher environmental standards. As a full member, Finland can now reap the benefits of the EU environmental policy-making processes. For example, with respect to transboundary pollution, which comes to Finland partly from the industrialised areas of Central Europe, regional problems near the Finnish borders are now considered an EU problem as well, and environmental investment funding for co-operation projects inside Russia and Estonia should hence be easier to raise. In his study, Rumpunen (1994: 76–7) points out that the Baltic Sea is also partly an EU matter in that it is surrounded by four EU countries as well as Eastern European countries.

Future Finnish environmental policy inside the EU
The previous Cabinet presented a report to parliament on 14 February 1995 on the future guidelines for Finnish goals and policies within the EU. However, this report was more of a political testament since the Cabinet changed after the March 1995 parliamentary elections. Nonetheless, the report and the parliamentary debate on the report yielded general guidelines for Finnish political goals within the EU. Most of them were also valid for the post-election Lipponen Cabinet, according to its Cabinet declaration. A general point seems to be that neither a majority of the parties nor the Cabinet wants the federalist structure of the EU to deepen. The most pro-Union line was driven by the SDP, but even they were restricted in foreign and security policy matters. However, the Cabinet report, and also the SDP, wanted stronger co-operation on monetary union and common market matters. The new Cabinet emphasised a higher degree of openness in the EU decision-making process. Almost all parties and members of parliament not opposing the EU seemed to be willing to give more power to the EU in matters of environmental protection. It was recognised that environmental problems are too important and

comprehensive to be solved on a national basis alone and that international measures internal and external to the EU are much more efficient than national regulation. Even the Greens supported a specific environmental programme that should be followed by the Cabinet in its EU policy. As mentioned earlier, the Lipponen Cabinet has emphasised environmental co-operation within the EU and probably sees Finland as a forerunner, certainly not a pusher, in environmental matters internal to the EU.

Conclusions

Environmental politics and policy are relatively late phenomena in Finnish society. The environmental awareness grew during the 1960s when signs of pollution became more visible than previously. The first warning bell was the pollution of water courses and especially the Baltic Sea. Water pollution was seen as *the* major problem and taking care of this problem started the late and slow process of institutionalising the environmental administration in the early 1970s. Environmental problems were first seen as sector-related problems that could be solved by sector legislation and very simple and light administration. This resulted in non-comprehensive environmental legislation and ongoing reforms inside the administration.

However, the private environmental sector, e.g. civic and grassroots organisations, was very strong. The reason for this might have been the weak institutionalisation of the public environmental sector at the early stages, but also the positive public opinion towards environmental protection. Today, the Greens are one of the strongest green parties in Western Europe, and there is a living tradition of non-violent environmental activism in Finland. There is great respect for environmental interest organisations, at least the originally domestic ones, for the environmental debate and agenda in Finland was basically formed on the basis of the activities and interests of the private sector. The Ministry of the Environment and its ministers have also been active in the formation of the political agenda, often too active according to other ministers and ministries.

The foreign policy environmental agenda seems to have been mostly the domain of the Ministry of the Environment and the Ministry for Foreign Affairs. Centralised foreign policy decision-making does not leave much room for private activity. Thus, the agenda has been dominated by politically feasible topics. In the

Finland 157

beginning, transboundary pollution and acidification problems were handled mostly in a Nordic context; marine pollution was handled within the Baltic Sea environmental co-operation; and later the multitude of environmental problems in Eastern Europe and the global issues of pollution, such as climate change and biodiversity, were handled mostly by UN bodies. Future EU environmental co-operation is seen as a possibility of obtaining concrete funds for environmental investments in Russia and Estonia and of influencing EU policies at the regional and global level.

Despite the late start and problematic institutionalisation phase of environmental policies, Finland has reached high standards of environmental protection. In comparison with the other new EU member countries, Finland is at the same level and will work to effect higher environmental standards in future EU policies.

References

Alho, K. and M. Widgrén (1994), *Suomen EU-valinta*, Helsinki, Elinkeinoelämän Tutkimuslaitos ETLA.
Aula, P. and L. Rosenblad (1995), *Argument och dagordningar under den finländska EU-kampanjen hösten 1994*, paper for XII Nordic Masscommunication Research Conference, Helsingör, Denmark, August.
Borg, O. (1991), Vihreät – vihreä liike politiikassa, in I. Massa and R. Sairinen (eds), *Ympäristökysymys*, Helsinki, Gaudeamus, 181–94.
Carson, R. (1963), *Äänetön kevät*, Helsinki, Tammi.
Donner-Amnell, J. (1991), Metsäteollisuus yhteiskunnallisena kysymyksenä Suomessa, in I. Massa and R. Sairinen (eds), *Ympäristökysymys*, Helsinki, Gaudeamus, 265–306.
Environmental Protection in Finland: National Report 1987 (1988), Helsinki, Ministry of the Environment.
Finland i siffror '94 (1994), Helsingfors, Statistikcentralen.
Hållbar utveckling och Finland – Statsrådets redogörelse till riksdagen om åtgärder för en hållbar utveckling (1990), Helsinki, Statens tryckericentral.
Helander, M. (1993), *De finländska ministeriernas internationella kontakter*, Ethnicity and Mobility, MOB.NO.24, 1992, Research Reports sls/sskh, Vasa.
Hermanson, A.-S. and M. Joas (1996), Finland, in P. M. Christiansen (ed.), *Governing the Environment: Politics, Policy and Organization in the Nordic Countries*, Research Nord: 5, Copenhagen, Nordic Council of Ministers, 103–77.
Hiltunen, H. (1994), *Finland and Environmental Problems in Russia and Estonia*, Foreign Policy Challenges 6, Helsinki, the Finnish Institute of International Affairs.

Implementation of Agenda 21 in Finland (1994), Ministry of the Environment Report, Finnish National Commission on Sustainable Development, Helsinki.

Jaatinen, P. (1991), Poliittisten puolueiden 'vihertyminen': ekologisen ympäristötematiikan profiloituminen pohjoismaisissa puolueohjelmissa aikavälillä 1970–1990, in J. Kanerva, *Suomalaisten Puolueohjelmien Retoriikasta*, Public. 63, Jyväskylä, Jyväskylä University, 42–53.

Jahn, D. and A.-S. Storsved (1995), Legitimacy through referendum? The nearly successful domino-strategy of the EU-referendums in Austria, Finland, Sweden and Norway, *West European Politics*, 18:4, London, Frank Cass, 18–37.

Jänicke, M. (1990), Erfolgsbedinungen von Umweltpolitik im internationalen Vergleich, *Zeitschrift für Umveltpolitik und Umweltrecht*, 3, 213–33.

Järvikoski, T. (1991), Ympäristöliike suomalaisessa politiikassa, in I. Massa and R. Sairinen (eds), *Ympäristökysymys*, Helsinki, Gaudeamus, 162–79.

Järvikoski, T. (1993), Luonnonsuojelu ennen ympärıstönsuojelua. Katsaus suomalaisen luonnonsuojelun varhaiseen aattelliseen ja osin toiminnalliseenkin kehitykseen, in J. Jokisalo and K. Väyrynen (eds), *Ympäristökysymysten yhteiskunnallisia ja eettisiä näkökulmia*, Oulu, 5–32.

Joas, M. (1994a), Tyngdpunkter i finsk utrikespolitik; fyra decennier, fyra indikatorer, *Politiikka*, 1, 39–40.

Joas, M. (1994b), Politiska besök 1960–1990 – En indikator på finsk utrikespolitik, in M. Joas, *Tanke, Ord och Handling – Studier i utrikespolitiska kvantiteter*, PhD thesis (unpubl.), Åbo Akademi.

Joas, M. (1995), *Local Environmental Protection Personnel: in the Municipal, Environmental and Governmental Context*, Meddelanden från Ekonomisk-Statsvetenskapliga Fakulteten vid Åbo Akademi, Ser. A:437, Åbo, Åbo Akademi.

Jyränki, A. (1981), *Presidentti – Tutkimus valtionpäämiehen asemasta Suomessa v. 1919–1976*, Juva, WSOY.

Kaila-Kangas, L., R. Kangas and H. Piirainen (1994), *Ympäristöasennebarometri*, Vesi- ja ympäristöhallinnon julkaisuja Sarja A 182, Helsinki, Vesi- ja ympäristöhallitus.

Kämäri, J. (1991), Saastumishaitat ja niiden säätely Suomessa, in O. Tahvonen (ed.), *Ympäristö, Hyvinvointi ja Talous*, Jyväskylä, 44–58.

Karvonen, L. (1984), High-level foreign policy coordination: a Finnish example, *Cooperation and Conflict*, 19, 135–55.

Karvonen, L. and B. Sundelius (1987), *Internationalization and Foreign Policy Management*, Aldershot, Gower.

Koskinen, K. (1994), *Ympäristönsuojelusta 'kestävään' kehitykseen' – Kansallinen ympäristöpolitiikka ja ekologinen modernisaatio*, Pori, Turun Yliopisto Satakunnan Ympäristöntutkimuskeskus.

Kunnat kestävää kehitystä etsimässä (1994), Helsinki, Suomen Kuntaliitto.

Luonnonvarat ja ympäristö (1995), Ympäristö 1995: 1, Helsinki, Tilastokeskus.

Meadows, D. H., D. L. Meadows, J. Randers and W. Behrens (1972), *The Limits to Growth*, London, Earth Island.

Nousiainen, J. (1991), *Suomen poliittinen järjestelmä*, Juva, WSOY.

Numminen, A. (1992), *Suomi ja kansainvälinen ympäristöyhteistyö*, Helsinki, Ulkoasiainministeriö.

Nuuja, I., R. Palokangas and V. Tarukannel (1993), *Uusi ympäristösuojelun hallinto ja lainsäädäntö*, Jyväskylä, Ympäristö-Tieto Ky.

Oittinen, V. (1993), Ekokriisi ja moraalinen eliitti: Piirteitä Pentti Linkolan ajattelun kehityksestä, in J. Jokisalo and K. Väyrynen (eds), *Ympäristökysymysten yhteiskunnallisia ja eettisiä näkökulmia*, Oulu, 171–91.

Persson, P.-E. (1983), Finlands miljöförvaltning – Ett decennium av födslovåndor, *Nordisk Administrativ Tidskrift*, 4, 348–58.

Pesonen, P. (ed.) (1994a), *Suomen EU-kansanäänestys*, Helsinki, Painatuskeskus Oy.

Pesonen, P. (1994b), EU-kannan pohja ja perustelut, in P. Pesonen (ed.), *Suomen EU-kansanäänestys*, Helsinki, Painatuskeskus Oy, 84–95.

Rannikko, P. (1993), Miljökampens vågor i Finland, *Nordisk Samhällsgeografisk Tidsskrift*, 17, 23–30.

Raumolin, J. (1990), *The Impact of Technological Change on Rural and Regional Forestry in Finland*, Keskusteluaiheita 343, Helsinki, ETLA.

Rouhinen, S. (1991), Ympäristöpolitiikka Suomessa, in I. Massa and R. Sairinen (eds), *Ympäristökysymys*, Helsinki, Gaudeamus, 219–47.

Rumpunen, J. (1994), Eta vai EU – integraatiovaihtoehtojen vaikutukset Suomen ympäristöpolitiikkaan, in J. Rumpunen, O.-P. Salmimies and J. Salovaara (eds), *Suomi ja Euroopan Unioni Vaikutukset ulko- ja turvallisuuspolitiikkaan, ympäristöpolitiikkaan ja pakolaispolitiikkaan*, Ulkopolitiikan haasteita 5, Helsinki, UPI, 38–82.

Rusanen, P. (1993), Dags för omvärdering av bostadspolitiken, *AH Uutiset*, 2, Asuntohallitus, 12–13.

Sänkiaho, R. (1994), Puoluesidonnaisuutta vai sitoutumattomuutta, in P. Pesonen (ed.), *Suomen EU-kansanäänestys*, Helsinki, Painatuskeskus Oy, 164–73.

Sänkiaho, R. and E. Säynässalo (1994), EU:n vaikutukset Suomen kehitykseen, in P. Pesonen (ed.), *Suomen EU-kansanäänestys*, Helsinki, Painatuskeskus Oy, 96–111.

Statsrådets beslut om åtgärder för förnyande av centralförvaltningen och regionalförvaltningen (1993), Helsingfors, Finansministeriet.

Storsved, A.-S. (1993a), The debate on establishing the Ministry of Environment in Finland in the light of environmental ideologies, *Environmental Politics*, 2:2, 304–26.

Storsved, A.-S. (1993b), *Det politiska spelet kring miljöadministrationens framväxt i Finland*, paper för Nordisk Statsviterkongress i Oslo, Norge 19–21 August.

Susiluoto, I. (1991), Yhteiskunnallinen ympäristökeskustelu Neuvostoliitossa, in I. Massa and R. Sairinen (eds), *Ympäristökysymys*, Helsinki, Gaudeamus, 326–48.

Tirkkonen, J. and M. Wilenius (1995), *Ilmastonmuutos, politiikka ja Suomi*, Suomen Akatemian julkaisuja 8/95, Helsinki, Edita.

Träskman, P. O. (1992), *Miljöbrott och kontroll av miljöbrottslighet*, Publikationer från institutionen för straff- och processrätt vid Helsingfors universitet A:5, Helsingfors.

Turun Sanomat, 19 April 1994, 1 June 1994 and 8 April 1995.

Vahtera, A. (1993), *Hyvinvoinnin harhakuvat*, Helsinki, Arator.

Valanta, J. (1992), Kehittyvätkö kunnat kestävästi? Kestävän kehityksen aluepoliittista tarkastelua, in P. Jokinen, I. Kantola and K. Koskinen (eds), *Myrkkyä, Rahastusta ja Retoriikkaa*, Sociological Research Reports, Series B 25, Turku, Turku University, 79–97.

Vuosikirja (1993), Turku, Ympäristöministeriö.

Vuosikirja (1995), Ympäristöministeriö, Painatuskeskus Oy.

Wahlström, E., E.-L. Hallanaro and T. Reinikainen (1992), *Miljöns tillstånd i Finland*, Vatten- och miljöstyrelsen och Miljödatacentralen, Helsingfors.

Ympäristö (1995), Ympäristöministeriö, 3.

Ympäristöhallinnon uudistaminen (1994), Muistio 3, Helsinki, Ympäristöministeriö.

Ympäristötilasto – Environment Statistics (1994), Environment 1994:3, Helsinki, Statistics Finland.

Germany: domestic obstacles to an international forerunner

A short review of the development of environmental policy

The establishment phase (1969–1974)
As late as 1969, 95 per cent of the German population could not make anything of the term 'environment' (Pötzl, 1982). One year later, almost 60 per cent of the population had still not developed an appropriate understanding of the term. A third, representative poll carried out in November 1971 presented a completely different picture: in the meantime, more than 90 per cent of the persons questioned had become familiar with the term 'environmental policy' (Schmidt, 1992).

The year 1969 can be regarded as the year of birth of a (federal) German environmental policy. As shown by the above-mentioned results of opinion polls, it could not have been any pressure exerted by public opinion that induced the new social-liberal federal government to adopt environmental policy as a new, independent area of politics immediately after entering into office. What, then, prompted the new government suddenly to pay attention to the new 'issue' of environmental protection of its own accord? The literature cites a bundle of factors (see Müller, 1986; Hucke, 1990; Barbian, 1992). First of all, the – in retrospect – 'easy conquest of the political agenda' (Barbian) surely cannot be explained without taking into consideration the overall political climate of reform which allowed the Social Democratic Party (Sozialdemokratische Partei Deutschlands, SPD) and the Free Democratic Party (Freie Demokratische Partei, FDP) to form a government coalition. To the FDP, which took over the province of environmental policy through Hans-Dietrich Genscher, the Federal Minister of the Interior, this field obviously offered a welcome opportunity to portray itself as a reform party, particularly in view of the new, highly and effectively publicised policy towards Eastern Europe ('Neue Ostpolitik') promoted by the SPD. A definitely (co-)decisive impetus, however, came from abroad. As early as 1968, the United Nations Educational, Scientific and Cultural Organisation had organised an international symposium with the title 'Man and the Biosphere'; the Council of Europe had declared 1970 the Year of Nature Conservation; and – this finally tipped the balance – the United Nations had called the first international 'Conference on the Environment of Man', to be held in 1972. In the course of making the necessary preparations for this conference, the federal government presented an initial 'immediate action programme' in 1970. This was followed by the first comprehensive 'Environmental programme of the federal government' in 1971. Since then, irrespective of the change in government that followed, the environmental policy of the federal government has been oriented along the principle of precautionary protection of the environment, the principle of causal responsibility (i.e. the polluter pays principle), and the principle of co-operation.

The passing of the environmental programme was preceded by a reorganisation of the federal government. On the basis of the organisational decree of 11 November 1969, the Chancellor transferred the Department of Water Industry, Air Pollution Control and Noise Abatement, which up to then had been part of the Federal Ministry of Health, to the sphere of responsibility of the Federal Ministry of the Interior (Bundesministerium des Inneren).

In the same year (1972), the Basic Law was amended to allow the federal government to become active in areas of environmental policy. However, the federal government was only partially successful. It had to content itself with the areas of waste disposal, air pollution control and noise abatement (article 74, no. 24 of the constitution). With respect to the areas of water resources as well as nature conservation and landscape management, the Bundesrat was merely accorded the competence to draw up skeleton legislation (article 75, nos 3 and 4 of the constitution). On the basis of this structure, the government was able to work out and pass special environmental laws within a relatively short period of time (Waste Disposal Act 1972, Federal Emmission Control Act 1974) and consequently realise the prioritised plans contained in the government's environmental programme. Progress was also made with respect to relevant institutions: following the establishment of the Council of Experts for Environmental Issues in 1971, the Federal Environmental Agency (Umweltbundesamt) was founded in 1974.

The relatively rapid preparation of new environmental laws can be explained by the resolute offensive taken by the officials and politicians working in the Ministry of the Interior at the time, as well as – and not least – by the fact that one returned to traditional patterns of regulation. Thus the Federal Emmission Control Act, which was classified as a 'guiding law' for environmental policy, was based on the principles of the nineteenth-century Prussian Industrial Code. Jochen Hucke (1990) accurately summarises the dilemma of a policy that hoped to cope with problems quickly by reviving established legal traditions:

> By taking recourse to the legal traditions of environmental policy, the basic patterns of which were conceived in the early phases of industrialization towards the end of the nineteenth century and which focused particularly on protecting private property against intervention of the state and third parties, significant obstacles and delays with respect to the further development and implementation of environmental policy were generated. It cannot be ignored that comprehensive protection of property basically contradicts the concept of the new environmental policy that environmental pollution be reduced as much as possible on the basis of the latest knowledge in pollution abatement technology.

In other words: the principle of precautionary protection of the environment proclaimed in the environmental programme of the federal government was not taken into consideration as adequately as it could have been, if one had not taken the traditional industrial codes as the model – even at the cost of somewhat delayed legislation – but the instruments already developed by the United States at the time with respect to environmental protection (e.g. environmental impact assessment). But now the implementation deficits of the 1970s, as they were revealed by implementation research projects (e.g. Hucke and Ullmann, 1980), were to a certain extent pre-programmed by the legislation.

Environmental policy on the defensive (1974–1978)
The oil crisis and economic recession changed the political priorities in favour of promoting economic revival and, consequently, marked

the beginning of a phase of stagnation and defensive action in environmental policy. Trade associations and labour unions, as well as their lobbyists in politics and public administration, declared environmental protection to be an obstacle to economic growth and a jobkiller – a highly effective argument in view of increasing unemployment. The decisive turning point came at the conference in the castle of Gymnich in 1975 (Müller, 1986; Hucke, 1990). Here, Chancellor Schmidt and leading representatives of the Employers' Association, trade associations and labour unions agreed on a kind of 'breather' in environmental policy and on reducing the investment-blocking effects of environmental obligations imposed on enterprises. Although the Bundestag and the Bundesrat passed altogether four laws on environmental protection (the Washing Agents Act, the Amendment to the Federal Water Act, the Waste Water Charges Act and the Federal Nature Conservation Act) in 1975 and 1976, the internal preparations in the government for these acts had all been completed by the spring of 1974. Moreover, particularly with respect to the Waste Water Charges Act, considerable concessions were made in the original draft concerning the amount of, and the starting date for, the collection of charges. Between 1975 and 1978, no new legislative plans were initiated in the field of environmental protection. Nonetheless, government officials in the Ministry of the Interior managed to maintain status quo in environmental legislation and policy, and this can be considered a remarkably 'successful act of defense' in view of the threatened 'mitigation' of the Federal Emmission Control Act (Müller, 1986).

The decade of consolidation (1979–1989)
The passivity of the legislator regarding environmental issues during the first 'Ice Age of environmental policy' (Müller, 1989) did, however, help pave the way for the phase of revival and consolidation that started around 1978. This phase was characterised by a wide network of citizens' initiatives and environmental groups, which were called into life as a result of the dissatisfaction that politically active and ecology-minded members of the population felt towards the omissions of governmental environmental policy. New environmental associations were founded, and existing organisations which were dedicated to traditional ideas of nature conservation, reoriented themselves along the comprehensive concept of environmental protection (Cornelsen, 1991; Hey and Brendle, 1994). Developments within the

parties took a parallel course. Due to the first successes of the 'green' factions in the 1978 elections to the Landtag and the establishment of the national Green Party (Die Grünen) in 1980, which was elected to the Bundestag for the first time three years later, the established parties were confronted with competition, which prompted them to revive environmental protection, at least as part of their programmes. Together with the increasing pressure exerted by ecological problems, reflected primarily in the intensive public discussion about forest damage (*Waldsterben*) and its causes, wide social consensus arose about the necessity of effective pollution control measures. On the basis of this consensus, the new government coalition of the Christian Democratic Union (Christlich Demokratische Union, CDU), the Christian Social Union (Christlich Soziale Union, CSU) and the FDP was able to push through a qualitatively thorough reform of environmental law. It manifested itself first in the Ordinance on Large Combustion Plants (Großfeuerungsanlagenverordnung) of 1984, which forced an investment volume of more than DM20 billion upon the energy sector (Müller, 1994):

> In the past, the legal situation and a broad interpretation of the protection of property made it extremely difficult to enforce upgrading requirements for plants polluting the environment and, hence, such enforcement was limited to individual cases, but within the framework of the new regulations ... binding time limits requiring the observance of considerably more stringent air-pollution control measures were set for the first time for all plants falling under the ordinance.
>
> (Hucke, 1990)

This concept was gradually introduced to other areas of environmental law, for example in amendments to water and waste laws. Even if the transition limits and exemptions were met with strong criticism from environmental groups, this reorientation in environmental policy did bring about measurable, medium-term success. Thus, for example, the emissions of SO_2, which is responsible for 'acid rain', decreased by 72 per cent between 1970 and 1989.

Despite these successes, the Chancellor revoked the Ministry of the Interior's competence for environmental policy by ordering the establishment of the Federal Ministry for the Environment, Nature Conservation and Nuclear Safety (Bundesministeriums für Umwelt, Naturschutz und Reaktorsicherheit, BMU) on 5 June 1986. The reason for this decision was widespread public criticism of the

Ministry of the Interior for its mismanagement of the consequences of the nuclear reactor accident in Chernobyl. The establishment of the BMU just eight months before the end of the legislative period, a move that surprised insiders as well, was motivated by campaign tactics (Pehle, 1988a, b).[1] Nevertheless, by transferring the relevant competencies from the Ministry of the Interior, the Ministry of Food, Agriculture and Forestry and the former Ministry of Youth, Family and Health to the new ministry, the federal government took into account the long-standing demand of environmental groups for a consolidation of competencies. Thus it also created a kind of 'atmosphere of setting off or starting anew' among government officials (Pehle, 1988a).

Walter Wallmann's term as Federal Minister for the Environment, which lasted barely a year, was marked by activities in the field of nuclear reactor safety and radiological protection. Thus the first law worked out by the new ministry was the Act on Precautionary Protection against Radiation Exposure of 19 December 1986. The new Minister for the Environment was not able to set other directions in environmental policy, since he had to act primarily as a 'crisis manager'. It was precisely the at times seemingly conceptless crisis management of the BMU, for example after the fire at Sandoz in Basel and numerous cases of water pollution by the chemical industry, which caused the 'new Minister for the Environment's loss of reputation in public opinion with respect to his political competence and ability to enforce measures' (Weidner, 1989). For this reason, government officials in the BMU hoped for a new offensive in environmental policy when, in May 1987, Klaus Töpfer, Minister for the Environment of Rhineland-Palatinate, was appointed successor to Walter Wallmann, who had been elected Hessian Minister President (Pehle, 1988b).

These hopes were only partially fulfilled. The positive directions set by the new minister were soon counteracted by the discrepancy between the policy propagated by him and the measures actually implemented. The reactions of the media to the first 'half-time stock-taking' of the Federal Ministry for the Environment resembled a 'devastating review' (Weidner, 1989; *Der Spiegel*, 15, 1989).

Environmental policy on the retreat (1990–1994)

A new field of activity opened up for environmental policy in the course of the reunification of Germany, especially in view of the ecological disasters discovered on the territory of the former German Democratic Republic, and these tasks were acknowledged and handled quickly, for example, by propagating the 'environmental union' (von Berg, 1990). Yet the debate about how to finance the reunification of Germany made environmental protection at best a 'subordinate campaign issue' right away (*Der Spiegel*, 47, 1990) during the parliamentary elections in December 1990. The ensuing discussion about 'Germany's viability as a commercial/industrial location' brought about a massive renaissance of the image of environmental protection as an economic obstacle, which many had thought a thing of the past (e.g. Hucke, 1990). Although German environmental engineering holds the top position world-wide with a world market share of 21 per cent and is actually one of the most dynamic growth markets as such, recording an annual volume of sales of about DM26 billion (Umweltbundesamt, 1993) and providing 680,000 jobs at present (see *Umwelt* published by the BMU, 9, 1994), and although the anti-pollution investments and expenditures of German enterprises come to a maximum 3.39 per cent of the gross production value (Umweltbundesamt, 1993), it was not possible to rob the 'sledge-hammer argument proclaiming environmental protection a job and investment killer' of its political effectiveness (Schmidt, 1992). The results shown in the balance-sheets of environmental protection in recent years reflect this attitude. Not even half of the measures relating to environmental policy that were put down in coalition agreements were put into reality (*Süddeutsche Zeitung*, 1 September 1994; *die tageszeitung*, 2 September 1994). Among others, the amendment to the Federal Nature Conservation Act which was announced more than six years ago, the Soil Conservation Act, and the ordinances on the utilisation of electronic scrap, old cars, waste paper and batteries fell by the wayside. Moreover, the measures implemented by the federal government during the period under discussion clearly reflect the defensive position of environmental policy.

The national climate protection policy of the federal government can be assessed in the same vein. The first relevant decision of the government to have reduced CO_2 emissions, which are responsible for the greenhouse effect, by 25 per cent by 2005 (related to the base year 1987) dates back to June 1990. At the same time, an interdepartmental Working Group on CO_2 Reduction was formed (Unfried, 1994). Nonetheless, the legislator did not implement any really far-reaching measures. Such measures as were passed, for example, a new Heat Shield Ordinance designed to reduce the heating energy required in new buildings, remained within the conventional limits of traditional administrative policy.

The coalition agreements that outline the political objectives of the conservative-liberal government, which was confirmed in office at the parliamentary elections in October 1994, deal with environmental policy only in passing. Mention is merely made that 'the ecological market economy' is to be expanded further. Yet this objective is not discussed in more detail. Moreover, the transferral of Mr Töpfer, the then Minister for the Environment, to the Ministry of Building and the appointment of Angela Merkel, hitherto head of the Ministry of Women and Youth and without any experience in environmental matters, as Minister for the Environment, were generally viewed as a 'sign of the Kohl government's reluctance to undertake ecological modernization' (*Die Zeit*, 48, 1994).

Institutional background

Laying the foundation: (environmental) policy in a federal state
Environmental policy takes concrete form in laws – not exclusively, but to a large extent. German federalism exhibits three special features in this respect: the distribution of legislative competence between the federal government and the *Länder* (states), the involvement of the *Länder* in the legislative process of the federal government and, finally, the enforcement of federal law through the *Länder*.

The legislative competencies of the federal government are defined by the Basic Law, which distinguishes between the exclusive and concurrent legislative powers as well as the skeleton legislation of the federal government. The Basic Law contains an enumerative catalogue of fields subject to regulation for each case in articles 73 to 75.

The Basic Law tersely states: 'The maintenance of relations to foreign states is the responsibility of the federal government' (article 32). For this reason, the list of areas where the federal government has sole legislative power also includes 'foreign affairs'. Thus 'foreign environmental policy' is basically regulated by the federal government. The major competencies of the federal government with respect to environmental policy can be found in the catalogue of concurrent legislation. The definition of 'concurrent legislation' in the Basic Law specifies that the *Länder* are entitled to legislative power 'as long as and to the extent that' the federal government does not make use of its legislative competence (article 72 in the Basic Law). The federal government, on the other hand, may enact laws in such an area only if the 'establishment of equal living conditions' in the territory of the Federal Republic of Germany or the 'maintenance of legal or economic unity' calls for a nation-wide solution. Article 72 was designed as a safeguard against excessive centralisation. But in particular the wording regarding equal living conditions has developed into a kind of 'general authorisation' to enact uniform legislation nation-wide. This becomes evident by the fact that the federal government has fully exploited the 24-point catalogue of concurrent legislation. In this context, regulation in the following areas is relevant to environmental policy: the rights of trade and industry, which include, among others, mining, the industrial and energy sectors; the peaceful utilisation of nuclear energy, which includes plant safety, radiological protection and the disposal of radioactive substances; roads and motor vehicles; and, finally, waste disposal, air pollution control and noise abatement. Regulation by federal law through concurrent legislation does not necessarily mean that the corresponding subject matter is regulated in such a way that the *Länder* are not left any room for action. Although, for example, a nation-wide regulation for waste disposal has existed since 1972, all *Länder* have also passed their own waste disposal laws, and these deviate considerably from one another in certain respects.

The right of the federal government to pass general provisions is tied to the same prerequisites as its right of concurrent legislation. Skeleton laws are to leave the *Länder* room to enact detailed legislation, and they are required to do so. The skeleton legislation of the federal government is relevant for the environment in the areas of nature conservation and landscape management as well as water resources. The latter can be taken as an example showing that also skeleton laws can at times contain very detailed regulations: the Waste Water Charges Act of the federal government leaves the *Länder* barely any room for enacting their own regulations.

The second special feature of German federalism, as stated above, concerns the involvement of the *Länder* in the legislative process of the federal government. This is realised through the Bundesrat, which consists of the members of the *Land* governments (not the parliaments). The distribution of votes – at least three, at most seven, votes for each *Land* – is based on the population of each state. The

Bundesrat participates in the preparation of every federal law. However, distinction must be made between bills requiring Bundesrat approval and so-called opposition bills. All laws amending the constitution require Bundesrat approval. They require a two-thirds majority in the Bundestag and the Bundesrat. The question of whether simple bills fall into the category of bills requiring Bundesrat approval is not conclusively regulated by the Basic Law. However, the view that all bills require Bundesrat approval if they extend into the range of competence of the *Länder* and/or affect the right reserved to the *Länder* to regulate the administrative enforcement of federal laws, has become generally accepted (and has been confirmed by the Federal Constitutional Court). The majority of federal laws require Bundesrat approval since – and this is the third special feature of the German federal state – the federal government, apart from a few exceptions, does not have its own administrative enforcement for federal laws; rather this falls under the authority of the *Länder*.[2] Thus hardly any law relating to environmental protection can be enacted without the approval of the Bundesrat. If the Bundesrat refuses to give its consent, the federal government or the Bundestag can demand that a mediation committee be convened. A compromise worked out by this committee must then again be accepted by the Bundestag and the Bundesrat. As far as laws are concerned that do not require Bundesrat approval, the Bundesrat is merely entitled to put in a suspensive veto, which can be rendered ineffective through another vote in the Bundestag.

The rights of participation of the Bundesrat illustrated above can become particularly problematic for the federal government and the supporting majority in the Bundestag if a majority of the *Länder* governments are led by the opposition party. This has been the case since the end of the 1980s: the federal government is made up of the CDU, the CSU and the FDP, but SPD-governed *Länder* governments constitute the majority in the Bundesrat. This means that environmental policy, to the extent that it is enforced by legislation, can be implemented only on the basis of compromises between the above-mentioned parties. Supplementary to this statement, and without wanting to limit it, it should be pointed out that conflicts between the federal government and the *Länder* are based not only on the constellation of the parties, but that the *Länder* governments frequently enter into coalitions against the federal government, including several or all parties.

Due to the mutual dependence of the federal government and the

Länder, numerous formal and informal modes of co-operation have developed between the *Länder* (co-operation at the 'third level') as well as between the federal government and the *Länder* (co-operation at the 'fourth level'):

> In environmental policy, a field of politics that is highly technical and dependent on enforcement, the network of interfederal co-operation is woven very tightly. The votes of the Environment Ministers Conference, which meets two times a year, to a large extent reflect the guidelines worked out in advance at the conferences of the heads of office, i.e. by the heads of the administrative authorities of the *Länder* departments of the environment. These in turn are based on the work of the working groups of the *Länder* as well as the joint working groups of the *Länder* and federal government, which consist of experts from different federal or *Land* authorities.
>
> (Müller-Brandeck-Bocquet, 1993)

The federal modes of co-operation are clearly dominated by the executive branches of government, not only but also with respect to environmental policy. It is up to the relevant ministers of the federal government and the *Länder* governments to reach compromises. As a consequence, particularly the *Länder* parliaments suffer a tangible loss of power. They are regularly put into a position where they are merely ratification organs for decisions taken somewhere else.

The legal setting

The constitutional debate As mentioned above, since 1972 the Basic Law has authorised the federal government to issue laws in all fields pertaining to environmental protection. However, a point of dispute was to what extent this also granted the federal government an authority to act and how far this authority extended. The prevailing opinion in the field of public law, which has developed since the 1970s, is that the protection of the natural basis of existence of man is a matter-of-course responsibility of the state, which, among others, can be deduced from article 2 of the Basic Law, which guarantees every person's right to freedom from physical injury. Hans-Peter Bull commented, however, on these facts very succinctly as early as 1973:

> If the state has any tasks at all, then one of them is to protect the natural ('biological') basis of existence of human life. This does not require any further constitutional reasoning; one must only refer to the fundamental rights, in particular article 2 of the Basic Law ... and the principle of social justice and the welfare state.

The claim that the state has a general and comprehensive duty to undertake environmental protection was, however, refused by the legal sciences. In its opinion, the state was not obliged to do more than safeguard a 'minimum ecological standard' (Bock, 1990).

The above is a shortened summary of the background situation of a twenty-year debate on the introduction of a corresponding supplement to the Basic Law. Many different proposals for formulations all failed to go through parliament, e.g. a proposal worked out in 1981 by a commission of experts set up by the federal government and introduced, among others, by the parliamentary party 'Die Grünen' as well as by the SPD-governed *Länder* through the Bundesrat (Kimminich, 1994). Finally, the Joint Constitutional Commission of the Bundestag and the Bundesrat, which was set up in the course of German reunification, attended to the matter. In view of the fact that a two-thirds majority is necessary both in the commission for passing corresponding recommendations and in the Bundestag and the Bundesrat for taking decisions on constitutional amendments, decisions were possible only on the basis of a compromise between the CDU/CSU and the SPD. This compromise was reached only after tough negotiations and literally at the last minute, with the CDU/CSU carrying through their standpoint in the end. The controversy centred around the so-called 'legal proviso', i.e. the question of whether decisions made by administrative authorities and court decisions should be subjected directly to the public/national objective of environmental protection or only to the framework of the 'simple' laws effective at the time. The position of the CDU/CSU, which put through the basic elements of its proposal, was as follows:

> The national objective of environmental protection can ... only be reconciled with other responsibilities of the state, the public interest and the rights of the individual by political decisions of the legislator, and not on a case-by-case basis through the administrative authorities or the courts. Environmental protection must not become a primary or even decisive issue, but must always be viewed in its relation to other objectives such as economic growth or the creation of jobs; and this could not be ensured if the executive and judicial branches were directly bound to the national objective of environmental protection in individual cases.
>
> (Joint Constitutional Commission, (Gemeinsame Verfassungs/ Commisssion) 1993)

The parties reached an agreement which became a valid constitutional provision (article 20a) after having passed the Bundestag and the Bundesrat in October 1994. It reads as follows: 'The state shall protect, also as part of its responsibility for future generations, the natural basis of existence within the framework of constitutional order by means of legislation and in compliance with the laws through executive power and legal decisions.' Since then, the legislator has been charged through the constitution to ensure the protection of the natural basis of existence; however, it is left to his political freedom of legal arrangement how and when he will fulfil this state function.

Environmental laws   German environmental law is extraordinarily fragmented. This is true in three respects: first, with respect to the territorial application of respective standards; second, with respect to the regulatory subject matter; and, third, with respect to legal quality.

The first aspect has been addressed several times in connection with the structures of the federal state. Even if the federal government covers almost all areas of environmental law through its competence of concurrent and skeleton legislation, the environmental legislation passed by the *Länder* is not insignificant.

The situation regarding regulatory subject matters is similarly unclear since there is no 'environmental skeleton law' or 'environmental code'. Taking up a proposal put forward by Peine (1992), I will distinguish between 'medium-related', 'causal', 'vital' and 'integrated' environmental law.

'Medium-related environmental law' comprises the preservation of air, water and soil. The Federal Emmission Control Act of 1974 is dedicated to controlling air pollution, and apart from that it also regulates the abatement of noise. A supplementary law also serving to control air pollution is the Federal Leaded Fuel Act of 1971. The second 'classic' environmental medium is covered by the Federal Water Resources Act of 1957. It is supplemented by the Waste Water Charges Act of 1976 as well as the Washing and Cleansing Agents Act of 1975. Soil is protected only fragmentarily, namely through the Nature Conservation Act. By granting the authority to demarcate certain protected areas, it can as a rule limit the conversion of rural land into urban, industrial and traffic uses. What is still missing is a general regulation of the qualitative preservation of soil and soil recovery. The latter, which is becoming an explosive topic in connection with contaminated sites, is regulated only to a limited extent in some *Land* laws.

'Causal environmental law' is occasionally described as 'substance-related'. This category includes atomic energy and radio-logical protection law, which is regulated, among others, by the Atomic Energy Law of 1957 and the Radiological Protection Act of 1986. The second group of 'substance-related' regulations is covered by the 'Chemicals Act'. The Chemicals Act (actually the Toxic Substances Control Act of 1980 is supplemented by special laws such as the Act on Fertilisers (1977) and the Act on DDT (1972). The third group comprises laws relating to food, drugs and cattle feed. The corresponding laws, all of which concern substances that can affect human health, were passed in the mid-1970s. The last group of substance-related regulations is made up of waste management laws. The Waste Avoidance and Waste Management Act enacted by the federal government in 1972 was developed further in the subsequent years into the Ecocycle or Closed Circuit Economy Act ('Kreis-laufwirtschaftsgesetz') of 1994, which was to ensure a closed cycle of product reutilisation.

'Vital environmental law' basically refers to the protection and preservation of wild plants and animals. In addition to the Nature Conservation Act of 1976, the Animal Protection Act (1972) and the Plant Protection Act (1968) need to be mentioned here.

Finally, 'integrated environmental law' aims to regulate pro-cedural aspects. It is concerned with the problem of balancing the interests of different parties. Relevant regulations can be found, for example, in the Town and Country Planning Code. According to this code, the urban development planning drawn up by the communes is to help 'safeguard an environment fit for human beings and to protect and develop the natural bases of existence' (article 1, section 5). The law on the Environmental Impact Assessment of 1990 can also be assigned to the category of 'integrated environmental law'.

A final aspect concerns the difference in legal quality of the respec-tive standards or statutory rules. Many of the legal provisions regard-ing the environment are not enacted as conventional parliamentary laws, but as ordinances. Even experts can hardly keep track of the large number of such laws. The idea behind ordinances is to relieve the legislator of the task of defining standards, e.g. technical details. For this reason, the competent ministers are authorised by law to issue ordinances. As a rule, they need the approval of the Bundesrat to do so. In many cases it would be misleading, however, to describe the concrete contents of ordinances as 'technical details'. One example will suffice to illustrate this point: the fundamental reform of Germany's air pollution control policy in 1984 was not based on a formal law, but on the Ordinance on Large Combustion Plants, and parliament was not involved in its formulation. The democratic-theoretical problem that becomes evident in connection with ordinances also applies to another group of statutory rules, namely administrative regulations, which are created in the same way. However, administrative regulations involve another problem. Even though they bind the executory administrative authorities (e.g. by requiring the observance of certain limit values with respect to issuing permits for plants), they do not generate any external effect. Among others, this is true with respect to the Technical Instructions on Air Quality Control (Technische Anleitung Luft). It applies to all combustion plants that do not fall under the Ordinance on Large Combustion Plants. Since the Technical Instructions on Air Quality Control have no binding effect on outside parties (i.e. they are only binding for the administrative authorities), they offer no legal basis for complaints from citizens who are affected by excessive emmissions. On 30 May 1991, Germany was obligated by the European Court of Justice to set by law the limit values specified in the Technical Instructions so that citizens may have legal security. Up until now, the federal government has not reacted.

Besides this isolated case of reform demanded by the EU, a fundamental revision of German environmental law has been on the agenda for a long time. The objective of the Ministry for the Environment is to obtain a 'self-contained codification of environmental law in the form of an environmental code' (*Umwelt*, 11, 1994). As early as 1990, several experts in jurisprudence drew up a draft for a 'General Part' of such an environmental code within the framework of a research project sponsored by the Minister for the Environment; the proposals for the 'Special Part' followed in 1994. Since the so-called 'professors' draft' did not limit itself merely to summarising existing laws, but also worked out a 'further development as regards content', the debate on the range of the legal reform as regards content is still underway.

Environmental policy and the political system

As mentioned above, the Federal Republic of Germany did not have an independent ministry for the environment until June 1986. The advantages and disadvantages of uniting important – but not all – areas of environmental protection in the Federal Ministry for the Environment (for more detailed information, see Pehle 1988a, b) are still being discussed heatedly today. A basic advantage accompanying the establishment of the Ministry for the Environment is that it is more likely that conflicts will be politicised. It rendered superfluous 'self-dealing', where a ministry – for example, the Ministry of Agriculture – in its capacity as representative of conflicting interests tends to veil rather than discuss differences of opinion. A minister who can gain a reputation only by successfully pushing through the interests of environmental protection in principle increases the ability of his staff to respond to conflicts in the voting process with other ministries, which is prescribed for draft bills.

Thus, as a rule it has proven beneficial only in cases bearing serious conflicts to exempt environmental interests from the decision-making power of a ministry that simultaneously represents the interests of polluters. Yet – and this is the reverse side of the coin – the only area taken from a so-called 'polluter hierarchy' is nature conservation. And taking this as an example, we can demonstrate the disadvantages accompanying the establishment of the Ministry for the Environment: shortly after the establishment of their ministry, the conservationists within the Ministry for the Environment complained that they were being excluded from the planning and decision-making processes of the polluters. Decisions relating to the environment taken by the Ministry of Agriculture could hardly be influenced 'from the outside' any more after the interruption of a previously intact flow of information.

The intentional exclusion of the Ministry for the Environment from the decision-making processes of other ministries is especially serious because the sphere of responsibility of the Ministry for the Environment is very limited. Particularly with regard to the environmental problems discussed most intensively by the public, the Ministry for the Environment is factually powerless. Thus the Ministry of Transport would be responsible for introducing a speed limit on the Autobahn in Germany. The same holds true for the introduction of road tolls, which environmental groups have been demanding for a long time. By means of such tolls, the 'environmental costs' caused by traffic (i.e. individual road users) could be charged to the actual polluters. The long-standing debate on the introduction of so-called 'ecological taxes' (see Wilhelm, 1990) addresses the competencies of the Ministries of Finance and Economics. The Ministry for the Environment can act only as a 'petitioner'.

Three authorities which are supposed to support the work of the ministry are directly subordinate to the Federal Ministry for the Environment. The best known and most important is the Umweltbundesamt, which was established in 1974 and has its headquarters in Berlin. In addition, there are the Federal Agency for Radiological Protection (established in 1989) and the Federal Agency for Nature Conservation (established in 1994).

The Umweltbundesamt supports the Ministry for the Environment, above all with respect to air pollution control, waste and water management, and environmental chemicals. Its primary task, as defined by law, is to perform the preliminary scientific work. Recently, however, the Umweltbundesamt's work in the fields of public relations and provision of central documentation and information services has gained importance. Thus the Umweltbundesamt has issued a biannual publication of environmental data since 1984. The co-operation between the Ministry for the Environment and the Federal Environmental Agency does not always run smoothly in all areas. The Federal Environmental Agency frequently tries to emphasise its own environmental policy, and its staff also publicly criticise the concepts put forward by the Ministry for the Environment.

The precarious situation of the Ministry for the Environment is made even more serious by the circumstance that it does not have a powerful lobby. In comparison, trade and industrial associations as well as the Deutsche Bauernverband (German Farmers' Association) have long-standing, intensive contacts with 'their' ministries, whereas 'one still cannot say that environmental groups have become the actual clientele of the Ministry for the Environment' (Weidner, 1989). Still today relations between the Ministry for the Environment and environmental groups are characterised by tension rather than co-operation. Hey and Brendle (1994) are of the opinion that a climate of mutual distrust and fear of contact is responsible for this. The representatives of the groups view the ministerial bureaucracy – also in the Ministry for the Environment – more as opponents than as co-players; for them, the administration is a 'closed system' designed to enact environmental policy from 'the top to the bottom'. Vice versa, the ministerial bureaucracy frequently considers the environmental groups to be incompetent, unable to reach compromises, and too 'radical' in the sense that they support unrealistic and non-realisable demands. As a consequence, the environmental groups are not viewed as potential allies by the Ministry for the Environment either, rather they are its most outspoken critics.

At present, however, there are more and more signs of a – albeit cautious – change in direction. For example, Greenpeace Germany forwarded a new concept some time ago, which the weekly newspaper *Die Zeit* (1994, 25) described as follows: 'Less action, more persuasion. Environmental lobbyists are seeking discussions with industry'. The same can be said for the German Association for the Protection of the Environment and Nature (Bund für Umwelt und Naturschutz Deutschland, BUND). In 1993 it found – to the surprise of many – an ally in the Federal Association of Young Entrepreneurs (Bundesverband Junger Unternehmer, BJU) in its struggle for an ecological tax reform. A year later, a second call for an ecological tax reform was jointly published by the BUND and sixteen heads of enterprises. In their joint statement of 1993, the BUND and the BJU affirmed that the contrasts between environmental groups and employers' associations, which have been so carefully maintained by politicians, are starting to disappear. The empirical content of this statement can still be (rightfully) disputed. Nonetheless, business and environmental organisations are slowly eliminating traditional points of conflict.

Despite, and also irrespective of, the fact that the number of members of environmental groups and the amount of income earned through contributions have grown enormously in recent years, the environmental lobby is still weak. The German environmental movement is highly fragmentary. In addition to the German Ring for Nature Conservation (Deutsche Naturschutzring), which is organised as an umbrella organisation, other groups such as Greenpeace, the BUND, the German Nature Conservation Association (Naturschutzbund Deutschland), and the World Wildlife Fund are trying to gain influence. The above-mentioned associations even compete with each other at times. Thus, for instance, environmental groups speak out in favour of intensively promoting wind energy to make Germany's 'energy mix' more environmentally acceptable. In their efforts, however, they have increasingly to face the resistance of nature conservation groups who complain that the landscape is ruined by wind power plants. This 'internal rivalry', as well as the inconsistency of the argumentation put forward by some environmental groups, contributes to the fact that the environmental groups, contrary to the interest groups of trade and industry, stand outside the political decision-making system; they address themselves primarily to the public.

Environmental policy at the federal level is rounded off by the Bundestag and the Bundesrat. Immediately after having established the Ministry for the Environment, the Bundestag set up an environmental committee that acts as a main consultant in connection with all environmental laws. One hears relatively little about the committee, which is considered a 'weak committee',[3] not least because of the defensive position which the Ministry for the Environment, the 'law workshop' for environmental issues, has been in for a few years (Mertes and Müller, 1987). It last hit the headlines in the summer of 1994, when it was involved in one of the few laws that the Ministry for the Environment was able to push through despite obstacles in the cabinet. The 'Kreislaufwirtschaftsgesetz', an amendment and further development as regards the provisions of the Waste Avoidance and Waste Management Act, was revised by the members of the government party in the environmental committee to such an extent that the substance of the law seemed endangered, also from the standpoint of the Ministry for the Environment.

The law was finally 'saved' by the Bundesrat: a law 'that the Minister for the Environment could only accept in the end, because the SPD-governed *Länder* in the Bundesrat pushed through those passages that had been struck out by members of the coalition' (*Süddeutsche Zeitung*, 1 September 1994). Several times in the past – and irrespective of the majorities held by the respective political parties – the Bundesrat had taken this kind of initiative; a role that optimises decisions in the opinion of many environmental politicians. Thus it fought for tightening the Ordinance on Large Combustion Plants presented by the federal government in 1983; and in the early 1990s, it also pushed through more stringent provisions for the Environmental Liability Law (Umwelthaftungsgesetz) and Ordinance on Packaging Material (Verpackungsverordnung) (Müller-Brandeck-Bocquet, 1993).

The cities and communes which are directly confronted with the concrete environmental problems, have no possibility of correcting the environmental policy of the federal government. Despite their right to be heard in the law-making process, the central association of local government bodies has not in the past been able to prevent the enactment of environmental standards that are 'hostile towards the communes' or that could not be implemented or only with great difficulty. This is true, for instance, with respect to the above-mentioned Ordinance on Packaging Material. A consequence of this ordinance was the establishment of the so-called 'Duale System', a system for registering and recycling packaging materials which is borne by industry and trade. In many places, the Duale System rendered useless the systems for collecting sorted waste. This met with harsh criticism from the German Congress of Municipal Authorities, which 'from the beginning [had expressed] doubt' about the concept developed in Bonn (*Süddeutsche Zeitung*, 18 March 1992). For the communes, the problems associated with waste are one of the most serious challenges that they have to face. One much-discussed attempt to solve the problem independently was undertaken by the city of Kassel when it introduced local taxes on non-returnable packaging. Since such a local tax was found permissible in a high court decision, many cities will probably copy this 'pilot project' (*Der Spiegel*, 35, 1994). The first German 'ecological tax' was introduced at the municipal level: many communes seem to be more able than the federal government or *Länder* governments to implement environmental policy. In many places, the Environmental Offices, which have been established in almost all large cities in the meantime, have been able to attain a significant potential for conflict in co-operation with the environmental committees of the local parliaments.

The tension between ecology and economy

Renewed opposition between environmental policy and economic policy

'The general resistance of enterprises and trade unions to environmental protection regulations died down in the 1980s. The positive effects that an economic policy oriented towards environmental protection could have on growth and employment were no longer seriously disputed' (Wilhelm, 1994). Also Schmidt (1992) stated that the 'associations representing capital and labor had thoroughly revised their respective philosophies on environmental policy' and 'One had learned a lesson from the forerunners in environmental policy, in particular Japan, the USA and Sweden; namely that environmental policy poses no obstacle to the transaction of business or the creation of jobs.'

As a matter of fact, at the end of the 1980s environmental policy seemed to be moving towards reconciling economy and ecology, and this development got wide social-political approval. At the beginning of 1989, the SPD decided to make environmental protection a central topic in their campaign for the elections to the Bundestag. Basically, their programme proposed to tighten the existing instruments of regulatory laws and supplement them with market-economic instruments of taxes and levies. The demand put forward by the SPD to introduce 'ecological taxes' was met with such a positive public response that the CDU came under political pressure. Thus in the autumn of 1989, the CDU also drew up a new environmental policy programme in which it spoke out in favour of developing the social market economy into an ecological-social economy. Wilhelm (1994) fittingly summarised this as follows: 'The years 1989 and 1990 marked a significant turning point in German environmental policy, because there was greater intervention than ever before, especially with new instruments. Nevertheless, this promising approach got stuck as soon as it was formulated and before it could be put into reality.'

As it were, the debate about environmental policy described above was pushed to the background overnight by the much more urgent problem of how to finance German reunification. Contrary to the plans of the SPD and the Green Party, environmental protection was only a 'secondary campaign topic' (*Der Spiegel*, 47, 1990) during the parliamentary elections in December 1990. The economic recession in the following years provoked widespread discussion about 'Germany's viability as a site for industrial enterprises'. In its wake, the argument that environmental protection was an obstacle to economic growth experienced a massive renaissance, and environmental policy was pushed even further into a defensive position. The argument put forth repeatedly by trade and industrial associations that the 'limit' in connection with costs for environmental protection had long since been reached (*Süddeutsche Zeitung*, 24 April 1992) not only aimed at preventing new environmental charges, but also wanted to 'loosen' existing regulations.

Although the Ministry for the Environment repeatedly tried to prove the economic profitability and justifiability of environmental protection measures and found allies among environmental politicians from all parties, e.g. the Declaration of Radebeul passed by all *Länder* Ministers of the Environment in May 1994, it was not able to move the political arena, which had become rigid as far as environmental protection was concerned.

The fact that economic and ecological issues were once again viewed as contrasts becomes evident through the circumstance that further developments of the instruments of environmental policy were blocked and that existing environmental protection regulations were 'loosened' by the legislator. For this purpose, a package of laws was passed in 1993. The law on investment facilitation and residential property (Investitionserleichterungs- und Wohnbaulandgesetz) as well as several investment acceleration laws (Investitionsbeschleunigungsgesetze) and the development planning simplification law (Planungsvereinfachungsgesetz) were decisive turning-points to the disadvantage of environmental protection. This package of laws was criticised not only by environmental groups. The Council of Experts for Environmental Issues (Sachverständigenrat für Umweltfagen, SRU), appointed by the federal government, also expressed unusually sharp and marked criticism in its Environmental Expertise of 1994: 'We do not understand and are concerned about the partially evident relapse into old ways of thinking, which can be summarized as "environmental protection is harmful to industrial sites".' The Council described the consequences of the law on investment facilitation and residential property as a 'restriction of procedural laws which served, amongst other things, to enforce ecologically compatible utilization of soil and areas' as well as a 'significant weakening of nature conservation and landscape protection' (SRU, 1994).

The partial 'release' of government and communal planning and approval procedures from the participation of the public, which the SRU definitively declared to be the 'wrong way', is, according to the will of the federal government, to be accompanied by extensive deregulation of environmental law. In the coalition agreement for the thirteenth legislative period, it is stated: 'the necessity and expediency of existing regulations [will be] examined with respect to the goal of deregulation. The planning and approval procedures relating to environmental law will be tightened and accelerated, and it will be examined whether private parties can also be involved' (*Umwelt*, 1, 1995). Also with respect to environmental issues, the federal government aims for a 'lean state' in future, in which the sovereign activities of the state are to be limited to a core area that has not been clearly defined. This also becomes evident in connection with the planned further development of substance-related environmental law, particularly in the field of waste management. The coalition agreement stated: 'In connection with enforcing the Kreislaufwirtschaftsgesetz, the necessary ordinances which regulate the responsibility of the industry for its products, especially scrap cars, electronic scrap and batteries, are presented. For this purpose, voluntary agreements of industry are to be given priority' (*Umwelt*, 1, 1995).

Such types of voluntary agreement had already existed in the past: between 1970 and 1990, about thirty voluntary agreements regarding environmental protection were concluded; and some of these were successful. A study of the Umweltbundesamt on the problem of voluntary self-commitment on the part of industry, however, shows an interesting point with regard to the aforementioned government plans. As far as the recycling of batteries is concerned, this study claims that a voluntary agreement had already been concluded between industry and the Ministry for the Environment as early as 1988. A study conducted by the University of Dortmund at the request of the Umweltbundesamt showed, however, that the rates of returned and recycled products quoted by the manufacturers were simply 'incorrect or unrealistic' (*Süddeutsche Zeitung*, 4 January 1995). This statement can obviously be interpreted as meaning that the Umweltbundesamt considers such self-commitment practical only if industry's conduct is subject to sufficient public control. Evidently, the federal government or the Ministry for the Environment is not convinced of the way batteries have been recycled so far either. How else can it be explained that the regulation of the 'product responsibility' for batteries appears in the federal government's catalogue of projects? If, however, it is true that industry has so far evaded the agreements that it concluded, doubts regarding the suitability of the instrument are in place. Self-regulation instead of government-imposed orders and prohibitions, as well as the exclusion of further financial charges on industry and trade, are the imperatives defined by the federal government for the next few years.

The discussion of economic instruments in environmental protection
Since the late 1980s, environmental groups and environmentally active scientists have intensively promoted the 'further development of environmental policy under market-regulating aspects' (Hansmeyer and Schneider, 1990). In the political arena, these attempts, as pointed out above, were barely met with any response after 1989–1990: Greenpeace – Germany's financially strongest and most popular environmental group – had some success in 'repoliticising' the subject of 'ecological taxes'. In advance of the parliamentary election campaign, it presented the results of a scientific study conducted

at its request about the effects of an ecological tax reform.[4] The conclusion of the study: an ecological reorganisation of the tax system – even if Germany did it on its own – would be 'legally possible, economically sensible, and socially compatible'. According to an Expertise prepared by the German Institute for Economic Research, a tax on all forms of energy and a simultaneous tax release for the factor of work as of 1995 would have resulted in a 21 per cent reduction in CO_2 emissions by 2005 and would, at the same time, have had a positive impact on the labour market (*Die Zeit*, 24, 1994). Neither the government parties nor the SPD took up the subject of ecological tax reform in their campaigns, probably not least because of the massive resistance announced by the leading industrial and trade associations against such a tax reform.

The attempts to continue handling the introduction of 'ecological taxes' or other economic instruments such as certificates or charges as a political taboo are met with increasing criticism. And such criticism comes from entrepreneurs as well. An increasing number of senior managers and entrepreneurs speaks up and vehemently criticises the defensive position taken by large employers' associations against an ecological modernisation of the economic system and the system of taxation (see, for example, *Der Spiegel*, 37, 1994 and 4, 1995). Even Daimler-Benz CEO Edzard Reuter pleaded 'for an unprejudiced discussion about ecological taxes' in the weekly *Die Zeit* (3, 1995). Although the breakdown of conflicts between environmental and trade associations announced jointly by the BUND and the BJU (see above) has not yet reached such leading trade associations as the Federation of German Chambers of Industry and Commerce or the Federal Association of German Industry, it has been accepted, in addition to the aforementioned individuals, for example by the Working Group of Independent Entrepreneurs (Arbeitsgemeinschaft Selbstständiger Unternehmer, ASU), which recommends that politicians test new models. With respect to air and water pollution control, the ASU is in favour of introducing certificates, and it is also open to discussions about 'ecological taxes' (*Die Zeit*, 43, 1994). 'Constant dripping wears away the stone': it seems as though the public discussion about the introduction of ecological taxes would be successful after all. Since the spring of 1995, corresponding concepts have been discussed by all political parties; however, no agreement between the different parties has yet been reached.

The concept of 'sustainable development'

Thus it seems that in the meantime the concept of 'sustainable development' is applied more stringently by some entrepreneurs and managers than by the politicians actually responsible. This criticism also includes the SRU. Although its Environmental Expertise of 1994 had the motto of 'permanent environmentally justifiable development' – a somewhat free translation of 'sustainable development' – and also provided a fundamental discussion of the term (Diefenbacher, 1994), its statements were of no significant help in the continuing 'struggle for the power of definition' of the still vague term. This can be attributed to the fact that the Environmental Expertise also defined sustainable development on the basis of the principle of precautionary protection of the environment. As Zimmermann (1990) proved quite impressively, the 'official governmental' adherence to the principle of precautionary protection of the environment is symbolic politics *par excellence*. Any reference to the principle of precautionary protection of the environment remains ineffective with regard to environmental policy until it can be determined how it is to be legally enforced in view of its collision with the legal principle of proportionality. The question at issue is how to define legal standards concerning the reasonableness of government interference in basic rights protected by constitutional law (e.g. property rights). If 'taking precautionary measures for the environment means acting as soon as there is the possibility of dangerous developments' (Töpfer, 1990), the concept of prevention becomes tied up in a circle of argumentation because, in the final analysis, its enforcement depends on the determination of the limits of danger and/or proof of concrete risks. In other words, a constitutional state cannot fulfil the principle of precautionary protection of the environment because 'its principle of operation as such – the risks, whose extent and probability are unknown' – is not compatible with the principle of precautionary protection (Zimmermann, 1990). For this reason, the definition of sustainable development as the 'leading concept for future environmental policy' (SRU, 1994) on the basis of the principle of precautionary protection does not take the matter one step ahead. The SRU, which wanted to define the concept more precisely, failed at the self-imposed task since it made no mention of the link between ecological and economic objectives, an especially problematic aspect in view of the more than four million unemployed (Vorholz, 1994). Not the discussion of the principle of precautionary protection, but the question as to the application and effects of polluter-oriented economic instruments, will decide the future of environmental policy. There is still no political-social agreement on what sustainable development concretely can or should mean for the further development of German environmental policy.

Main points of German foreign environmental policy

Global environmental problems

'We have to take responsibility beyond our borders in a European and worldwide environmental partnership ... Successful foreign environmental policy – disarmament in man's struggle against nature – will decide the survival of the German people and all people around the world', wrote Klaus Töpfer, Minister for the Environment, in his outlook for the twelfth legislative period (*Umwelt*, 2, 1991). His successor, Angela Merkel, sustained the priority of international co-operation for the thirteenth legislative period as well: 'In order to be able to confront effectively today's requirements in environmental protection, we must turn our attention more to the global context ... Germany will continue to act as a driving force behind this new global cooperation in environmental and development issues' (*Umwelt*, 1, 1995).

As far as the global dimension of environmental policy is concerned, the public discussion in Germany is currently absolutely dominated by climate problems. In advance of the summit in Rio de Janeiro, the federal government had tried to take an internationally leading position with respect to reducing CO_2 emissions. As early as June 1990, the cabinet took the decision to reduce German CO_2 emissions by 25 per cent by 2005, related to 1987. One year later, the first CO_2 reduction programme of the federal government was passed, which raised the goal to 25–30 per cent in view of German reunification. The Bundestag supported the objective of the government by passing a corresponding resolution in September 1991. With reference to internal government papers, Unfried (1994) shows that at the beginning of the 1990s the federal government was anxious:

> to take on the role of forerunner in environmental policy within the EU and internationally. An opportunity presented itself to the government in the form of a national resolution to reduce emissions. The advantage

offered by this resolution was that these 'symbolic' politics made possible a corresponding foreign policy success for a short period ... Furthermore, German reunification made it easier for the federal government to uphold its resolution to reduce emissions in the years after 1990, since enormous potential for reduction became evident in East Germany, which was caused by the effects of the economic breakdown and beginning reorganization. Thus, in Rio in 1992, Germany was still in a better starting position with respect to a national reduction of emissions than, for example, other states of the EC.

Germany was able to hold this 'head start' due to the favourable starting year, 1987: according to the Ministry for the Environment, CO_2 emissions dropped by about 15 per cent in all of Germany in the six years up to 1993 due to the industrial collapse of East Germany, whereas they continued to rise in the 'old' German *Länder*. Thus public criticism of the lack of concrete national climate protection measures was relatively strong despite the decrease in emissions recorded for all of Germany.[5] For this reason, the federal government decided 'to set an example' before the Climate Conference in Berlin (*Süddeutsche Zeitung*, 24 February 1995). In accordance with the aforementioned new orientation of the federal government with respect to environmental policy, it planned to have public and industrial power plant operators voluntarily agree to an improvement of the efficiency at their plants. If such voluntary commitments were made, the federal government would give up the heat utilisation ordinance it had been planning for a long time (*Süddeutsche Zeitung*, 24 February 1995).

The trade associations complied with the expectations of the federal government and published the Declaration of the German Industry on Climate Protection in March 1995. At first this declaration was generally interpreted as meaning that German industry had obligated itself to reduce its CO_2 emissions by 20 per cent by 2005 (e.g. *Süddeutsche Zeitung*, 11, 12 March 1995).

In advance of the summit in Berlin, 'many states found it increasingly difficult to consider Germany a forerunner' (*Süddeutsche Zeitung*, 21 February 1995). For German environmental diplomats, who had little to show except the 'free effects' provided by East Germany in connection with gas reductions, the 'worldwide first commitment of an economy to support climate protection' – as it was described by the Head of the Chancellor's Office – came at the best conceivable time. Thus it was possible to represent the German position in a more credible way, the aim of which was to obtain a mandate for the working out of a binding climate protocol. In this respect, the self-commitment of German industry to protect the climate contributed indirectly to the partial success of the Berlin Conference, which was aimed at precisely this mandate.

Nevertheless, it soon became evident that it would not be possible to add a corresponding national plus to this temporary advantage of German foreign environmental policy. If read carefully, the self-commitment turns out to be but a 'mere promise of industry' (Vorholz, 1995). The trade associations had declared their willingness only to 'undertake special efforts to reduce their specific CO_2 emissions or their specific energy consumption by up to 20 per cent by 2005 (base year: 1987)'. The decisive element of this declaration is the adjective 'specific'. It means that German industry wants to try to reduce its CO_2 emission per unit of value added, and this says nothing about total emissions: if total production rises, total emissions will probably also increase, even if the specific emissions were reduced, as was already the case in the German paper industry in the 1980s. In this industry, specific emissions dropped by 20 per cent, while total emissions rose by 7 per cent (Vorholz, 1995).

In view of the foreseeable limited effects of the self-commitment to climate protection, which, by the way, include the East German free effects since 1987 was chosen as the reference year and remain below the target strived for by the federal government, the question remains whether the federal government has not attained a Pyrrhic victory. At any rate, the Federal Association of German Industry agreed on the self-commitment only on the condition that the federal government would then definitely refrain from introducing energy taxes. This unjustified demand goes far beyond the concessions offered by the federal government – i.e. abandonment of the heat utilisation ordinance. It remains to be seen whether the trade associations will be able to abolish the freedom of legal arrangement with respect to environmental policy in the long run by pointing to their voluntary self-commitment. They opened a corresponding front in the spring of 1995.

Prittwitz (1990) has pointed out that the interests in environmental policy are not bipolar, i.e. with polluters and parties concerned about pollution taking opposite sides. Rather the interests of third parties – called 'helper interests' by Prittwitz – play an important part. The position of Germany with respect to global environmental problems is obviously also determined by the interests of these third parties. Such 'helper interests' became particularly evident in a positive sense when Germany stopped producing and using CFCs, which destroy the ozone layer. A similar decision was taken by the Bundestag in March 1991 in the form of the CFC and Halogen Ordinance, which stipulated that Germany would have completely withdrawn from the 'CFC industry' by January 1995 as the very first state in the world. The industry, which hoped for new markets for 'environmentally friendly products', had at its disposal substitute materials. Thus the Association of the Chemical Industry was able to present a credible voluntary self-commitment to stop using CFCs. CO_2 emissions can, however, be reduced only to a limited extent by means of technical innovations. That is the reason why there have not yet been any powerful intergovernmental 'helper interests' and why none are in sight. In this respect, environmental policy-makers will have to continue looking for allies.

European environmental problems
In addition to the characteristics of the national 'triangle of interests' with regard to specific problems, the respective foreign environmental policy is significantly determined by geographical location:

> Due to its geography, its links to the North, South, East and West, Germany is integrated in the entire European ecological cosmos. In every political area of environmental protection, the transnational interdependence is obvious. The Germans are involved as 'wrongdoer' and 'victim', polluter and party concerned with environmental pollution.
>
> (Strübel, 1992)

The development of European anti-air pollution policy and Germany's role in this connection show how fundamentally a country's self-definition can change to concern and what significance this has when building up efficient international environmental regimes.

At the UN conference in Stockholm in 1972, the delegation from Bonn was among those vehemently disputing the results presented in particular by Swedish scientists on the relationship between transboundary air pollution and environmental harm (for this and the following, see Pehle, 1991a). In the subsequent years, the government in Bonn substantially delayed internationally co-ordinated measures to reduce SO_2 emissions. Supported by Great Britain, it was partially successful with its proposal to keep the text of the Geneva Air Pollution Control Convention, which had been signed by 34 states in 1979, as vague as possible. Three years later, however, the German delegation came up with a surprise at a Conference on the Increasing Acidification of the Environment held in Sweden. It unexpectedly supported the demand to pass an international emission reduction programme with clear-cut, verifiable goals and obligations. All of a sudden Germany, next to Sweden, became a decisive driving force behind the so-called '30 Per Cent Club', named for its objective to reduce annual SO_2 emissions or the flow of CO_2 emissions across borders by this percentage. This change in attitude can be attributed to the intense national discussion about forest damage in Germany. German foreign environmental policy was fundamentally revised due to the country's new perception of itself as a country affected by environmental pollution. 'Helper interests' were also ready in the form of the growing pollution control technology industry.

A similar change of mind can be observed with respect to Germany's attitude towards international efforts to protect or restore the Baltic Sea (List, 1991; Pehle, 1995). The first international conference on marine environmental protection in the Baltic Sea – organised by Sweden in Visby in 1969–1970 – was dedicated to the problem of oil pollution. No results were achieved because the German representatives refused to sign a corresponding agreement.[6] When the Convention on the Protection of the Marine Environment of the Baltic Sea Area, called the Helsinki Agreement, had been signed by all states bordering the Baltic Sea in 1974, it was once again the federal government that prevented the agreement from coming into effect under international law until 1980. The reason for the inglorious delay of the ratification process is provided in the literature 'EC Problems':

> For Denmark and the Federal Republic of Germany it resulted from the fact that the EC, after issuing its first comprehensive directive in the field of water protection in 1976, was supposed to enter into an agreement about these issues for its member states. However, this was refused by the eastern participating states, putting the two EC states into the difficult situation of having to decide between adherence to European law and their regulatory interests relating to environmental policy.
>
> (List, 1991)

It is, however, a remarkable point that Denmark was able to get out of the dilemma three years before Germany. Evidently, the regulatory interests of the federal government with respect to environmental policy were not yet particularly marked in the 1970s.

The federal government was a vigorous supporter of the revised version of the Helsinki Convention presented in 1992. It also presented an ambitious national 'Programme for the Restoration of the Baltic Sea', which focused on twenty-seven high-priority sewage treatment plant projects in the new *Länder*, particularly in Mecklenburg–Western Pomerania. The German programme for reductions in the flow of nutrients from agriculture into the North Sea and the Baltic Sea shows, however, a structural weakness. According to estimates, half the nutrients discharged into these seas from German territory can be traced back to agriculture, only about 30 per cent comes from local sewage treatment plants. Whereas considerable expenditures are spent on modernisations of the latter – the Ministry for the Environment estimates that an investment volume of DM4–6 billion will be necessary (*Umwelt*, 3, 1991) – the main polluters are left alone. An important formal reason for this is that Germany has still not implemented the Nitrate Guideline of the European Community. The 'triangle of interests' developed by Prittwitz will prove helpful when determining why this is so. The restoration of sewage treatment plants is supported by 'helper interests', i.e. by the 'environmental industry'. Due to the powerful polluter interests, it has been impossible to integrate agriculture, i.e. the German Farmers' Association, in the restoration programme.

An analysis of the international efforts undertaken to restore the River Rhine, which are co-ordinated by the International Commission for the Protection of the Rhine River (Internationale Kommission zum Schutz des Rheins), shows that German foreign environmental policy always sets positive marks when the planned measures have conformed with the technological philosophy that continues to dominate governmental environmental policy. As is generally known, the water quality of the River Rhine has been considerably improved in recent years. Germany has contributed significantly to this; after all, 70–80 per cent of the total pollution load comes from German emitters (Strübel, 1992). The restoration of the River Rhine has been achieved by laying down emission limit values on the discharge of industrial and communal waste water, and taking into consideration the principle of using the best possible technical means available. It was not without reason that the restoration concept propagated by the International Commission for the Protection of the Rhine River focused on 'end-of-pipe technologies', which is still the dominating orientation in Germany. Strübel (1992) credits the national and international lobbying activities of the waterworks for their decisive contribution to the restoration of the River Rhine (the International Working Group of the Waterworks near the River Rhine was founded as early as 1970). Without the pressure exerted by the waterwork associations, which were concerned about the quality of the drinking water, Germany would probably not have commissioned the International Commission for the Protection of the Rhine River to work out a detailed and efficient restoration programme.

Summary

Mr Töpfer's term in office as Federal Minister for the Environment was marked by a clear-cut emphasis on international co-operation in environmental policy. However, Malunat (1994) considers this symbolic politics, claiming that it was an attempt to divert attention from national environmental problems. The concentration on foreign environmental policy was particularly suitable for 'winning back some of the trust among its own population that had been lost through national environmental policy'. It must, however, be doubted whether the activities of the Ministry for the Environment within the field of foreign environmental policy have been addressed to the German public – at least in recent years – because, faced with economic recession and increasing unemployment, the public has averted its attention from environmental issues.[7] The assumption put forth by Weidner (1991) seems much more plausible: 'that the Federal Minister for the Environment used international environmental policy as a vehicle to overcome obstacles in his own country'. The strategy of putting the national decision-making system under pressure by concluding agreements on environmental measures at the international level may prove to be counterproductive under certain circumstances. For instance, the Ministry for the Environment will suffer a double loss of prestige if it successfully supports ambitious objectives at international environmental conferences without being able to implement them at the national level: it loses international credibility and, at the national level, criticism is expressed of an environmental policy that does not live up to the promises behind it. A relevant example is the protection of the marine environment discussed above: Germany will not be able to meet its obligation to reduce the discharge of nutrients into the North Sea and the Baltic Sea by 50 per cent by the end of 1995. Although this has been quite clear for some time now, the Ministry for the Environment still upholds the reduction goals and target year verbally. Not only has this invoked the criticism of German environmental groups regarding the poor implementation of international environmental agreements, other states have also distanced themselves from the German position. At the same time, the overall assessment of German foreign environmental policy is still positive. However, euphoria is long gone. Malunat (1994) has summarised it as follows: 'The federal government played its part well on the international stage'. Yet he immediately modifies this statement by adding, 'even if it is no longer playing a leading part'. The loss of its former leading role in international environmental policy (see, for example, *Die Zeit*, 28, 1993) can above all be ascribed to national barriers against a modernisation of environmental policy. So far, these barriers have meant that the conventional patterns of regulatory policy are not abandoned. As will be discussed in the final section, this has also affected Germany's role in the environmental policy of the EU considerably.

The institutional foundation of foreign environmental policy

Formal competence
The Ministry of the Interior, which had been quite successful within environmental policy for many years, suffered an international defeat in the mid-1980s, i.e. before the handling of the Chernobyl crisis triggered the foundation of the Federal Ministry for the Environment. This defeat showed to what extent national environmental protection depended on international co-operation and how important it was to have experts and powerful representatives at the international level: Federal Minister of the Interior Mr Zimmermann's proposals for the introduction of motor vehicles with catalytic converters failed within the EC, and consequently he suffered a considerable loss of prestige in Germany.

In view of the fact that 'low-ranking government employees of the Federal Ministry of the Interior and staff of the politically subordinate Umweltbundesamt were usually concerned with the international representation of the Federal Republic with respect to environmental issues', Prittwitz (1984) demanded that the 'field be politically upgraded', thus thinking of the Ministry of Foreign Affairs:

> Also the Department for Foreign Affairs – which is responsible for international relations and has comparably good prerequisites for exerting political influence on the international level – could conduct systematic foreign environmental policy in cooperation with the relevant departments responsible for environmental protection.

With respect to the demand that foreign environmental policy be upgraded, the ministerial bureaucracy active in environmental protection agreed completely with Prittwitz's analysis, but not with the suggestion to transfer foreign environmental policy to the Ministry of Foreign Affairs: 'Negotiations in the field of environmental protection are so specialised that, although they do include issues of foreign policy, they could not be handled by the Department for Foreign Affairs and, if so, then only less effectively', claimed a section head in the newly founded Ministry for the Environment.[8] For the section heads responsible for issues related to international environmental protection, the establishment of the Ministry for the Environment, which was assigned the overall responsibility for foreign environmental policy without this having been explicitly discussed, was simply a logical step. They considered it a positive aspect that they were represented on the international stage by 'only a minister for the environment' after the foundation of the Ministry for the Environment. Probably, a 'Federal Minister for the Environment could not have pushed through completely the US values for motor vehicles in Brussels either' (Interview, BMU). Nevertheless, the transfer of the responsibility for foreign environmental policy to the newly created Ministry for the Environment was the only correct decision, because:

> In the entire international scene one had been wondering for a long time why the Federal Republic of Germany, which had become more and more progressive since 1981–1982, still did not have an independent ministry for the environment. That was never completely understood abroad ... Now we are in a better position – and more frequently in a position at all – to be present on a high international political level.
> (Interview, BMU)

Thus the establishment of the Ministry for the Environment was a step long overdue, namely 'pursuing the diplomatic preparation of decisive international agreements on a drastic reduction of air and water pollution with the political seriousness it deserved' (Mayer-Tasch, 1986).

This positive, fundamental attitude of the 'foreign environmental politicians' in the newly founded Ministry for the Environment was supported even more when the second German Minister for the Environment, Klaus Töpfer, established an independent 'Sub-Department for International Co-operation' as one of his first official acts. It originally comprised four sections and was subordinate to the central department. After a second internal reorganisation in 1990, the 'international' department was upgraded again. Another section was added and integrated as sub-section GII into the newly established department G ('Fundamental and economic issues of environmental policy/international co-operation'):

> The fundamental idea behind this reorganisation (was) that general issues would be handled in a central sub-department, so that the general aspects of international co-operation would not be handled separately by the individual sections ... This does not exclude that, as in the past, individual technical issues of international co-operation will remain the responsibility of specialised sections.
>
> (Interview, BMU)

Not only the responsibility for 'technical details' inevitably remained with the individual departments. As before, they handled all special technical problems, irrespective of whether they were international in scope or not, and the section heads of the specialised departments also maintained international contacts. The 'new' sub-department is, among other things, responsible for the drawing up of general concepts and guidelines of foreign environmental policy. When doing this, it is dependent on the preparatory work performed by the specialised sections. In other words, the internal need for co-ordination has risen with the establishment of the Sub-Department for International Co-operation. This is a problem which, in the opinion of the staff in the ministry concerned, should not be underestimated. At the same time, Töpfer's decision was (and is) considered to be correct: 'The technical issues have to be handled by special sections, but the representation of expert political knowledge towards the outside can be handled easier and more centrally through this sub-department' (Interview, BMU).

Even if international co-operation within the field of environmental protection has become a focal point in the work of the Ministry for the Environment since the 'era of Töpfer', this says little about the status of foreign environmental policy in overall government policy.

The status of foreign environmental policy

At its establishment, the Ministry for the Environment was assigned the task of representing Germany internationally in matters of environmental policy. This was evidently considered quite natural, because this aspect was not mentioned explicitly in the organisational decree issued by the chancellor at the time. Vice versa, however, this means that the Ministry for the Environment can or may represent only policies expressly assigned to it. Thus it is by no means the case that all areas of German foreign environmental policy are represented by the Ministry for the Environment. This point will be illustrated by means of the following examples.

In January 1994, the freighter 'Sherbro' lost several containers holding plastic packages containing the pesticide 'Apron Plus'. A large number of these 'poisonous bags' were washed on to German beaches. For several days, stories about these packages were headline news in the German press. Minister for the Environment Töpfer described the threat to the beaches of the North Sea as a 'warning that forces us to take action' (*die tageszeitung*, 25 January 1994). Action was, however, necessary internationally, so in this case it was not the German Minister for the Environment but the Minister of Transport who became active. At a conference convened in Paris, he supported a catalogue of measures that, in his words, was designed to reduce the probability of ship accidents in the interests of the environment. The following day, the German press spitefully commented on the lacking expert knowledge of the minister and his European colleagues. They had merely decided what had been effective international law for a long time. The Ministry for the Environment, which would probably have been able to present more expert-like arguments, did not comment on the insufficient representation of the federal government. The Chairman of the Environmental Committee of the Bundestag, a member of the CDU party, said in its place that: the agreements of Paris were 'probably not more than an attempt to calm the enraged public'. What was necessary was 'completely new regulations' on sea transportation of hazardous substances. Furthermore, the exportation of pesticides that are not allowed to be used in the EU should be prohibited (*Süddeutsche Zeitung, die tageszeitung,* both 28 January 1994). Such consequences of the 'poison bags scandal' were probably not placed on the international agenda by the federal government because the representation of Germany's environmental policy interests had been transferred to the Ministry of Transport.

The Ministry for the Environment also 'stood on the outside' in connection with another intensively discussed issue – the protection of drinking water. The debate was triggered by an EU Commission initiative for Amending the Guideline on Drinking Water. The main point of discussion in Germany was the planned changes in pesticide limit values. The leading role in the negotiations in Brussels was not taken by the Ministry for the Environment but the Ministry of Health, which, however, turned out to be an 'ally' of the Ministry for the Environment. Both ministries declared that they strictly opposed any 'softening' of the limit values (*Süddeutsche Zeitung,* 3 November 1994). The representation of interests was further complicated by the fact that the Ministry of Agriculture was responsible for the handling of the approval of pesticides, which is closely connected to the protection of drinking water. For a long time, there was insecurity about the position taken by the Minister of Agriculture in Brussels with respect to approval guidelines for pesticides. However, considerable public pressure, which was also supported by the state ministries of health (*Handelsblatt,* 15–16 October 1994), caused the Ministry of Agriculture to assume a relatively environmentally friendly negotiating position. Due to the incomplete technical competencies of the Ministry for the Environment – thus, the temporary conclusion – German foreign environmental policy is in part handled by 'polluter departments'. With respect to the question of whether the positions taken in these cases at the international or supranational level can actually be called 'foreign environmental policy' or should be described as the representation of interests in foreign affairs, has not been decided in the arena of environmental policy; it can at best be influenced 'from outside' by the actors involved in environmental policy.

Vice versa, the foreign environmental policy propagated by the Ministry for the Environment is not completely without influence from other areas of politics either. A prominent example is the formulation of the German position in advance of the Berlin Climate

Conference. The Ministry for the Environment had prepared a paper on Germany's position for a preparatory meeting in Geneva in the summer of 1994. This paper included a catalogue of measures for reducing CO_2 emissions. Four days before the conference was scheduled to begin, the parliamentary undersecretary from the Ministry of Economic Affairs informed the Minister for the Environment that the proposals worked out by the Ministry for the Environment could not be presented as the position of the German government in Geneva: 'I can only agree to such a presentation, when it is agreed between the federal departments' (*Der Spiegel*, 34, 1994). The co-ordination between the Ministry of Economic Affairs and the Ministry for the Environment, which had at least been attempted at the request of the Ministry for the Environment in the week before the 'veto' of the undersecretary, had taken place in an 'angry atmosphere' and had led to nothing but the Ministry of Economic Affairs' refusal of all proposals submitted by the Ministry for the Environment. The 'political isolation' of the Minister for the Environment in the cabinet (*Der Spiegel*, 34, 1994) had allowed the Ministry of Economic Affairs to undermine completely his initiative regarding foreign environmental policy.

A similar situation occurred when the Minister for the Environment wanted to start an initiative for the introduction of an EU-wide energy tax during the German Presidency of the Council. This project completely conformed with government policy. The Ministry of Economics informed the Ministry for the Environment publicly and without much ado: 'We do not have any ready formulas for a CO_2 energy tax' (*Die Zeit*, 8 July 1994). Thus the German initiative was implausible from the beginning in the Council of Environmental Ministers. Actually no one was surprised when the 'environment ministers of the European Union ... rejected the introduction of an EU-wide energy tax as proposed by Germany' (*Süddeutsche Zeitung*, 17–18 December 1994), because the Minister of Economics had made it sufficiently clear 'between the lines' that not the entire federal government but *de facto* only the Minister for the Environment seriously championed the energy tax.

In anticipation of the results of a research project currently underway, it should, in summary, at least briefly be indicated how the ministerial bureaucracy in the Ministry for the Environment assesses the problem: the Ministry for the Environment is obviously 'excluded' by other ministries, particularly when the government's comments or position papers on environmental issues within the EU are concerned. At the official level, it is evidently common practice to let the Ministry for the Environment participate at least 'after a fashion', i.e. the Ministry for the Environment is called in at such a late stage that comments can be drawn up only without preparation – frequently 'overnight' – or not at all any more. In the event that the Ministry for the Environment is in charge, competing departments frequently try to 'wall in' the environmental politicians. I would like to close this section by describing this strategy with an anecdote that seems most suitable for illustrating the status of the Ministry for the Environment in formulating and implementing German foreign environmental policy. When a ministry negotiates a guideline in Brussels, the official responsible for this task usually travels to Brussels alone to represent the position of his department. When the Ministry for the Environment negotiated the European guideline on the environmental impact assessment, the section head responsible for the matter at the time told me that two 'chaperones' from the Ministry of Transport, one from the Ministry of Economics, Ministry of Defence and Ministry of Agriculture respectively, and two observers from the *Länder* accompanied him. They had all been instructed to make sure that the Ministry for the Environment did not go too far in Brussels: 'An unbelievable extravagance. We travelled in a group the size of a soccer team. The other delegations merely smiled condescendingly'.

Foreign environmental policy in Germany is anything but a focal point of the government's work. At least in the recent past, the Ministry for the Environment has frequently been hindered much more energetically in its efforts to develop or present its own ideas for further international co-operation in environmental protection than in its national initiatives on environmental policy.

Germany and the environmental policy of the EU

The discussion about European environmental policy
As far as public opinion about the environmental policy of the European Community is concerned, a distinction can be made between three phases.

'Phase one' began around 1983, after the German federal government had made a surprising attempt to push through the US exhaust gas limit values for passenger cars as an EC directive. After

the initiative of the Federal Minister of the Interior, Mr Zimmermann, had failed in the face of the resistance put up by France,
Great Britain and Italy, there was a 'great political fuss' (on this
and the following, see Weidner, 1991). The public, which had
become more aware of ecological issues through the discussion
about forest damage at that time, got the impression that the EC
hindered Germany from taking effective measures, particularly
against air pollution. This opinion was definitely supported by the
public relations work of the German federal government, because
in this way it could divert attention from its contradictory strategy
regarding European policy, i.e. its refusal to introduce a speed limit
on the German Autobahn.

> In other areas the German federal government also strived for stricter
> guidelines. In this respect, the conservative-liberal government, rela-
> tively soon after taking office, took on the difficult role of 'forerunner'
> on the stage of supranational environmental policy with its many
> obstacles. It concentrated on areas where there was very high pressure
> to act in Germany.
>
> (Weidner, 1991)

As with the introduction of motor vehicles with catalytic converters,
it repeatedly met with resistance that was very difficult to
overcome. The ministerial bureaucracy, which was definitely used to
the incrementalistic 'policy of small steps', also considered
Germany's European partners to be a hindrance. Thus in 1987, for
instance, the competent section head in the Ministry for the Environment criticised the negotiations on the European directive for large
combustion plants as follows: 'this directive, which we have been
discussing for more than three years without making any significant
progress ... is an absolutely negative example' (Interview, BMU).

Quite appropriately, Gündling and Weber (1988) characterised
the attitude prevalent in Germany at least up to the mid-1980s as
follows:

> In public opinion Europe stands for the blown-up bureaucratic
> apparatus in faraway Brussels, which does nothing but delay urgently
> needed measures of environmental protection, water them down to
> ineffectiveness, or prevent them entirely. Concerned citizens and asso-
> ciations who see the slow and catastrophic deterioration of the envi-
> ronment day by day, more and more frequently demand that
> Germany return to going its own way in environmental policy.

After environmental protection had been designated an objective of EC policy in the Single European Act, opinions became more complex. 'Phase two' of the public discussion about EC environmental policy was marked by slowly growing differentiation. Scientific literature tried to make clear 'that Europe is not only a problem for environmental protection, but also a chance' (Gündling, 1988). This point of view prevailed in the press as well, which now had a better understanding of the vacillation of the European Commission and Council of Ministers between 'promoting economic interests' on the one hand and 'precautionary environmental policy' on the other. 'Does the EC Commission want environmental protection or not? It does not know itself,' concluded the *Süddeutsche Zeitung* (10–11 March 1990) and pointed out that the Commission, on the one hand, complained about the poor implementation of the Directive on Drinking Water in several member states – including Germany – while, on the other hand, it simultaneously presented a proposal for a directive on marketing pesticides that would undermine the Directive on Drinking Water.

Since about 1994, public opinion seems to have changed to such an extent that it is justifiable to speak about 'phase three' of the public discussion. At the end of Germany's Presidency of the Council, Germany's role in European environmental policy was criticised more and more often: 'The pacemakers of the European Union, which the Germans like to consider themselves, have become obstacles' (*EU Magazin*, 12, 1994; see also *Das Parlament* of 6 January 1995). The resistance of the federal government is directed primarily at the new regulatory philosophy of the European Commission. Up to the beginning of the 1990s, the Commission favoured the German approach, which – based on regulatory law – aimed at implementing regulations that referred to emissions or technology. Now it has become quite obvious that the Commission counts on the self-regulatory power of economics and societies, and France and Great Britain are vigorous supporters of this.[9] On the basis of various examples, the German press demonstrates and criticises the fact that the government's enthusiasm for environmental policy 'is diminishing considerably with respect to laying out procedural measures such as the introduction of economic regulatory instruments or the expansion of public participation' (*Das Parlament*, 6 January 1995). Germany has been left behind, so to say; it is trying to prevent, or at least delay, the new regulatory philosophy from being put into concrete terms by the Council of Ministers and, thus, it implements the decisions taken in Brussels into national law only haltingly, insufficiently and frequently with delay.

Three examples predominate in current news reports: first, the Joint System for Environmental Management and Environmental Plant Inspection, called 'Ecological Audit' in short, which the German government refused to approve for a long time in the Council of Ministers. Second, the directive on public access to official environmental files and information, to which Bonn was opposed for a long time, and which was finally implemented into national law in July 1994, i.e. with a delay of eighteen months. Third, there is the environmental impact assessment, which has for many years been at the centre of discussion about the insufficient implementation of European rules into German environmental law. In this respect, two court judgments caused a stir, both of which concerned the two-year delay in implementing the directive on the environmental impact assessment. The federal government had held the legal opinion that an environmental impact assessment was necessary only for projects started after the German law on environmental impact assessment had come into effect. This interpretation had already been rejected by the European Court of Justice in the summer of 1993 on the grounds that the directive makes the assessment of environmental compatibility mandatory for certain projects starting in 1988. The delayed implementation of the environmental impact assessment into German law could not cancel this provision, since it took precedence. In December 1994, the Higher Administrative Court of Koblenz followed the judgment of the European Court of Justice and repealed the decision to approve officially the construction of a new highway since no environmental impact assessment had been conducted. It can be expected that this much-discussed judgment will become a precedent for numerous projects, for which the planning work was started between 1988 and 1990, that would be subject to an environmental impact assessment (*Süddeutsche Zeitung*, 30 December 1994 and 9 January 1995). Not only did the judgment give reason to remind the public of the careless implementation of European environmental law, it was also an occasion to point out that the law on environmental impact assessment basically cannot be applied by the authorities because the federal government has still not passed the administrative regulations needed for this purpose, although these were announced more than four years ago (*Süddeutsche Zeitung*, 9 January 1995).

The Federal Republic of Germany has been markedly lagging behind developments in European environmental policy for several years – this conclusion is quite evident. The change in paradigm at the European level in favour of instruments of constitutional law illustrates quite clearly that the federal government has basically lost its ability to influence the formulation of European environmental policy. As a result of this change, which was met with an almost complete lack of understanding among the national decision-makers, Germany has, so to speak, to a large extent become detached from the train of European environmental policy. This inability to interpret the 'signs of the time' and, hence, to manoeuvre German environmental policy to a siding, can best be illustrated by the comments made by Bavaria's Minister for the Environment, Goppel. These comments could also be applied to 'official' environmental policy:

> The high scientific-technical standard of our country is reflected in the numerous, highly differentiated and sophisticated quality standards. They characterize German environmental law. This applies to limit values for pollution as well as to orders regarding minimization and optimization ... Purely bureaucratic procedures are of no use to the environment. For this reason, I demand that we break with the inappropriate, procedure-oriented environmental policy of the EU.
>
> (*Süddeutsche Zeitung*, 23 February 1995)

The problem with this standpoint is by no means that Goppel insists on high quality standards; rather it is the fact that he plays off qualitative regulations against procedure-oriented environmental law. It would be appropriate to strengthen the instruments of regulatory law to achieve effective public control over an industry 'left to itself' precisely because the federal government counts on more self-commitment by industry. Or to put it differently: in order to ensure that the modernisation of technology is environmentally compatible, a 'modernisation of democracy' (Zilleßen *et al.*, 1993) is absolutely essential. But precisely this is rejected by German environmental policy. In view of the circumstance that Germany does not only not execute the European trend towards developing further procedural instruments, but also severely thwarts it at the national level by eliminating already existing rights of participation (see above), it does to a large extent detach itself from the process of developing European environmental policy further. The criticism that there is no German 'environmental concept for the EC' expressed by Weidner as early as 1989 is still an accurate description of the problem today.

Outlook: setbacks and successes

The circumstance that the federal government has let itself be more or less 'run over' by the developments made in environmental policy by the EU can actually be ascribed to the fact that a consistent Europe-oriented strategy has never been worked out for this field of politics. Thus the 'Bonn–Paris' axis, which has played a determining role in many other European policy issues, does not apply in this connection. On the contrary, France has opposed Germany several times with respect to European environmental matters in the recent past.[10] For instance, a legal action filed with the European Court of Justice by the European Commission against the German Ordinance on Packaging Materials can be ascribed to an initiative made by the French government. The reason for lodging the complaint: German discrimination against non-returnable bottles constituted an obstacle to trade for the European beverage industry (*EU-Magazin*, 12, 1994).

The federal government has in general been on the defensive within the EC regarding its waste policy. The European Directive on Packaging Materials, for example, which was passed in December 1994 (against the votes of Denmark, the Netherlands and Germany), was, so to speak, a reaction against the fact that Germany was inundating Europe with its waste exports. The directive specifies that at most 45 per cent of a packaging material may be recycled. For all that, the defence strategy asserted by the federal government was partially successful and, in the opinion of the federal government, it was possible to avoid the worst: if it can be proven that there are corresponding recycling plants in the country, the upper recycling limits defined in the compromise that was finally worked out can be exceeded.

When one tries to pursue environmental politics without any future-oriented strategies, one has to be content with such types of success. As a matter of fact, all German 'reports of successes' in Brussels have been limited to such examples lately. Thus Germany's solo initiative prohibiting the production and marketing of PCP was finally confirmed by the Commission following severe disputes.[11] The fact that the European Commission revised its amendment to the Ordinance on Drinking Water, which had been vehemently discussed in Germany, in such a way that it also seemed acceptable to the

German waterworks can be attributed to 'protests from Germany' (*Süddeutsche Zeitung*, 5–6 January 1995).

In advance of the compromise finally reached in connection with the Directive on Drinking Water, which still needs to be passed by the Council of Ministers, the German government had already speculated on admitting a decision on the directive only after the enlargement of the EU had taken effect: 'The Ministry of Health is playing for time: After Austria and the Scandinavian countries enter the Community, the circle of countries saying no will be considerably enlarged', reported, for example, the *Handelsblatt* on 3 November 1994. At present, however, it seems doubtful whether the Scandinavian politicians responsible for environmental policy will find an ally in the federal government in connection with their plans to raise the standards of European environmental policy.

Notes

1   The establishment was realised at the initiative of Heiner Geissler, General Secretary of the CDU at the time, in view of the upcoming elections to the Landtag in Lower Saxory: 'At the time, I went to see the Chancellor and advised him to form an independent environmental agency and to make Walter Wallmann ... the new and first Minister for the Environment of the Federal Republic of Germany. That was a clear signal and – I am utterly convinced of this – helped us win the elections to the Landtag in Lower Saxony' (Geißler, 1993).

2   As a rule, the *Länder* execute federal laws as 'their own affairs', and the federal government's supervisory power is limited to the question of the legality of the administrative activities. An exception important with respect to environmental protection is nuclear energy.

3   It is no coincidence that the 'Bündnis 90/DIE GRÜNEN' party refrained from taking over the chairmanship of the environmental committee of the Bundestag after the 1994 elections, even though they could have claimed this position.

4   The special point was that Greenpeace had commissioned the German Institute for Economic Research (Deutsches Institut für Wirtschaftsforschung), an institution whose seriousness is not doubted, not even by the federal government because it also calls on this institute regularly.

5   All experts agree that the reduction goal can be achieved only through a marked reduction in the consumption of energy, which in turn seems possible only through an increase in energy prices. In this connection, Chancellor Helmut Kohl promised the President of the Association of German Industry that Germany would not enforce a price rise for energy on its own as early as the autumn of 1992, i.e. before the oblig-

ations entered into in Rio had been confirmed (*Die Zeit*, 47, 1992).

6 The reason for this refusal was that the government in Bonn feared 'that participating in a convention together with the German Democratic Republic would be the same as acknowledging East Germany under international law' (Dieter, 1993).

7 According to an opinion poll conducted by the 'Research Group Elections' in March, 65 per cent of the West German voters considered unemployment the 'most important political issue', whereas only 12 per cent named environmental protection. In Eastern Germany, 85 per cent named unemployment, and the issue of environmental protection was not even indicated here by the research group (*Süddeutsche Zeitung*, 26–27 March 1994). During the parliamentary elections, unemployment was a decisive issue for 40 per cent of all German voters, whereas environmental protection was decisive for only 6 per cent (*Der Spiegel*, 40, 1994).

8 In the following, I will quote from interviews that I have conducted with various section heads in the Ministry of the Environment in October 1987. These statements are entitled 'Interview, BMU'. For information about the context of these discussions, please see Pehle (1988b).

9 The criticism expressed by the different member states of the environmental legislation influenced by Germany is perceived as follows in Germany: 'already at an early time the federal government tried to influence the formulation of European environmental laws in such a way that it would create an advantage in know-how and a competitive advantage for its own highly developed environmental technology' (*EU-Magazin*, 12, 1994).

10 The reason for this may be that the French 'environmental industry' is steadily gaining significance. More than about one-third of the turnover on the European market for environmental protection products is transacted by German enterprises, which rank first within the EU. In the meantime, the French economy ranks second, with a share of 21 per cent.

11 The discussion about the German prohibition of PCP is another example of the Franco-German 'opposition in environmental issues'.

References

Barbian, Thomas W. (1992), Geschichte der Umweltpolitik, in Franz Joseph Dreyhaupt *et al.* (eds), *Umwelt-Handwörterbuch*, Berlin, Bonn, Regensburg, 154ff.

Berg, Michael von (1990), Umweltschutz in Deutschland. Verwirklichung einer deutschen Umweltunion, *Deutschland-Archiv*, 6, 897ff.

Bock, Bettina (1990), *Umweltschutz im Spiegel von Verfassungsrecht und Verfassungspolitik*, Berlin.

Bull, Hans-Peter (1973), *Die Staatsaufgaben nach dem Grundgesetz*, Frankfurt am Main.

Cornelsen, Dirk (1991), *Anwälte der Natur. Umweltschutzverbände in Deutschland*, München.

Diefenbacher, Hans (1994), Für eine dauerhaft-umweltgerechte Entwicklung. Das Gutachten 1994 des Sachverständigenrats für Umweltfragen, *Blätter für deutsche und internationale Politik*, 8, 1014ff.

Dieter, Robert (1993), *Das Umweltregime der Ostee. Völker- und europarechtliche Aspedte*, Tübingen.

Geißler, Heiner (1993), Heiner Geißler im Gespräch mit Gunter Hofmann und Werner A. Perger, Frankfurt/Main.

Gemeinsame Verfassungskommission (1993), *Bericht der Gemeinsamen Verfassungskommission* (Zur Sache 5, 1993), Bonn.

Gündling, Lothar (1988), Umweltschutz in einer übernationalen Wirtschaftsgemeinschaft, in Lothar Gündling and Beate Weber (eds), *Dicke Luft in Europa. Aufgaben und Probleme der europäischen Umweltpolitik*, 21ff.

Gündling, Lothar and Beate Weber (eds) (1988), *Dicke Luft in Europa. Aufgaben und Probleme der europäischen Umweltpolitik*, Heidelberg.

Hansmeyer, Karl-Heinrich and Hans Karl Schneider (1990), *Umweltpolitik. Ihre Fortentwicklung unter marktsteuernden Aspekten*, Göttingen.

Hartkopf, Günter and Eberhard Bohne (1983), *Umweltpolitik, Bd. 1. Grundlagen, Analysen und Perspektiven*, Opladen.

Hey, Christian and Uwe Brendle (1994), *Umweltverbände und EG. Strategien, Politische Kulturen und Organisationsformen*, Opladen.

Hucke, Jochen (1990), Umweltpolitik: Die Entwicklung eines neuen Politikfeldes, in Klaus von Beyme and G. Schmidt Manfred (eds), *Politik in der Bundesrepublik Deutschland*, Opladen, 382ff.

Hucke, Jochen and Arieh A. Ullmann (1980), Konfliktregelung zwischen Industriebetrieb und Vollzugsbehörde bei der Durchsetzung regulativer Politik, in Renate Mayntz (ed.), *Implementation politischer Programme. Empirische Forschungsberichte*, Königstein, Ts., 105ff.

Kimminich, Otto (1994), Umweltverfassungsrecht, in Kimminich, von Lersner and Storm (eds), *Handwörterbuch des Umweltrechts*, second edn., Berlin, 2462ff.

List, Martin (1991), *Umweltschutz in zwei Meeren. Vergleich der internationalen Zusammenarbeit zum Schutz der Meeresumwelt in Nord- und Ostsee*, München.

Mayer-Tasch, Peter-Cornelius (ed.) (1986), *Die Luft hat keine Grenzen. Internationale Unweltpolitik: Fakten und Trends*, Frankfurt/Main.

Malunat, Bernd M. (1994), Die Umweltpolitik der Bundesrepublik Deutschland, *Aus Politik und Zeitgeschichte*, 49, 3ff.

Mertes, Michael and Helmut G. Müller (1987), Der Aufbau des Bundesumweltministeriums, *Verwaltungsarchiv*, 4, 459ff.

Müller, Edda (1986), *Innenwelt der Umweltpolitik. Sozial-liberale Umweltpolitik – (Ohn)macht durch Organisation?*, Opladen.

Müller, Edda (1989), Sozial- Liberale Umwelt- politik von der kornere eines neuen Politikbereiches, *Aus Politik und Zeitgeschichte*, 47/48, 3ff.

Müller, Edda (1994), Zur Verwendung wissenschaftlicher Ergebnisse in der Umweltpolitik. Ein Kommentar aus der Regierungspraxis, in Axel

Murswieck (ed.), *Regieren und Politikberatung*, Opladen, 49ff.

Müller-Brandeck-Bocquet, Gisela (1993), Von der Fähigkeit des deutschen Föderalismus zur Umweltpolitik, in Volker von Prittwitz (ed.), *Umweltpolitik als Modernisierungsprozeß. Politikwissenschaftliche Forschung und Lehre in der Bundesrepublik*, Opladen, 103ff.

Pehle, Heinrich (1988a), Das Bundesumweltministerium: Neue Chancen für den Umweltschutz? Zur Neuorganisation der Umweltpolitik des Bundes, *Verwaltungsarchiv*, 2, 184ff.

Pehle, Heinrich (1988b), Das Bundesministerium für Umwelt, Naturschutz und Reaktorsicherheit (BMU) – alte Politik im neuen Gewand?, *Gegenwartskunde*, 2, 259ff.

Pehle, Heinrich (1991a), Umweltpolitik in Schweden und Deutschland, *Nordeuropa-Forum*, 3, 17ff.

Pehle, Heinrich (1991b), Umweltpolitische Institutionen, Organisationen und Verfahren auf nationaler und internationaler Ebene: Wirkungsvoll oder symbolisch, *Politische Bildung*, 2, 48ff.

Pehle, Heinrich (1996), *Umweltschutz in der Ostseeregion. Schweden und Deutschland als Vorreiter im Umweltregime für die Ostsee?*, in Bernd Hennigsen and Bo Stråth (eds), *Deutschland, Schweden und die Ostsee-Region*, Baden-Bachn, 54ff.

Peine, Franz-Joseph (1992), Geschichte des Umweltrechts, in Franz Joseph Dreyhaupt *et al.* (eds), *Umwelt-Handwörterbuch*, Berlin, Bonn, Regensburg, 242ff.

Pötzl, Norbert F. (1982), Riesenhaft dimensioniertes Stückwerk. Die Umweltpolitik der sozialliberalen Koalition, in Wolfram Bickerich (ed.), *Die dreizehn Jahre. Bilanz der sozialliberalen Koalition*, Reinbeck b. Hamburg, 103ff.

Prittwitz, Volker von (1984), *Umweltaußenpolitik. Grenzüberschreitende Luftverschmutzung in Europa*, Frankfurt, New York.

Prittwitz, Volker von (1990), *Das Katastrophenparadox. Elemente einer Theorie der Umweltpolitik*, Opladen.

Prittwitz, Volker von (ed.) (1993), *Umweltpolitik als Modernisierungsprozeß. Politikwissenschaftliche Forschung und Lehre in der Bundesrepublik*, Opladen.

Schmidt, Manfred G. (1992), *Regieren in der Bundesrepublik Deutschland*, Opladen.

SRU (1994), Umweltgutachten 1994 des Rates von Sachverständigen für Umweltfragen: Für eine dauerhaft-umweltgerechte Entwicklung, *Bundestag-Drucksache 12/6995*.

Strübel, Michael (1992), *Internationale Umweltpolitik. Entwicklungen, Defizite, Aufgaben*, Opladen.

Umwelt. Eine Information des Bundesumweltministeriums, verschiedene Ausgaben.

Umweltbundesamt (1993), *Umweltschutz – ein Wirtschaftsfaktor*, Berlin.

Unfried, Martin (1994), *Regierungspolitik gegen Klimakatastrophe. Die deutschen CO_2-Minderungsbeschlüsse von 1990/91 und die Schwierigkeiten einer querschnittsorientierten Umweltpolitik*, unpublished master's thesis at the University of Erlangen-Nürnberg.

Vorholz, Fritz (1994), Schlechte Noten. Das Umweltgutachten 1994 wurde vorgelegt, *Die Zeit*, 9, 24.

Vorholz, Fritz (1995), Rechnen schwach. Umweltschutz: Die Regierung fiel auf ein leeres Versprechen der Industrie herein, *Die Zeit*, 12, 28.

Weidner, Helmut (1989), Die Umweltpolitik der konservativ-liberalen Regierung. Eine vorläufige Bilanz, *Aus Politik und Zeitgeschichte*, 47–48, 16ff.

Weidner, Helmut (1991), Umweltpolitik – Auf altem Weg zu einer internationalen Spitzenstellung, in Werner Süß (ed.), *Die Bundesrepublik in den achtziger Jahren. Innenpolitik, Politische Kultur, Außenpolitik*, Opladen, 137ff.

Wilhelm, Sighard (1990), *Ökosteuern. Marktwirtschaft und Umweltschutz*, München.

Wilhelm, Sighard (1994), *Umweltpolitik. Bilanz, Probleme, Zukunft*, Opladen.

Zilleßen, Horst et al. (eds) (1993), *Die Modernisierung der Demokratie. Internationale Ansätze*, Opladen.

Zimmermann, Klaus (1990), Zur Anatomie des Vorsorgeprinzips, *Aus Politik und Zeitgeschichte*, 6, 3ff.

The Netherlands: a net exporter of environmental policy concepts

One of the stereotypes of the Netherlands is that of a small, clean and neatly organised country. There can be no doubt that it is small. Of all fifteen EU member states, only Belgium and Luxembourg are smaller. At the same time, the Netherlands has the sixth-largest population in the EU. With an average 366 inhabitants per km², it is one of the most densely populated states in the world. This fact justifies some doubts about the actual cleanness of the country. Although backyards may be swept and tidied several times a week, environmental problems are severe and ubiquitous. Well-developed industries, highly intensive agriculture, intense traffic and a generally high level of consumption all contribute to this. An additional factor is the geographical situation of the Netherlands, surrounded by other heavily industrialised regions and downstream of the Rivers Rhine, Meuse and Schelde. This is not to say that the Dutch do not try to clean up their country. Given the tendency to be neatly organised, considerable efforts have also been put into the organisation of environmental policy. Policy programmes, expounding principles, plans and approaches to deal with all kinds of environmental problems, have abounded in the past decades. The National Environmental Policy Plan, published in 1989, in particular, received, broad international attention. The policy concepts contained in the plan were actively propagated by the Dutch government in the international context, including the EU. Together with relatively firm stands taken in several international environmental negotiations, the plan gave the Netherlands a reputation as one of the more environmentally progressive states in Europe.

This chapter will first review the broad lines of domestic environmental policy in the Netherlands. After a concise historical sketch, the main characteristics of the institutional context will be described. This will be followed by an analysis of the evolving relationship between economy and ecology in Dutch policy. The second part of the chapter will deal more specifically with the foreign policy aspects of the environmental field. First, the most important substantive themes on the 'foreign environmental policy agenda' will be outlined. Subsequently, attention will be paid to the way international and EU environmental negotiations are prepared domestically. Finally, the Dutch perception of European integration and its relationship with environmental issues will be discussed.

Environmental problems and policies in the Netherlands: an overview

The beginning: local problems, local policies

The first environmental policy measures in the Netherlands were aimed at urban pollution. By the end of the Middle Ages, local authorities were already attempting to regulate, for instance, the disposal of waste and the use and discharge of water in the expanding towns (Diederiks and Jeurgens, 1989). In the nineteenth century, the pace of urbanisation rapidly accelerated. Large concentrations of people emerged around the new industrial centres. Sanitary conditions were poor and cholera epidemics occurred. In accordance with prevalent ideas about state intervention, the responsibility for improving the situation was largely left to the communities. Measures included the provision of clean drinking water and the abolishment of open sewers, but these measures were taken only reluctantly. The construction of genuine sewage systems was not taken up seriously before 1900 (van Zon, 1986).

The precursors of present-day environmental policy in the Netherlands were thus closely linked to issues of public health and hygiene. The only way for public authorities to influence environmental impacts of industrial activities in a somewhat broader sense was through the Nuisance Act (Hinderwet), established in 1875, but with origins in Napoleonic times. Through a licensing procedure, the act sought to control the danger, damage and nuisance caused by industrial (and increasingly also other) installations. For about a century, the Nuisance Act remained uncontested as the basic legal tool for environmental policy in the Netherlands. From the 1970s, its function was gradually taken over by several more specific laws (see below), and in 1993 it was merged entirely into the Environment Act (Wet Milieubeheer, cf. Brussaard *et al.*, 1993).

In the Netherlands, as in most other Western countries, nature conservation was a second cornerstone of public involvement with environmental degradation. Around the turn of the century, concern mainly among the urban elites about the rapid reclamation of land and the loss of natural areas led to the establishment of the Dutch Foundation for the Protection of Birds (Nederlandse Vereniging tot Bescherming van Vogels, 1899) and the Foundation for the Preservation of Natural Monuments in the Netherlands (Vereniging tot Behoud van Natuurmonumenten in Nederland, 1906) (Gorter, 1986; van Noort, 1988).

As in the other north-west European democracies, the years after World War II were characterised by rapid economic growth and the development of the welfare state. A typical feature of the Netherlands in this period was the far-reaching division of social and political life according to religion and the culture of government by consensus and compromise between the highest levels of those confessional 'pillars' (Lijphart, 1968). In the mid-1960s, the first protests against the dominant ideology of economic growth and mass consumption emerged. Inspired, among other things, by Rachel Carson's *Silent Spring* (1962) and a limited number of Dutch publications (Briejèr, 1967), environmental pollution was among the central issues of the new movement. At the same time, the 'pillarised' structure of Dutch society started to erode, making room for other, more unconventional ways of political participation. The environmental protest groups that accompanied some large industrial and infrastructural projects in the late 1960s were thus part of a more general tendency and heralded a profound change in the perception of, and approach to, environmental problems (Boender, 1985; van Noort, 1988; Cramer 1989).

The early 1970s: the alarm phase
Between 1968 and 1972, the consciousness of environmental problems quickly spread beyond the limited circles of experts and activists. This is not the place for a profound analysis of the social and political backgrounds of this development, but some factors may be mentioned.

Apart from the processes of 'depillarisation' and democratisation and the related rise of new protest movements, which stimulated the susceptibility to a broader range of social problems than before, it cannot be denied that some of the negative consequences of industrial society started to become visible during the 1960s, also to the general public. Most conspicuous was the problem of water pollution, e.g. the accumulation of foam in water courses caused by detergents and the serious (and malodorous) pollution of surface water by organic waste from the sugar and potato starch industries. Although these kinds of problems were not unique to the Netherlands, the high population density and the relatively late, but rapid industrialisation after World War II may have added to their urgency (Tellegen, 1983).

The public interest in environmental problems was further strengthened by the stream of alarming publications in this field in the late 1960s and early 1970s. The *Limits to Growth* report to the Club of Rome (Meadows, 1972) was, in particular, a bestseller: it was estimated that about half of the world sales of the book took place in the Netherlands (Groen, 1988).

The rising concern about pollution led to the preparation of the first specific environmental laws in the late 1960s (see below). The issue was given more political weight through the establishment of the Ministry of Public Health and Environmental Hygiene (Volksgezondheid en Milieuhygiëne, VoMil) in 1971. This happened in the context of the formation of the Biesheuvel Cabinet, which was – as most other cabinets in the decades after the World War II – dominated by the Christian Democrats. One of the first products of the new ministry was the so-called Emergency Memorandum on Environmental Hygiene (Urgentienota Milieuhygiëne, 1971–1972), which explored the policy field and attempted to set out a strategy for future policies. The document illustrated the way environmental problems were perceived at the time.

The first part of the Emergency Memorandum contained an extensive and fundamental analysis of the character and causes of environmental problems, taking into account a wide variety of social, economic and technical aspects. A considerable gap existed, however, between this analysis and the second part of the document. It worked out plans in thirteen priority areas, including, first of all, water pollution, but also, for instance, air pollution, soil degradation and noise. The measures proposed for each area remained largely unrelated and continued to have a strong focus on public health and hygiene. In fact even the hygienic aspects of outdoor recreation and the abatement of mice and rats were among the thirteen priorities listed in the memorandum (for a more extensive analysis, see, among others, van Tatenhove, 1993; Leroy, 1994).

The 1970s: cleaning up

Although the complexity of environmental problems was explicitly acknowledged in the first part of the Emergency Memorandum, it expressed a fairly optimistic view on the development of the policy field. It was estimated that the trend of further environmental degradation could be 'substantially adjusted' within five to ten years. After that, efforts should be directed at setting strict environmental limits to future economic, technical and social development (Urgentienota Milieuhygiëne, 1971–1972: 22). Thus at the same time, the memorandum reflected both the widespread sense of serious and profound crisis and the unshattered belief in the power of state intervention to solve such a crisis. The reality of the 1970s turned out to be different, however.

The first environmental laws had already been adopted before the new ministry was founded, notably the Surface Water Pollution Act (Wet Verontreiniging Oppervlaktewater, 1969, which had been discussed since 1964) and the Air Pollution Act (Wet Luchtverontreiniging, 1970). Several other laws followed in the course of the 1970s, for instance, regarding seawater pollution (1975), chemical waste (1976), waste (1977) and noise (1979). The basic philosophy of this legislative programme was characterised by Leroy (1994) as a combination of generalisation and differentiation. Generalisation refers to the widening of the use of the environmental licence as the main instrument to control pollution from the Nuisance Act to all new legislation. The dominance of the licence – an instrument hardly able to stimulate novel approaches to problems – stressed the basically reactive character of environmental policy in the 1970s. Differentiation or 'sectorisation' refers to the tendency to divide the environmental policy field into several small sectors, each to be governed by their own laws and regulations. This tendency made it very difficult to ensure the necessary coherence between the measures (van Tatenhove, 1993). In spite of the ambitions of the Emergency Memorandum, all attention in this period was directed only at the control of the wide variety of existing sources of pollution. The

Social Democratic intermezzo under Prime Minister Den Uyl between 1973 and 1977 did not change much in this respect.

In the field of water pollution, for instance, the levy under the new Surface Water Pollution Act provoked a rapid decrease in industrial discharges and made possible a massive and successful effort to set in place an extensive system of public sewage treatment. It was particularly effective in reducing the most basic form of water pollution, i.e. organic (oxygen-demanding) substances (cf. Bressers, 1983; Andersen, 1994). One of the main focuses of air pollution policy in the 1970s was the health effect of SO_2 in urban areas. Concentrations of SO_2 in the air actually decreased around 1974, but this was due only partly to measures to reduce the sulphur content of fuels. The main reasons for the lower concentrations were the oil crisis and the increased use of the natural gas that had been found in the northern part of the country some years earlier. After 1977, however, concentrations of sulphur in the air started to increase again (SO_2 Beleidskaderplan, 1979–1980). It was not until the early 1980s that policies were introduced to deal with emissions from industrial sources.

Perhaps the best illustration of the necessarily reactive character of environmental policy in this period was the emergence of the issue of soil pollution. The discovery of heavy pollution under a residential area at the end of the 1970s marked the development of an extensive programme to clean up old industrial sites and waste dumps all over the country, often at very high costs. Because of this complication, a comprehensive law on soil protection, which had already been announced in the Emergency Memorandum, was first adopted in 1986 and had to be preceded by temporary *ad hoc* legislation (Brussaard *et al.*, 1993).

The 1980s: the response to fragmentation

It became more and more apparent that the gradual emergence of Dutch environmental policy was inadequate. Except for some specific problems, the environmental situation continued to deteriorate. The rapidly growing body of environmental measures could hardly keep track of existing problems. The essence of the diagnosis at the end of the 1970s was that sectorisation had turned into fragmentation.

Difficulties were first felt in the procedural field. The authority to grant licences was distributed among a multitude of public agencies. All three basic levels of government were involved (central government, provinces and municipalities) as well as several functional branches of government. With the General Environmental Provisions Act (Wet Algemene Bepalingen Milieuhygiëne) of 1980, a start was made to come to a single licensing procedure. In its attempts to streamline and simplify procedural arrangements, the new act, in a sense, anticipated the ideology of 'deregulation', which started to emerge in Dutch politics in the first half of the 1980s.

It soon became clear, however, that more fundamental organisational and conceptual factors lay at the heart of the problem. Because of the fragmented institutionalisation of the new policy field, it had become almost impossible to take into account the connections both between the 'sectors' of environmental policy and with other policy fields such as physical planning, water management or agricultural policy. Therefore, the key word for innovation in the 1980s became 'integration' (for more detail, see van Tatenhove and Liefferink, 1992; van Tatenhove, 1993).

Apart from bottlenecks perceived in the implementation and the effectiveness of policies, a more profound understanding of the seriousness, scale and complexity of environmental problems also played a role in this period. The rise of the issue of 'acid rain' may be exemplary of this change. Air pollution policy in the 1970s focused on the health effects of single pollutants in predominantly local settings. The long-range transport of particularly SO_2 was acknowledged, but its impact was supposed to be limited to sensitive lakes in Scandinavia. Reports about damage to forests and aquatic ecosystems in Germany and also the Netherlands in the beginning of the 1980s necessitated a re-appraisal of the existing policy approach. First, acidification involved a large variety of sources, from refineries to cars. An effective policy would have to encompass all source categories. Second, it stressed the international aspect not only of the pollution of seas and the protection of Antarctica, but also of apparently 'domestic' environmental problems. Third, concern about the health of forests and lakes helped to introduce more ecocentric elements into environmental policy. The increased attention paid to problems such as the eutrophication of water and soil or the disposal and processing of household and chemical waste had to a large extent a similar effect (cf. Leroy, 1994).

Consistent with the central role of planning in the Dutch administrative system (see below), the first impulses for a more integrated approach to environmental policy were worked out in a series of annual 'Indicative Multi-year Programmes' for the Environment (Indicatieve Meerjarenprogramma's Milieubeheer, IMP), starting in 1984 for the period 1985–1989. They were published by the Ministry of Housing, Physical Planning and Environment (Volkshuisvesting, Ruimtelijke Ordening en Milieubeheer, VROM), which was established through reorganisation in 1982. This departmental reorganisation was an indication of the recognition that environmental problems had increasingly transcended the narrow frame of public health.

According to the IMPs, policies were to be developed along two complementary lines. First, 'effect-oriented policies' were no longer directed at the old sectors of the environment, but at five themes: acidification, eutrophication, diffusion of substances, disposal of waste, and disturbance (including noise, odour, local air pollution, etc.). Later, climate change, dehydration and squandering were added. Policy objectives were formulated for each theme, encompassing all relevant sources and policy levels and including also the international level to an increasing degree. Second, coherent 'source-oriented' policies were to be developed for various groups of polluters, such as traffic and transport, industry and refineries, and households (or consumers). At the same time, a shift was to be made from the 'command-and-control' approach of the 1970s to more communicative strategies.

In the terms of the IMPs, the target groups were supposed to 'internalise' responsibility for the environment in their daily activities. The slightly moralistic overtone in the discussion about 'internalisation' was aptly summarised in the appeal to behave like a 'guest in one's own house'. This was the title of the political testament of the Minister of the Environment, the Liberal Pieter Winsemius, who instigated the new policy approach (Winsemius, 1986). From a pragmatic point of view, the establishment of a more collaborative relationship with actors in society was meant to increase their commitment to environmental policies. In a more general sense, the emergence of the concept of 'internalisation' reflected the tendency towards declining confidence in the state's problem-solving capacity, which could be observed in many Western democracies in this period.

Towards the 1990s: the emergence of a global view
The IMPs of the 1980s were presented as the first products of a new, comprehensive system of long-term environmental policy planning.

Two publications, from 1988 and 1989, respectively, finalised the establishment of this system: the first national 'state of the environment' report with the ominous title 'Concern for tomorrow' (Rijksinstituut voor Volksgezondheid en Milieuhygiëne (RIVM), 1988), and the first National Environmental Policy Plan (Nationaal Milieubeleidsplan, NMP, 1988–1989). On the basis of the alarming situation sketched in the former report, the first part of the NMP offered a broad, analytical perspective on environmental policy-making. In the second part, concrete targets and measures were proposed for the years 1990–1994 and beyond. Not only the structure of the document, but also the striking gap between the analysis of the problem and some of the suggested measures were reminiscent of the 1972 Emergency Memorandum. For all that, the NMP contained a number of substantial policy proposals and raised considerable controversies, which even played a role in a government crisis in May 1989. However, both the domestic upheaval and the broad international interest in the NMP may have contributed to a certain overestimation of the novelty and importance of the NMP. It has no doubt been an influential vehicle for the further development and the 'export' of the theme-oriented policy organisation and the target group approach (cf., for example, the EU's Fifth Environmental Action Plan; EU, 1993; Kronsell, 1997), but it should be noted that the conceptual basis of this had already been laid in the IMPs of the mid-1980s. Moreover, it turned out to be more difficult than anticipated to implement several of the concrete policy proposals in the NMP (cf., e.g. NMP-Plus, 1989–1990).

The end of the 1980s witnessed a temporary upswing in public attention for environmental issues in the Netherlands. The conclusions of the 1988 report and the political fuss about the NMP no doubt played a role in this connection. But the appearance of the Brundtland Report *Our common future* (WCED, 1987) did not go unnoticed in the Netherlands, and in 1988 even the Queen's Christmas address was devoted to the topic of the environment. In particular, concern about global environmental problems, such as the greenhouse effect and the depletion of the ozone layer, rapidly increased in this period. After the 1992 Rio Conference, however, public interest in the environment declined rapidly, basically due to increasingly pressing economic problems.

International environmental policy was also given a prominent place in the NMP. Not only did the seriousness of global environmental change as such provoke Dutch efforts at the national and the international level, but it also stressed that effective policies abroad were necessary to reach the ambitious domestic environmental targets, for instance, in the fields of water and air pollution. This trend was carried out in follow-up programmes. The second NMP even formulated reduction targets for acidifying substances in neighbouring countries (NMP2, 1993–1994: 80). On the one hand, this approach acknowledged that processes of growing international interdependence and globalisation have an ecological dimension as well, and it confirmed the Dutch commitment to international environmental negotiations. On the other hand, it made the success of Dutch environmental policy explicitly dependent upon foreign policy measures and the uncertain outcomes of international agreements.

The institutional context

Legal framework
Environmental protection was not included in the Dutch constitution until 1982. This happened in the framework of the most encompassing revision of the constitution since 1815. During the first preparations of the revision in the mid-1960s, only general reference was made to the 'liveability' of the country and to the protection of public health. In the final text, 'protection and improvement of the environment' (in a broad sense) was added as an explicit field of government care (cf. Tonnaer, 1990: 16ff.). As described above, however, a firm legal basis for environmental policy had already been built up during the 1970s in the form of a considerable number of specific environmental laws.

The sectoral laws of the 1970s had two major features (cf. Drupsteen, 1990; Tonnaer, 1990: 140ff.). The first one was their procedural character. The laws themselves mainly provided the legal framework for concrete norms, such as emission limits or requirements to products or processes. The instrument most commonly used to lay down such norms was (and still is) the government decree (Algemene Maatregel van Bestuur). A government decree is issued under the responsibility of the entire cabinet, but without formal intervention by parliament. Mostly, however, drafts for more substantial decrees are announced and discussed in the policy programmes periodically issued by the government, and this offers parliament an opportunity of giving its comments at a relatively early stage. Ministerial regulations are issued by a single minister and usually refer to a more limited subject matter. The established concrete, but still general norms, together with the relevant policy plans and programmes, form in turn the basis for the authorisation of specific plants or activities.

The second characteristic of the first generation of environmental laws in the Netherlands was the strong and, at first, almost exclusive reliance on licensing systems. The Surface Water Pollution Act, the Air Pollution Act and many others, all, in principle, prohibit polluting activities *unless* an authorisation has been obtained. In most cases, licences are granted by provinces or municipalities (see below).

In 1980, a start was made with the establishment of an integrated law on the environment, the General Environmental Provisions Act (Wet Algemene Bepalingen Milieuhygiëne). New chapters were added to it subsequently. At first, for instance the chapters on licensing, environmental impact assessment and finance had had a predominantly procedural focus. Gradually, however, focus shifted to arrangements with a more substantive character. The new integrated planning system (see below) was laid down in the act. In the beginning of the 1990s, a number of the earlier sectoral laws were incorporated into it. This operation included the Nuisance Act, regulating a wide variety of small sources, and laws on waste and chemical waste. In order to reflect its evolving status as a genuine framework law, the General Environmental Provisions Act was then renamed the Environment Act.

Organisation at the state level

For the elaboration and implementation of environmental policies, the Ministry of VoMil was set up in 1971. As pointed out above, the main focus of the new ministry was public health, but from the beginning, the environmental policy field came under the responsibility of the minister himself. The only exception was a short period in 1981–1982, during which a state secretary (*staatssecretaris*, hierarchically positioned immediately below the level of a cabinet minister) was the first in charge of environmental policy.

However, several important aspects of the environmental policy remained under the care of other governmental departments. This created a need for extensive co-ordination. The succession of the Ministry of VoMil by the Ministry of VROM in 1982 only partly solved this problem of fragmentation.

Most conspicuously, the entire area of water pollution was deeply rooted in the domain of water management and still comes under the competence of the Ministry of Transport and Public Works (Verkeer en Waterstaat). The ministry's powerful Directorate-General for Public Works (Rijkswaterstaat) deals with both water quantity – an important issue in the 'Low Countries' – and water quality. Together with its branches at the provincial level, it is responsible for, among other things, licensing discharges into the larger water courses in the Netherlands, the so-called 'state waters'. The control of smaller water courses is the competence of the provinces, but in most cases it has been delegated to the waterboards (*waterschappen*). These are public, semi-autonomous and semi-democratic institutions, traditionally charged with the water quantity management within their territory (cf. Drupsteen, 1990; Andersen, 1994).

Physical planning is a major, well-developed policy field in the Netherlands. Plans and programmes at the national, provincial and municipal levels have attempted to control the use of every inch of available space in the densely populated country. They have been established through heavy, time-consuming procedures of public participation and political decision-making. Physical planning obviously has close links to environmental policy. Until 1982, the two policy fields were handled separately by the Ministry of Housing and Physical Planning (Volkshuisvesting en Ruimtelijke Ordening) and the Ministry of VoMil, respectively. The new Ministry of VROM formally brought them together. The initial focus on 'command-and-control' strategies in environmental policy and the long-established tradition of detailed planning in physical planning, however, made it difficult to achieve an integration in practice. An important test case was the publication of a number of basic long-term policy plans around 1990, including the first NMP in 1989 and the Fourth Memorandum on Physical Planning (Vierde Nota over de Ruimtelijke Ordening, 1988–1989). Strong criticism of the lack of co-ordination between the two documents was an important factor behind the development of a 'region-oriented' approach, which arose as a third policy approach after the 'source-oriented' and 'target group-oriented' policies, which had been introduced in the 1980s (see above). The region-oriented policies as they are implemented at this moment in the Netherlands aim to integrate environmental and physical planning within a designated region. A further characteristic of this approach is the involvement of a large variety of governmental and non-governmental actors in a consensual model of decision-making (Driessen and Glasbergen, 1994). It can, therefore, be regarded as an attempt by the Ministry of VROM to overcome not only the separation between environmental policy and physical planning, but also the rivalries with other governmental departments, at least at the regional level (van Tatenhove, 1993).

The Ministry of Agriculture, Nature Conservation and Fisheries (Landbouw, Natuurbeheer en Visserij) is responsible not only for agricultural policy, but also, since 1982, for the protection of natural reserves and landscapes. It has often been criticised for systematically marginalising nature conservation *vis-à-vis* traditional agricultural interests. It is important to note, however, that issues of nature conservation seldom led to struggles between the Ministries of VROM and Agriculture. Consistent with the focus of the Ministry of VROM, controversies between them were mainly about typical pollution issues, such as manure from livestock industry and pesticides.

Finally, the Ministry of Economic Affairs (Economische Zaken) has no direct competences in the field of pollution control or environmental management. It does, however, co-ordinate industrial and energy policy, which renders it a major party in various environmental problems, such as acidification or the greenhouse effect.

The Netherlands has no genuine environmental agency. Tasks in the field of policy implementation and control, which are delegated to a broad executive body in some other countries, are carried out by various institutions in the Netherlands. As mentioned above, practically all licences are granted by local, provincial or state authorities. The only specialised agencies involved in environmental licensing are the water boards. An important role in monitoring and collecting environmental data is played by the RIVM (National Institute of Public Health and Environmental Protection), which dates back to the beginning of this century. Since 1988, it has biannually published the national 'state of the environment' reports (see above).

The role of local and provincial government
As pointed out above, care for public health and the environment was originally largely in the hands of local government. The rise of environmental concern around 1970, however, led to a host of legislation at the state level. As a result, local autonomy was gradually replaced by various, often precisely defined, executive tasks. A rela-

tively high degree of centralisation is not uncommon in the Netherlands. It should be noted, however, that in other policy fields local autonomy has remained considerably greater than in the environmental field. Although national and provincial physical plans can overrule the municipal level, the municipal physical 'designation' plan (bestemmingsplan) can, for instance, still be regarded as the core of the Dutch physical planning system (Brussaard *et al.*, 1993; Grossman and Brussaard, 1989).

One of the most important executive tasks at the lower governmental levels is the issuing of authorisations under most of the sectoral environmental laws. Communities, for instance, administer licensing under the Nuisance Act (merged into the Environment Act in 1993; see above). Sources of pollution on a somewhat larger scale are, in principle, controlled by the provinces. This applies, for instance, to the Air Pollution Act. Within the rules and requirements laid down at the central level, there is room for discretion and negotiation on the part of the licensing authorities. In addition to their tasks in the field of licensing, municipalities are responsible for the removal of household waste and for the local sewage system.

Generally, the 'vertical' co-ordination between different levels of government in the Netherlands is characterised by relatively clear-cut hierarchical relations, and there can be little doubt that the focus in environmental policy-making is much more at the state level than in, for instance, some of the Scandinavian countries.

The role of private interests

The Dutch policy system has strong neo-corporatist traits. Policy-making is characterised by a tendency towards bargaining and co-operation with interest groups, both in the formalised context of advisory bodies to the government and in more informal contacts. As van Putten (1982) points out, this particularly applies to the 'new' policy sectors associated with the emergence and growth of the welfare state. After an initial, relatively conflictual phase, the Ministry of VROM also adopted a more consensual approach in the course of the 1980s.

An important formal channel for the participation of private interests in environmental policy-making is the Council for the Environment (Raad voor het Milieubeheer). This consists of representatives of lower public authorities, public utilities, employers' and workers' organisations, and various societal interests including environmental and consumer organisations, as well as independent experts. It attempts to focus itself on the broad lines of environmental policy and works with *ad hoc* committees for specific subjects.

The co-operative approach of the Ministry of VROM has been reflected particularly in its discussions with various polluting sectors since the mid-1980s. This strategy was part of the so-called 'target group policy' and aimed at developing and implementing specific policy goals in close collaboration with those who actually control the sources of pollution. By 1994, the strategy had led to some 100 covenants covering all major industrial sectors (*NRC-Handelsblad*, 21 November 1994).

The emergence of the relatively regularised, target group approach can be interpreted as a decisive step towards more closed and stable policy communities between the state and polluting sectors, bringing the environmental policy field more in line with the basically consensual policy style in the Netherlands. The policy process in the 1970s was characterised by a struggle for independence and legitimation on the part of the newly established ministry (van Tatenhove, 1993). The new approach institutionalised a more harmonious relationship between the parties involved. To the extent that it grants private actors a certain influence on the form and content of policies in exchange for an active and committed role in policy implementation, it can even be said to possess neo-corporatist traits (cf. Liefferink and Mol, 1997; see next for a more detailed discussion).

With regard to the role of environmental organisations, the last decade has shown two opposite tendencies. On the one hand, a growing number of environmentalists have turned from the fundamental, idealistic views of the 1970s to a more pragmatic approach and have sought active involvement in government policy-making. This process has gone hand in hand with an increasing professionalisation of the organisations and a steady growth in membership. The Foundation for the Preservation of Natural Monuments (Vereniging tot Behoud van Natuurmonumenten), an organisation focusing on the purchase and management of natural areas, grew from around 200,000 members in 1981 to more than 800,000 in 1996. The Dutch branch of Friends of the Earth (Vereniging Milieudefensie) almost doubled its size, from 15,000 members in the beginning of the 1980s to 27,000 in 1990. Greenpeace the Netherlands counted 30,000 members in 1985 and 830,000 in 1990. Altogether, Dutch environmental organisations have around 2 million members on a population of about 15 million. The task of influencing the government has been performed particularly by the Society for Nature and Environment (Stichting Natuur en Milieu, SNM), an umbrella organisation with which most environmental groups in the Netherlands co-operate. SNM has a staff of about fifty and is dependent on the government for more than half of its funding. This dependency is, in itself, an illustration of the rather symbiotic relationship between the environmental movement and the state (Jamison *et al.*, 1990: 121–184; Hey and Brendle, 1994: 249ff.). On the other hand, the growing importance of the target group approach has tended to diminish the role of environmental organisations at the sector-specific level. In the negotiations on most of the recent covenants, representatives from environmental groups were absent, among other things due to the fact that they did not want to commit themselves beforehand to a process the outcome of which was as yet unclear. As a result, talks about specific goals and operational measures became a matter almost entirely between the government and the relevant industries or branch organisations.

The environmental planning system

Planning is an important feature of Dutch politics. There is a long tradition of meticulous plans at all three levels of government, particularly in the field of physical planning, but long-term plans and projections have also been very influential in social-economic policy. The Central Planning Bureau (Centraal Plan Bureau, CPB) was founded in 1945, and during the first decade of its existence it was led by the economist and later Nobel prize winner, Jan Tinbergen. The CPB's short- and medium-term economic forecasts have since been a major basis of macro-economic policy. In addition, the CPB publishes studies of the economic ramifications of specific problems, such as energy supply or environmental protection. The collection of statistical data is organised accordingly in the Netherlands. The first comprehensive environmental statistics were published in 1974 (CBS, 1974).

As pointed out earlier, policy planning has played a substantial role in the environmental field from the beginning. Around 1990, with the first NMP, the present 'integrated' form of environmental planning was established. Parallel to this, the first integrated plan on water management was published (Derde Nota Waterhuishouding, 1988–1989). This covered both quality and quantity aspects, which had been dealt with separately until then. New editions of policy programmes in the fields of nature conservation (Natuurbeleidsplan, 1989–1990), transport (Tweede Structuurschema Verkeer en Vervoer, 1989–1990) and the structure of agriculture (Structuurnota Landbouw, 1989–1990) further contributed to the excessive amount of plans in this period.

On the one hand, the encompassing character of each of these plans demonstrated the priority given to 'integration'. On the other hand, the mere existence of *five* plans covering core issues, or in any case notable aspects of environmental policy, showed that there was still something left to be integrated. Whether this should have been attempted is another matter. Various critics have commented on both the substantive and procedural shortcomings of the present stage of integration and have cautioned against hasty further steps in this direction (for instance: Drupsteen, 1990; Brussaard and Enter, 1990).

The two NMPs (NMP, 1988–1989; NMP2, 1993–1994) were not strictly binding. They laid down the policy objectives and intentions for the four years following their publication as well as the broad orientation of the policy field for the four years succeeding that. When formulating their own (obligatory) environmental policy plans, the provinces formally have to 'take into account' the national plan, i.e. they can deviate from it if sufficiently motivated. The same applies to authorities at all levels of government in concrete decision-making contexts. The political weight of these kinds of plans is considerable, however, and it is not easy to neglect them. The implementation of the policy plans is worked out and monitored in annual 'Environment Programmes'. Whereas communities are not obliged to formulate broad environmental plans, all three levels of government have to make such operational programmes annually.

Environment and economy in the Netherlands: an evolving relationship

The relationship between environmental policy and economic activities in the Netherlands can be described at two levels. At the practical level, the ever closer co-operation between economic actors and environmental policy-makers has been the most outstanding feature of the past decade. Since the late 1980s, the debate at a more conceptual level, dealing with questions of ecology *vis-à-vis* economic growth and development, has focused on the interpretation and elaboration of the notion of sustainability. Both levels will be characterised and discussed here, starting at the more fundamental level.

Sustainable development: the reception of the Brundtland Report
The debate in the Netherlands about the relationship between economy and the environment was revitalised with the publication of the Brundlandt Report (WCED, 1987). The concept of sustainable development was actively taken up by policy-makers and non-governmental actors alike. Despite, or perhaps thanks to, its broadness, the concept functioned as a nucleus around which ideas about the basic orientation of environmental policy centred. A review article by Waller-Hunter (1993) forms the basis of the following discussion.

The alarming tone of the 'Concern for tomorrow' report (RIVM, 1988) constituted fertile soil for the reception of the Brundtland Report in the Netherlands. The report convincingly sketched the precarious state and ongoing deterioration of the Dutch environment. It recommended reductions of up to 90 per cent in the use and emission of various polluting substances and thus stressed the need for radical changes in the present mode of production and consumption.

The NMP of 1989, a key document in the recent history of Dutch environmental policy, emphatically took the concept of sustainable development as its point of departure. This implied, as pointed out earlier, more attention being paid to the global scale of many environmental problems, but also the endorsement of the idea of inextricable linkages between environmental problems, environmental management and socio-economic development. The NMP sought to work out the Brundtland recommendations for the Dutch context along three lines:

- integrated life cycle management: closing the product cycle as much as possible by making better use of raw materials and waste products and using more renewable resources;
- energy-extensification: improving energy efficiency and making better use of non-finite energy sources, together with stabilisation and reduction of energy demand and consumption;
- quality improvement: raising the quality of production processes and products so that their life time could be extended and raw materials could be used more efficiently (NMP, 1988–1989: 105).

According to the NMP, close co-operation with economic actors was needed to achieve these goals. This gave a further impulse to the concretisation of the target group approach.

Spaargaren and Mol (1992) interpreted the focus on the restructuring of production–consumption cycles in the NMP as a shift from a traditional 'end-of-pipe' approach towards the political programme of ecological modernisation. This programme was characterised by notions such as 'clean technology, economic valuation of environmental resources, alteration of production and consumption styles, prevention, and monitoring of compounds through the production–consumption cycles' (*ibid.*: 338–9). It is interesting to note that the Dutch environmental movement can be observed to move in the same direction, but from a more or less opposite point of departure. Starting from the ideology of de-industrialisation and de-modernisation of the 1970s, the environmental movement now seems to meet the government with growing consensus, at least in principle, about 'the ecologizing of production and consumption' (*ibid.*: 341; Cramer, 1989). In comparison with other countries, Weale has considered the NMP 'perhaps the most serious attempt to integrate environmental concerns into the full range of public policy' (Weale, 1992: 125) and to achieve a 'union of economy and ecology' (*ibid.*: 135).

The Brundtland Report, the concept of sustainability and its elaboration in the NMP and other documents provoked a lot of official and unofficial reactions. Perhaps the most remarkable was a report prepared by the Social Economic Council (Sociaal Economische Raad, SER). In its evaluation of the Brundtland Report, the SER followed the general conclusion that economic growth and care for the environment are not principally opposed and that, in many cases, they are able to reinforce each other. More importantly, however, the SER stressed the importance of sustainability as an essential condition for economic development: eventually it should even transcend the pursuance of socio-economic goals (SER, 1989). Considering the status of the SER as one of the most influential advisory bodies to the government, comprising all established interests in social and economic policy at a high level, this is indeed a notable statement.

The idea of sustainable development itself and its basic premises were hardly attacked at the fundamental level in the Netherlands. This observation supports the thesis referred to above of a growing consensus about the basic lines of environmental policy, away from inadequate 'end-of-pipe' solutions towards more radical changes, but without breaking with modern, industrial society. With regard to the implementation of 'sustainable' policies, however, non-governmental organisations, both in the field of development and the environment, were considerably more critical.

In reading the second NMP (NMP2, 1993–1994), one can indeed get the impression that little progress had been made since the end of the 1980s. The concept of sustainable development was still referred to in rather abstract terms and concrete policy objectives were generally of the same magnitude as in the first NMP, i.e. far below the level that was regarded as 'sustainable' by the environmental organisations and by the 'Concern for tomorrow' report. A notable change had, however, been carried through in the way environmental policy was made. The shift towards a more collaborative relationship between public and private actors had in fact already been initiated in the mid-1980s but corresponded very well with the basic ideas of the Brundtland Report. Even though its impact in terms of environmental quality is difficult to assess as yet, the new approach deserves closer attention.

Internalisation, target group management and voluntary agreements

By the early 1980s, the difficulties of the sectorised 'command-and-control' approach of the 1970s could no longer be denied, as described at the beginning of this chapter. The development of new strategies was inspired particularly by the idea of integration, both within the environmental policy field and within other policy fields. Around 1985, the concept of 'internalisation' was introduced to denote attempts to reduce the gap between the regulator and those regulated. Although the concept itself seems to have lost some of its original attractiveness among policy-makers, internalisation is indeed a major key to an understanding of the rather radical changes that have taken place in the relationship between the different actors in environmental policy-making in the Netherlands.

Internalisation has two different aspects. On the one hand, it refers to the need to increase the polluters' willingness to contribute to the solution of environmental problems by appealing to their sense of 'social responsibility'. On the other hand, as a kind of counter-effort on the part of the government, it entails paying serious attention to the needs and wishes of groups affected by environmental policies and taking them into account in the design of measures (cf. particularly IMP-M, 1985–1989; IMP-M, 1986–1990; Winsemius,

1986). At this point, the issue of integration becomes crucial again, as the lack of co-ordination between the many regulations they were confronted with was felt by economic actors to be one of the major shortcomings of the 'old' approach.

In accordance with the bargaining-oriented character of Dutch politics, ways to work out the idea of internalisation in practice were mainly sought in the improvement of communication and co-opera-tion with polluters. For a number of major areas, including, for instance, agriculture, traffic and transport, refineries, construction, and waste utilities, so-called 'target group management structures' were set up by the Ministry of VROM. These constituted the frame-work for negotiations between the relevant public actors (ministries, provinces, municipalities, water boards) and specific sectors of the target groups, usually represented by branch organisations. Not only were problems and emissions mapped and possible solutions explored, but policy goals and concrete measures were also laid down in commonly agreed documents or covenants. The participat-ing branch organisations were responsible for communicating the outcomes to their members and for ensuring proper implementation (Klok and Kuks, 1994).

As pointed out above, covenants have become extremely popular in Dutch environmental policy. Nevertheless, the status of environ-mental covenants is still unclear and controversial. Some covenants are formulated as 'gentlemen's agreements', which means that they cannot be enforced by the courts. Others have a more binding char-acter, but uncertainty still exists as to the consequences of this in practice. Because negotiations with industry are usually carried out with intermediary organisations, individual members of such organi-sations are not legally bound by the outcomes of such negotiations. In some sectors, moreover, the degree of organisation is low, so that parts of the sector are not represented at all. This leads to the para-doxical situation that the most effective way for public authorities to enforce compliance with a covenant – which is in the end an agree-ment under *civil* law – is with the help of *public* law, namely simply by introducing customary legislative instruments. This also points to a notable aspect of the position of the public authorities in covenants: as soon as the possible introduction or the content of future legisla-tion is at stake, the government can bind itself only to a 'best effort' obligation to adhere to the covenant. Or, to put it more directly: provisions in covenants can always be overruled by public law (more extensively, for instance, van Vliet, 1992; van Buuren, 1993; van Acht, 1993; van de Peppel and Herweijer, 1994; van de Peppel, 1995).

In addition to problems in the field of implementation and enforcement, Klok and Kuks (1994) identified two other serious shortcomings of covenants and the target group approach in general. First, the strong focus on often rather specific target groups entails the risk of shifting the problem of fragmentation from the traditional environmental sectors (water, air, soil, etc.) to industrial sectors. Relations across target group networks are difficult to establish. Second, the making of covenants is a rather closed process. This limits the opportunities for public and political participation and control, for instance by environmental organisations (see above).

The establishment of voluntary agreements with polluters has, nevertheless, considerable advantages, which may account for the rapid spread of these agreements in the past five years. The advantages include flexibility and speed, particularly in comparison with the lengthy process of the enactment of a formal law. Furthermore, the direct participation of polluters in policy formation is widely claimed, not least by industry itself,[1] to increase their commitment to environmental policy goals. The approach would thus indeed contribute to the internalisation of environmental responsibility. An important advantage for the target groups is, finally, that covenants reduce uncertainty about the future course of government policies. Even though public authorities cannot fully bind themselves in this respect, the agreements make drastic changes in the character or content of policies very unlikely.

The foreign environmental policy agenda

In the past 25 years, environmental policy in the Netherlands has become a wide-ranging and highly structured, perhaps even over-structured, undertaking. Since the 1980s, all policies have been explained and justified with the help of various objectives, approaches and classifications. The Netherlands' international environmental policy has not been saved from this tendency. The two NMPs (NMP, 1988–1989; NMP2, 1993–1994), in particular, attempted to embed international issues in encompassing schemes and to develop more general principles and objectives for the actions to be taken by the Dutch government in the international arena. This

section will first present a discussion of the basic orientation of
Dutch foreign environmental policy, concentrating on the present
situation. Then it will present an outline of the country's main
substantive priorities in international co-operation as they emerge
from the thematic discussions of environmental problems and policies in the two NMPs.

Basic orientation

A priority put forward, particularly in the first NMP, is the stimula-
tion of international co-operation with regard to sustainable development and the reinforcement of institutional structures. In this field,
the document made a number of relatively far-going suggestions
(NMP, 1988–1989: 181ff.). One of these was the improvement of
continental and global management structures. The NMP stressed
the importance of organisations, such as the United Nations Environment Programme (UNEP), which are able to develop more integrated views on complex international problems than specific
conventions. For this reason, UNEP should be transformed into a
well-resourced and effective 'global environment authority'. It should
be able to set binding standards that could be enforced by the International Court of Justice; even the introduction of qualified majority
voting was proposed. Other international institutions, such as the
Organisation for Economic Co-operation and Development (OECD),
the Economic Commission for Europe (ECE) and the EU, should also
be reinforced and their capacity enlarged. Another point underlined
in this context was the establishment of international funds for the
financial support of sustainable policies in developing countries,
primarily in the field of climate change. In the second NMP, a strong
interest in the institutional conditions of international environmental
policy was retained, but the actual policy proposals reflected the
reality of intergovernmental co-operation somewhat better. In
conformity with promises made in Rio de Janeiro, the Netherlands
confirmed its willingness to reserve 0.1 per cent of its GNP for activities in the field of environment and development, provided that
other countries made similar contributions. The role of international
funds in spending this money was less strongly emphasised, however.
The Global Environment Facility was to function as a co-ordinating
body, but, for instance, with regard to greenhouse policies, the strategy of 'joint implementation' was suggested as an important alterna-

tive. Joint implementation entails raising the cost-effectiveness of environmental investments by (co)financing policies in other, mostly developing, countries. In this essentially bilateral relationship, the interests of the donor (including the industrial interests, for instance, of anti-pollution equipment producers) can obviously be better articulated than in a global fund (NMP2, 1993–1994: 58 and 75). The idea of decision-making by a qualified majority in an extended version of UNEP was not repeated in the second NMP.

Two additional priorities of the NMPs were the integration of environmental aspects into other international policies – in the Netherlands often referred to as 'external' integration – and the facilitation of the exchange of information, knowledge and technology. As a special point of interest with regard to external integration, the issues of the environment and foreign trade were discussed quite extensively in the second NMP. Unilateral measures for the sake of environmental protection but with negative impacts on international trade should be made only in the last instance. International agreements including as many countries as possible (in order to avoid 'free rider' positions of non-participating states) should, therefore, be preferred and stimulated, if necessary with material and/or financial support (NMP2, 1993–1994: 67–70). The transfer of technology and scientific knowledge could also play a role here. In line with the increasingly co-operative relationship with the target groups of Dutch environmental policy (see above), industry would be required to take part in such efforts (NMP, 1988–1989: 185).

This short discussion makes it clear that the Netherlands explicitly aims at playing the role of initiator and stimulator in international environmental policy. 'Active environmental diplomacy' (NMP2, 1993–1994: 57 and 68; Herijking van het buitenlands beleid, 1994–1995), supported by institutional reinforcement at the international level, when possible, forms the basis of this approach. It should be based on a consistent and credible policy at the domestic level (NMP2, 1993–1994: 57). Genuine forerunner positions are, however, the exception rather than the rule. Except for certain specific sectors that are particularly important to the Netherlands, such as refining, the chemical industry and goods' transport, this cautiousness can hardly be attributed to specific features of the Dutch economic interest. Other small member states with a stronger reputation as forerunners in environmental policy, especially Denmark, have a comparably open economy and are generally not less vulnerable to competitive disadvantages. It can rather be connected to the Dutch ambition to be a constructive, consensus-oriented partner in international environmental negotiations and to avoid unnecessary, potentially counterproductive conflicts. Unilateral measures are regarded as an option worth considering only if the domestic situation requires immediate action and/or if other countries may be realistically expected to follow the Dutch example. In that case, not only competitive risks are taken into account, but so is the possibility of taking a technological lead (NMP, 1988–1989: 184–5; NMP2, 1993–1994: 69).

Major issues
As described at the beginning of this chapter, environmental problems have, since the mid-1980s, no longer been approached along sectoral lines, but with the help of 'effect-oriented' environmental themes and 'source-oriented' target group policies (IMP-M, 1985–1989). The difficulty of bringing all environmental problems under a limited amount of headings was illustrated by the fact that the number of themes was soon extended from five to eight. The themes of climate change and acidification can be considered the two 'standing' international themes in Dutch environmental policy. Bottlenecks in the implementation of international agreements occurred particularly with regard to eutrophication. The remaining themes (diffusion, waste disposal, disturbance, dehydration and squandering) have so far had less obvious international ramifications, but some new trends are emerging, as will be pointed out at the end of this section.

Climate change   The international character of the theme of climate change is evident. In view of the global scale of the problem, a worldwide approach is, in principle, preferable. Around 1990, apart from setting preliminary national goals for the emission of CO_2, most efforts were, therefore, directed at the UN level. The establishment of an international climate convention and financial arrangements to support policies in developing countries were to form the framework of activities at lower levels, such as energy-saving programmes and the use of financial instruments in the EU and the OECD (NMP, 1988–1989: 129–32). With these standpoints, the Netherlands turned out to be one of the more progressive countries in international climate policy. Because international decision-making did not proceed as quickly as desired, the domestic debate gradually shifted to co-operation at a more regional level and ultimately to the question of unilateral action to achieve the domestic goal of a 3–5 per cent reduction of emissions by the year 2000 relative to 1989–1990 (NMP-Plus, 1989–1990: 20). The Ministry of Economic Affairs, among others, argued that an energy tax should cover all of the OECD, or at least all of the EU, so as to avoid unacceptable competitive disadvantages. Others, including the Ministry of VROM, promoted a national tax for small energy consumers only, irrespective of the action taken by the EU. As a compromise, it was decided that no decision should be taken until the outcome of the negotiations in Brussels was known, but to start preparations for the introduction of unilateral measures to be implemented at a later date, if necessary (see further: Jaarsma and Mol, 1994). A suggestion was also made to explore the possibility of establishing an energy tax together with a number of north-west European countries (NMP2, 1993–1994: 73). In the course of 1995, it became clear that higher economic growth and lower energy prices made the national reduction target of 3–5 per cent, and actually even stabilisation, very difficult to achieve. The need for additional policy measures to raise energy efficiency was slowly realised. As the EU level had not been able to take decisions on a tax on energy either, this opened the way for a limited 'small users' tax' from 1996. Large industrial emitters were to improve energy efficiency through voluntary agreements with the government. In order to revitalise the EU process, the Dutch government convened an informal ministerial meeting of eight member states basically in favour of an EU tax, but so far the impact of this meeting has been limited (cf. *Europe Environment* 471).

Acidification Dutch policy in the field of acidification has been guided by relatively ambitious national deposition targets. For the realisation of these targets, the country has been, and remains strongly, dependent on efforts made abroad. In the first NMP, it was stated that 'the deposition levels being aimed at in the Netherlands are totally unfeasible unless acidification is also tackled energetically in the neighbouring countries' (NMP, 1988–1989: 135). The second NMP even went so far as to formulate concrete objectives for the reduction of emissions in other countries, amounting to 85 per cent for SO_2, 60 per cent for NO_x and 50 per cent for ammonia (NMP2, 1993–1994: 80). The Dutch position in international negotiations evolved according to this dependency. After a short period in the early 1980s of basically following Germany in its campaign for international action against forest die-back, the Netherlands started to play an active role on its own in European acidification policy. Particularly in the EU, where more specific measures for car emission and large combustion plants were formulated, diverging sectoral interests often prevented close collaboration between Germany and the Netherlands, although their basic environmental goals in this field were largely correspondent (cf. Liefferink, 1996). In the ECE, consistent with the national approach based on deposition, the Netherlands was one of the main promoters of the use of so-called 'critical loads' as a starting point for emission reductions. Critical loads are differentiated deposition targets that take into account the regional characteristics of the environment. The most recent ECE protocol on SO_2, signed in the spring of 1994, aims at a 60 per cent closure of the gap between 1990 emissions and critical loads by the year 2000, although many exemptions and longer lead times have been granted to individual countries.

Eutrophication   This theme involves the problem of excess amounts of nitrogen and phosphorus in the environment. Because the transport and accumulation of these nutrients take place mainly in soil, groundwater and surface water, the international aspects of the problem primarily refer to what is in Dutch policy programmes called the 'fluvial' level, i.e. the geographical scale of river basins and coastal seas. The Netherlands' downstream position along the Rivers Rhine and Meuse once again makes it dependent upon its neighbours.

The most relevant institutional frameworks in this context are the International Rhine Convention, particularly the Rhine Action Plan under this convention, and the North Sea Action Plan, a political agreement among the North Sea states. Both action plans require a 50 per cent reduction in the emissions of nutrients in 1995 relative to 1985. Although other countries appear to have problems in achieving these objectives as well (cf. NMP2, 1993–1994: 85), the Netherlands cannot be regarded as a forerunner in this field. The use of high amounts of fertilisers and the production of large surpluses of animal manure in certain parts of the country cause considerable losses of nitrogen and phosphorus that are difficult to control. Full compliance with the action plans in 1995, particularly for nitrogen, has proved to be unfeasible. The need for further reductions (up to 75 per cent) was merely stated in the second NMP in general terms (NMP2, 1993–1994: 85; Milieuprogramma, 1996–1999).

Attempts to set up a similar programme for the River Meuse have been in a deadlock for a long time. The project became the victim of an unfortunate package deal between Belgium and the Netherlands, involving the reduction of pollution along the Belgian part of the River Schelde and the deepening of the Dutch part of it in the interests of the Antwerp harbour. However, the ongoing federalisation of Belgium has helped partly to uncouple the issues, and this finally resulted in the signing of the Meuse Treaty by all parties involved at the beginning of 1995 (*NRC-Handelsblad*, 1 December 1994).

Recently, the EU also started to play a significant role in the field of eutrophication through its directive on the discharge of nitrates from diffuse sources (Directive 91/676/EEC). The Dutch position in this case was also defensive rather than stimulative, which can be related to the specific problems of highly intensive agriculture in the Netherlands. Limits on the amount of nitrogen that can be applied to land, as specified in the directive, were considered too strict for the Dutch situation. In the end, an alternative system for complying with the water quality objectives also contained in the directive was accepted. Due to difficulties and delays in Dutch manure policy, however, the implementation of this alternative system also gives rise to problems (cf. Liefferink, 1996).

In the fields of climate change and acidification, in conclusion, the Netherlands explicitly attempts to play a leading and stimulative role. The Dutch ambition to bring about institutional improvement can be observed particularly in the initial phase of the relatively new area of greenhouse policies; but more recently, problems in achieving the domestic reduction target have weakened the Dutch position. The same applies to the theme of eutrophication, where serious implementation problems, especially with regard to nitrogen, diminish the opportunities of taking active international stances.

Emerging themes on the Dutch foreign environmental policy agenda include integrated preventive policies (control of production processes, chemicals, etc.) and the co-ordination of international transport in relation to a wide range of environmental impacts (air pollution, noise, spatial aspects). Regarding the former issue, the domestic target group approach clearly moulds Dutch positions in international negotiations (cf. Milieuprogramma, 1996–1999: 37). The negative impacts of the continuous growth of both air and inland traffic are increasingly seen as a problem that requires co-ordination at the European level (cf. NMP2, 1993–1994). However, the issue of transport and environment is particularly controversial in the Netherlands. On the one hand, the space demand and the serious environmental consequences of the transport sector in a densely populated country such as the Netherlands stress the need for vigorous action. On the other hand, the Netherlands has a proportionally very high share in European goods transport and tries to maintain its status as a 'gateway to Europe'. This generates a strong economic interest in adequate infrastructure and an incentive to compete with other countries exactly on this point. This conflict is likely to intensify in the next years and to have repercussions on Dutch foreign policies in this field.

The institutional setting of foreign environmental policy

General framework
Foreign environmental policy is a form of environmental policy, but it is also an aspect of foreign policy. In order to co-ordinate the Dutch input in international environmental negotiations with other foreign policy interests, the Ministry of Foreign Affairs (Buitenlandse Zaken, BuZa) was assigned a considerable role in the domestic preparation of this input, at least formally. The general procedure and the special arrangements made for the different stages in EU decision-making will be described below.

Formally speaking, the central co-ordinating body in this field is the Co-ordination Commission for International Environmental Affairs (Coördinatie Commissie voor Internationale Milieuvraagstukken, CIM). The CIM is chaired by the Ministry of BuZa, but it is composed of civil servants from several ministries. As the CIM is the highest administrative body in this field, a lot of preparatory work on technical issues is done at lower levels, often only between the ministries directly involved. Highly controversial issues, on the other hand, cannot be solved by the CIM and will be passed on to the political level.

Within the Ministry of VROM, the Directorate for International Environmental Affairs (Directie Internationale Milieuzaken) co-ordinates all international efforts. The directorate has grown rapidly from a handful of people in the 1970s and 1980s to almost forty in the 1990s. Now, it has specialised divisions for co-operation in different regions (EC/OECD, Eastern Europe, global issues).

The Directorate for International Environmental Affairs was established in the early 1970s and initially had to assert itself against the Directorate General for Foreign Economic Relations (Directoraat-Generaal voor Buitenlandse Economische Betrekkingen) of the Ministry of BuZa, which claimed important aspects of the field under its competence. As far as the EU is concerned, the distribution of issues on the different sectoral councils in Brussels now determines which ministry takes the lead in the domestic preparation process. Issues negotiated in the Environment Council are usually assigned to the Ministry of VROM. In other international environmental issues strongly related to economic and trade interests (General Agreement on Tariffs and Trade, co-operation with Eastern and Central European countries), however, the Ministry of BuZa continues to play a leading role. International water policy, furthermore, is co-ordinated by the Ministry of Transport and Public Works, whereas the Ministry of Agriculture, Nature Conservation and Fisheries is responsible for international issues of nature conservation.

Co-ordination of EU policies
While the positions of the Dutch delegations to international conferences and negotiations in the environmental field are generally co-ordinated under the auspices of the CIM, the domestic preparation of EU environmental policies takes place largely within the co-ordination structure for matters of European integration and co-operation (for a historical account and a detailed description of the present situation, cf. van den Bos, 1991). In this case, the CIM functions as a sub-committee to the Co-ordination Commission for European Integration and Association Problems (Coördinatie Commissie voor Europese Integratie- en Associatieproblemen, CoCo). The CoCo is a high-level administrative committee, composed of representatives from all ministries and chaired by the (politically appointed) State Secretary for European Affairs, the second person in charge at the Ministry of BuZa. It meets weekly in order to prepare the Dutch input for all meetings of the EU Council of Ministers. In addition, it sometimes co-ordinates broader international issues with an important EU aspect, such as climate policy. In highly controversial issues, final decision-making is left to the cabinet.

The Dutch input at the level of the EU Council working groups, including the ones for the environment and for trade barriers, is also co-ordinated by the Ministry of BuZa, but direct, informal contacts between the officials involved play an important role as well. In this network, as van den Bos (1991: 97ff.) demonstrated, the Directorate for International Environmental Affairs of the Ministry of VROM, due to its size and its expertise, holds a particularly strong position when compared with the positions of other 'technical' ministries in the various networks around their specific issues.

In the EU Council Working Group on Environment itself, the Netherlands is represented by an official based at the Permanent Representation in Brussels. For a long time, this function has been performed by a diplomat from the Ministry of BuZa, assisted from 1990 by a second diplomat. Since 1993, the second person responsible for environmental affairs in the Dutch Permanent Representation to the EU has been an official from the Ministry of VROM (Pellegrom, 1994). This change marks the formal acknowledgement of the role of the Ministry of VROM in Brussels, but at the same time facilitates the 'encapsulation' of environmental policy goals by the essentially diplomatic machinery in Brussels. In practice, though, the attachés to the Permanent Representation are usually assisted by experts from the home ministries. In almost all cases, an expert is sent by the Ministry of VROM. Depending on the subject, other ministries (Economic Affairs, Agriculture) may delegate an additional expert.

The role of private actors

The direct involvement of Dutch private actors in the domestic preparation of international environmental policy-making varies strongly. For instance, a wide range of public interests, including environmental and developmental organisations, but also trade unions and churches, participated actively both in the general debate about the operationalisation of the idea of sustainable development and in the preparation of the Dutch input in Rio de Janeiro in 1992. A group of representatives from these organisations was even included in the Dutch delegation to Rio.

In more specific issues, participation differs from case to case. With regard to EU environmental policy, industry usually follows policy developments on a routine basis through its national and European branch organisations. If the interests of a specific sector threaten to be affected by emerging EU legislation, they follow a 'multi-channel' approach, involving various national, bilateral and multinational routes to articulate their interests with the EU Commission and Council. This has recently occurred, for instance, in relation to the packaging directive (Lievaart, 1994). In many fields, however, environmental legislation in the Netherlands tends to be ahead of corresponding EU initiatives. In most of these cases, agreement between public and private actors about the character and details of policy measures has already been reached domestically. When the issue appears on the agenda in the EU, the Dutch government will usually base its position on the existing national arrangement, and Dutch industry can basically limit itself to following the negotiations from a certain distance (for instance, for the field of acidification, cf. Liefferink, 1996). An interesting development in this context is the repeated attempts recently made by the Dutch government actively to involve industrial actors in the making of international environmental policy. These attempts are inspired both by the collaborative target group approach and by the perceived need to bring about reductions in foreign emissions of several substances in order to achieve domestic environmental targets. An example is the bilateral talks held in 1990 between the Dutch government, Dutch refineries and their counterparts in neighbouring countries, which aimed at joint efforts to limit sulphur emissions.[2]

Dutch environmental organisations are among the most active in EU environmental policy. The SNM, the main channel by which the Dutch environmental movement influences government policy (see above), in particular, recognised the importance of the international and EU levels at an early stage. It was among the founders of the European Environmental Bureau (EEB) in 1974, and it has continued to be one of the bureau's driving forces. The actual influence of the EEB and other Brussels-based environmental organisations on policy processes is often fairly limited, however. At the same time, lobbying the national government with regard to EU policy-making is not always an effective strategy for organisations such as the SNM either, because the Dutch delegations to the Council often represent 'environmentalist' views already, relatively speaking. As pointed out above, the crucial decisions have in most cases already been taken earlier in the context of domestic policy-making.

The Netherlands, European integration and environmental policy

Changes in the attitude towards European integration
The Netherlands was one of the founding members of the EU. During the four decades of the EU's existence, the country has come to be

known as one of the most steadfast supporters of the process of European integration. Generally speaking, this reputation seems to be justified. The Netherlands has indeed quite consistently promoted the development of common policies in an ever-wider range of areas. The basic political rationale for this position was shared with the other founding members: the stability of the western part of the continent, particularly the embedding of Germany in a firm political structure. In the economic dimension, the Netherlands was convinced that its interests as a small, strongly export-oriented country in the centre of Europe were best served with a large, integrated market, in the broadest sense of the word. The preference, moreover, was to have decisions in the EU made in a supra-national rather than an inter-governmental fashion. An active role of the Commission was stimulated and the re-introduction of qualified majority voting in the Single European Act was welcomed as the resumption of the project of establishing a genuinely 'federal' Europe after the 'Euro-sclerosis' of the 1970s and early 1980s. The argument behind this attitude was that majority voting would prevent the large member states from imposing their views upon the others and thus effectively increase the political weight of the smaller member states.[3] Recently, however, the traditional 'integrationist' position of the Netherlands has been questioned and discussed more and more openly.

The shock that provoked the start of the process of re-evaluation was not the Danish referendum in 1992, but rather the run-up to the Maastricht Treaty, which occurred when the Netherlands held the Presidency in the second half of 1991. Consistent with the views just sketched, the Dutch government had drawn up a draft with strong federal traits, including a considerable enlargement of the powers of the European Parliament and supra-national arrangements for the establishment of the European Political Union. On 30 September 1991, against the Hague's probably somewhat naive expectations, the draft was rejected by all member states. 'Black Monday', as it was later called, drew attention primarily to the unreality of the Dutch ideas about European integration. Soon, however, it also triggered doubts about the actual content of these ideas. The general tendency of the debate was still moderate in comparison to what other countries had experienced: the merits for the Netherlands of the EU and the achieved level of integration were hardly called into question. A more selective approach to the 'Europeanisation' of new policy fields guided by a stricter interpretation of the principle of subsidiarity was advocated, however, also in relation to elements of environmental policy, such as the protection of surface water, groundwater and soils. In addition, the doctrine of a strengthening of supranational institutions was criticised, and the value of retaining the right of veto was emphasised, at least with respect to certain 'vital' issues. In a sense, the negative responses abroad, even to the final, considerably weakened version of 'Maastricht', supported this argument: what could in the end be the advantage of putting important aspects of the future of the country into the hands of others who showed so little commitment to the ideas of European integration?

A new element was added to the debate at the end of 1994, when it became clear that the Netherlands was in the process of becoming one of the biggest financial contributors to the EU. Due to massive subsidies in the agricultural sector, the 'net result' of EU membership had long been positive for the Netherlands, but the reform of the Common Agricultural Policy under the MacSharry scheme, in particular, and the simultaneous enlargement of the structural funds diminished incomes and raised expenditures. Since 1995 the Dutch net contribution has been among the largest, measured as a percentage of GNP (which itself is in fact not among the very highest in the EU). The perception of this inequality and the fact that the possibility of reversing the effect is probably very limited are bound to add to the increasingly reserved attitude towards the EU.

In the course of 1995, a broad evaluation and reorientation of Dutch foreign policy was carried through (Herijking van het buitenlands beleid, 1994–1995) in the light of the rapid changes in the world political system after the end of the Cold War. In this debate, the traditional Dutch emphasis on international law and institution-building, which had long been formulated in idealistic or moralistic terms, was questioned. This resulted in a closer and more explicit link between the relatively abstract priorities and the 'self-interest' of a small industrial state such as the Netherlands in a stable world political order with well-functioning international markets. The strengthening of supra-national decision-making structures in the EU, for instance, should not be pursued dogmatically, but primarily as a means of safeguarding the achievements of the internal market in an extended EU. It cannot be claimed that the reorientation radically changed the basic attitude towards European integration. The shift in the domestic argumentation on EU policies may, however, be interpreted as yet another indication of an increasing pragmatism *vis-à-vis* the EU level.

The Dutch position in EU environmental policy

The EU is regarded by the Dutch government as the first and foremost framework for international environmental policy (NMP2, 1993–1994: 58–9). There are obvious geographical and economic reasons for this perception, since the EU comprises all the direct neighbours and almost all the major trade partners of the Netherlands. In addition, there are factors more directly related to environmental policy interest. The broad range of issues covered by the EU, for instance, provides relatively favourable opportunities of integrating environmental considerations into other policy fields at the international level. Policies endorsed by the EU can also carry more weight in international co-operation at the global level than can unilateral actions (*ibid.*). It should also be realised, however, that the strategic choice between the EU and other possible frameworks often simply does not exist in view of the obligations contained in the EU Treaty (stressed, for instance, by Kakebeeke, 1993: 24).

Together with the Dutch ambition to play an active and innovative role in international environmental policy described above, the great importance attached to the EU justifies the expectation of an engaged and constructive approach to EU environmental policy. Although the Dutch role in Brussels in this field can hardly be called passive, the motivation behind it is, in practice, not always as constructive as might be concluded from the policy documents. Interviews carried out by the author in the Hague revealed that EU policies with regard to the environment are often seen by policy-makers primarily as a potential burden on domestic policy goals and processes. Not only is Dutch legislation in most cases stricter than the values discussed in Brussels, but the process of give-and-take in and around the Council can also interfere with carefully constructed domestic compromises. This reinforces the tendency, which is to some extent naturally present in all member states, to defend domestic policy solutions with great vigour in Brussels and, more than that, to present them explicitly as 'examples' for the EU level.

The Dutch 'forerunner' position thus often takes the form of attempts to promote domestically applied strategies and tools at the EU level rather than attempts to provoke the other member states by employing unilateral measures. In promoting EU policies, the Netherlands can draw upon its own strongly systematised approach to environmental policy-making and planning. The approach of the Dutch IMPs and NMPs was, for instance, advanced quite successfully as a model for the EU's Fifth Environmental Action Programme (European Communities, 1993; cf. Kronsell, 1997). Similar to the Dutch plans, the EU programme describes policy objectives along the lines of themes and priority target groups. In dealing with those target groups, emphasis is envisaged to shift from direct regulation to a broader package of instruments, including, for example, environmental charges and also more communicative strategies and voluntary agreements. At the instigation of the Dutch government, talks were indeed started in the early 1990s between the Commission, the member states and representatives from relevant industries about the management of different types of waste (tyres, chlorinated hydrocarbons, etc.). Most of these pilot projects were broken off before they had reached the executive phase, however, in view of a lack of interest from both the Commission and most other member states. The case illustrates the difficulty of putting into practice new approaches in EU policy-making, even if they have in principle been endorsed by the other partners.

As mentioned earlier, 'going-it-alone' in practice seldom occurs in Dutch EU policy. One example is the unilateral introduction of tax incentives for small cars equipped with catalytic converters in 1988–1989 (cf. Holzinger, 1994). Remarkably enough, this step was induced mainly by domestic motives. The possible 'exemplary' effect on negotiations in Brussels started to play a role only in the discussion later (Liefferink, 1996). One year later, the first NMP formulated general factors to be taken into account in future decisions on a Dutch *Alleingang*. Apart from the benefit to the environment and possible competitive disadvantages, the possibility that other countries might be 'inspired to take the same measures' was now referred to (NMP, 1988–1989: 184–5). More than once, moreover, the suggestion has been made to form smaller groups of countries that could go further than the EU as a whole (NMP, 1988–1989: 185; NMP-Plus, 1989–1990: 72; NMP2, 1993–1994: 73).

Conclusions

It is an awkward task to summarise a review article such as this because the value of such an article derives from its broad treatment of a wide variety of characteristics and phenomena, occurring and developing over a period, rather than from one or two clear-cut arguments. Nevertheless, it is possible to identify three features of Dutch environmental policy that mark its history and present state and may help to distinguish it from the development of environmental policy in other countries.

The first feature is the response to the problem of fragmentation in the institutionalisation of the policy field. Although problems of fragmented competence and poor co-ordination are by no means unique to the Netherlands, the kind of solutions sought for these problems are probably unique to some extent. The integration of different aspects of environmental policy – of different environmental 'sectors', of effects and sources, or of policy formation and implementation – is basically attempted with the help of comprehensive and detailed strategic plans and programmes. Although most are not strictly binding, these plans are something like the building blocks of Dutch environmental policy.

A second important feature is the continuous trend towards a closer and more co-operative relationship between environmental policy-makers and their target groups. Particularly since the 1980s, the state has actively tried to bring about a process of 'internalisation' of environmental responsibility among industry and other polluting actors by involving them more closely in the process of environmental policy-making. At the moment, this strategy has led to a large number of voluntary agreements with a broad range of target groups.

In the international arena, finally, the Dutch approach is characterised by its willingness to play an active, stimulative role. Rather than in genuine forerunner positions, however, this approach expresses itself mainly in the ambition to improve the institutional context of international environmental policy-making. Dutch policy principles and concepts are actively promoted in an international context. In international negotiations on specific issues, also in the EU framework, well-established domestic policies often form the firm basis of the Dutch position.

Notes

1 Cf., for instance, the President of the Association of Dutch Christian Employers (Nederlands Christelijk Werkgeversverbond, NCW), J. C.

Blankert, in *NRC-Handelsblad*, 21 November 1994.

2   At the bilateral level, the talks were successful only to a limited extent. But together with a French initiative, they helped shift the issue to the EU level (Liefferink, 1996).

3   This argument is correct to the extent that the voting rules in the Council give an advantage to the smaller member states. While, for instance, Germany and France control ten votes each, the Netherlands has five and Luxembourg has two.

References

Andersen, M. Skou (1994), *Governance by Green Taxes*, Manchester, Manchester University Press.

Boender, K. (1985), *Milieuprotest in Rijnmond, sociologische analyse van milieusolidariteit onder elites en publiek*, Rijswijk, Sijthoff.

Bressers, J. T. A. (1983), *Beleidseffectiviteit en waterkwaliteitsbeleid: een bestuurskundig onderzoek*, dissertation, Enschede.

Briejèr, C. J. (1967), *Zilveren sluiers en verborgen gevaren*, Leiden, Sijthoff.

Brussaard, W. and J. H. Enter (1990), Het stelsel van milieubeleidsplanning in relatie tot ruimtelijke ordenings- en waterhuishoudingsplanning, *Tijdschrift voor Milieu en Recht*, 5, 222–30.

Brussaard, W. *et al.* (eds) (1993), *Milieurecht*, third edition, Zwolle, W. E. J. Tjeenk Willink.

Carson, R. (1962), *Silent Spring*, Boston, Houghton Mifflin.

CBS (Centraal Bureau voor de Statistiek), *Algemene milieustatistiek 1973*, C14/1974, 's-Gravenhage, Staatsuitgeverij.

Cramer, J. (1989), *De groene golf, geschiedenis en toekomst van de Nederlandse milieubeweging*, Utrecht, Jan van Arkel.

Derde Nota Waterhuishouding (1988–1989), Tweede Kamer 1988–1989, 21250, 1–2.

Diederiks, H. A. and C. Jeurgens (1989), Nijverheid versus milieu in Holland 1500–1900, *Holland. Regionaal-historisch tijdschrift* 21: 4–5, 190–208.

Driessen, P. P. J. and P. Glasbergen (1994), Het gebiedsgerichte milieubeleid, in P. Glasbergen (ed.), *Milieubeleid, een beleidswetenschappelijke inleiding*, fourth edition, Den Haag, VUGA.

Drupsteen, Th. G. (1990), Twintig jaar milieuwetgeving; tijd voor bezinning, *Tijdschrift voor Milieu en Recht*, 5, 194–201.

European Communities (1993), Towards sustainability (Fifth Environmental Action Programme, 1993–2000), *Official Journal*, C138, 17 May 1993.

Gorter, H. P. (1986), *Ruimte voor natuur. Tachtig jaar bezig voor de natuur van de toekomst*, 's-Graveland, Vereniging tot Behoud van Natuurmonumenten in Nederland.

Groen, M. (1988), *Naar een duurzaam Nederland*, Den Haag, SDU.

Grossman, M. R. and W. Brussaard (1989), Planning, development and management: three steps in the legal protection of Dutch agricultural land, *Washburn Law Journal*, 28: 1, 86–149.

Herijking van het buitenlands beleid (1994–1995), Tweede Kamer 1994–1995, 24337, 1–2.

Hey, C. and U. Brendle (1994), *Umweltverbände und EG. Strategien, politische Kulturen und Organisationsformen*, Opladen, Westdeutscher Verlag.

Holzinger, K. (1994), *Politik des kleinsten gemeinsamen Nenners? Umweltpolitische Entscheidungsprozesse in der EG am Beispiel der Einführung des Katalysatorautos*, Berlin, Edition Sigma.

IMP-M (Indicatief Meerjaren Programma Milieubeheer) 1985–1989, Tweede Kamer 1984–1985, 18602, 1–2.

IMP-M (Indicatief Meerjaren Programma Milieubeheer) 1986–1990, Tweede Kamer 1985–1986, 19204, 1–2.

Jaarsma, E. and A. P. J. Mol (1994), De rol van onderzoek in het beleidsproces rond regulerende energieheffingen, *Milieu. Tijdschrift voor milieukunde*, 9: 3, 120–8.

Jamison, A., R. Eyerman, J. Cramer and J. Læssøe (1990), *The Making of the New Environmental Consciousness. A Comparative Study of the Environmental Movements in Sweden, Denmark and the Netherlands*, Edinburgh, Edinburgh University Press.

Kakebeeke, W. J. (1993), Milieu als internationale prioriteit, in G. Spaargaren *et al.* (eds), *Internationaal milieubeleid*, second edition, 's-Gravenhage, SDU Uitgeverij Koninginnegracht.

Klok, P.-J., and S. M. M. Kuks (1994), Het doelgroepenbeleid, in P. Glasbergen (ed.), *Milieubeleid, een beleidswetenschappelijke inleiding*, fourth edition, Den Haag, VUGA.

Kronsell, A. (1997), Policy innovation in the garbage can: the EU's Fifth Environmental Action Programme, in D. Lifferink and M. S. Andersen (eds), *The Innovation of EU Environmental Policy*, Copenhagen, Scandinavian University Press.

Leroy, P. (1994), De ontwikkeling van het milieubeleid en de milieubeleidstheorie, in P. Glasbergen (ed.), *Milieubeleid, een beleidswetenschappelijke inleiding*, fourth edition, Den Haag, VUGA.

Liefferink, D. (1996), *Environment and the Nation State: the Netherlands, the European Union and Acid Rain*, Manchester, Manchester University Press.

Liefferink, D. and A. P. J. Mol (1997), *Voluntary agreements as a form of deregulation? The Dutch experience*, paper prepared for the workshop 'Deregulation and the environment', European University Institute, Florence, 9–11 May in U. Collier (ed.), *Deregulation in the European Union: Environmental Perspectives*, London, Routledge.

Lievaart, M. (1994), *Verpakkingsafval: de relatie tussen de totstandkoming van nationaal en EG-beleid*, Wageningen, Landbouwuniversiteit Wageningen, Vakgroep Sociologie.

Lijphart, A. (1968), *Verzuiling, pacificatie en kentering in de Nederlandse politiek*, Amsterdam, De Bussy.

Meadows, D. (1972), *The Limits to Growth*, New York, Universe Books.

Milieuprogramma 1996–1999, Tweede Kamer 1995–1996, 24405, 1–2.

Natuubeleidsplan (1989–1990), Tweede Kamer 1989–1990, 21149, nos 2–3.

NMP (Nationaal Milieubeleidsplan) (1988–1989), Tweede Kamer 1988–1989, 21137, 1–2.

NMP-Plus (Nationaal Milieubeleidsplan-Plus) (1989–1990), Tweede Kamer 1989–1990, 21137, 29–21.

NMP2 (Nationaal Milieubeleidsplan 2) (1993–1994), Tweede Kamer 1993–1994, 23560, 1–2.

Pellegrom, S. (1994), *National Civil Servants in EC Environmental Policy: A New Elite and its Role in European Integration*, paper presented at the ECPR 22nd Joint Sessions of Workshops, Madrid, 17–22 April.

RIVM (Rijksinstituut voor Volksgezondheid en Milieuhygiëne) (1988), *Zorgen voor morgen*, Alphen aan den Rijn, Samsom H. D. Tjeenk Willink.

SER (Sociaal Economische Raad) (1989), *Our Common Future*, SER, Report 89/06, Den Haag.

SO_2 *Beleidskaderplan* (1979–1980), Tweede Kamer 1979–1980, 15834, 1–2.

Spaargaren, G. and A. P. J. Mol (1992), Sociology, environment and modernity: ecological modernization as a theory of social change, *Society and Natural Resources*, 5, 323–44.

Structuurnota Landbouw (1989–1990), Tweede Kamer 1989–1990, 21148, 2–3.

Tellegen, E. (1983), *Milieubeweging*, Aula pocket 734, Utrecht/Antwerpen, Het Spectrum.

Tonnaer, F. P. C. L. (1990), *Het Nederlands milieurecht in ontwikkeling*, Alphen aan den Rijn, Samsom H. D. Tjeenk Willink.

Tweede Structuurschema Verkeer en Vervoer (1989–1990), Tweede Kamer 1989–1990, 20922, 15–16.

Urgentienota Milieuhygiëne (1971–1972), Tweede Kamer 1971–1972, 11906, 1–2.

van Acht, R. J. J. (1993), Afdwingbare milieuconvenanten?, *Nederlands Juristenblad*, 67:14, 512–17.

van Buuren, P. J. J. (1993), Environmental covenants – possibilities and impossibilities: an administrative lawyer's view, in J. M. van Dunné (ed.), *Environmental Contracts and Covenants: New Instruments for a Realistic Environmental Policy?*, Lelystad, Koninklijke Vermande.

van de Peppel, R. A. (1995), *Naleving van milieurecht. Toepassing van beleidsinstrumenten op de Nederlandse verfindustrie*, Deventer, Kluwer.

van de Peppel, R. A. and M. Herweijer (1994), Het communicatieve sturingsmodel, in P. Glasbergen (ed.), *Milieubeleid, een beleidswetenschappelijke inleiding*, fourth edition, Den Haag, VUGA.

van den Bos, J. M. M. (1991), *Dutch EC Policy-making. A Model-Guided Approach to Coordination and Negotiation*, Amsterdam, Thesis Publishers.

van Noort, W. (1988), *Bevlogen bewegingen, een vergelijking van de anti-kernenergie-, kraak- en milieubeweging*, Amsterdam, Sua.

van Putten, J. (1982), Policy style in the Netherlands: negotiation and conflict, in J. Richardson (ed.), *Policy Styles in Western Europe*, London, George Allen & Unwin.

van Tatenhove, J. P. M. (1993), *Milieubeleid onder dak. Beleidsvoerings-processen in het Nederlandse milieubeleid in de periode 1970–1990; nader uitgewerkt voor de Gelderse Vallei*, Wageningen, Pudoc, Wageningse Sociologische Studies 35.

van Tatenhove, J. P. M. and J. D. Liefferink (1992), Environmental policy in the Netherlands and in the European Community, a conceptual approach, in F. von Benda-Beckmann and M. van der Velde (eds), *Law as a Resource in Agrarian Struggles*, Wageningen, Pudoc, Wageningen Studies in Sociology 33.

van Vliet, L. M. (1992), *Communicatieve besturing van het milieuhandelen van ondernemingen: mogelijkheden en beperkingen*, Delft, Eburon.

van Zon, H. (1986), *Een zeer onfrisse geschiedenis, studie over niet-indus-triële verontreiniging in Nederland 1850–1920*, Den Haag, SDU.

Vierde Nota over de Ruimtelijke Ordening (1988–1989) (final version), Tweede Kamer 1988–1989, 20490, 9–10.

Waller-Hunter, J. H. (1993), 'Sustainable development', van Brundtland tot UNCED, in G. Spaargaren *et al.* (eds), *Internationaal milieubeleid*, second edition, 's-Gravenhage, SDU Uitgeverij Koninginnegracht.

WCED (World Commission on Environment and Development)(1987), *Our Common Future*, Oxford, Oxford University Press.

Weale, A. (1992), *The New Politics of Pollution*, Manchester/New York, Manchester University Press.

Winsemius, P. (1986), *Gast in eigen huis, beschouwingen over milieuman-agement*, Alphen aan den Rijn, Samsom H. D. Tjeenk Willink.

Denmark: the shadow of the green majority

Introduction[1]

Denmark has with the peninsula of Jutland and more than 500 islands, a coastline of about 7000 km, and domestic environmental policy has, compared with other countries, to a considerable degree focused on the aquatic environment. Denmark has less heavy, smoke-stack industries than the other Nordic countries and is mainly dominated by food processing industries. The many bays and fjords are vulnerable to discharges from these industries as well as to run-off nutrients from Denmark's intensive agricultural production. The interior Danish sea waters (the Belts and the Kattegat) are affected both by domestic and transfrontier pollution, but water exchanges slowly with the Baltic Sea, reducing the impact of pollution from Eastern Europe. With regard to air pollution, Denmark is less affected than the other Nordic countries. Thanks to the lime layers settled in Denmark's underground, acidification of lakes and forests is limited, and Denmark is, due to the reliance on coal for energy supply, itself a net exporter of air pollution.

This profile of environmental policy-making will show how domestic environmental policy-making has often been propelled by the particular parliamentary traditions in Denmark. The fragmented system of political parties has created a practice of minority, multi-party governments. Coupled with the existence of the Danish parliament's so-called 'green majority' from 1982 to 1993, environmental policy was often promoted by the opposition parties, and rather ambitious environmental targets were set. However, the so-called 'green majority' could not compensate for the government's lack of ability to provide for consistent policy measures and a high international profile. Because the government was in practice more concerned with economic and other policies, the opposition was unable to give environmental policy a coherent and offensive form. If one can be a forerunner by jumping from hillock to hillock, that was Denmark's position in the 1980s.

While Denmark has sometimes been portrayed as the most environmentally friendly member state in the EC/EU (Spiegel, 1992), the conflictual development of environmental policy at the domestic level coupled with Denmark's reluctant attitude towards European integration has tended to make its European environmental policies defensive; Denmark has tended to focus more on opt-outs and guarantees than the attainment of high standards at the European level. Denmark has supported the development of a common European environmental policy, but has, at the same time, wished to maintain its right to be 'cleaner than the rest'.

Environmental problems and policies in Denmark: an overview

Historical background
The cholera epidemics of the 1850s triggered the first hygiene regulations and led to the institutionalisation of the authorities that were the first to deal with pollution control in Denmark. Water was the main object of concern, its hygienic as well as environmental properties. Local hygiene commissions as well as local farmers' commissions became responsible for pollution control matters (Nue, 1980). In 1880, the first legislation on industrial pollution prohibited the location of specific industries within the town district of Copenhagen and made restrictions possible in other cities (von Eyben, 1989).

Sewers and sewerage were little known outside Copenhagen until the turn of the century. In 1901, two members of parliament submitted a bill for a sewer act, and this bill was passed as one of the reforms in the period following the 1901 change in the political system. In 1926, the first Water Supply Act was passed. During the social reform of the 1930s, work commenced on a water course act because many water courses had become polluted by cities and industries. In 1949, the Water Course Act was passed, regulating discharges to all fresh waters. The Water Course Act established the first permit scheme for industrial pollution and mandated the local farmers' commissions to license dischargers. Until the beginning of the 1970s, regulation was very fragmented and a by-product of health legislation. The concept of the environment was interpreted narrowly, leaving legislation to focus mostly on relationships between neighbours so that firms and farms did not pollute their closest neighbours (Grønnegård Christensen, 1987).

The 1970s: the institutionalisation phase
Only in the 1960s did concern about pollution begin to increase. In the late 1960s, a study commission, the Pollution Council (Forureningsrådet), was established to report on the extent of pollution and the remedies available. In the years from 1969 to 1971, the Pollution Council issued twenty-nine reports on the state of the environment. These reports covered a wide range of problems: water pollution, air pollution, soil pollution and waste. Based on the Pollution Council's recommendations, a broad reform was prepared by the new Ministry for Pollution Control, established in 1971.[2] To underline the significance of environmental policy, a separate Minister for Pollution Control was appointed by the government.

In 1972, a separate Hazardous Waste Act on the management of chemicals and oil was passed in response to incidents at some chemical industries (Nielsen, 1985; Pedersen, 1987). This act established a public system for the management of hazardous waste and included a compulsory system for the delivery of hazardous waste and a national chemical incinerator to be operated by the association of municipalities. Some years later, this act was followed by the Act on Chemical Substances and Products, seen as one of the most important laws next to the Environmental Protection Act (Moe, 1994). It established a system requiring mandatory approval and labelling of chemical products.

In 1973, after two years of extensive negotiations between the Ministry for Pollution Control and the most important interest organisations, parliament finally adopted the Environmental Protection Act, which entered into force on 1 October 1974. The law was passed with the votes of the Social Democrats (in government) and the Conservative Party, which had close links to the Federation of Danish Industries. The policy approach was in many ways exemplary, at least on paper: fragmented regulations were replaced by a general framework act and an integrated permit system for industrial pollution, and a separate Ministry of Environment was institutionalised and given substantial resources. Moreover, the implementation of decisions on guidelines and technical standards was removed from parliament and left to negotiations between the major interest organisations and public officials from the Ministry of Environment on a neo-corporatist basis. Traditionally, the key elements of Danish policy style have been the emphasis on consensus-seeking and a striving to reach an understanding among those regulated.

Some of the key officials in the Ministry of Environment came from the Ministry of the Interior. They brought with them a line of thinking about the relationship between national and local authorities that stemmed from the 1968 reform of local authorities, which gave municipalities more power and established fourteen regional counties. The municipalities were thus made the main responsible units for the implementation of environmental policy; a choice which was not discussed in the political arena, however (Andersen, 1989). So, while the responsibility for the implementation of environmental laws lies with the local authorities in many countries, the combination of environmental responsibility and exceptionally strong interests in local tax revenues has become troublesome in Denmark (cf. Andersen, 1994a).

When the environmental protection law entered into force in the mid-1970s, other political issues had come to dominate the political agenda. Unemployment had increased considerably, and Denmark had been thrown into a bitter debate on the future of energy supply, in particular on the use of nuclear power. Itself without energy sources, Denmark had relied exclusively on imported oil and coal when the energy crisis broke out in 1973. In the end, the government abandoned nuclear power as an option and chose a policy of energy savings, efficiency measures and supply diversification including wind and solar energy. The availability of oil and gas in the North Sea also changed the policy options. Despite these measures, coal remained the most important source of energy. The early development and refinement of a comprehensive national energy planning system made Danish energy policy relatively advanced (Lucas, 1985).

The 1980s: compliance issues and non-point sources of pollution
In the early 1980s, environmental issues were gradually put on the agenda again. There were many indications that the local authorities had not implemented the regulations and laws of the 1970s in the way they should have had (Miljøstyrelsen, 1985; DIOS, 1987). Using the legal options for access to public files, environmentalists began to

investigate whether industries were in compliance with environmental permits, and to what extent local authorities had enforced these permits. The environmentalists found that most of both the larger and smaller companies investigated had breached their environmental permits, and they attracted media attention by reporting such breaches to the police for prosecution (Larsen and Christensen, 1985). The police had difficulties in treating such breaches as violations of the law since the local authorities had often been privy to them. The local authorities often responded by issuing new and more lenient permits to the industries in question. As a result, a more intense debate on environmental policy began to emerge.

Incidents of eutrophication of the interior Danish seawaters in the early 1980s turned attention to nutrient pollution from agricultural run-off, mainly caused by nitrogen. But changes in EU membership had changed the structural development of Danish agriculture, and this only reinforced intensification. Encouraged by the government, which wanted to maximise the benefit of the Common Agricultural Policy (CAP), farmers invested and specialised their production so as to increase production as much as possible. Livestock production became concentrated in the western part of Jutland on sandy soils where the yield from crops was small and which were the most vulnerable to nitrate leakage.

In October 1986, national television transmitted the now famous picture of a bucketful of dead lobsters. This picture brought the conflicts that had been apparent in environmental policy for some years out into the public arena. While the phenomenon of eutrophication had previously been limited to bays and fjords, its effects on the quantity of oxygen in the Kattegat had now become a problem. In response to the dead lobsters (and fish), the influential Nature Conservation Society demanded a 50 per cent reduction in discharges from agriculture, cities and industries. Within less than four weeks, its demands had been accepted and made official policy in a resolution issued by the Danish parliament. The outcome, the Plan for the Aquatic Environment (1987), as well as its successor, the Plan for Sustainable Agriculture (1992), introduced ambitious and binding guidelines for waste water treatment as well as new restrictions on agricultural practices, mainly with regard to manure spreading (Landbrugsministeriet, 1991). Despite the fact that two-thirds of all nitrate leaching to marine waters from the Nordic countries stemmed from Denmark (Bernes, 1993), the plan did nevertheless become one of the most disputed and controversial domestic environmental issues (Miljøstyrelsen, 1990; ATV, 1990; Schrøder, 1990; Røjel, 1990; Dubgaard, 1991; Andersen and Hansen, 1991).

Air pollution has not been an issue to the same extent as water pollution, and certainly not compared with the situation in the other Nordic countries. Most air emissions stem from power plants, which are organised into two regional monopolies. In 1984, the government reached an agreement with the management of these monopolies for a substantial reduction in air pollution within the framework of quotas allocated within a national air pollution control 'bubble'. Later these targets were strengthened, although this received little public attention, because these air polluters are an exclusive group that remains outside media attention. With regard to vehicle emissions, Denmark was more vociferous at the EU level. Without a national car industry, Denmark pushed for US standards (Holzinger, 1994).

The 1990s: a new approach develops

In 1993, the independent Danish Economic Council published a twenty-year account of environmental policy which was rather critical of the results attained (Det Økonomiske Råd, 1993). The balance showed that the content of nitrate in the groundwater had increased and that the average oxygen content in Kattegat had deteriorated by about 25 per cent, depleting fish resources. With regard to air pollution, SO_2 emissions had declined by about 50 per cent from 1972 to 1992, while NO_x emissions had increased by 50 per cent. CO_2 emissions had remained stable over the period. The Economic Council concluded that: 'The environmental policy pursued in Denmark over the last 20 years has not resulted in substantial improvements of the marine environment nor of ambient air quality. However, due to economic growth, and the derived increase in the use of resources, this does not imply that environmental policy has been useless.' Still, the council stressed the ineffectiveness of the predominant regulatory approach and recommended the use of market instruments. The findings of the Economic Council confirmed other studies and reports published in the same period, reports which were critical of the prevailing approach to environmental policy (Andersen, 1993; DMU, 1991).

During the first part of the 1990s, a new approach to environmental policy-making gradually broadened the range of instruments applied. Not only were economic instruments introduced, but voluntary agreements were also applied in a number of cases. While these instruments have been directed mainly towards traditional target groups such as producers and polluters, more attention has also been paid to consumers and the role that they play in bringing about changes. For example, a public labelling system for organic farm products – the red 'Ø' – has been successful in extending the sales of organic foods, which are now available in most regular supermarkets and shops. The role of the public sector as a consumer has also changed. Public procurement has been used to signal to producers the importance of environmental concerns, and local as well as state institutions have begun to specify the environmental product standards to which they give priority when they invite tenders for supply. In addition, the Ministry of Environment has embarked on a new and more product-oriented environmental strategy, in which life cycle assessments will play a crucial role (Miljø- og Energiministeriet, 1995).

Another topic of environmental policy-making in the 1990s has been policy integration. As a follow-up to the Brundtland Report, the Ministries of Energy and Transport were required to draw up plans for sustainable development and for CO_2 reductions. The Ministry of Energy has presented a rather impressive plan, Energy 2000, with detailed prescriptions for CO_2 reductions. Although Energy 2000 builds on the tradition of national energy plans, it goes beyond supply diversification and supply security, which were the main concerns in previous plans. Instead, Energy 2000 has made an ambitious effort to integrate environmental targets with energy planning. The aim is to have reduced CO_2 emissions by 20 per cent and energy consumption by 15 per cent by the year 2005 (the baseline year is 1988). Energy 2000 is a catalogue of policy initiatives which will make these targets attainable. Both CO_2 taxation and the reform of existing energy taxes (making them reflect the actual energy use and environmental load) are important measures in this catalogue. Other measures are improved standards for appliances and the extension of wind energy and other renewables, as well as a substitution of coal with natural gas and improved efficiency in the remaining coal-based power plants. The Ministry of Transport has, on the other hand, aimed only at stabilising CO_2 emissions and has been more concerned with its traditional task of extending the highway network and with the new fixed links across the Great Belt and the Øresund.

Partly to improve policy integration, the responsibility for implementing the Plan for the Aquatic Environment was given to the Ministry of Agriculture rather than the Ministry of Environment. The Ministry of Agriculture took the opportunity to elaborate its own sub-plan, the Plan for Sustainable Agriculture, and it seems as if the shift in the responsibility for implementation was important in changing the course of thinking in the Ministry of Agriculture, although it also used the opportunity to water down some of the details in the original plans. The Ministry of Agriculture has generally become more independent of agricultural organisations (Daugbjerg, 1995).

An attempt to establish a more comprehensive environmental planning model was made with the Nature and Environment Policy Report released in 1995 (Miljøministeriet, 1995). The report itself paralleled the annual reports of the key economic ministries and this made observers raise the question of whether the Ministry of Environment had promoted itself to a cross-sectoral 'over-ministry' of the same rank as, for example, the Ministry of Finance. Although there is no doubt that the Ministry of Environment in Denmark is a relatively important ministry, a closer look at the Nature and Environment Report revealed that most of the sectoral policies remained in the hands of the sectoral ministries. The most innovative step in the report was the introduction of the concept of environmental utilisation space in Danish policy. This concept refers to the amount of resources that can be consumed at a sustainable level per capita (Opschoor and Weterings, 1994). On a political level, its significance lies in its focus on individual consumption patterns, and it may thus signal a new post-Brundtland phase in environmental policy-making, in which the conflictual relationship between environmental and economic growth once again comes under scrutiny.

Institutional context

The Ministry of Environment and Energy

The Ministry of Environment, which was founded in 1971, was merged with the smaller Ministry of Energy in 1994. Organisationally, the Ministry of Environment and Energy consists of a small leading 'Departement' and three relatively large administrative agencies: the Danish Environmental Protection Agency (Miljøstyrelsen), the Danish Energy Agency (Energistyrelsen) and the National Forest and Nature Agency (Skov- og Naturstyrelsen). In addition, three research agencies come under its domain; Denmark's Environmental Research Institute (Danmarks Miljø Undersøgelser, DMU) is the most important of these.

When first established, the Ministry of Environment was itself a merger of existing administrative units from other ministries. Nature conservation was transferred from the Ministry of Culture, planning regulations were transferred from the Ministry of Housing, and raw material management was transferred from the Ministry of Public Works. Later, units were transferred from the Ministry of Agriculture, notably within forest and nature management. The Ministry of Energy was established in 1979, mainly as an offshoot of the Ministry of Trade; it became responsible both for off-shore industry and energy planning. The Ministries of Environment and Energy were merged in 1994, mainly because climate policies required more and better co-ordination between environmental and energy policies.

The agencies of the combined ministry are formally subordinate to the 'Departement', but because most environmental issues are technically complicated and because the 'Departement' has often lacked the expertise to challenge the recommendations made by its agencies, the 'Departement' has recently redefined the roles of the agencies and itself. The agencies will prepare cases directly for approval by the minister, and the 'Departement' will devote more attention to international co-ordination, e.g. in relation to EU negotiations and inter-ministerial co-ordination, to ensure that environmental policies are better integrated in other sectoral policies (Bjørnskov, 1994).

The administrative agencies
The oldest and most important agency is the Danish Environmental Protection Agency. It has about 350 employees and is responsible for traditional areas of pollution control regarding water, air, chemicals, waste and soil, as well as for subsidy programmes for cleaner technologies and aid to Eastern Europe (Christiansen, 1996: 49). The Environmental Protection Agency supervises the local authorities, and it issues guidelines for the administration of the environmental framework laws at the local level. Furthermore, many decisions taken at the local level can be appealed to the agency.

From 1978 to 1990, the head of the Environmental Protection Agency was Jens Kampmann, who was Denmark's first Minister of Pollution Control from 1971 to 1973. During the 1978–1990 period, the agency developed into a relatively powerful and independent agency. Unusual for an administrative agency, it was allowed to voice its own opinions in the public debate if only it made clear that the opinions were not necessarily those of the Minister of Environment (Pedersen and Geckler, 1987).

The Danish Energy Agency, founded in 1976, made up the greater part of the former Ministry of Energy. It has two main responsibilities: the management of Denmark's sub-soil resources, mainly in the North Sea where oil and gas are explored; and energy planning and savings, which includes the extension of renewable energy sources. The Energy Agency is a more traditional agency, which has adhered to more normal patterns of subordination to its minister and ministry. Since the merger of the Environment and Energy Ministries, the Energy Agency has also become responsible for the management of the CO_2 tax. Using part of the tax proceeds, subsidies are offered for district heating and energy efficiency measures in industries and for local energy savings consultants authorised by the agency.

The National Forest and Nature Agency is responsible for the practical management of Denmark's state forests as well as for the preservation of wetlands and natural reserves. It was established only in 1987, the result of a merger between former units in the Environment and Agricultural Ministries. Because of the great number of responsibilities it must manage on the practical level, it employs a large proportion of the total number of employees in the Ministry of Environment.

Prior to 1988, the Danish Environmental Protection Agency controlled about ten different research institutions and laboratories. In 1988, these research institutions were united within one independent environmental research institute, the DMU. Among the various reasons for this development was the wish to make the research institutions independent of the Environmental Protection Agency. While subordinate to this powerful agency, the research institutions were seen as having to provide the scientific background for policies often already developed in the agency. With the creation of the DMU, the research institutions acquired a more independent position which did, to some extent, improve their credibility outside the Ministry of Environment.

Local authorities

Denmark has an administrative tradition for local administration and decentralisation that is stronger than that found in many other countries; local municipalities enjoy considerable autonomy. They collect their own income taxes, and although they also receive grants from the state, local taxes are their most important source of revenue. Local taxes make up about one-third of all taxes, and in few other places in the EU do local authorities have such a share in taxation. In addition, the municipalities and counties have broad discretionary powers within the limits of the law. In environmental policy, most guidelines are not binding for the local authorities, and enforcement is an issue for the municipal authorities, rather than for the police.

The roots of decentralisation are to be found in the constitutional conflict that took place in the late nineteenth century between the ruling class in Copenhagen and the farmers and smaller landholders of the countryside, who struggled for independence and local self-governance (Østergård, 1990). The farmers' movement was mainly inspired by the poet, priest and educator, N. F. S. Grundtvig (Thodberg and Thyssen, 1983). When Copenhagen's ruling class forced parliament out of operation with a rule by decree in the 1890s, the farmers eventually seized power in both houses of parliament in 1901. Since then, the profound scepticism of rule from Copenhagen has ensured that much of the competence regarding most public services is decentralised to the local authorities (Mørch, 1982).

The local authorities were thus allocated an important role in the implementation of most environmental laws. They were given responsibility for the management of sewage treatment plants, water supply and waste management facilities. Furthermore, they were given the responsibility for issuing permits to companies required to have a permit for their operation according to the Environmental Protection Act. Local authorities were also given the responsibility for monitoring compliance with such permits. While the 277 municipalities are responsible for issuing permits and controlling most of the industrial and agricultural polluters, the fourteen counties are responsible for the more specialised and heavy industrial sectors. While the municipalities generally have more practical management responsibilities, the counties are more responsible for the monitoring and control of environmental quality as such. The environmental administrations are very small, especially in the smaller municipalities with less than 5000 inhabitants, and often they do not function very well. These administrations have difficulties in ensuring compliance and in dealing with more advanced technical issues, e.g. in relation to cleaner technologies (Andersen and Jørgensen, 1995).

A comprehensive system of national, regional and local planning was introduced in the 1970s in the Planning Act. One of the main purposes of the Planning Act was to enable a better co-ordination of policies between the different public authorities. Environmental protection was among the issues incorporated into this planning system. The municipalities were obliged to draw up plans for water supply, waste management, waste water treatment, noise abatement, etc., and these sectoral plans were to form part of the general municipal plan. Within this larger plan, the sectoral plans were to be co-ordinated with other local plans, e.g. for roads and social welfare. The counties were also obliged to elaborate water supply plans, waste management plans and water quality plans dealing with the same issues at the regional level, again incorporating them into the general regional plan. Furthermore, the counties were obliged to ensure that the municipal plans were not in conflict with the regional plan. There was no plan at the state level, but the Minister of Environment had a general say and could intervene in the regional and local planning process if interests differed or were in conflict. While the planning system has lost some of its political significance today, it remains formally in place, and the local authorities are still obliged to present sectoral plans, including for environmental issues (Kristensen *et al.*, 1987).

Interest organisations

A key element in Danish policy-making is the corporatist system of decision-making. Major interest organisations are closely involved in negotiations for the drafting of legislation as well as in the subsequent implementation. Such negotiations are expected not only to facilitate the approval of a bill in parliament but also to legitimise its subsequent implementation. The most important organisations representing groups targeted by legislation are the Federation of Danish Industries (Dansk Industri) and the Agriculture Council of Denmark (Landbrugsrådet).

The Federation of Danish Industries is an umbrella organisation, and it is normally the most important partner for the environmental authorities when drawing up new legislative proposals. The federation or some if its sub-associations are involved every time new administrative decrees are tabled, and it is quite influential during the implementation stage when actual guidelines are drawn up.

The Agriculture Council of Denmark is an umbrella organisation comprising three independent organisations of farmers: the Danish Farmers' Union, the Danish Family Farmers' Union and the Danish Commercial Farmers' Union. Historically, the Agriculture Council has been more adverse to the idea of pollution control. In 1973, the Agriculture Council demanded economic compensation for pollution control requirements, and although the Pollution Council had identified the problems of large livestock farms and manure disposal, the new framework law was written without paying much attention to agriculture. In fact, it was often said that the Environmental Protection Act did not apply to 'Greenland, the Faroe Islands and agriculture'. (Most Danish laws include an exemption clause for Greenland and the Faroe Islands.) The Agriculture Council resisted environmental regulation for about ten years, and as recently as 1985, its president declared that the very idea that agriculture polluted stemmed from 'a Marxist way of thinking' (Andersen and Hansen, 1991).

Today, despite its resistance, agriculture has become subject to more detailed environmental regulation. However, to avoid the fertiliser tax advocated by environmentalists, the Agriculture Council has gradually had to accept a more and more fine-meshed net of command-and-control regulations. The Danish Family Farmers' Union is, on the other hand, more friendly to the idea of restrictions on agricultural practices, and therefore the Agriculture Council has not always been able to act unanimously. Once one of the strongest and most powerful organisations in Denmark, its power is now gradually declining, partly due to the role of environmental issues. Although it seems still to possess a kind of veto right on crucial issues, it was not powerful enough to stop a recently passed pesticide tax.

The most important environmental or 'green' organisations, in terms of membership, activism and influence, have been the Danish Society for the Conservation of Nature (Danmarks Naturfrednings-forening), the World Wildlife Fund, Greenpeace Denmark, NOAH (the Danish section of Friends of the Earth), the Ornithological Association and the Anglers' Association. A host of smaller green organisations and consumer groups have been active as well.

The Society for the Conservation of Nature was established in 1911 and merged the interests of local citizens with those of concerned scientists in a powerful alliance (Rehling, 1994). In 1937, the Conservation Act was passed, granting the organisation semi-official status in recognition of its growing influence. At the suggestion of the then Prime Minister, Thorvald Stauning, the society was entrusted with the right to initiate proposals for the preservation of sites and landscapes. Delegating responsibility to a private organisation was conspicuous, but not unusual for the decentralised and corporatist Danish policy style that developed during the first half of the twentieth century. For many years, the society remained a careful and venerable organisation, which came to regard itself almost as a public institution. With a current membership numbering about 250,000, it has become the largest environmental organisation in Denmark. Since the mid-1980s, it has developed into a more independent environmental interest group (Svold, 1989).

As with the Society for the Conservation of Nature, all environmental organisations have been granted the formal right to appeal local environmental licences and permits to the Environmental Appeal Board. Yet the membership figures and influence of other environmental organisations are somewhat less impressive. Although Greenpeace has been regarded as less 'serious' than the Nature Conservation Society, it has been quite influential in lobbying parliament's Environment Committee and the Ministry of Environment on matters regarding international conventions. NOAH, the grassroots organisation which was established after an event at the University of Copenhagen in 1968, has been weakened substantially over the last few years. It has refused to accept the appeal right in the Environmental Protection Act, claiming that the appeal right is a symbolic gesture, offering no real opportunities for environmentalists to influence pollution control. The Anglers' Association is small as well, but has been influential in its own field, i.e. the protection of water courses, thanks to continuous lobbying of local and national authorities.

The Environmental Appeal Board

Apparently, Denmark is the only EU member state that has a 'high court' of the environment: the Environmental Appeal Board (Basse, 1987). The establishment of this institution in 1974 resulted from industrial concerns that the Environmental Protection Agency would otherwise become too powerful. Decisions taken by local authorities and appealed to the Environmental Protection Agency may thus, in the end, be appealed to the Environmental Appeal Board. Although only issues of principal interest can be appealed to this institution, its rulings are final and decisive for the administration at lower levels of government. The Appeal Board does not hesitate to overrule decisions taken by the Environmental Protection Agency. It has served as a brake on a rather zealous Environmental Protection Agency, especially in the early 1980s.

The Appeal Board combines a legal body with a corporatist interest mediation body. Headed by a judge, the board consists of experts nominated by interest organisations (industrial, agricultural and other) and by the Environmental Protection Agency. Through this body, interest organisations are consulted and negotiated with on important cases. Although environmental organisations are not represented on the Appeal Board, their rights to complain were enlarged and formalised in the 1981 and 1991 amendments to the framework law. The board can thus be seen as an institutionalised procedure of traditional neo-corporatist interest mediation.

Parliament's green majority

To understand why environmental policy became an issue of some salience in Denmark, it is necessary to consider the particular parliamentary situation that existed during most of the 1980s, which allowed the Committee on the Environment and Regional Planning (Miljø- og planlægningsudvalget) of the Danish parliament to play an important, but unpredictable, role as a promoter (cf. also Andersen, 1996).

Denmark has a parliamentary tradition for minority governments, i.e. governments which do not control a majority in parliament (Damgaard, 1992). When Poul Schlüter's Conservative government, consisting of four centre and right parties, seized power in 1982, it was a minority government, as were its predecessors. Poul Schlüter's main concern was with economic policies as well as maintaining power after several years of Social Democratic rule. His government had to accept that policies on the environment as well as security and other issues could be decided by majorities of the opposition.[3] To avoid having to resign should the government be outvoted in such instances, he introduced a new constitutional practice.

The economic and financial policies of Schlüter's government were based on a close alliance with the small Social Liberal Party (De Radikale). But with respect to environmental issues, the Social Liberals often did not support the government. So together with the Social Democrats and two left parties, the Social Liberals formed the alternative, so-called 'green majority'.

During most of the period from 1982 to 1993, the green majority often influenced environmental policy. The Minister of Environment was often questioned and required to present plans to parliament's Committee on the Environment and Regional Planning, which played an independent role in promoting new policies and initiatives. Its activities peaked in the parliamentary year 1986–1987, during which it raised 1103 written questions and conducted forty-three consultations with the minister. In 1993–1994, the number of written questions had declined by 50 per cent, but the number of consultations increased to sixty-seven, or more than one each week (Christiansen, 1996: 41). The Committee on the Environment and Regional Planning did not work out an all-embracing strategy; its members brought smaller and larger issues to the committee on an *ad hoc* basis, and there was little systematic use of the power which the committee possessed.

From 1982 to 1988, Christian Christensen of the small Danish Christian Party held the post as Minister of Environment. Christian Christensen was often accused of being a victim to zealous officials in his ministry, but the Christian Party was also eager to present itself as a 'green' party. Since Christian Christensen held the only portfolio for his party in the fragile minority government, he had a good position to do so. It was difficult for the coalition parties to turn down his proposals and ideas, since their reluctance could endanger the participation of the Christian Party in the government and thus the fate of the government as such. In fact, he willingly accepted many of the ideas and proposals emanating from the Committee on the Environment and Regional Planning, and most of the important plans were drawn up during his period as minister.

In 1988, Poul Schlüter persuaded the Social Liberals to join his new minority coalition government, and Lone Dybkjær was assigned the environment portfolio. As one of the architects of environmental policy while serving on the Committee on the Environment and Regional Planning, her effort was intended to bring some order into the many new, but fragmented, regulations. Still in 1990, the Social Liberals left the government again, and the green majority was re-established. The years from 1990 to 1993 were calmer regarding environmental issues, reflecting the shift to other issues on the political agenda. But the green majority did manage to introduce a CO_2 tax, which opposed the policy of the government. In 1993, the Social Democrats returned to power.

Because of the particular parliamentary position and the existence of the green majority, environmental issues often escalated on the political agenda and the neo-corporatist system came under pressure. The members of the Committee on the Environment and Regional Planning were particularly eager to demonstrate that they would impose more ambitious targets or deadlines than would the government. The interest organisations began to hesitate in negotiations with the government, because they did not know what would happen when parliament began to intervene. In order to reach a compromise, they often made concessions to the government, but since the government did not hold a majority they did not know whether the compromise would hold, or whether they would be asked to give new concessions. The 1980s has been characterised as a 'restless' epoch in environmental policy with little consistency in reform initiatives (Garde, 1993).

In the 1980s, the corporatist system lost its grip on policy-making, and in the more loosely coupled political system, interest organisations began to lobby for their interests rather than negotiate. Environmental policy-making thus became more fragmented and less coherent than, for instance, in the Netherlands, and it lacked the stability that characterised German environmental policy during the same period. Until recently, there has been no national environmental policy plan in Denmark, but rather a number of sectoral targets and plans, many of which were rather ambitious.

When Schlüter resigned in 1993 and the Social Democrats returned to power (in coalition with the Social Liberals, the Centre Democrats and the Christian People's Party), the former green majority did, in a way, gain control of the environmental policy institutions. While the Conservative-led government had been reluctant to ensure the implementation of the often ambitious policy goals and did little to clarify technical problems, the new government was eager to revitalise most of the plans and initiatives previously approved by parliament. The new Minister of Environment and Energy, Svend Auken, declared that 'green issues would be the red thread of the government's policy', and the government programme listed a number of important environmental policy initiatives, such as a CO_2 tax on industrial emissions as well as a plan for job creation in the environmental sector. The government also initiated an update on energy and transport policies.

Despite the escalation of many environmental issues, the basic corporatist arrangements for environmental policy-making remained in place. The standard operating procedure for new proposals has been to try to sort out differences in preparatory committees, where organised interests are consulted. Still, in comparison with other countries, the Danish political system appears to have fostered a relatively open attitude to policy ideas from outside the established circles.

The economy and the environment

The Brundtland Report, released by the World Commission on Environment and Development in 1987, acquired a significant role in the Danish debate on environmental policy. There was special interest in its recommendations to halve energy consumption and to use economic instruments, as well as in its emphasis on the need for cleaner technologies. For the green majority, the Brundtland Report provided an important rationale for many of the policy goals pursued and was an ample point of reference (Verdenskommissionen, 1988).

Simultaneously with the release of the Brundtland Report, the Environmental Protection Agency embarked on a new policy that was based on cleaner technologies. The aim was to develop specific cleaner technologies for selected industrial processes by means of subsidised pilot projects, and to show by means of example how pollution control at the source could be compatible with economically profitable solutions for the individual firm (Miljøstyrelsen, 1986). In contrast to the former, more legalistic, going-by-the-book strategy, the cleaner technology programme placed the officials of the environmental agency in a practical dialogue with members of industry about the development of cleaner technologies.

In 1988, Minister of Environment, Lone Dybkjær of the Social Liberal Party published an influential discussion paper entitled 'Simple and effective', which indirectly suggested a political bargain between environmentalists and Schlüter's Conservative government and emphasised the combination of economic effectiveness, regulatory reform and improved environmental protection (Miljøministeriet, 1988). Its practical focus was on both cleaner technologies and the use of economic instruments as means to be used for simplifying and deregulating the environment, while at the same time improving performance. The discussion paper prepared the way for a reform of environmental laws (cf. above): in the revised Environmental Protection Act, the use and development of cleaner technologies, rather than end-of-pipe measures, were accorded a key role.

In the course of the reform, twenty-one environmental laws were merged into four main laws: the Environmental Protection Law, the Planning Law, the Nature Protection Law and the Contaminated Soil Law. The reduction in the number of laws was more or less a symbolic gesture to the business community, because the merger only reorganised existing laws under common headings and did not reduce the complexity of regulation. Among the twenty-one laws were two laws from 1861, one prohibiting unchained dogs in a Copenhagen deer park and another regulating the speed of vessels on the Gudenå water course, which had little practical significance anyway (Garde, 1993: 80). The most important result was the restriction of the right to complain to the Environmental Appeal Board: only cases of principal interest could now be appealed; the remaining cases were to be sorted out by the Environmental Protection Agency. In other words, more effort was to be devoted to making environmental policy more effective (Miljøministeriet, 1989).

In 1987–1988, a number of economic instruments were introduced, such as a national waste tax, a CFC tax and packaging taxes. They provided increased revenue for the Ministry of Environment during a period when public spending was being restricted. The waste tax, for example, financed more than half of the ministry's budget. Previous reservations against the use of economic instruments were lifted; and in the years that followed, more and more emphasis was placed on the role of economic instruments for a more preventive environmental policy. In 1993, taxes were reformed to include a substantial package of 'green' taxes. This reform shifted the burden of taxation from income to other sources of revenue, including that based on pollution. During 1994 and 1995, discussion focused on how to introduce taxes in order to fulfil several of the environmental targets not yet attained. A political compromise was reached on a pesticide tax and on a substantial increase in the part of the CO_2 tax relating to industrial emissions. In the future, the CO_2 tax will be DKr600/ton CO_2 (about US$ 100) on industrial heating, while the tax will be DKr90 for industrial processes, although specific sectors vulnerable to international competition may enjoy exemptions. Green taxes and energy taxes have now become important for the state budget, providing about 10 per cent of total revenue (Andersen, 1994b).

The principle of integrating economy and ecology gained support in the early 1990s, not least in academic and administrative circles. For the many key positions occupied by professional economists in most ministries and interest organisations, this was probably important for the consensus that evolved. The influential and independent Economic Council has since 1993 extended its activities to include environmental policy aspects. The environmental expertise of the council has been institutionalised by the appointment of a separate expert in environmental economics. The Ministry of Taxation as well as the Ministry of Finance have released comprehensive reports on economic instruments and the integration of environmental concerns in economic policies (Skatteministeriet, 1992; Finansministeriet, 1994). High unemployment has also provided a stimulus to rethink environmental policy in terms of the know-how, export and jobs that the environmental sector could produce (Metals miljøudvalg, 1988). A report published by the Ministry of Trade and Industry estimated that the energy and environment sector accounts for 70,000 jobs and DKr22 billion in annual exports (Erhvervsfremmestyrelsen, 1994). The Danish experience with windmill sales was important in showing how being at the forefront can produce know-how and subsequent export. All in all, the conventional view of a conflict between environmental policy and economic policies has been in retreat. Perhaps this new line of thinking was most clearly expressed by Minister of Environment, Svend Auken, when he spoke about Denmark as an experimentarium for a new, more environmentally friendly lifestyle:

> Denmark can be made an experimentarium for a new lifestyle that combines modern industrial production and welfare with ecological responsibility. It requires that we give a high priority to research and technological innovation, but perhaps we can also develop new models of governance and organisation, which pass on and develop the co-operative traditions as well as the traditions of public participation and discussion.
>
> (Miljøministeriet, 1995)

Foreign environmental policy agenda

Historically, Denmark's profile in international environmental policy has been less pronounced than Norway's and Sweden's, but it is becoming more articulate. One reason for Denmark's lower international profile could be that Denmark has been less exposed to transfrontier pollution than its Nordic neighbours. For Denmark, transfrontier pollution occurs mainly in marine waters, where it does not cause visible effects that can be clearly distinguished from those emanating from domestic sources. Oil spills from international shipping are an exception. With regard to air pollution, Denmark is little affected because of lime layers in the underground. In fact, Denmark is itself a net exporter (Bernes, 1993: 45). Denmark's more recent involvement in international environmental policy is best explained by an increased awareness that a high domestic level of environmental policy can be difficult to maintain for a small and open economy. But there is also a certain pressure for involvement emanating from Denmark's growing environment industry.

Denmark is a signatory to a large number of international environmental agreements, and Denmark has usually been an active proponent of relatively stringent environmental standards (Miljøstyrelsen, 1988). Despite its relative dependence on coal as an energy source, Denmark has supported policies to reduce emissions of SO_2 and NO_x. In the early 1980s, Denmark joined the 30 Per Cent Club, and at the EU level, Denmark supported relatively high standards in the Directive on Large Combustion Plants as well as in the Directive on Vehicle Emissions. With regard to CFCs, Denmark joined the Montreal Club and advocated a quick phase-out of substances hazardous to the ozone layer.

In response to the increased significance of EU environmental policy and Europeanisation, the Ministry of Environment formally listed the following environmental issues as the most important to Denmark: 1) nutrient eutrophication of marine waters; 2) radioactive waste discharged or dumped at sea; 3) oil pollution by ships in marine waters; and 4) nuclear safety (Miljøstyrelsen, 1988).

With regard to nutrients and eutrophication, Danish targets are similar to those set in the Paris Convention on the North Sea, and they also inspired the targets set in this convention. Before 1987, the year when Denmark proposed making its own standards for sewage treatment and agricultural run-off from the Plan for the Aquatic Environment applicable to all countries in the Paris Convention, Denmark had not submitted any proposals, except for joint Nordic proposals and proposals regarding procedures for the

Paris Convention. Sætevik (1988), who studied the convention, classified Sweden and the Netherlands as the most active members (Sætevik, 1988: 99).

Radioactive waste discharged from nuclear processing plants, such as Sellafield and La Hague, can be monitored in the Baltic Sea, and the discharge and dumping of radioactive waste has been a traditional concern for Denmark (Ringius, 1994). In the London Convention on radioactive waste materials, Denmark co-ordinated its position closely with that of the other Nordic countries. Because Danish straits and belts are subject to considerable international shipping activity, oil spills and subsequent pollution of Danish beaches have also become a recurrent problem, which Denmark has tried to prevent through OILPOL (prevention of sea pollution by oil), MARPOL (prevention of sea pollution by ships) and the Helsinki Convention (HELCOM). The main problem is no longer the making of formal rules, but rather the lack of compliance, not least by Eastern European ships; but it is difficult and costly to detect the responsible party. About 300 oil spills are reported annually, and they damage especially the tourist industry, which depends on an attractive coastline.

Barsebäck, the nuclear power plant located across the Øresund only 20 km from the centre of Copenhagen, also remains a recurrent concern and issue of dispute with Sweden. Several times, the Danish parliament and government has requested the Swedish government to close down Barsebäck, or at least to give the closure of Barsebäck first priority in the Swedish plan for the phasing out of nuclear power. Swedish governments over the years have shown little obligingness for Danish concerns about the vicinity of Barsebäck. The date for the closure of Barsebäck remains uncertain.

The Danish foreign environmental policy agenda is not steady. Compared with the issues listed as the most important in the late 1980s, several new issues have emerged as perhaps even more important.

Nutrients and agriculture
Now that the EU Directives on Urban Waste Water (91/271) and on Nitrate (91/676) have been passed, Denmark cannot expect much more at the EU level with regard to eutrophication initiatives, except for improvements in monitoring and ensuring compliance among member states with regard to these directives. However, the eutro-

phication issue may be addressed in the broader context of agricultural policy. In that regard, Denmark supports reform measures that improve the conditions for organic farming, protect environmentally sensitive areas, etc. Environment Commissioner, Ritt Bjerregård's proposal to start a debate on future reforms of the CAP reflects such Danish concerns, but it may be difficult for Denmark to support her clear position fully because of concerns about the future of Danish agriculture (*Environment Watch*, 1995b).

Climate change

Denmark is a signatory to the Rio Climate Convention and has been relatively active in its efforts to meet its own CO_2 target, which is to reduce emissions by 20 per cent (baseline year: 1988). Because of national energy planning and Energy 2000, very detailed accounts can be made of CO_2 emissions and reductions. Currently, Denmark is about 6 per cent behind its reduction target, according to official sources, but an increase in the CO_2 tax combined with voluntary agreements is expected during 1995 and is supposed to ensure the attainment of the reduction target. Denmark was thus among the few countries at the 1995 Berlin Conference that could present a relatively optimistic report.

Denmark can be expected to try to keep the EU moving ahead on the climate issue and to stick to the stabilisation target agreed upon earlier among the EU member states. No doubt Denmark's position will be to support the intentions of the Dublin Declaration of the European Council, that the EU should take the lead over the US and Japan in the control of CO_2 emissions.

Economic instruments

Denmark has been an active proponent of CO_2 taxes at the international and EU levels. Although economic instruments have not been so willingly accepted by other EU member states, Denmark has continued to advocate their use. In the domestic context, there has been a certain pressure to 'export' the use of economic instruments, not only to put Danish industries on an equal footing with those of other member states, but probably more importantly because CO_2 and other taxes are seen as more effective policy instruments with regard to the concurrent implementation deficits in EU environmental policy.

Waste export

A recent priority has been the Basel Convention and the ban on the export of waste and hazardous waste to Third World countries. Together with the other Nordic countries, Denmark proposed to insert the political agreement previously achieved on such a ban directly into the text of the convention. This priority created a controversy within the Commission, which as a signatory to the convention maintained that it, and not Denmark, formally has the right to submit such proposals. The case is an interesting one in light of the possible influence of the Nordic bloc. The Commission actually elaborated a less stringent proposal and required Denmark to withdraw its own proposal. But since Norway – as a more independent member of the convention – had supported the Danish proposal, it would formally remain, whether or not Denmark withdrew its support. In the end, Denmark exchanged views with the Commission, but did not withdraw its independent proposal.

Eastern Europe

Denmark is running a major programme that supports and transfers environmental technologies and know-how to Eastern Europe. The environmental aid programme was proposed by the former green majority in 1989 and was reinforced after the change of government in 1993. The environmental aid programme had three purposes: to increase Danish exports to Eastern Europe, to reduce Danish unemployment and to reduce pollution, in particular transboundary pollution from Eastern Europe (Ringius *et al.*, 1995). The three goals conflict, and the programme has been criticised for giving more support to the environment industry in Denmark than to Eastern Europe. In fact, this industry was looking for a new market and a considerable industry was built up following, for instance, the Plan for the Aquatic Environment, which served to increase the business of one of the main producers of sewage treatment plants, Krüger, which has become one of the largest engineering companies in Denmark.

But there can be little doubt that the government has been concerned about the quality of the environment in Eastern Europe, and that it also wanted to support green interests, which, for instance, were important in organising the campaigns in the Baltic countries against Soviet rule. For the same reason, and in the broader context of Denmark's policy towards Europe, it has been a deliberate policy to expand EU programmes, such as the PHARE programme, to address also the Baltic countries. To what extent Denmark is directly affected by pollution from Eastern Europe remains a relatively open question. Occasional oil spills from ship traffic and the persistent threat from nuclear installations still seem to represent the most urgent environmental impacts of Eastern Europe on Denmark.

Institutional framework for international environmental policy

With regard to EU policies, Denmark has a well-developed tradition for parliamentary consultation before decisions are agreed to. In order to understand the mechanisms that allow parliament's majority to influence Danish foreign environmental policy, a short summary of these complex consultation procedures will be given.[4]

Parliamentary control

The most influential committee in the Danish parliament is the European Committee (formerly named the Market Committee), which receives and approves the mandates given to ministers or top level officials in Council negotiations. Parliament's European Committee has a formal and extensive right of access to documents, but it normally becomes active only in the last stage of Council negotiations (Grønnegård Christensen *et al.*, 1994). Some have described the European Committee as a second chamber of parliament.

In an area such as environmental policy, where public interest and media attention abound, parliament's European Committee is keen on questioning the Minister of Environment and on controlling as much as possible the decisions he will deliver to Brussels. The minister needs a political mandate from the committee, i.e. majority support for his position must be established. According to most observers, ministers regard their presentation and subsequent interrogation in the committee as a rather troublesome and onerous event, and some ministers need to meet practically every week.

Still, the European Committee lost some of its influence when decision-making by qualified majorities was introduced in the Council. Where unanimity applies, the European Committee is more influential, since its consent is necessary for EU initiatives to succeed. For instance, it was because of the position of the European Committee that Denmark blocked the Directive on Vehicle Emissions in 1985

(Holzinger, 1994). With the increased use of qualified majorities, the mandate from the committee needs to be more flexible so as not to bind ministers unreasonably, and the European Committee has lost some of its close grip on ministers because of this. Furthermore, the committee has a control problem because Council meetings are closed, and it is difficult to know whether the Danish minister actually follows a given mandate as loyally as the committee would like him to. The use of qualified majorities implies that the European Committee needs to know more about the positions of other member states before it can give the Danish minister a realistic mandate.

Ministerial co-ordination
Before issues reach parliament's European Committee they are, however, co-ordinated at three different levels: the special interministerial committee for the environment, the interministerial EU committee and the ministerial foreign policy committee. The formal procedures for determining Denmark's policy in the Council and the Committee of Permanent Representatives (COREPER) are relatively centralised in the Ministry of Foreign Affairs, but at the same time, the individual ministries and agencies play a pivotal role since, in practice, instructions are worked out by the sectoral ministries. As parliament enters the process at a rather late stage, the possibilities of influencing the course of the negotiations are generally limited, and this may explain the difficulties which the green majority has had influencing Denmark's position in EU environmental policy, especially in areas with decision-making by qualified majority in the Council.

The special interministerial committees, which consist of officials from the ministries involved, report to the ministerial EU Committee, which is the highest co-ordinating body at the administrative level, and which consists of the permanent undersecretaries (Departementscheferne). The ministerial EU Committee reports to the interministerial foreign policy committee, consisting of the ministers involved, and this committee is responsible for sorting out disagreements within the government. The government's European Committee finally reports to parliament's European Committee.

The Ministry of Foreign Affairs formally plays a key role by being represented on all twenty-nine interministerial committees, and by chairing the EU Committee. In practice, sectoral ministries tend to control the policy-making process, and the function of the special committees for interministerial co-ordination is rather to provide a forum for compulsory consultation with other ministries. The sectoral ministries are responsible for participation in working groups in the Commission and Council phases, and while they formally report to the interministerial special committees, and thus to the Ministry of Foreign Affairs and the European Committee, actual policy networks mean that a great deal of information flows directly between sectoral ministries and the different attachés at the Permanent Representation in Brussels (Jacobsen, 1994). In environmental policy, both time-pressure and the large number of directives pending often cause mandates to be very broad, leaving sometimes considerable discretionary powers to the two environmental attachés in Brussels, especially in matters that have not attracted a great deal of attention in Denmark. In practice, fewer and less detailed instructions are prepared when national officials participate in the meetings in the working groups under COREPER (Jacobsen, 1994: 214).

In the wake of the Danish 'no' to Maastricht, the consultation process was extended so as to allow the major interest organisations better possibilities of expressing their views before decisions are made. The special interministerial committee for the environment has invited up to thirty-eight different interest organisations to attend its meetings. This is the largest number of organisations invited for any special committee.

The EU debate

Denmark became a member of the EU in 1973 after a referendum in which 63.4 per cent voted in favour of membership (Haahr, 1992). Despite this majority, groups that were sceptical towards or against membership of the EU have received 20 to 25 per cent of the vote since the first direct elections to the European Parliament in 1979, and they have held up to five of the sixteen Danish seats. The issue of membership has remained a very sensitive one, as evidenced by the narrow defeat of the Maastricht Treaty in the 1992 referendum.

Although the EU had already taken the first steps towards a common environmental policy in 1972, this policy was of limited significance for Denmark's national environmental policy in the 1970s, partly because of its broad framework character (Bungarten,

1978; Hildebrandt, 1992). More important were directives related to product standards, in particular chemicals, which conflicted with Denmark's environmental and occupational health and safety legislation. Denmark regarded itself as one of the forerunners in environmental policy, domestically as well as internationally, and in the first decade of EU membership Denmark tended to ignore such directives as threatened the level of protection, and tried to refrain from implementation. At the same time, Denmark did not regard the EU as a forum for European or international environmental policy-making, and so directed its efforts towards various international conventions and agreements instead.

The 'policy of ignorance' came to an end in 1983, when the labelling system for chemicals had to be changed according to EU standards in a way that Denmark regarded as a deterioration. Denmark had developed a rather strict labelling system for chemical substances – one of the few preventive instruments that had been introduced at that time in environmental policy – but it did not comply with the three EU directives in force (67/548 with daughter directives; 73/173; 77/728). According to the EU directives, for instance, warnings on carcinogenic organic solvents could vary according to the solvent (Ege and Haffar, 1995: 54). The Commission threatened Denmark with legal proceedings at the European Court of Justice, and because the Court had already in 1979 ruled against Italy in a similar case, it was evident that Denmark had to comply with the harmonised EU labelling rules. Denmark gave in, but tried to remedy the EU labelling system by requiring additional directions for product use from the producers.

The development of the single market was scheduled to be discussed at the 1985 intergovernmental conference in Luxembourg, and because of this, concerns about the possible conflicts between the free movement of goods and environmental standards began to deepen. Along with the fate of the labelling system for chemicals, the decision-making process regarding the control of vehicle exhaust emissions was also important to these concerns. During the discussions on vehicle exhaust emission regulations in the early 1980s, Denmark supported the introduction of US standards in the EU and had, along with Sweden, Norway, Austria and Switzerland, formed the so-called 'Stockholm Group', which agreed to introduce US standards domestically. Because of the resistance, in particular from Italy, the UK, France and their national car producers, the Luxembourg compromise reached in 1985 fell short of the US standards (Arp, 1993; Holzinger, 1994). Faced with the risk of having to impose a standard more lax than the preferred US standards, the green majority in the Danish parliament asked Minister of Environment Christian Christensen to block the Luxembourg compromise, if necessary by means of a veto. They were able to block these standards, but only because Council decisions still required unanimity in 1985.

Against this background, it is not surprising that the insertion of an environmental policy section in the Rome Treaty included in the Single European Act was viewed with suspicion in Denmark. Not only would the Single European Act promote harmonisation of technical and environmental standards, it would also change the decision-making procedures so that in the future decisions could be taken with a qualified majority of votes in a Council where Denmark controlled only three of seventy-six votes. Because of the unclear boundaries between harmonisation and environmental policy measures, this change was perceived as a real threat to domestic environmental standards, not least by the parties of the green majority in the Danish parliament. For example, with the vehicle emission standards case, Denmark would have been outvoted had the new voting procedure been in force, and would have been forced to impose emission standards considerably more lax than those in the US or in neighbouring Sweden.

The ratification of the Single European Act by Denmark was blocked in late 1985 by a majority in the Danish parliament. Although arguments about the loss of national sovereignty were decisive, concerns about national environmental standards were significant too. The one-sided focus on creating an internal market gave the impression that the EU would sacrifice environmental standards for trade and economic growth. The government evaded the block by parliament by calling for a referendum. It argued that it had achieved concessions at the intergovernmental conference that would allow Denmark to maintain a stricter environmental policy at the national level. These concessions were embodied in the so-called 'environmental guarantee', Article 100A(4), in the revised treaty. The Danish Ministry of Foreign Affairs argued that Article 100A(4) would allow a member state to operate higher environmental standards than the harmonised EU measures. Despite the legal and political confusion that surrounded the article, it was an asset to the government's ratification campaign, and the referendum resulted in a defeat of the parliamentary majority. In February 1986, 56 per cent of the Danes voted to ratify the Single European Act.

Before the referendum, questions were already being raised as to whether the interpretation of Article 100A(4) given by the Ministry of Foreign Affairs would be shared by the Commission and the European Court of Justice. In Brussels, the interpretation was less far-reaching than in Copenhagen: that Article 100A(4) would allow a member state to *maintain* higher standards, but would not allow it to introduce new and higher standards in areas that had already been subject to harmonisation measures (see Krämer, 1992 for the Commission's argument). Although this interpretation was at first denied by the Danish Ministry of Foreign Affairs, the environmental guarantee remained a sensitive and troublesome policy option, which Denmark was careful not to invoke. The government seemed to have taken great care not to make use of it, since it would have immediately tested the promises made by the government prior to the referendum.

The case of the directive regarding the wood preservative PCP would have become the first test case for the environmental guarantee. But it was Germany and not Denmark which asked for the Commission's permission to make use of it. The Commission's approval was subsequently challenged by France in an appeal to the Court, and in 1994 the Court made a careful decision in which it asked the Commission to provide a better justification for the use of the guarantee. The Court was careful not to interpret the full meaning of Article 100A(4). Following the ruling in the PCP case, the Danish Ministry of Foreign Affairs withdrew its most optimistic statements and admitted that the guarantee would not apply to the introduction of new and stricter standards in areas that had become harmonised (Udenrigsministeriet, 1994). From the text of Article 100A(4), it follows that the use of the guarantee requires notification and acceptance from the Commission, but the Danish Ministry of Foreign Affairs maintains the opinion that if the Commission does not reply to a notification, use of the guarantee can be regarded as justified.

A ruling by the European Court of Justice in 1987 on the approval system of which Denmark's 1979 law on chemical substances formed the basis, confirmed the general scepticism towards EU environmental policy: the approval system was overruled (Ege and Haffar, 1995: 78). But in a similar product-related test case, the famous 1988 bottle case, the Court surprisingly refused the Commission's claim that Denmark's legislation was incompatible with the internal market. The Court found that Denmark's requirement for a bottle return system was proportionate and justified, despite the possible limitations on the free circulation of goods. Although the Court based its ruling mainly on Article 36, its decision was generally read as an important precedent for taking the environment more into consideration. The political decision to introduce US vehicle emission standards, reached the same year with pressure from the European Parliament, was another turning point in EU environmental policy that helped show the possibilities of realigning market harmonisation with stricter environmental standards.

Nevertheless, Denmark kept a relatively low profile in EU environmental policy-making in the years from 1987 to 1992, when member states such as Germany and the Netherlands were somewhat more actively involved. Denmark generally supported the use of Article 130 as the legal basis of EU environmental policy, because this article provided for minimum standards that allowed individual member states to maintain or introduce stricter domestic standards. This reserved position may be explained by the limited number of votes in the Council of Ministers as well as by the reluctance of the minority government to market the policy of the green majority. Copenhagen remained the centre of environmental policy-making, and Brussels was still regarded as a distant place as well as a suitable location for sending officials found to be impossible at home, such as had become the case with officials in the Environmental Protection Agency who had been too zealous during the preparation of the Plan for the Aquatic Environment. The first Danish officials in DG-XI did not arrive until 1987.

Issues relating to environmental policy played a more limited role in the two referendums on the Maastricht Treaty. Denmark had supported the introduction of decision-making by qualified majorities under Article 130, and the Maastricht Treaty was not perceived as carrying any great dangers to environmental policy, nor any great improvements. Following the narrow Danish 'no' in the 1992 referendum, the Danish government achieved four exemptions from the Maastricht Treaty at the Edinburgh Summit (regarding economic and monetary union, defence, police and Union citizenship). In the period from the Danish 'no' and up to the Edinburgh Summit, the UK and Denmark both emphasised the need for a more subsidiary approach to European integration. Thus two declarations were issued at the end of the summit: a joint declaration on subsidiarity and a declaration ensuring Denmark's right to maintain higher environmental standards than those of the EU (Det europæiske Råd, 1992; Maastricht ratification, 1992). In this way, Denmark's traditional opt-out position in environmental policy unexpectedly contributed to support UK preferences for a more subsidiary approach to environmental policy, a development which paradoxically seems to have added to the defeat of the Commission's proposal for the common CO_2 tax.

The change of government in Denmark in January 1993 and the appointment of the experienced Svend Auken as Minister of Environment was a turning point for the Danish 'opt-out position' in environmental policy. The change of government brought parties from the former green majority into power, i.e. the Social Democrats and the Social Liberals. Although also in coalition with two smaller parties that formerly supported the Conservative-led government, the change generally provided a new impetus to environmental policy-making. Svend Auken gave international and EU environmental policies a priority that was higher than that given by previous environment ministers and he very actively flagged Denmark's green policies at the international level, e.g. in climate policies. Since the recent enlargement of the EU, Denmark has tried to extend the traditional co-operation among the Nordic countries into the EU Council of Ministers. And with a more experienced corps of diplomats, Denmark has sometimes been able to act as a leader for this group. This policy of active coalition-building represents a significant change from the earlier defensive stance.

The placement of the European Environment Agency in Copenhagen and the subsequent appointment of Ritt Bjerregård as Environment Commissioner was further evidence of the new and more active Danish position. Considerable support has been given to consolidate the resource-poor agency, the location of which was seen as an opportunity to move the centre for policy initiatives to the North. In particular, the insufficient implementation of EU environmental policy, legally as well as practically, in most of the member states was seen as a sincere caveat (Erhardtsen, 1993).

Despite the recent more activist position taken by Denmark in EU environmental policy-making, there is still much emphasis on the role of the environmental guarantee and the opportunities it offers for opting out of the harmonised EU measures. At the intergovernmental conference in 1996, Denmark requested that the guarantee be broadened, not only to what was actually promised in 1986 (both to maintain and introduce higher environmental standards), but so that it also be included in other parts of the treaty relating to environmental aspects of other sectoral policies (in particular Article 43 concerning the CAP). It is also more likely that Denmark will actually use the opportunities offered by Article 100A(4). The more mixed approach of activism, alliance-building and opting out shows that Denmark has overcome its initial paralysis and now seeks to exploit the possibilities that the EU offers to further its own objectives in EU environmental policy-making.

Notes

1   I would like to thank Eskild Holm Nielsen, Aalborg University Centre, for comments on an earlier draft of this chapter.
2   The Danish ministry is sometimes mentioned as the first environmental ministry in Europe (and internationally), but it was actually preceded by the French Ministry of Environment, established in January 1971 (Bungarten, 1978).
3   In security policies, the alternative majority gave birth to Denmark's policy of NATO 'footnotes' in the cruise missiles issue.
4   This summary is based on J. Grønnegård Christensen *et al.*, (1994), *Åbenhed offentlighed og deltagelse i den danske EU-beslutningsproces*, Copenhagen: Rådet for Europæisk Politik.

References

Andersen, Mikael Skou (1989), Miljøbeskyttelse – et implementeringsproblem, *Politica*, 21:3, Århus, Politica.
Andersen, Mikael Skou (1991), Hvordan er effektiviteten af den danske regulering af vandmiljøet sammenlignet med reguleringen i andre lande?, *Rapport fra konsensuskonference 31.1.–4.2.1991*, 18.1–18.15, København: Undervisningsministeriets Forskningsafdeling.
Andersen, Mikael Skou (1994a), *Governance by Green Taxes: Making Pollution Prevention Pay*, Manchester and New York, Manchester University Press.
Andersen, Mikael Skou (1994b), The green tax reform in Denmark: shifting the focus of tax liability, *Journal of Environmental Liability*, 2:2, 47–50.
Andersen, Mikael Skou (1996), Denmark, in Martin Jänicke and Helmut Weidner (eds), *National Environmental Policies: A Comparative Study of Capacity Building*, Berlin and New York: Springer 157–74.
Andersen, Mikael Skou and Michael W. Hansen (1991), *Vandmiljøplanen:*

Fra forhandling til symbol, Harlev J, Niche.

Andersen, Mikael Skou and Ulrik Jørgensen (1995), Evaluering af indsatsen for renere teknologi 1987–1992, *Orientering fra Miljøstyrelsen*, 5, Copenhagen.

Arp, Henning A. (1993), Technical regulation and politics: the interplay between economic interests and environmental policy goals in EC car emission legislation, in D. Liefferink, *et al.*, *European Integration and Environmental Policy*, London: Belhaven Press, 150–72.

ATV (Akademiet for de Tekniske Videnskaber) (1990), *Vandmiljøplanens tilblivelse og iværksættelse*, Vedbæk, ATV.

Basse, Ellen Margrethe (1987), *Miljøankenævnet*, Copenhagen, GAD.

Bernes, Claes (1993), The Nordic environment: present state, trends and threats, *Nord*, 1993:12, Copenhagen, Nordic Council of Ministers.

Bjørnskov, Leo (1994), Styrelserne får mere ansvar, *Miljø-Intern*, 56, March, Copenhagen, Miljøministeriet, 4.

Bungarten, H. H. (1978), *Umweltpolitik in Westeuropa*, Bonn, Europa Union Verlag.

Christiansen, Peter Munk (1996), Governing the environment: politics, policy and organization in the Nordic countries, *Nord*, 1996:5, Copenhagen, Nordic Council of Ministers.

Damgaard, Erik (ed.) (1992), *Parliamentary Change in the Nordic Countries*, Oslo, Scandinavian University Press.

Daugbjerg, Carsten (1995), *Policy Networks and Policy Choices in Changing Environments: Environmental Policy in Swedish and Danish Agriculture*, paper to the Political Studies Association Annual Conference, York University, 18–20 April, Aarhus, Department of Political Science.

Det europæiske råd i Edinburg den 11.–12. december 1992 – Formandsskabets konklusioner.

Det Økonomiske Råd (1993), Dansk Økonomi, Copenhagen.

DIOS (Dansk Institut for Organisations Studier) (1987), *Tilsynsundersøgelse 1986*, Copenhagen.

DMU (Danmarks Miljøundersøgelser) (1993), Miljø og samfund – en status over udviklingen i miljøtilstanden i Danmark, *Faglig rapport nr. 93*, Kbh: DMU.

Dubgaard, Alex (1991), *The Danish Nitrate Policy in the 1980s*, report 59, Copenhagen, Statens Jordbrugsøkonomiske Institut.

Ege, C. and D. Haffar (1995), *EU's miljøpolitik*, Copenhagen, CASA.

Environment Watch (1995a), Bjerregaard makes disastrous debut as EU environment Commissioner, 4:2, 1–3.

Environment Watch (1995b), Bjerregaard sets sights on environmental reform of EU farm policy, 4:10.

Erhardtsen, B. (1993), EU's miljøpolitik truer erhvervslivet, *Dagbladet Børsen*, 22 November.

Erhvervsfremmestyrelsen (1994), *Miljø/Energi – en erhvervsøkonomisk analyse*, Copenhagen.

Finansministeriet (1994), *Betænkning om grønne afgifter og erhvervene*, Copenhagen.

Garde, Johan (1993), *Lovbemærkningers sandhedsværdi: Om miljølovrefor-*

men 1990–1991, Copenhagen, GAD.

Grønnegård Christensen, J. (1987), Hvem har magten over miljøpolitikken: politikerne, embedsmændene eller organisationerne, in A. Dubgård (ed.), *Relationer mellem landbrug og samfund*, report 36, SJI, Copenhagen, 65–77.

Grønnegård Christensen, J. *et al.* (1994), *Åbenhed, offentlighed og deltagelse i den danske EU-beslutningsproces*, Copenhagen, Rådet for Europæisk Politik.

Haahr, Jens Henrik (1992), *Folkeafstemningen 2. juni 1992 om dansk ratifikation af Maastricht traktaten*, Århus: Dept. of Political Science.

Hildebrandt, P. (1992), The European Community's environmental policy 1957–1992: from incidental measures to an international regime, *Environmental Politics*, 1:4, 13–44.

Holzinger, Katharina (1994), *Politik des kleinsten gemeinsamen Nenners? Umweltpolitische Entscheidungsprozesse in der EG am beispiel der Einführung des Katalysatorautos*, Berlin, Sigma.

Jacobsen, C. Boye (1994), Den danske forvaltnings EU-opbygning, *Nordisk Administrativt Tidsskrift*, 75:3, 211–23.

Krämer, Ludwig (1992), *Focus on European Environmental Law*, London, Sweet and Maxwell.

Kristensen, Erik Basse *et al.* (1987), Nye perspektiver i miljøplanlægningen, *Vand og Miljø*, 6, 275–7.

Landbrugsministeriet (1991), *Handlingsplan for en bæredygtig udvikling i landbruget*, Copenhagen.

Larsen, V. J. and P. Christensen (1985), *Håndbog for kratluskere: hvordan man afslører en miljøforbryder*, Harlev J, Niche.

Lucas, Nigel (1985), *Western Energy Policies: A Comparative Study*, Oxford, Clarendon Press.

Maastricht ratification and Denmark – note by the Presidency, Brussels: 9 December 1992.

Metals miljøudvalg (Kampmann-udvalget) (1988), *Betænkning om miljøregulering og økonomisk vækst*, Copenhagen, Dansk Metalarbejderforbund.

Miljøministeriet (1988), *Enkelt og Effektivt*, Copenhagen.

Miljøministeriet (1989), *Renere teknologi – Konferencegrundlag*, Copenhagen.

Miljøministeriet (1995), *Denmark's Nature and Environment Policy*, Copenhagen.

Miljøstyrelsen (1985), *Miljøtilsyn*, Copenhagen.

Miljøstyrelsen (1986), *Udviklingsprogram for renere teknologi*, Copenhagen.

Miljøstyrelsen (1988), *Det europæiske miljøsamarbejde*, Copenhagen.

Miljøstyrelsen (1990), *Vandmiljø 90*, Redegørelse fra Miljøstyrelsen 1/90, Copenhagen.

Moe, Mogens (1994), *Miljøret – miljøbeskyttelse*, Copenhagen, GAD.

Mørch, Søren (1982), *Den ny Danmarkshistorie*, Copenhagen, Gyldendal.

Nielsen, Wittus (1985), *Cheminova*, Copenhagen, Gyldendal.

Nue, Claes (1980), Den danske miljøbeskyttelseslovs tilblivelse, *Retfærd*, 15, Århus, Modtryk.

Opschoor, H. and R. Weterings (1994), Environmental utilisation space: an introduction, *Netherlands' Journal of Environmental Sciences*, 9, 198–205.

Østergård, Uffe (1990), *Peasants and Danes: Danish National Identity and Political Culture*, working paper 75, Aarhus, Centre for Cultural Research.

Pedersen, Carl Th. (1987), *Den kemiske industris miljøforhold*, Odense, Universitetsforlaget.

Pedersen, Jørgen Flindt and Rolf Geckler (1987), Græsrødder og embedsmænd, in Rolf Geckler and Jørgen Grønnegård Christensen, *På ministerens vegne*, Copenhagen, Gyldendal.

Rehling, David (1994), *Indlæg ved Nordisk Parkkongres*, Vejle 25 August, unpublished manuscript.

Ringius, Lasse (1994), *Regime Lessons from Ocean Dumping of Radioactive Waste*, working paper 1994:9, Oslo, CICERO.

Ringius, Lasse *et al.* (1995), *Denmark's Environmental Aid to Central and Eastern Europe: Present and Future Trends*, working paper 1995:3, Oslo, CICERO.

Røjel, Jørgen (1990), *Fra Anarki til Hysteri*, Copenhagen, Samleren.

Sætevik, Sunneva (1988), *Environmental Cooperation between the North Sea States*, London, Belhaven.

Schrøder, Hans (1990), *Et økologisk råd*, Copenhagen, Rhodos.

Skatteministeriet (1992), *Skattepolitisk redegørelse*, Copenhagen.

Spiegel (1992), Alarm für die Umwelt, *Spezial 1/92*, Hamburg.

Svold, Claus (1989), *Danmarks Naturfredningsforening – fra pæn forening til agressiv miljøorganisation*, Århus, PLS Consult.

Thodberg, C. T. and A. P. Thyssen (eds) (1983), *N. F. S. Grundtvig. Tradition and Renewal*, Copenhagen: The Danish Institute.

Udenrigsministeriet (1994), Besvarelse vedr. EF-domstolens afgørelse i PCP-sagen, *Folketingets miljø- og planlægningsudvalg*, bilag nr. 401.

Verdenskommissionen (1988), *Vores fælles fremtid*, Copenhagen, FN-forbundet and Mellemfolkeligt Samvirke.

von Eyben, W. E. (1989), *Miljørettens grundbog*, Copenhagen, Akademisk forlag.

Norway: a case of 'splendid isolation'[1]

Introduction[2]

When Norway applied for EU membership, together with Sweden and Finland, European environmentalists welcomed the possibility of a Nordic enlargement. They expected the new Nordic member states to support their demand for a more progressive environmental policy at the European level, and their expectation was directed not least at Norway, a country whose prime minister had led the Brundtland Commission, and a country with a reputation for being active in international environmental co-operation.

For the Norwegian membership supporters, these arguments were also central. Both the responsibility for the global environment and the self-interest of Norway in participating at the EU level when solving international environmental problems were regarded as important reasons for joining the EU from an environmental point of view. Norway's position as a net importer of pollution was one of the core arguments behind the wish to act as a 'pusher' at the European level, and in this respect environmental arguments on EU membership reflected a more general Norwegian position in foreign environmental policy.

As we know, Norway did not become a member in the end, and among the membership opponents, who eventually became the winners in this struggle, environmental issues had also been placed at the top of the agenda prior to the referendum. The international dimension was important to them as well, and their arguments were part of a more general argument concerning Norwegian goals in foreign environmental policy. They emphasised Norway's role as a 'forerunner' in the international community and questioned the country's possibility of playing this role if it were to become an EU member.

The discussion on the environmental aspects of EU membership can thus serve to illustrate a few more general characteristics of Norwegian foreign environmental policy. It can also be used to illuminate dilemmas that Norway has been forced to cope with to an increasing extent in the relationship between domestic and international levels of environmental policy-making. The purpose of this chapter is to describe these general characteristics, both at the national and international level, and to use them as a general framework for an analysis of the environmental aspects of the EU debate.

In describing the development of issues on the national environmental policy agenda in the first section, it is argued that focus has been broadened from the protection of waterfalls and efforts to clean up industrial pollution initiated in the early 1970s, to the integrationist approach of the 1990s. It is then shown how the development of the legal framework and the administrative apparatus – established for the implementation of environmental regulation at the national and the sub-national levels of government – has resulted in a high degree of institutionalisation. I then elaborate on the national follow-up to the Brundtland Report, which aimed to integrate economy and ecology.

In the second part of the chapter, the international dimension of Norwegian environmental policy is discussed. In the first section, some core issues on the foreign environmental policy agenda are presented, and it is argued that the implementation problems experienced by Norway, particularly with respect to energy-related environmental issues, have resulted in a more defensive Norwegian position on the international arena. The way in which the increasing importance of trans-sectoral issues on the agenda has also led to a broadening of the institutional context within which foreign environmental policy is made is then discussed. Finally, an analysis is made of the discussions prior to the EU referendum to identify some of the questions that were on the agenda at that time: should Norway emphasise the pusher or the forerunner role, and to what extent can these roles be combined within the EU? What is the role of the supranational versus the national levels of government, and what are the capabilities of the two levels for effective environmental regulation?

The national environmental policy agenda

Historical background[3]

Traditionally, the Norwegians have attached great importance to the value of 'untouched nature'. As observed by today's anthropologists, the unique way in which the Norwegians perceive their relationship with the environment can be explained only by using a long historical perspective (Witoszek, 1993). One of the characteristics of the Norwegian environment is its wilderness: about two-thirds of the country is classified as mountainous. The abundance of mountains, along with the large number of fjords, lakes and waterfalls, has been important to the formation of environmental consciousness and has been a driving force behind the development of an environmental policy.

Even if the historical roots of environmental policy can be traced back to medieval laws regulating the rights to hunt and fish, an emerging environmental concern could not be observed until the late nineteenth century. The creation of the conservationist movement was influenced by members of the British nobility who began to explore the Norwegian mountains in the 1820s. The attraction of the mountainous landscape also inspired the Norwegian urban elite, many of whom were natural scientists, to take an interest in environmental, and particularly conservationist, issues in the 1870s and 1880s. In 1914, the conservationist movement became formalised through the establishment of the National Foundation for Nature Preservation (Landsforeningen for naturfredning). The first measures to protect natural areas were taken during the last part of the nineteenth century, and in 1910 the first Nature Preservation Act (Lov om naturfredning) was passed. A new Nature Conservation Act was passed in 1954 resulting in a legal framework for establishing national parks. The first national park was established in Rondane in 1962. The act also resulted in the establishment of the Council for Nature Conservation (Statens Naturvernråd), an advisory body in which environmental interests were given substantial influence.

A controversial nature conservation issue that remained on the agenda for a long time concerned the protection of waterfalls. The first conflicts over the regulation of waterfalls occurred at the beginning of the twentieth century. These conflicts were caused by the accelerating industrialisation which occurred after Norway had broken away from the union with Sweden in 1905. To a large extent, the industrialisation was based upon the exploitation of hydro-electric power, and developers soon ran into conflicts with conservationists. In the 1960s, the conservationists claimed that no single waterfall had yet been saved. Subsequently, the preservation of waterfalls became an important mobilising factor for the upsurge of the environmental movement in the early 1970s, as will be elaborated below.

Problems of pollution have played a less important role in the development of an environmental policy in Norway. A low degree of urbanisation, low population density and late industrialisation are some of the explanations given for this. Although some initiatives had already been taken in the nineteenth century, it was not until the late 1950s that more attention was paid to the problems of water pollution, and that initiatives resulted in the Water Act (Vannvernloven) in 1971. The problems of air pollution appeared on the agenda even later. In 1961, a licensing procedure for air pollution was amended to the Neighbourhood Act (Granneloven), and the corporate Smoke Damage Council (Røykskaderådet) was established and given the authority to award licences to industrial polluters.

The pressures of increasing problems became the most important reasons for the growing, though still limited, awareness of industrial pollution. The industrialisation that had accelerated at the beginning of the century was followed by continuous industrial growth after World War II. The Labour Party, which won the election in 1945 and stayed permanently in office until 1963, gave high priority to industrialisation as a means of post-war reconstruction. The development of hydro-electricity from water courses was an important part of this strategy and resulted in the establishment of various industries, including ferro-alloy industries and aluminium smelters, both of which produced raw or semi-processed materials for export. As will be discussed below, these industries, which were considered powerful symbols of the development of the welfare state and of a successful social democratic growth policy, became the main targets of environmental regulation years later.

The 1970s and the early 1980s: conflicts and clean-ups
As in other countries, international events such as the publication of Rachel Carson's book *Silent Spring* and a growing environmental concern in general were important factors in the upsurge of the environmental movement in the 1960s and 1970s in Norway. Certain

national historical peculiarities may also explain, however, why certain issues were brought on to the political agenda. The environmental movement, which experienced what has been called 'the Golden Age' in the 1970s (Gundersen, 1991), was based on an alliance between traditional conservation interests and more radical environmentalists committed to ecological and populist ideologies (Knutsen, 1991: 10). The ideological contents of Norwegian populism were influenced by historical cleavages in Norwegian politics, several of which could be traced back to pre-industrial society (Rokkan, 1967). The core values in this populist ideology were related to local communities, households and decentralised decision-making. The ideology was anti-capitalist, anti-technocratic and anti-industrial (Knutsen, 1991: 6).

These ideas influenced the environmental movement as well. During the 1970s, it became increasingly occupied with theoretical questions, and debates were focused on fundamental issues, such as energy consumption, growth rates and the rate of oil extraction. These issues were all part of a general criticism of modern industrial society, a criticism that was an important element of the populist ideology. The growing environmental concern led to what has been described as a 'green cleavage' in Norwegian politics, cross-cutting the industrial left–right dimension and revitalising the old populist ideology (Valen, 1981). These characteristics of the Norwegian political system are important not only because they explain the kind of environmental issues pursued by the environmental movement, but also because they have been an important background for the strong resistance to Norwegian EU membership in 1972 as well as in the 1994 referendums (Aardal and Valen, 1995).

The upsurge of environmentalism began with 'the Mardøla action' in 1970. The controversy concerning the regulation of the Mardøla waterfalls resulted in a major confrontation between a coalition of developers and representatives from some local communities, on the one hand, and conservationists and representatives from other local communities, on the other (Gleditsch *et al.*, 1971). The action was given extensive press coverage, and although the activists lost the struggle, the Mardøla case has been seen as a point of 'take-off' for the environmental movement. Ten years later, 'the Alta action' occurred, representing the culmination of the conflict over the regulation of waterfalls. The environmental dimension of the case became intertwined with questions such as the minority rights of the Laps, civil disobedience and the legitimacy of democracy in general. The 'Alta action' has been regarded as one of the major issues for citizens' initiatives, political mobilisation and confrontation in Norwegian politics (Knutsen, 1991: 10).

The struggles over the regulation of the waterfalls have resulted in several conservation plans, designed to protect the remaining waterfalls. In 1973, parliament (the Storting) approved the first Conservation Plan (Verneplan I), which was strongly criticised by environmentalists for being insufficient. New plans were approved in 1980, in 1986 and in 1993 (Verneplan II–IV). One of the conservationists' most important points of criticism was the lack of a comprehensive plan, resulting in piecemeal and arbitrary regulation. In 1985, a comprehensive plan (Samlet Plan) was approved, which laid down the general guidelines for the disposition of the remaining hydropower resources. The last plan was approved by parliament in 1993 and settled (at least temporarily) the conflict over the waterfalls. Other nature conservation laws were also passed during this period.

As previously mentioned, the attention paid to the problems of pollution grew during the 1960s. In the 1970s, the Ministry of the Environment (Miljøverndepartementet) and the Pollution Control Agency (Statens Forurensingstilsyn, SFT) were established, and from then onwards this policy area was given high priority. However, before the establishment of the SFT, the first initiatives thoroughly to revise the emission permits of all major industrial polluters had already been taken. New and more comprehensive regulation was imposed on different industrial branches (e.g. the ferro-alloy, aluminium smelting, and paper and pulp industries), many of which were the cornerstones of post-war industrialisation. In 1974, the Ten-Year Action Plan for Cleaning Up Pollution from Older Industries (Tiårsplan for opprydding i forurensing fra eldre industri) was approved. This plan became an important precedent for major improvements carried out over the next ten to fifteen years.

Financial incentives, such as subsidised loans, state guarantees for private loans and even state grants, were given to support the implementation of the new regulation. Local pollution was the main target, but the acid rain issue soon appeared on the agenda, making the reduction of sulphur emissions a priority to be used as a basis for international negotiations. The measures taken were by and large reactive in their character, and the installation of end-of-pipe technology became the dominant strategy. The regulations were implemented within a context of economic growth, and in some cases, e.g. the paper and pulp industry, they were parts of otherwise necessary structural changes. The level of conflict was low, not least because regulation was accompanied by generous financial support, and the results were impressive. From 1975 to 1985, sulphur emissions were reduced by 37 per cent.

During the last half of the 1970s, attention was also paid to the solution of water pollution problems emanating from the municipal sector and from agriculture. By 1973, initiatives had already been taken to clean up Norway's biggest lake, Mjøsa. But in 1976, a dramatic and sudden occurrence of blue algae in the lake triggered the drawing up of a major action plan targeted at industrial, agricultural and municipal polluters. Generous grants given to the municipalities and to the agricultural sector were an important precedent for what has been described as a successful implementation. For industrial polluters, the measures taken were part of the industrial action plan mentioned previously. Although new problems occurred in the 1980s, the Mjøsa action plan resulted in major improvements of the water quality in the Mjøsa area (Hallén, 1981).

The mid-1980s: a broadening of the agenda

In 1981, after several years of preparation, the new Pollution Control Act (Forurensingsloven) was approved. The act replaced the separate regulations of air and water pollution and introduced the principle of integrated pollution control. It covered all forms of pollution from stationary sources: water, air and noise pollution and waste from industry, agriculture, municipal and off-shore activities. For industry and for the municipalities, individual permits were still the main tool of regulation, and the SFT was given extensive discretion to issue permits in each individual case. Two regulatory instruments, environmental taxes and the principle of legal liability for polluters, were briefly discussed, but were postponed when the law was passed (see below).

When the first permits were given as a part of the Ten-Year Action Plan in the 1970s, branch guidelines were established to ensure equal treatment for all companies within the same branch. In a report to parliament in 1985, the 'recipient principle' was introduced, making regulation dependent on the cleaning capacity of different recipients. General regulation has been introduced for a few smaller industries, but individual permits based upon the recipient principle are still the main instrument aimed at the major polluters. Other fundamental principles presented in this report included the 'polluter pays principle' and a priority given to preventive rather than reactive (end-of-pipe) measures.

Although the activity of the environmental movement declined and less attention was paid to environmental issues in general after the defeat of the environmental movement in the 'Alta action', new issues soon appeared on the agenda. In the mid-1980s, a new generation of environmental activists entered the stage. Their main target was industrial pollution, and they used unconventional means of participation. Activities were directed at combating specific pollutants: in particular, hazardous waste. One important organisation was Nature and Youth (Natur og Ungdom) another was Bellona, which was established in 1986. In contrast to what had been the case for the environmental movement in the 1970s, these organisations were less involved in theoretical, fundamental environmental questions. Their activity was directed at specific issues and particularly at what they saw as the implementation and enforcement deficits of the environmental regulation imposed on industry.

Government responded quickly to the growing awareness of these problems. Although the Ten-Year Action Plan had already resulted in stricter regulation, problems of implementation and enforcement had so far received less attention. The Minister of the Environment announced that this would be given priority, and measures were subsequently taken. Between 1986 and 1989, the budget for the Ministry of the Environment was doubled, resulting in a substantial increase in the amount given to pollution control. The SFT was thus able to extend its control and enforcement activities. Controls became more frequent, and the penalties for companies violating their licences became more severe. In 1987, several well-known companies were reported to the police for violation of the Pollution Control Act.

The courts became more important in the policy of pollution control. The prosecution established a separate office for the investigation of environmental crimes, and in 1989 the principle of legal liability of polluters was established as an amendment to the Pollution Control Act (Stordrange, 1990). Moreover, the principles of regulation concerning licensing procedures were changed, and environmental taxes were introduced in 1988.

Problems of agricultural pollution received little attention prior to the late 1980s, except in the 'Mjøsa action'. A change in attitude was initiated by the sudden and dramatic 'invasion' of algae on Norway's west coast in 1988. This invasion highlighted the problems of eutrophication. But the change in attitude was also initiated by the obligation to implement the North Sea Declaration. A co-operation between the Ministry of the Environment and the Ministry of Agriculture evolved, resulting in several measures to integrate environmental considerations in agricultural policy, both at the institutional level and through the establishment of new means of regulation. Emphasis has now been put on the improvement of technical facilities with the aim of reducing point discharges from storage facilities, and on measures to encourage changed cultivation practices, for example. The regulation is carried out through directives based on the Pollution Control Act and supported by 'soft' means, such as guidelines and technical advice available to farmers. Economic means have also been introduced, both through changes in the profile of subsidies and through a tax on fertilisers. Since 1989, the Ministry of the Environment has been represented in the annual negotiation between the state and the agricultural organisations on the size and profile of the subsidies given to agricultural production (Mydske *et al.*, 1994).

Although less public attention was paid to nature conservation in the 1980s, important regulation was also introduced in this policy area. In addition to the conservation plans for waterfalls previously mentioned, a comprehensive plan for national parks was completed and approved by parliament in 1993 (parliamentary report 62, 1991–1992). In contrast to earlier plans, which had resulted in the establishment of national parks covering mainly mountainous landscapes on state land, this plan aimed at the conservation of other biotopes, including those on private property. Questions concerning the possible expropriation and the amount of compensation to be given were controversial (Berntsen, 1994: 257–60). The economic aspects were also brought to the fore in controversies concerning the drawing up of the Coniferous Forest Conservation Plan (Barskogplanen), in which the government stated its reluctance to include what has been considered a scientific minimum of productive forests into the plan due to large compensation costs.

From the 1980s to the 1990s: the follow-up to the Brundtland Report

The broadening of the agenda in the late 1980s was influenced by the presentation of the Brundtland Report and initiatives taken at the national level to follow up on its recommendations. Global environmental issues, and in particular the issue of global warming, were placed at the top of the agenda, and concepts such as 'sustainable development' and 'an integrationist approach' became catchwords. These issues will be discussed in more detail in the sections 'institutional aspects of an integrationist approach' and 'the concept of sustainable development', as well as in the second half of the chapter, which regards international issues.

The institutional context

The Ministry of the Environment

Before the Ministry of the Environment was established in 1972, the administration of environmental issues was divided among different ministries. When the first Nature Preservation Act was approved in 1910, the Ministry of Education was made responsible for its administration (Berntsen, 1994: 52). In 1965, the administration was moved to the Ministry of Local Government (Kommunal- og Arbeidsdepartementet), where it remained until the establishment of the new Ministry of the Environment (Berntsen, 1994: 124). Pollution control issues were, on the other hand, located within the Ministry of Industry (Industridepartementet).

One important reason for the establishment of a separate ministry was the desire to obtain a better co-ordination of the administration of different environmental issues, the responsibilities for which had been divided among different ministries. However, it was not only co-ordination *within* the environmental sector that was at stake in discussions prior to the establishment of the Ministry of the Environment. Perhaps even more important was the question of the role to be given to the Ministry of the Environment in relation to *other* ministries. As mentioned previously, environmental ideologies based on an ecological approach had been developed in the late 1960s, and advocates of this approach played an important role in the preparatory work leading up to the establishment of the Ministry of the Environment. They wanted a superior planning ministry to have the sole responsibility for the exploitation and allocation of all natural resources. However, this radical proposal had little chance of being approved, as could be expected. It met severe opposition, particularly from the Ministry of Finance (Jansen, 1989).

When the Ministry of the Environment was established in 1972, the administration of the Local Planning Act (Bygningsloven) and the Nature Conservation Act was moved to the Ministry of the Environment from the Ministry of Local Government. Departments for pollution control and for organisation and economy were established within the Ministry of the Environment. The administration of both air and water pollution control was moved to the Ministry of the Environment from the Ministry of Industry. A department of resources was added two years later. In 1972, the Ministry of the Environment had 103 employees, of whom 32 occupied new positions (Lægreid, 1983). Surveys carried out in the mid-1970s showed that the recruitment patterns for the Ministry of the Environment were markedly different from those of other ministries. The employees were younger, many had been educated as natural scientists, and they were more inclined to support environmental organisations. In addition, the bureaucrats in the Ministry of the Environment were willing to promote professional (often pro-environmentalist) considerations, even if these were opposed to political signals from above (Lægreid, 1983). This differed from policies in other ministries. Although data are old, one could argue that at least some of these characteristics are still valid.

The Ministry of the Environment was made responsible for physical planning and for the development of a system of annual budgets and accounts for natural resources. This was, however, far from the integrationist model demanded by the environmentalists. In the first years after its establishment, the Ministry of the Environment gave priority to the implementation of pollution control measures and emphasised the necessity of developing a collaborative relationship with industry. According to Jansen (1989), the Ministry of the Environment succeeded in carrying out this strategy. The Ministry of the Environment experienced further difficulties when trying to play an integrative role (Lægreid, 1983: 370).

In 1989, the Ministry of the Environment was reorganised as part of the follow-up to the recommendations made by the Brundtland Commission. The purpose was to make the Ministry of the Environment more capable of playing an integrative role *vis-à-vis* other parts of the state administration. The pollution control department was divided into separate departments for water and air pollution, and within these departments, specialised sections were set up to focus on agriculture and transport, for example, to make the Ministry of the Environment better equipped to deal with the respective ministries (Mathiesen, 1992). In addition, the increasing importance of international issues resulted in the establishment of the department for international environmental co-operation. Shortly thereafter, the departments of air pollution and international co-operation were merged, reflecting both the interdependence of these areas and the need to co-ordinate measures taken at the national and international level.

Environmental agencies

At present, there are five environmental management bodies under the authority of the Ministry of the Environment, of which only two are environmental agencies: the SFT and the Directorate for Nature Management (Direktoratet for Naturforvaltning). The SFT and the Directorate for Nature Management are responsible for the implementation and enforcement of environmental laws in the area of pollution control and nature conservation. They are directly subordinate to the Ministry of the Environment, which has the power to reconsider and change all decisions taken at lower levels.

As already described, industrial pollution has been governed by the principle of integrated pollution control, administered by the SFT, since the approval of the Pollution Control Act in 1981. The first measures for setting up a system of integrated pollution control were taken, however, in 1974 when the existing regulatory bodies were merged into the new regulatory agency. Before the SFT was established, the administration of water and air pollution had been divided between two different bodies, both subordinate to the Ministry of Industry. The Central Office for Water Supply and Waste Water (Statens vann- og avløpskontor) was responsible for water pollution. The Secretariat for the Smoke Damage Council (Røykskaderådets sekretariat) prepared the decisions taken by the Smoke Damage Council (Røykskaderådet).

Today the SFT is responsible for the administration of the pollution control policy. For the major industrial polluters, the SFT is responsible for the issuing of licences on the basis of the Pollution Control Act, and for carrying out controls. For agricultural pollution and discharges from municipal waste water, the SFT has an advisory role in that it is responsible for the development of guidelines for the control activities carried out by the environmental departments at the county level (see below). The SFT is also responsible for the co-ordination of activities and measures aimed at reducing air pollution in the transport and energy sectors. In addition, the agency is responsible for the implementation of the Product Control Act and for hazardous waste (SFT, 1992). During its 20 years of existence, the SFT has expanded enormously. In the late 1980s, when the regulation of industrial pollution, and particularly the implementation of problems, were at the top of the agenda, the allocation of more resources to the SFT was regarded as the main instrument for improving the situation. Today the SFT is a well-institutionalised body, with a number of employees not much lower than that in the Ministry of the Environment.[4]

The other main agency in the field of environmental policy is the Directorate for Nature Management. The Directorate for Nature Management was transformed from the former Directorate for Wildlife and Freshwater Fish (Direktoratet for vilt og ferskvannsfisk) in 1985. Agricultural interests wanted the new agency to be located below the Ministry of Agriculture. Resistance from environmental interests, however, resulted in the establishment of the agency under the environmental authorities (Berntsen, 1994: 249). Today the Directorate for Nature Management is responsible for the administration of nature conservation laws, such as the Nature Conservation Act and the Wildlife Act. In addition, the agency has been given responsibility for the administration of the Planning and Building Act, and for participating in international negotiations on agreements concerning nature conservation. At present, the Directorate for Nature Management has 125 employees (Direkforatet for Naturforvaltruing, 1995).

Horizontal integration: conflicts and the distribution of competence between the Ministry of the Environment and other ministries
In a parliamentary report on the follow-up to the Brundtland Commission (parliamentary report 46, 1988–1989), the government emphasised the trans-sectoral dimensions of environmental issues and the necessity for developing an integrationist approach. At the central level, this was to be achieved by giving all the ministries the responsibility for carrying out a policy of sustainable development within their respective sectors. 'Sector responsibility approach'

became the keyterm. In addition, the institutional capacity of the environmental administration was strengthened. As described above, the Ministry of the Environment was reorganised in 1989 to improve the capacity for dealing with environmental issues belonging to the spheres of other ministries.

Several other initiatives were taken to achieve better integration. All the ministries were made responsible for building environmental considerations into their planning and budget processes, and they are expected to identify and assess the likely environmental effects of their policies. Various planning and budget reports, such as the four-year, long-term programmes prepared by the Ministry of Finance and the national budget proposals, routinely include environmental data. Several interministerial committees have also been established to address environmental policies relevant to different ministries (Organisation for Economic Co-operation and Development, OECD, 1993: 79ff.).

However, it would be a great exaggeration to conclude that integration has been accomplished. There are numerous examples of conflicts between the Ministry of the Environment and other ministries over issues that have had severe environmental consequences. The Ministry of Finance has played an increasingly important role in environmental policy. As will be elaborated in other parts of this chapter, the role of the Ministry of Finance in defending the principle of cost-effectiveness has influenced Norwegian behaviour in environmental policy, both in the national and international arena. Moreover, disagreement between the Ministry of the Environment and the Ministry of Industry and Energy[5] has been observed in several cases. Energy policy and the problems of implementing national climate policy goals and international commitments of NO_x reductions while simultaneously increasing the rate of petrol production are examples of the issues that will be discussed later in this chapter. In addition, questions concerning the ecological consequences related to the opening of new oil and gas fields for exploration activities have been on the agenda (Natur og Miljø Bulletin 2, 1995). Conflicts have also prevailed in the relationship between the Ministry of the Environment and the Ministry of Transport. The reluctance of the Ministry of Transport to accept regulation within its sector has been seen as the main reason for the postponement of the Action Plan on NO_x reductions.

The behaviour of the environmental organisations illustrates the present situation concerning the (in)ability of the government to give substance to an integrationist approach. In criticising the government for its evasiveness, the organisations are not targeting the Minister of the Environment. They are targeting the unwillingness of the other ministries to integrate environmental considerations into their respective sectors. One can easily agree with the conclusions drawn in the Environmental Performance Review made by the OECD, in which it was stated that:

> Integration does not operate in practice as satisfactorily as it should. ... These sectors [transport, agriculture, manufacturing and energy] do not always seem to work as closely with the Ministry of Environment as might have been expected in view of their role in environmental protection and degradation. There is scope for developing both formal and informal co-ordination mechanisms.
>
> (OECD, 1993: 80)

Vertical integration: the role of local government

According to parliamentary report 46, the integration of environmental considerations into different sectors of government was not to take place only at the central level of government. The decentralist dimension and measures taken to integrate environmental considerations into institutions located at the sub-national levels of government were also important parts of the integrationist strategy. Local government has traditionally played a central role in the Norwegian political system, most importantly in the development of the welfare state, but also in environmental policy issues. In the mid-1980s, a general trend in the direction of decentralisation ran parallel to signals given in report 46, resulting in several measures taken at the sub-national level to strengthen the institutional framework for the development of a local environmental policy. As will be described below, this applied both to the regional (county) and the municipal level.

The regional (county) level   In general, the development of administration at the regional level has been characterised by a duality of institutions and a dilemma between two different considerations: on the one hand, the preference of the central government for the development of deconcentrated state institutions as a means of national standardisation and regulation; and on the other hand, the values of decentralisation and the establishment of representative bodies elected in local constituencies. This general dilemma has been an important factor in the development of institutions responsible for environmental issues at the county level. Since the first initiative taken at this level in 1971, the responsibility for environmental issues has been moved back and forth several times between the (state) county prefect's office and the locally elected county governments. In 1971, nature conservation consultants were appointed to the county prefects' offices. In 1977, when directly elected county governments were established, the responsibility for environmental issues was transferred to these new bodies. These issues were, however, moved back to the state administration again in 1982, when separate environmental departments were established at the county prefects' offices. At present, experiments are being carried out in one of the counties, once again bringing the responsibility back to the democratically elected bodies (Nenseth, 1994).

The departments at the county prefect's office were given responsibility for the administration of municipal sewage treatment, municipal waste and agriculture, as defined by the Pollution Control Act. In 1993, the responsibility for the regulation of smaller industrial polluters was also delegated to the county level. In addition, the environmental departments are supposed to play an advisory role in the process of physical planning at the municipal level, ensuring that environmental considerations are taken properly into account. Another important obligation was the preparation of nature conservation plans (Thorén *et al.*, 1991). The environmental departments are important actors in the implementation of national environmental regulation at sub-national level, since they are given the responsibility for ensuring that municipalities carry out central directives on the implementation of national environmental goals. On the other hand, the institutions of the county government play a role in environmental policy as well. They are supposed to mediate and aggregate local preferences in regional planning processes – processes in which the participating actors have been forced to consider the environmental consequences of policies carried out to an increasing degree in recent years.

The municipal level   Traditionally, the municipalities have been responsible for several policy areas with substantial environmental consequences. Among the most important have been the policies of land use and physical planning, central to a whole range of environmental issues, from nature conservation to patterns of transport and energy consumption. Other important local issues have been waste water treatment and waste disposal. As already described, local government was seen as an important instrument in the strategy of the follow-up to the Brundtland Report. In 1987, a decentralist experiment called Environment Protection in the Municipalities (Miljøvern i kommunene, MIK) was set up as a joint project initiated by the Ministry of the Environment and the Association of Local Authorities (Kommunenes Sentralforbund).

The most important parts of the experiment were the establishment of separate political bodies responsible for environmental issues at the local level and the appointment of environmental advisers in the ninety municipalities chosen to take part in the experiment. All the participating municipalities were obligated to work out comprehensive environmental plans, and the intention was that these plans should be integrated into the regular planning processes at the local level. In 1992, the MIK experiment was transformed into a reform resulting in the establishment of political and administrative units with the responsibility for environmental issues in all the municipalities (Hovik and Johnsen, 1994).

The MIK experiment resulted in the establishment of a political and administrative framework, but it did not imply more decentralisation *per se*. To what extent this is going to be carried out in the future is still being considered. An evaluation of the MIK programme has shown that participation in the experiment resulted in more activities directed at environmental issues at the local level, more co-operation with environmental organisations and higher priority given to environmental questions among local politicians. The goal of the experiment, i.e. increased local participation, thus seems to have been achieved. Most recent data show that there is a tendency to standardise the activities carried out because the municipalities give priority to issues considered important to the central government. Hence it seems that the intention of the experiment, i.e. to make the municipalities more capable of implementing national environmental policy goals, will also be accomplished (Hovik, 1994; Hovik and Reitan, 1994).

The role of interest organisations
In comparative literature, Norway has often been classified as a neo-corporatist political system (Olsen, 1981; Katzenstein, 1985). Organised interests have been given institutionalised rights of participation

in all phases of governmental policy-making through a well-developed system of committees and boards. The major organisations have been invited to participate in these bodies, particularly those representing economic interests. In addition, a 'hearings commission' has permitted organisations to comment on drafts for legal proposals and other government documents that are considered important to them (Egeberg, 1981). The characteristics described above are, however, not equally accurate for the Ministry of the Environment. The system of corporate representation is less developed, and the population of participating organisations is different. Comparatively speaking, economic organisations are given less access, and environmental organisations are given more (Lægreid, 1983: 377). On the other hand, the hearings commission is well developed within the Ministry of the Environment.

Although interest representation is less common in the environmental sector, corporate bodies have been developed both in the area of nature conservation and, until 1991, in pollution control policy. As described previously, a Council for Nature Conservation was established by 1954. Although the main idea behind the establishment of such a body was to make use of the scientific expertise in the organisations, another motive was to give environmental interests influence (Berntsen, 1994: 107). The council has played an important role in the development of nature conservation policy. An example is the new plan for national parks approved by parliament in 1993; this was strongly based upon the work of the council (Berntsen, 1994: 257ff.). In the area of pollution control, the Smoke Damage Council, which existed until 1981, gave permits to major industrial pollutants. The council members' scientific expertise was an important precondition for its establishment.

In 1990, in the wake of the United Nations Conference on Environment and Development (UNCED) in Bergen, a new body called the Norwegian National Committee for UNCED (Den norske nasjonalkomiteen for UNCED) was established. The Prime Minister, the Minister of the Environment and representatives from environmental organisations and major economic organisations were appointed members. The committee participated in the preparation of the Norwegian position at the Rio Conference and in the drawing up of the Norwegian national report presented there (Berntsen, 1994: 266).

Although participation has been institutionalised, there are indications that environmental organisations prefer informal channels of

influence. An ongoing research project on the role of these organisations in policy-making shows that they often consider participation
through established channels to be of little value if it is not combined
with informal contact. These studies also show that environmental
organisations frequently use informal channels of influence when
making contact with both the state administration and parliament
(Klausen, 1995; Rommetvedt and Opedal, 1995).

The role of parliament and the political parties

The role that politicians play in environmental policy seems to
depend on the different stages of issue attention cycles for environmental questions (Downs, 1972) rather than on the growth in
problem pressure. Since environmental issues were placed on the
political agenda in the 1970s, the attention paid to these questions
has gone up and down in the electorate as well as in the political
parties. As described previously, environmental issues played a
prominent role in the political debates of the 1970s, whereas less
attention was paid to these questions in the early and mid-1980s.
Since the local election in 1987, a renewed interest in environmental
issues has been observed, culminating in 1989 when the follow-up of
the Brundtland Commission was one of the core issues on the agenda
during the election campaign. Since then, the interest in environmental issues has been declining. Time series data from 1975 show the
pattern in quantitative terms: in 1977, when asked in a questionnaire
to choose the most important determinant for party choice, 25 per
cent of the respondents chose environmental issues. In 1985, the
corresponding figure was as low as 5 per cent. In 1989, it reached a
record of 37 per cent. And in 1993, it was again down to 7 per cent
(Aardal and Valen, 1995: 183).

As previously described, the upsurge in the attention paid to environmental issues in the early 1970s resulted in the occurrence of a
green cleavage at the party level, cutting across the industrial
left–right dimension. According to Knutsen, on the one hand, this
new cleavage can be explained by a theory of post-materialism.
Knutsen argues that the three bourgeois centrist parties and the left
socialists, which were the parties located at the 'green' pole of this
dimension, were 'taken over by post-materialist forces' (Knutsen,
1991: 34). On the other hand, he emphasises the pre-industrial cleavages in Norwegian society, which were an important background for
populist ideology. The declining interest in environmental issues in

the early 1980s was followed by a lower level of conflict. Since then, some analysts have pointed to the *consensus* that can be seen among the political parties on environmental issues (Bjørklund and Hellevik, 1988; Aardal, 1993).

One of Aardal's main conclusions is that Norway has experienced what he describes as a 'silent evolution' resulting in the incorporation of environmental issues into all political parties (Aardal, 1993: 439). A quantitative analysis of party programmes shows a substantial increase in the percentage of programmes devoted to environmental issues, most notably between 1985 and 1989 (Knutsen, 1991: 26). In 1989, when the popularity of environmental issues was at its highest, all parties were strongly committed to environmental policy. Since then, the parties have been forced to pay attention to these questions and to develop positions on new issues emerging on the agenda, even if the popularity of environmental issues has declined. On the one hand, this can indicate support for the consensus hypothesis. On the other hand, there are also cases – and the EU issue is one of them – where the level of conflict is high and the cleavage between the political parties remains the green one developed during the early 1970s.

On the parliamentary agenda, more and more importance has been attached to environmental issues. The parliamentary register shows that the number of issues passing through the assembly each year, including all kinds of documents from annual budgets to questions during the 'question time' to reports to parliament, has almost doubled since the mid-1970s (from 47 in 1975–1976 to 75 in 1993–1994). Since 1987, annual reports on the state of the environment have been issued by the Ministry of the Environment followed by general debate. This new institution, combined with the increasing number of reports presented to parliament on environmental issues, has given the politicians numerous opportunities to discuss issues within this policy area. In most cases, decisions are in reality made by the parliamentary sub-committees after negotiations among the participating parties. During the 1970s and 1980s, environmental policy, together with local government issues, was located with the Committee for Local Government and Environmental Issues (Kommunal- og miljøvernkomiteen). A reorganisation of the committee structure in 1993 resulted in the creation of the Committee for Energy and Environmental Policy (Energi- og miljøkomiteen), aimed at a better co-ordination of energy and environmental issues.

Some analysts have asked what the political consequences have been of the institutionalisation of environmental policy. The breakdown of the former consensus on these issues in the early 1970s took place at the same time as the first initiatives were made to establish a legal and administrative framework for environmental policy. The conflicts over environmental issues that could be observed during the next ten years ran parallel to an extensive institutional development. Some observers have interpreted the declining interest in environmental issues in the mid-1980s as a result of the co-optation of environmental issues into the political system, which in turn led to the institutionalised settlement of conflicts within the state apparatus (Gundersen, 1991).

The rapid institutionalisation of environmental policy, both at the political and administrative level, and the declining level of political conflict have been explained by the 'political opportunity structure' of the Norwegian political system (Kitschelt, 1986; Aardal, 1993). The concept refers, on the one hand, to the openness of the political system to societal demands and, on the other hand, to the capacity of the system to convert these demands into policies and to the capacity for implementation (Kitschelt, 1986: 63). On the input side, emphasis has been on various factors: the many small parties, cross-cutting political cleavages, an electoral system with proportional representation, and a threshold of 3 per cent giving small parties and new ideas easy access (Aardal, 1993). On the output side, we can point to the development of a legal framework and an administrative system given the resources to carry out successful regulation in several subareas of environmental policy. Together these factors may have contributed to the de-politicisation of environmental policy.

The integration of the environment and the economy

The basic ideas

According to Albert Weale, the central idea behind the ideologies of sustainable development and ecological modernisation is the challenge of the conventional assumption that there is a zero-sum trade-off between economic prosperity and environmental concern (Weale, 1992: 31). In Norwegian politics, the validity of this wisdom has been at the core of the environmental debate. In the early 1970s, the perception of a fundamental conflict between protection of the environment and economic growth emerged as an important dimension of the green cleavage within the party system. This conflict was so important that the cleavage has been called the 'growth-protection dimension' (Aardal, 1993).

The parties located at the green pole of this dimension were fundamentally critical of industrial society and economic growth in general, and argued in favour of giving environmental considerations priority in what they saw as a zero-sum game in relation to economic growth. At the other pole, advocates of the growth ideology argued for the need to balance the two values, also basing their argument on the assumption that there was a trade-off. However, it should be added that, even at that time, early signs of the perception of a more collaborative relationship could be observed on the growth side (Jansen, 1989: 56).

The concept of sustainable development and the arguments put forward by the Brundtland Commission were echoed in the report to parliament on the Norwegian follow-up: a healthy environment is a precondition for economic prosperity, the government argued. It is a wrong composition of growth (i.e. the exploitation of non-renewable resources and non-sustainable patterns of consumption) that causes environmental degradation, not economic growth *per se*. Economic growth offers the possibility of protecting the environment through investments and new technical solutions. Changes in patterns of consumption and the development of cleaner technologies were some of the keywords given to describe the new strategies (parliamentary report 46, 1988–1989: Chapter 6). Although the government has promoted the strategy of sustainable growth enthusiastically, it has met resistance not only from the environmental organisations and some political parties, as could be expected, but also within the governing party's own youth organisation, the Norwegian Labour Youth (Arbeidernes Ungdornsfylking, AUF) and even from the cabinet. Both the AUF and the Minister of the Environment have been critical of the Brundtland strategy of sustainable economic growth.

Ecological modernisation and new means of regulation
As described previously, several measures have been taken to implement a policy of sustainable development within different sectors of society, both at the institutional level and through new means of regulation. With respect to regulatory instruments, emphasis has been put on both positive and negative economic means and changes

in the licensing procedure for industrial pollutants. Except for new directives for physical planning at the local level, planning instruments have been less developed, perhaps unexpectedly because of the strong planning traditions in the Norwegian political system (Østerud, 1979). In parentheses, it could be added that in its environmental performance review on Norway, the OECD recommended a strengthening of the strategic planning function within the Ministry of the Environment (OECD, 1993: 80).

The discussion below will focus on the most important changes that have taken place: changes within the existing system of administrative regulation, new environmental taxes, and the development of new positive economic means of regulation.

Changes in the licensing procedure
Although initiatives to increase the use of taxes in pollution control policy had already been taken in the early 1970s, the licensing procedure was still the most important instrument. Within the present system of individual permits, changes have, however, taken place. In 1987, the SFT launched a programme for a thorough revision of the licences held by all major industrial polluters, imposing stricter regulation and introducing new regulatory principles. Emphasis was still put on the recipient principle introduced in 1985. Other important keywords were the 'critical load' approach, life cycle analyses, and the obligation of companies to develop their own control systems (Internkontrollforskriften), which were amended to the Pollution Control Act in 1989. In his annual report to parliament in 1990, the Minister of the Environment stated that the implementation of the programme was in progress. He emphasised that the companies given new permits were obligated to consider all possible means for reducing pollution – from new factor inputs to energy conservation and waste recycling. They were also obligated to carry out comprehensive technical analyses aimed at the detection of all possible opportunities for a reduction of polluting substances in industrial processes and products.

These new regulatory principles, which have been called the 'second generation' of measures directed at industrial polluters, were considered more in line with the thoughts of the Brundtland Commission and the concept of sustainable development. However, it would be an exaggeration to describe the development in the late 1980s as leading unequivocally in the direction of ecological modernisation, as the concept has been interpreted (Weale, 1993; Andersen and Lief-ferink, 1993). That description would be particularly inaccurate for the relationship between the state and economic actors. The changes in the licensing procedure took place at the same time as stricter control procedures and new efforts directed at the prosecution of environmental crimes were introduced. More recent interviews give the impression that the relationship between the environmental authorities and industrial actors has developed in a more collabora-tive direction, particularly in the 1990s. In 1992, an interministerial committee was established to review the existing regulatory system within pollution control policy, particularly with reference to admin-istrative regulation. The committee presented its report in the spring of 1995 and recommended a continuation of the licensing procedure for major industrial polluters (NOU, 1995).

Environmental taxes
Economic instruments with environmental consequences were used in Norway long before they were classified as environmental taxes. As early as 1931, a petrol tax was introduced, and in 1971 parlia-ment approved a tax on heavy crude oil, differentiated on the basis of the sulphur content of oil. Yet more serious attention was not paid to the possibility of using economic instruments in environmental policy until the late 1980s. Some years earlier, the Pollution Tax Committee (Forurensingsutvalget) had been established to consider the use of environmental taxes, but the conclusions drawn by this committee were, by and large, negative: emphasis was put on the different recip-ient conditions in various parts of the Norwegian environment, thus making standardised taxes inefficient.

The Brundtland Commission became a catalyst for change. In 1987, higher priority for the use of economic instruments was announced in the Minister of the Environment's annual report to parliament. As part of the budget processes in 1988 and 1989, taxes were introduced on a number of products and factor inputs. In the follow-up report in 1989, the government proclaimed the introduc-tion of new environmental taxes and the raising of existing ones an important part of the strategy for sustainable development. In evalu-ating the pros and cons associated with different regulatory instru-ments, it was still pointed out that administrative regulation allowed for the possibility of differentiation. However, more importance was attached to the principle of cost-effectiveness and the economic incentives for developing new technology. The push to think more in terms of cost-effectiveness, particularly driven by the Ministry of Finance, was based on an emerging recognition of the scope of environmental degradation and the extensive costs related to a policy of sustainability. The push was also a result of the increasing popularity of market mechanisms in general, which spilt over into environmental policy.

Parliamentary report 46 was followed up by the establishment of the Environmental Tax Committee (Miljøavgiftsutvalget), which was given the task of considering the use of economic instruments. The first report from the committee resulted in the introduction of a carbon tax in 1991. Although the tax has been raised several times since 1991, the government has also permitted new exceptions. One of the reasons for this was the substantial resistance to the carbon tax, particularly from the process industries. At present, several environmentally motivated taxes are in effect in Norway, but the enormous upsurge that these instruments experienced some years ago seems to have been replaced by a harsher political reality in which the willingness to pay for the environment is lower. In its performance review, the OECD gave Norway credit for having taken the lead among the OECD countries in the development of economic instruments in environmental policy. Yet the OECD also commented on what the organisation described as 'a number of limitations or difficulties in the current situation', pointing to the fact that many of these taxes remained unchanged between 1991 and 1993, even though prices increased by around 5 per cent (OECD, 1993: 86).

The relationship between environmental taxes and the general system of taxation has also been part of the debate about the integration of the environment and the economy in the 1980s. The fiscal motivations behind the introduction of environmental taxes and the questions of earmarking have been two of the central concerns in these discussions. A Green Tax Commission (Grønn skattekommisjon) has recently been established to review the relationship between the systems of taxation. The intention is to propose changes in the present tax system, giving it a more 'green' profile.

Positive financial incentives
During the 1970s and early 1980s, industrial companies received financial support earmarked for the implementation of regulation imposed on them by the SFT. The incentives elicited mainly reactive

solutions, and the money was primarily spent on the installation of end-of-pipe technology. In the last half of the 1980s, this was changed. The state would no longer pay for compulsory measures, nor would it finance the installation of end-of-pipe technologies. Financial incentives were to be given to waste-minimising programmes, treatment facilities for hazardous waste, and the development of cleaner technologies. These changes were all part of a strategic plan presented by the Ministry of the Environment and aimed at the development of a new, more prevention-oriented policy of pollution control.

The foreign environmental policy agenda

Basic orientation
The historical background of Norway's position on foreign environmental policy issues involves an interest in developing international agreements to counteract the degradation of the Norwegian environment caused by transfrontier pollution. According to OECD data, Norway is probably the OECD member country most exposed to transfrontier air pollution. Over 90 per cent of the acid precipitation over Norway originates abroad (OECD, 1993: 111). Marine pollution is also a problem, because of the direction of ocean currents: Norway is located not only downwind, but also downstream from the rest of Europe.

During the 1970s, a growing awareness of the international causes of national degradation became a driving force behind initiatives taken at the regional level to establish international agreements. Norway started to play the role of pusher in international environmental co-operation. Parallel to the pusher role was the pursuit of the forerunner role at the national level. The intention was to make international efforts more credible by doing the right things at home.

Following the Brundtland Report, the principle of cost-effectiveness was introduced. It has gradually been recognised that the costs of environmental regulation, particularly those associated with implementation, are high for Norway compared with other countries. The Ministry of Finance has been given an increasingly important role in the policy process, emphasising cost-effectiveness as a governing principle of Norwegian environmental policy, both at the national and the international level. The principle has been the rationale behind the strategy of 'joint implementation' – a strategy which has been strongly supported by Norway. Another principle supported by Norway concerns the necessity of developing a scientific basis for international environmental agreements. As will be described below, this has been used by Norway in work with the whaling issue. This principle should not, however, become an excuse for not using the precautionary principle, which is also a governing principle in Norwegian foreign environmental policy (Skjærseth and Rosendal, 1995: 164).

With these general keywords to describe the basic orientation of Norwegian foreign environmental policy, a few of the issues considered internationally important will be presented below. The issues have been chosen because they seem to be the most important on-going cases relevant to this chapter.[6]

Marine pollution

Norway's role in international environmental co-operation can be traced back to the beginning of the 1970s when initiatives were taken to establish international regulation to prohibit the dumping of toxic waste in the North Sea. Norway took the lead, together with other Scandinavian countries, to draw up the Oslo Convention, which was signed by all thirteen European maritime countries in 1972. The convention regulated the dumping of industrial wastes, sewage sludge and other wastes. Norway also played an active role in the creation of the Paris Convention in 1974, which extended the ban on dumping to land-based sources. However, in this convention, the role of Norway has been described as ambiguous: on the one hand, Norway apparently played an active role at the international level, but, on the other hand, it resisted regulations that were opposed to the interests of Norwegian industrial companies. The same conclusion has been drawn from the evaluation of Norway's role in the re-negotiation of the Paris Convention in 1992 (Skjærseth and Rosendal, 1995: 168ff.).

During the North Sea Conferences in 1987 and 1990, Norway supported the work leading up to the Hague Declaration in 1990. Measures were taken within all relevant sectors to implement the goals of the declaration. However, these measures have been insufficient to reach the reduction targets. The most recent data from the SFT show that the discharges of nutrients will be reduced by 45 per cent for phosphorus, but only by 30 per cent for nitrogen by 1995. The targets will not be met for hazardous substances either. Only in the case of four out of ten specified toxic substances that have been given priority due to the declaration, has the goal of a 50 to 70 per cent reduction been met (SFT, 1994: 34 and 43).

Acidification
During the 1970s and early 1980s, Norway took the lead in establishing an agreement among the European countries to reduce the emissions of SO_2. In 1968, a Swedish scientist had launched the theory that sulphur emissions from Great Britain and Central Europe caused acidification of southern Scandinavian lakes. Norway, and in particular Gro Harlem Brundtland, the then Minister of the Environment, became an important actor in the efforts taken to convince other European countries that measures had to be taken. The Ministry of the Environment gave financial support to, and relied on, the results from a major research programme entitled 'The effects of acid precipitation on forests and fish' (Roll-Hansen and Hestmark, 1990). Gradually, the aim of the programme became to produce scientific information that could be used in international negotiations.

By the early 1970s, Norway had already started to implement measures to reduce SO_2 emissions, and when the international target of a 30 per cent reduction was agreed upon in the Economic Commission for Europe (ECE) convention of 1985, Norway had already met the target. The reduction was, however, obtained not only through regulations (among the most important was the licensing procedure for major industrial polluters and the regulation of the contents of sulphur in heavy crude oil), but also through a reduced oil consumption. As a result, the target was reached easily and inexpensively. Norway wanted to continue playing the role of a forerunner and decided to pursue the national goal of a 50 per cent reduction by 1995. This goal was also met without excessive costs.

Against the background of this 'record' of being both a forerunner and a pusher, the international community was taken by surprise when Norway accepted a best available technology (BAT) requirement only reluctantly for new plants in the negotiations on the revised sulphur protocol (the Geneva Protocol) in 1993. Norway initially opposed the principle, even though its application would have had no consequences for Norway (Natur og Miljø Bulletin 9, 1993). The reason was that such a requirement would contradict the principle of cost-effectiveness and the freedom of each country to choose its own means of regulation. The Norwegian position had been strongly influenced by the Ministry of Finance, which had advocated cost-effectiveness as a fundamental principle of Norwegian foreign environmental policy. The Ministry of Finance was afraid that a deviation from this principle would negatively affect its application within other environmental policy areas. A conflict between the Ministry of Finance and the Ministry of the Environment, which wanted Norway to support the BAT requirement in the negotiations, became apparent and resulted in the defeat of the Ministry of Finance. Norway also supported the 'critical load' approach on which all the countries had, at an early stage, agreed to base the agreement.

For Norway, the nitrogen part of the acidification story has been more complicated than the reduction of sulphur emissions. When the issue was placed on the agenda in the early 1980s, Norway had the ambition of playing a progressive role in this case as well. This was, however, to be changed within the next years. Norway supported the Sofia Protocol in 1988, in which all the signatory countries committed themselves to having stabilised the emissions of NO_x to the 1987 level by 1994. Ten of the countries also signed a declaration of intent to reduce emissions by 30 per cent by 1998. Norway was initially reluctant to sign this declaration because of what were seen as implementation problems. The consequences of a reduction would be severe for domestic and coastal traffic, because the principal polluters (84 per cent of the NO_x emissions in 1988) were mobile sources. A 30 per cent reduction would therefore be particularly difficult for Norway, it was argued. Pressure on the Labour government, from the opposition in parliament and from environmental groups, eventually resulted in the signing of the declaration (Laugen, 1995).

The government has been reluctant to propose measures to achieve the reduction target. Between 1987 and 1992, emissions were reduced by 7 per cent. The reductions were due to new requirements for exhaust gas from private cars, reduced production in the ferro-alloy industry, reduced flaring in the North Sea, and NO_x-reducing measures in the production of fertilisers (SFT, 1994: 16ff.). Though growth in the production of oil and gas led to an increase in No_x in 1993, the stabilisation goal is still within reach. Estimates from the SFT show that a reduction of 11 per cent by 1998 is expected to be reached by measures already taken. If a 30 per cent reduction is to be achieved, however, new regulation has to be imposed, both upon mobile sources and industry and oil production (SFT, 1994: 19).

During the last two years, the Minister of the Environment has given ambiguous answers as to whether sufficient measures will be taken to meet the target. In January 1995, an explicit answer was given: the minister admitted that Norway would not be able to implement its goal of a 30 per cent reduction of NO_x by 1998 (*Aftenposten*, 12 January 1995).

Climate change

In parliamentary report 46, the Brundtland government proposed a national stabilisation of CO_2 emissions by the year 2000. The proposal implied that emissions were expected to *increase* during the 1990s. The Prime Minister was strongly criticised for being inconsistent, proposing a target that according to the Brundtland Commission was insufficient. Environmental issues were at the top of the political agenda, and the parliamentary debate escalated, resulting in a goal of stabilisation by the year 2000, using 1989 as the base year. Eventually, it was decided to try to carry out the Conservative Party's proposal. Norway could, as the first country in the world establishing a national goal on CO_2, maintain its role as a forerunner.

Two committees were established to propose measures for the implementation of the stabilisation goal. The Interdepartmental Group on Climate Change (den interdepartementale klimagruppen) was to make a study of possible measures for reducing emissions from all greenhouse gases. The work of the Environmental Tax Committee (Miljøavgiftsutvalget), resulted in the introduction of a carbon tax in 1991, as described earlier. However, when the main conclusions of the working groups were presented, the costs of implementation had already become obvious. First, Norway is highly dependent on the hydrocarbon sector, which contributes about 30 per cent of Norway's export revenue (OECD, 1993). Second, energy production is heavily based upon the use of hydro-electric power, and this makes reductions particularly expensive. The conflict between, on the one hand, dependence on a growing production of oil and gas and, on the other hand, the intent to play the role as a forerunner in international climate policy has been a difficult dilemma for Norway to handle.

The principle of cost-effectiveness has been seen as the main strategy to be applied if the aim is to escape this dilemma. The principle was strongly recommended by the Environmental Tax Committee and became the background for the Norwegian position in the negotiations on the Climate Convention starting in 1991. Norway supported the demand for quantitative emission reductions, but doubt has been cast as to the extent to which Norway was really committed to this strategy (Bolstad, 1993). Norway strongly supported the principle of joint implementation – a mechanism that would make it possible to combine an increasing production of oil and gas with measures for reducing CO_2 emissions. By 1991, there was already an apparent unwillingness to uphold the national goal *unless* there was a possibility of implementing it in other countries as well. The minister was reluctant to give any clear response to this question, and the meaning behind his evasiveness was confirmed by the Norwegian performance in Rio.

Since the Rio Conference, the announced Climate Action Plan has been postponed several times. The use of a carbon tax has been the main instrument in Norwegian climate policy so far; and although it is among the highest in the world, it has been considered insufficient. In addition to the process industries, which received exemptions when the tax was introduced, other industries have been exempted due to economic problems and successful lobbying.

At present, only 60 per cent of the CO_2 emissions are covered by the tax. From 1989 to 1993, CO_2 emissions decreased by 4 per cent, even though the emissions from the petrol sector increased by 13 per cent. SFT estimates show that emissions are expected to increase by 13 per cent between 1989 and 2000 if no new measures are taken. Approximately 70 per cent of this will be caused by an increased production of oil and gas (SFT, 1994: 9–11).

In early January 1995, a long-expected confirmation was given: not only would the NO_x target be given up, but so would the target of stabilising CO_2 emissions by the year 2000, using 1989 as the base year (*Aftenposten*, 12 January 1995). The day after this announcement, Svend Auken, the Danish Minister of Environment and Energy, criticised Norway's role in the negotiations on the follow-up to the Climate Convention. Auken expressed his disappointment with the Norwegian reluctance to support the Danish proposal of quantitative emission reductions in the preparatory work to the Berlin meeting (Natur og Miljø Bulletin 1, 1995). Finally, in June 1995, the Minister of the Environment presented the delayed Climate and NO_x Action Plans (parliamentary report 41, 1994–1995). The government wanted to give priority to energy-saving programmes, the development of renewable sources of energy, and voluntary agreements with industrial actors and branches. It was also announced that the carbon tax was to remain at its present level until the presentation of the conclusions from the Green Tax Commission in 1996. Both political parties and environmental organisations have expressed their disappointment with the plan.

The whaling question

The Norwegian position on minke whaling has been an important issue on the international environmental agenda and has damaged the Norwegian reputation as a forerunner in environmental policy. A growing concern for these whales resulted in moratoria for several whale species between 1979 and 1982. A total ban on whaling was approved by a majority on the International Whaling Commission (IWC) in 1982. By then, Norway had already stated its reservation about what was considered a decision made without scientific support. The international community considered the minke whales a threatened species, however, and increasing international pressure on Norway resulted in a national moratorium in 1986. Two years later, a five-year integrated research programme on whales and seals was introduced. The programme was the largest fisheries research programme ever launched in Norway. One of the first major objectives of the programme was a stock assessment of the north-east Atlantic minke whales. The results were presented in 1990 in connection with a comprehensive assessment of whale stocks carried out by the IWC. Although the IWC Scientific Expert Committee accepted the Norwegian assessments, the IWC itself rejected the recommendations made by this committee. Before the 1995 IWC meeting, a miscalculation in the Norwegian figures was discovered. A new stock assessment or management procedures have not yet been agreed upon within the Scientific Expert Committee.

Norway decided to resume minke whaling in 1992, basing its position on scientific recommendations. The Norwegian Foreign Minister argued that Norway had used a scientific basis for agreements on environmental protection and natural resource management for many years. The subject of minke whaling was therefore 'bigger than whales ... If countries are forced to accept rules prohibiting the use of certain resources without a sound basis, the very foundation of international co-operation and agreement on environmental issues will be endangered', the Foreign Minister argued (Statement on Minke Whaling, 29 June 1993: 2). In addition, the government had domestic reasons to pursue the whaling issue (Skjærseth and Rosendal, 1995: 177). Negotiations about membership of the European Economic Area (EEA) were coming up, and an emerging conflict between the centre and the periphery within the Labour Party could be observed. For the Brundtland government, it became important to show the people in northern Norway that Norway's resources were governed by Norway itself. The whaling question has not been controversial domestically, since all parties have supported the government's position. Support has also come from the National Foundation for Nature Conservation.

The institutional context of foreign environmental policy

The general institutional framework

The development of the institutional context of foreign environmental policy mirrors the increasing importance of trans-sectoral issues on the agenda and the interdependence of environmental policy and foreign policy in general. When the international dimension of environmental issues was first brought up in the early 1970s, the Ministry of the Environment was given sole responsibility for the administration of this policy area. In the 1990s several ministries are involved. The Ministry of Foreign Affairs is responsible for the co-ordination of foreign policy in general, and thus also for the Norwegian performance in international environmental negotiations. The leader of the Norwegian delegations in negotiations is normally a representative from the Ministry of the Environment, but it may also be a representative from the Ministry of Foreign Affairs, from other ministries or from subordinate environmental agencies. The Ministry of the Environment is normally responsible for the co-ordination of a common position on the basis of the diverging interests of various other ministries which also have strong interests in the outcomes of the negotiations. In the implementation phase, all the affected ministries are expected to take the necessary measures within their respective sectors. The Ministry of the Environment is, however, often given a special responsibility for co-ordination.

In the 1970s and 1980s, the Ministry of the Environment played a more dominant role. When the Ministry of the Environment was established, the responsibility for the co-ordination of international environmental co-operation was transferred to this new ministry from the Ministry of Foreign Affairs. The need for co-ordination of issues administered by different parts of the Ministry of the Environment was one important reason for the establishment of an international section within the Department for Organisation and Economy in 1975 (Kvamme, 1983). Another reason was the growing importance that Norway attached to international issues during the 1970s.

Since the late 1980s, the number of issues has increased, and new actors have become involved. As described previously, the reorganisation of the Ministry of the Environment in 1989 resulted in the establishment of the Department for International Environmental Co-operation and Polar Affairs, which was soon merged with the air pollution department into the Department for International Co-operation, Air Management and Polar Affairs. While the international department is responsible for global and regional air pollution issues, other departments are responsible for international issues within their respective fields of administration. For example, the Department for Nature Conservation is responsible for the administration of international nature conservation conventions.

The international environmental issues brought on the agenda in the wake of the Brundtland Report are, to a greater extent, transsectoral, involving implementation costs across different sectors of society. They are also more intertwined with other parts of foreign policy, e.g. trade policy. As a result, ministries influenced by implementation costs as well as the Ministry of Finance and the Ministry of Foreign Affairs have played an increasingly important role in the preparation of Norwegian positions in international negotiations. The Ministry of Foreign Affairs is responsible for the co-ordination of other international commitments that Norway has undertaken and for ensuring that the established positions are in accordance with the general orientation of foreign policy. As described in the discussion on the negotiation on the revised sulphur protocol, the Ministry of Finance firmly supports the principle of cost-effectiveness. Another goal of the Ministry of Finance is to avoid making commitments that are too expensive to implement. The other ministries also participate in negotiations if they are expected to become involved in the implementation of the potential outcome. For example, the Ministry of Industry and Energy is involved with climate policy, the Ministry of Transport is involved with the NO_x protocol and the Ministry of Agriculture is involved with the Convention on Biodiversity; all protecting their own sector interests (Skjærseth and Rosendal, 1995: 166ff.). The Ministry of the Environment is thus given the key role as co-ordinator of the different positions held by different parts of the state administration.

The institutional context of EEA participation

After the rejection of EU membership, the EEA institutions continued to be the main point on the Norwegian agenda for co-operation with the EU. The EEA agreement is based on a so-called 'two-pillar' system, where the EU and the European Free Trade Area (EFTA) are given one vote each in decisions taken by the EEA Council. The council can accept or reject regulation approved by the EU, but it cannot change the contents of the proposals. If the EFTA countries refuse to accept EU regulation, the EU can dismiss its co-operation with EFTA for the policy area in question (Bugge and Thrap-Meyer, 1992).

The EU Commission has the exclusive right to propose new regulation to be carried out within the EEA, although the EFTA countries are granted participation in the expert committees working under the EU Commission. Even though the members of these committees are appointed in their capacity as experts, the committees also serve as an arena for preliminary talks among representatives from different countries. Norway and the other remaining EFTA countries are thus given an opportunity to participate in the policy-making process at an early stage.

Within the framework of the EEA agreement, the EFTA countries are also granted the right to participate in the 'comittology committees' (or 'implementation committees' as they have also been called) in policy areas covered by the EEA treaty. However, the right to participate does not include the right to vote on cases and in committees when relevant. The participation covered by the EEA agreement is estimated to cover approximately 70 per cent of these committees.

On the domestic side, several initiatives have been taken to co-ordinate national measures to follow up on the EEA agreement. A position has been established at the Norwegian Embassy in Brussels for a secretary working with environmental issues. He or she is formally subordinate to the Ministry of Foreign Affairs and receives instructions from the Norwegian EU ambassador, but works closely with the Ministry of the Environment. All ministries have appointed co-ordinators for EEA issues, and the government has established a special interministerial co-ordination committee. In addition, since the EEA agreement came into force on 1 January 1994, twenty special committees have been established to deal with EEA issues.

European integration and environmental policy

On 28 November 1994, 52.2 per cent of the Norwegian electorate voted against EU membership. For the second time since 1972, a majority of the people had rejected a proposal strongly advocated by the government and supported by key political and economic actors. Norway was to remain outside the EU. Arguments concerning environmental policy were used by both sides in the EU struggle, and they were core issues on the agenda during the election campaign. In an opinion poll carried out on the day of the referendum, 20 per cent of the supporters and 17 per cent of the opponents of EU membership stated environmental issues as their main reason for voting the way they did.

The arguments put forward by the two sides on environmental policy reflect the general orientation of Norwegian foreign environmental policy. This orientation can be summarised in two core questions: to what extent would Norway be able to play the role as a pusher in international environmental policy if it were a member of the EU, and to what extent would it be able to play the role as a forerunner? In this respect, the arguments embodied a general dilemma that has been crucial in the EU debate; namely the trade-off between influence and governability, on the one hand, and the loss of sovereignty, on the other (Østerud, 1994). The discussion below addresses these two questions.

The 'pusher' argument

For the supporters of EU membership, the relationship between the scope of environmental problems and the boundaries of EU jurisdiction was a central premise for preferring regulation at the European level. Statistical evidence was frequently used to symbolise the dependency of actions taken within the EU. One example was that 96 per cent of all sulphur, causing acid lakes in the south of Norway, originated abroad, and more than 40 per cent of that originated in EU countries (SFT, 1994). It was argued that an improvement in EU policy would be of far greater importance than what Norway could do alone, both for Norway and for the European environment as such (parliamentary report 40, 1993–1994: 80).

Importance was attached to the institutional properties of the EU – properties such as decision-making rules allowing for majority voting and supra-national enforcement and surveillance mechanisms. Emphasis was also put on the possibility, and responsibility, that

Norway would get, particularly in co-operation with other 'green' member states, of pushing the EU in a more progressive direction. Neither the capacity of the EU institutions for effective environmental regulation nor Norway's possibility of influencing environmental policy-making was questioned. In general, the picture drawn of future EU environmental policy was optimistic.

The arguments pursued by the opponents of EU membership were based on a fundamentally different perception of the working of the European institutions. First, arguments were made, in general, against the importance attached to the EU as an arena for international environmental co-operation. It was maintained that global environmental problems needed global institutions to be solved, and that the EU had often shown itself to be reluctant to make commitments in the global arena. If Norway were to stay a pusher, it could not be tied to a common – more defensive – European position in international negotiations. At the European level, the ECE was seen as a more appropriate arena. Emphasis was also put on traditional international environmental agreements (parliamentary recommendations 209, 1993–1994, from the members of the Standing Committee for Foreign Affairs, represented by the Centre Party, the Left Socialist Party and the Christian People's Party, 79ff.).

The governing capacity of the EU in the field of environmental policy – or rather what was perceived as the lack of it – was one of the core arguments used by the opponents. Their perception was one of an institutional bias within the EU resulting in a systematical subordination of ecological values to the requirements of economic growth. It was argued that the most fundamental goal of the EU was the realisation of the four freedoms[7] to improve the growth rates of the Community, and that the institutional framework within the EU was designed for the fulfilment of this objective. The whole rationale behind the Single European Act was to improve growth rates by exploiting the comparative advantages of the different countries. The consequences would be more transport, more centralisation and higher levels of energy consumption (recommendations from the Centre Party, 60 and the Left Socialist Party, 64). The problem, according to one of the representatives, was that: 'Both the Single European Act and the Economic Union have been established to produce more economic growth than the nation-state alone has the capacity of doing' (Gunn Karin Juul, parliamentary debate, April 27 1994 – author's translation).

The 'forerunner' argument

The self-perception of Norway as a clean, environmentally progressive country was an important background for the strength of the forerunner argument on the agenda prior to the referendum, and this perception reflected a more general vision of Norway as 'the different country' (No: *Annerledeslandet*). The EU opponents emphasised what they saw as the special qualities of Norwegian society: a well-developed welfare state, a mixed economy, a high level of environmental protection, decentralisation and grassroots participation. It was proclaimed that a rejection of EU membership would also mean the support of a new policy orientation and priority given to these values.

Two dimensions need to be distinguished in the forerunner argument. The first one concerns the extent to which Norway can be characterised as a forerunner today compared with the EU. The second dimension concerns the possibility of taking a future forerunner position. Looking at the present situation, Norway is neither better nor worse off than the average European country when compared on a number of environmental indicators. A comparison of Norwegian and EU environmental *policies* shows the same pattern: namely, that in some areas Norway is better off, whereas in others the EU is better off (Dahl, 1994). How important these different issues are, and to what extent they reflect fundamental differences that are important particularly for the possibility of playing a *future* forerunner role, has, however, been the object of much controversy.

Most discussions prior to the referendum concerned areas in which Norway has a higher level of protection than the EU, and where EU regulation is based on maximum directives. The most important case in this category is the regulation of hazardous substances in products. In this policy area, Norway and the EU use different classification and labelling criteria based on different risk analyses. In the EU, a more comprehensive scientific verification is needed for a substance or product to be classified and labelled as hazardous than is the case in Norway (Dahl, 1994: 41ff.). This difference has been used by Norwegian opponents of EU membership to demonstrate that Norway is more willing than the EU to support the precautionary principle (parliamentary recommendation 209: 80).

In cases where Norway has higher standards than the EU and regulation is carried out through maximum directives, Norway would have been given a transitional four-year period to comply with EU standards. During this period, the EU would commit itself to a review of existing regulation with the aim of developing higher standards. The main question was what would happen if these four years were to pass without such an improvement taking place. The government responded with reference to the so-called 'environmental guarantee', arguing that Norway would be allowed to maintain its own higher standards even after this transitional period (parliamentary report 40: 113). This argument was questioned by the EU opponents, who emphasised that the EU had not issued any legally binding guarantees allowing Norway to maintain higher standards, and that it was highly uncertain whether Norway would be able to use the environmental guarantee if such a situation were to occur.

In conclusion, it can be said that the pusher and forerunner arguments were important on the EU environmental agenda in Norway for the supporters and opponents of EU membership, respectively. Membership supporters considered the possibility of being a forerunner within the EU as good, and emphasised the possibility of being a pusher. The strength of their argument rested on the possible positive consequences for Norway of measures taken within the EU, compared with what Norway could accomplish alone. The opponents questioned the possibility of being a pusher and gave higher priority to the role as a forerunner, both for domestic reasons and with a view to international negotiations. They argued that, in some important areas in which regulation is carried out through maximum standards, Norway could not maintain its forerunner role if it joined the EU. Just as important, however, was their perception of future environmental policy in a broader sense. Their vision of Norway as a future forerunner reflected their perception of the 'different country' in which environmental values were given higher priority. To what extent such a perception reflected the real preferences of the Norwegian electorate is, however, another story, even if a majority voted against EU membership.

Conclusions

The purpose of this chapter has been to describe the development of Norwegian environmental policy, both at the national and international level, as part of an analysis of the environmental aspects of the EU membership debate. Although the number of topics covered has been extensive, an attempt has been made to illuminate some more general features characterising the development in this policy area. In summary, the first point concerns the factors explaining the national interest taken in environmental issues since the early 1970s: that Norwegians have traditionally attached value to 'untouched nature' and that Norway's self-perception has been that of a clean and environmentally friendly country. To a large extent, this background also explains the early interest Norway had in working in the international arena, i.e. in developing international environmental agreements. Norway's exposure to transfrontier air and water pollution and damage from acid precipitation, in particular, in the early 1970s was also an important factor motivating Norway to choose a high profile and become an example for the international community, both as a forerunner at the domestic level and as a pusher in international negotiations.

Another characteristic pointed out concerns the basic structure of the Norwegian economy. Norway is strongly dependent on the exploitation of natural resources, and the industrialisation that has taken place in this century has to a large extent been based upon the development of hydro-electricity from water courses. Since the mid-1970s, petrol production has come to occupy an increasingly dominant position in the Norwegian economy. As energy-related environmental issues, such as NO_x and in particular climate policy, have become more important on the international agenda, Norway has, to an increasing extent, been forced to cope with the dilemma between contradictory environmental and economic interests. Norway has experienced increasing problems in the implementation of both international environmental agreements and unilateral commitment, such as the CO_2 goal; and the credibility of the forerunner position has come into question.

Finally, this chapter has discussed the environmental aspects of the EU membership debate. This discussion was based on the two dimensions along which the basic orientation of Norwegian foreign environmental policy has been located, namely the role as a forerunner and as a pusher, respectively. The question was whether Norway could play these roles successfully if it were a member of the EU. As is known, Norway voted against EU membership, and for the opponents, who won the referendum, the perception of a future forerunner role *outside* the EU remained important as part of a more general vision of Norway as a 'different country'. Now Norway is a different country in the sense that it is still outside the EU. But is Norway also different in the sense that it is an environmental forerunner ready to take a leading position in international environmental co-operation? Prediction is a dangerous business within the social sciences, so conclusions should not be drawn too hastily. Nevertheless, an ambiguous and not too optimistic answer can be given on the basis of lessons learned from the past. Although, in some respects, Norway still intends to be a forerunner when confronted with conflictual environmental and economic interests, it has shown to be neither better nor worse than the members of the EU it decided not to be a part of. The 'different country' is still not so very different.

Notes

1 The expression 'splendid isolation' is normally used to refer to the British foreign policy at the end of the nineteenth century. With a combination of skilful diplomacy and power play, Great Britain succeeded in bending the political situation on the European continent to its own will without itself getting involved in any major conflicts.

2 I would like to thank Francesco Kjellberg, Per Kristen Mydske, Jon Naustdalslid and Arild Underdal for comments on earlier drafts, Morten Egeberg and Jo Saglie for generously giving access to their data on EU issues, and officials in the Norwegian Ministry of the Environment and the SFT for useful information. Thanks also to participants in the workshop 'Makt- og miljøforum' at Sundvollen in Norway on 23–24 August 1995 for their comments.

3 This section is based on a summary of Berntsen (1994).

4 In 1994, the Ministry of the Environment had 270 employees and the SFT had 238 employees (Statskalenderen, 1994).

5 The Ministry of Industry was merged with the Ministry of Energy on 1 January 1993. In January 1997 the ministries were separated again.

6 The idea that international environmental co-operation should promote development in the Third World is also a governing principle of the Norwegian policy (Skjærseth and Rosendal, 1995: 164). Due to limited space, I have chosen not to discuss the Norwegian position on the relationship between development and environment and trade and environment. Other important issues on the Norwegian foreign environmental agenda not discussed in this chapter are the environmental problems at the Kola Peninsula and the bilateral co-operation that has been established between Norway and Russia to cope with these problems.

7 The free flow of capital, goods, services and labour.

References

Aardal, B. (1993), *Energi og miljø. Nye stridsspørsmål i møte med gamle strukturer*, Oslo, Institutt for samfunnsforskning.

Aardal, B. and H. Valen (1995), *Konflikt og opinion*, Oslo, NKS-forlaget.

Andersen, M. S. and D. Liefferink (1993), *New Nordic Member States and the Impact on EC Environmental Policy*, Aarhus/Wageningen, Department of Political Science University of Aarhus/Department of Sociology, Agricultural University of Wageningen.

Berntsen, B. (1994), *Grønne linjer. Natur- og miljøvernets historie i norge*, Oslo, Grøndal Dreyer/Norges Naturvernforbund.

Bjørklund, T. and O. Hellevik (1988), De grønne stridsspørsmål i norsk politikk, *Politica*, 4, 414–31.

Bolstad, G. (1993), *Inn i drivhuset*, Oslo, Cappelen.

Bugge, H. C. and R. Thrap-Meyer (1992), *EøS-avtalen i et miljørettslig perspektiv*, Oslo, Senter for EF-rett, Universitet i Oslo.

Carson, R. (1963), *Silent Spring*, Harmondsworth, Penguin Books.

Dahl, A. (1994), *EUs og Norges miljølovgivning: likheter og forskjeller*, Oslo, Fridtjof Nansens institutt.

Direktoratet for Naturforvaltning (1995), *informasjonsbrosjyre*.

Downs, A. (1972), Up and down with ecology – the 'issue-attention cycle', *Public Interest*, 28, 38–50.

Drivhuseffekten. Virkninger og tiltak (1991), rapport fra den interdepartementale klimagruppen.

Egeberg, M. (1981), *Stat og organisasjoner. Flertallsstyre, partsstyre og byråkrati i norsk politikk*, Oslo, Universitetsforlaget.

Gleditsch, N. P., Å. Hartmann and J. Naustdalslid (1971), Mardøla-aksjonen, *Tidsskrift for samfunnnsforskning*, 12, 177–210.

Gundersen, F. (1991), Utviklingstrekk ved miljøbevegelsen i Norge, *Sosiologi idag*, 2, 13–35.

Hallén, A. (1981), *Mjøsaksjonen 1977–80. Studiar av iverksettingsprosessane*, Oslo, Norsk institutt for by- og regionforskning.

Hovik, S. (1994), Prioriteringer i kommunalt miljøvern, in J. Naustdalslid and S. Hovik (eds), *Lokalt miljøvern*, Oslo, Tano.

Hovik, S. and V. Johnsen (1994), Kommunal organisering og lokalt miljøvern, in J. Naustdalslid and S. Hovik (eds), *Lokalt miljøvern*, Oslo, Tano.

Hovik, S. and M. Reitan (1994), Kommunal vilje til lokalpolitisk innsats, in J. Naustdalslid and S. Hovik (eds), *Lokalt miljøvern*, Oslo, Tano.

Innstilling S. nr. 209 (1993–1994), innstilling fra Stortingets Utenrikskomite om medlemskap i den europeiske union.

Jansen, A. I. (1989), *Makt og Miljø. Om utformingen av natur- og miljøvernpolitikken i Norge*, Oslo, Universitetsforlaget.

Katzenstein, P. (1985), *Small States in World Markets*, Ithaca, Cornell University Press.

Kitschelt, H. P. (1986), Political opportunity structures and political protest: anti nuclear movements in four democracies, *British Journal of Political Science*, 16, 57–85.

Klausen, J. E. (1995), *Miljøpolitiske nettverk på sentralnivået*, working paper, Oslo, Norsk institutt for by- og regionforskning.

Knutsen, O. (1991), From old politics to new politics: the development of environmental policy as a party cleavage. To be published in K. Strøm and L. Svåsand (eds) (1997), *Challenges to Political Parties: the Norwegian Case*, Michigan, Michigan University Press.

Kvamme, A. (1983), *Handlingsmiljø og miljøvern*, Hovedoppgave, Bergen, Institutt for offentlig administrasjon og organisasjonskunnskap, Universitetet i Bergen.

Lægreid, P. (1983), Miljøverndepartementet. Ny organisasjon i etablert miljø, *Nordisk administrativt tidsskrift*, 4, 365–83.

Laugen, T. (1995), *Compliance with International Environmental Agreements*, Master's thesis, Oslo, Department of Political Science, University of Oslo.

Mathiesen, R. (1992), *Effekter av organisasjonsendring. En case-studie av organisasjonsendringen i Miljøverndepartementet 1989*, Hovedoppgave, Oslo, Institutt for statsvitenskap, Universitetet i Oslo.

Miljøressurser (1976), Naturressurser og forurensinger, SSB Statistiske analyser, 22.

Miljøvern og europeisk samarbeid (1992), delrapport til Europautredningen fra en arbeidsgruppe nedsatt av statssekretærutvalget for Europautredningen, *Miljøvernministrenes miljøpolitiske redegjørelser* (1987–1994).

Mydske, P.K., A. Steen and A. Tarud (1994), Land-use and environmental policy in Norway, in K. Eckerberg, P. K. Mydske, A. Niemi-Iilahti and K. H. Pedersen, *Comparing Nordic and Baltic Countries – Environmental Problems and Policies in Agriculture and Forestry*, Copenhagen, Nordic Council of Ministers.

Natur og Miljø Bulletin (1993–1995), Norges Naturvernforbund.

Nenseth, V. (1994), Miljøvern på fylkesnivå, in J. Naustdalslid and S. Hovik (eds), *Lokalt Miljøvern*, Oslo, Tano.

Norwegian Whaling (1993), statement by the Minister of Foreign Affairs on 29 June.

NOU (1992:3), *Mot en mer kostnadseffektiv miljøpolitikk*.

NOU (1995:4), *Virkemidler i miljøpolitikken*.

OECD (1993) *Environmental Performance Review*, Norway, OECD.

Olsen, J. P. (1981), Integrated organizational participation in government, in P. C. Nystrom and W. H. Starbuck (eds), *Handbook of Organizational Design 2*, Oxford, Oxford University Press.

Østerud, Ø. (1979), *Det planlagte samfunn*, Oslo, Universitetsforlaget.

Østerud, Ø. (1994), *Antinomies of Supra-national State-building. Centralization, Sovereignty and Democracy in the EU*, working paper, Oslo, Department for Political Science, University of Oslo.

Rokkan, S. (1967), Geography, religion and social class: crosscutting cleavages in Norwegian politics, in S. M. Lipset and S. Rokkan (eds), *Party Systems and Voter Alignments*, New Haven, The Free Press.

Roll-Hansen, N. and G. Hestmark (1990), *Miljøforskning mellom politikk og vitenskap*, Oslo, NAVFs utredningsinstitutt.

Rommetvedt, H. and S. H. Opedal (1995), Miljølobbyisme og næringskorporatisme? Norske miljø- og næringsorganisasjoners politiske påvirkning, *Nordisk administrativt tidsskrift*, 3, 279–302.

Skjærseth, J. B and G. K. Rosendal (1995), Norges miljø-utenrikspolitikk, in T. L. Knutsen, G. M. Sørbø and S. Gjerdåker (eds), *Norges utenrikspolitikk*, Bergen/Oslo, Chr. Michelsens institutt/Cappelens akademiske forlag.

Statens Forurensingstilsyn (1992), *informasjonsbrosjyre*.

Statens Forurensingstilsyn (1994), *Forurensing i Norge*.

Stordrange, B. (1990), Erstatning for forurensningsskader, *Lov og Rett*, 131–48.

Stortingsforhandlinger (1994), 25, 26–27 April.

Stortingsmelding (1984–1985), 51, Om tiltak mot vann- og luftforurensinger og om kommunalt avfall.

Stortingsmelding (1988–1989), 46, Miljø og Utvikling. Norges oppfølging av Brundtlandkommisjonens rapport.

Stortingsmelding (1991–1992), 62, Ny landsplan for nasjonalparker.

Stortingsmelding (1991–1992), 64, Norges oppfølging av Nordsjødeklarasjonen.

Stortingsmelding (1993–1994), 40, Om medlemskap i den europeiske union.

Stortingsmelding (1994–1995), 41, Om norsk politikk mot klimaendringer og utslipp av nitrogenoksyder (NO_x).

Stortingsregistre (1975–1976 and 1993–1994).

Thorén, A. H., O. Glesne and S. Nyhuus (1991), *Miljøvern i norsk forvaltning*, Oslo, NKS-forlaget.

Utenriksministerens redegjørelse i Stortinget 18. mai 1993 om hvalsaken (1993).

Valen, H. (1981), *Valg og politikk – et samfunn i endring*, Oslo, NKS-forlaget.

Weale, A. (1992), *The New Politics of Pollution*, Manchester, Manchester University Press.

Weale, A. (1993), *Environmental Protection and the Four Freedoms*, paper presented at the COST Conference, Maastricht 3–4 December.

Witoszek, N. (1993), Narrative of place: inside and outside in Norwegian tradition, in N. Witoszek and E. Gulbransen (eds), *Culture and Environment*, Oslo, Centre for Environment and Development/Centre for Technology and Culture, University of Oslo.

Index

Note: 'n.' after a page reference indicates the number of a note on that page. Organisations and institutions specific to one country appear under that country's entry.